Barbara Burman   Ariane Fennetaux

T0385846

The Pocket

A Hidden History of
Women's Lives, 1660–1900

YALE UNIVERSITY PRESS

NEW HAVEN AND LONDON

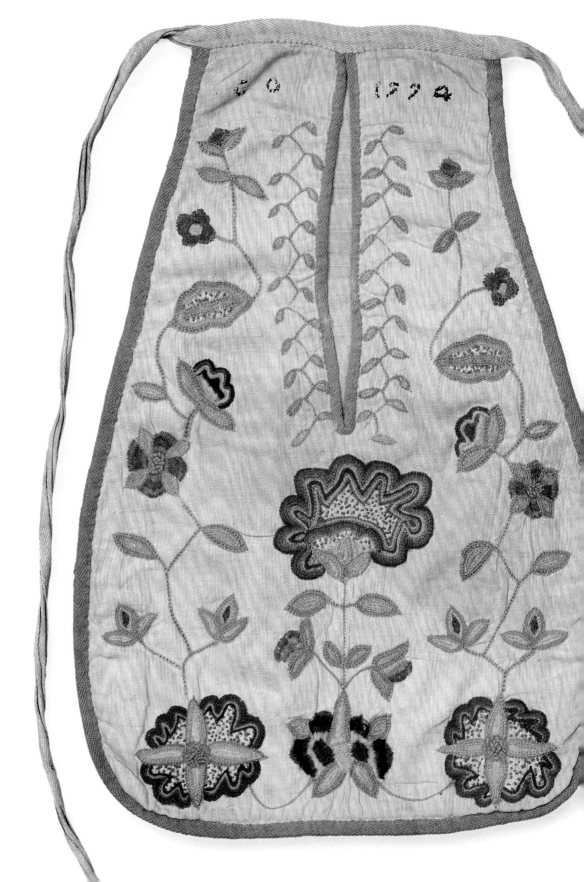

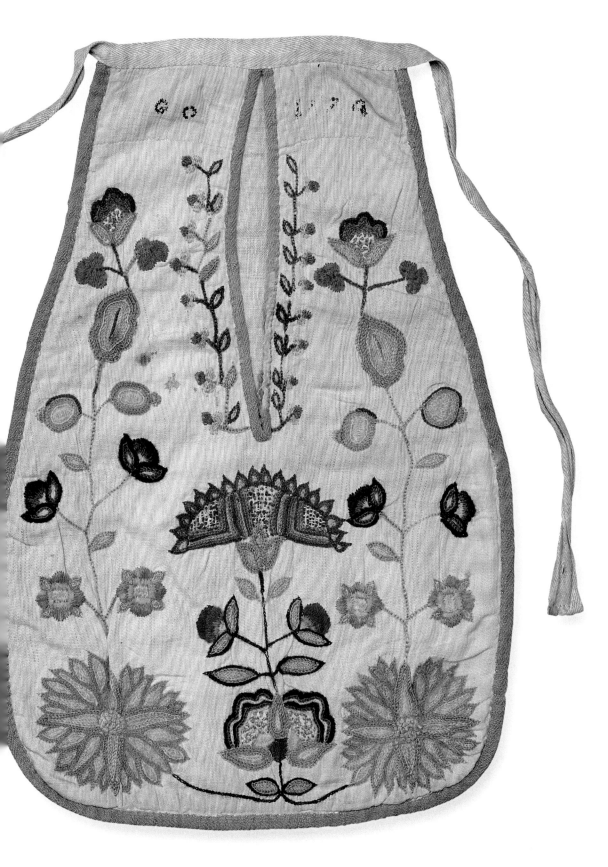

First published in hardback by Yale University Press 2019
This edition published in paperback 2020
302 Temple Street, P. O. Box 209040, New Haven,
CT 06520-9040
47 Bedford Square, London WC1B 3DP
yalebooks.com | yalebooks.co.uk

ISBN 978-0-300-253740 PB
Library of Congress Control Number: 2018955377

10 9 8 7
2027 2026 2025

Designed by Myfanwy Vernon-Hunt, this-side.co.uk
Cover design by Alice Marwick
Printed in China

Front cover image: One of a pair of embroidered pockets
marked with the initials 'G O', 1774 (L 41 cm and 42 cm).
Manchester Art Gallery, MCAG.1951.107/2.

Back cover image: Embroidered pocket, early to mid-18th
century (L 36.2 cm). Fashion Museum Bath, BATMC VI.14.1.

Frontispiece: Pair of embroidered pockets marked with the
initials 'G O', 1774 (L 41 cm and 42 cm). Manchester Art Gallery,
MCAG.1951.107/2.

This publication was made possible by the generous funding
of the Paul Mellon Centre; LARCA (CNRS-UMR 8225), the
Université Paris Diderot via Global Matters; the Association
for Art History; and the Arts & Humanities Research Council.

CONTENTS

6   Acknowledgements

9   List of Abbreviations

10   INTRODUCTION
'small things forgotten'

CHAPTER ONE
22   **'Oh, pockets – pockets – pockets!'**
Revealing Pockets: Practice and Polemics

CHAPTER TWO
52   **'work'd pocketts to my intire sattisfaction'**
Making and Getting Pockets

CHAPTER THREE
84   **'So many things'**
Pockets and the Labours of Consumption

CHAPTER FOUR
110   **'they say there is no bottom to them?'**
Pockets, Possession and Promise

CHAPTER FIVE
142   **'for the play and coach'**
Pockets, Mobility and Sociability

CHAPTER SIX
162   **'I turn my Hand to any Thing to get a Penny'**
Pockets and Work

CHAPTER SEVEN
186   **'I always have the last sheet
of my journal in my pocket'**
Pockets, Privacy and Memory

CONCLUSION
216   **'this is the sort of pocket our great
grandmothers used to wear'**
The Demise and Afterlife of Tie-On Pockets

224   Appendix: Pockets in the Old Bailey

226   Notes

240   Archives

244   Bibliography

258   Index

264   Picture Credits

ACKNOWLEDGEMENTS

This book has its roots over a decade ago in the 'Pockets of History' research project generously funded by the Arts and Humanities Research Council at the University of Southampton. For their vital contributions in shaping the initial stages we are particularly indebted to members of the project's Steering and Expert User Groups; to Mary M. Brooks, Dinah Eastop, Kate Gill, Maria Hayward, Nell Hoare, Frances Lennard and colleagues at the former Textile Conservation Centre (now Centre for Textile Conservation and Technical Art History, University of Glasgow); Alison Carter and Sue Washington of Hampshire County Museum Service (now Hampshire Cultural Trust); Seth Denbo; the Visual Arts Data Service. Rosemary Harden of the Fashion Museum Bath and Susan North of the Victoria and Albert Museum provided invaluable impetus and expertise and raised our game. We are immensely grateful to Jonathan White for his enthusiasm from the start and for his scholarship, which he will recognise at numerous points in this book. Students on the MA History of Textiles and Dress at Winchester School of Art were stimulating companions at this early stage of the book: Helen Brookes, Katy May and Katharine Wheaton deserve special credit for their resourceful engagement with the material evidence.

Museum objects underpinned our research; meaningful study of them was a collaborative occupation dependent on the expertise and generosity of curators, other staff and volunteers, to whom we owe vast gratitude, at the following museums and organisations: Abbey House Museum, Leeds; Amgueddfa Cymru–National Museum Wales; Bankfield Museum, Halifax; Blaise Castle House Museum, Bristol; Bolton Museums; Bowes Museum, Barnard Castle; Burrell Collection, Glasgow; Carmarthenshire County Museum; Chertsey Museum; Clare Ancient House Museum, Suffolk; Dorset County Museum, Dorchester; Embroiderers' Guild; Fashion Museum Bath; Gallery of Costume, Manchester Art Gallery; Gawthorpe Textiles Collection, Gawthorpe Hall; Hampshire Cultural Trust; Hereford Museum Service; Horsham Museum and Art Gallery; Killerton, Devon (National Trust); Maidstone Museum and Art Gallery; Meg Andrews Antique Costumes and Textiles; Museum of Cambridge; Museum of London; National Army Museum; National Museums Scotland; Norfolk Museums Service; Nottingham City Museums and Galleries; Oxfordshire County Council Museum Service; Royal Albert Memorial Museum and Art Gallery, Exeter; Royal School of Needlework; Salisbury and South Wiltshire Museum; School of Historical Dress, London; Swaledale Museum; Victoria and Albert Museum and Museum

1 George Smith (1829–1901), *Temptation: A Fruit Stall*, 1850, oil on panel (63.5 × 76.1 cm). Victoria and Albert Museum, London, FA.186[O].

of Childhood; Wilson Art Gallery and Museum, Cheltenham; Worthing Museum and Art Gallery; York Castle Museum. Not least, we thank those private collectors of other wonderful artefacts who gave so freely of their time.

We also thank the staff at Bedfordshire Archives and Record Service; British Library; Centre for Buckinghamshire Studies; Christ's Hospital School Museum, Horsham; City of Westminster Archives Centre; Guildhall Library, City of London; Hampshire Record Office; Huntington Library, San Marino; Kent History and Library Centre; London Metropolitan Archives; The National Archives; National Art Library, V&A; Surrey History Centre; the Special Collections of the University of St Andrews Library ; Victoria and Albert Museum Archive; The Women's Library, London School of Economics.

We are grateful for funding from the Association for Art History and the Paul Mellon Centre. To the Université Paris Diderot, we extend a very special *merci*! For their outstanding support over time, we especially thank the directors of the LARCA research group (Laboratoire de Rercherches sur les Cultures Anglophones, UMR 8225), the late Robert Mankin, the late François Brunet and Mélanie Torrent. We are very grateful to Paris Diderot's Global Matters for their generous support.

We thank too those who shared their suggestions, expertise and research and who supported us in various professional guises over the long development of the study: the late Judy Attfield, Jeremy Aynsley, Dale Barter, Jennie Batchelor, Christopher Breward, Una Brogan, Clare Browne, Nolwenn Bruneel, Dawn Chappell, Helen Clifford, Barrie J. Cook, Valerie Cummings, the late Leonore Davidoff, Hilary Davidson, Angela Davies, Susan C. Djabri, Alice Dolan, Edwina Ehrman, Pascale Gorguet-Ballesteros, Tom Gray, Mike Halliwell, Jennie Harding, Karen Harvey, Lesley Hoskins, Ariane Hudelet, Cora Kaplan, Matthew Keagle, Beth Kowaleski-Wallace, Frédérique Lab, Arlene Leis, Beverly Lemire, Sarah Lloyd, Bridget Long, Alison Matthews David, Marion Maule, Lesley Miller, Sara Pennell, Lara Perry, Elen Phillips, Nicola Pink, the Premières Modernités reading group at Paris Diderot, Giorgio Riello, Suzanne Rowland, Philip Sykas, Nancy Tanner, Jennie Tiramani, Shelley Tobin, Sally Tuckett, Carole Turbin, Sophie Vasset, Jane Whittle. To John Styles we owe a particularly special debt of gratitude. We thank the anonymous readers who engaged with the manuscript at various stages. Their thoughtful insights have been an invaluable stimulus.

At Yale University Press, we are indebted to Mark Eastment and Sophie Neve for their guidance and confidence in the book. Very gratefully, we also acknowledge Clare Davis for her enthusiasm and exemplary attention to production standards, Lydia Cooper for her amazing efficiency in steering the project smoothly and cheerfully, Myfanwy Vernon-Hunt our gifted designer and Rosemary Roberts, our utterly stellar copy-editor.

If co-authors are allowed to thank each other in print, then we do; it was a long but immensely enjoyable and creative voyage of discovery together. Across the Channel, from Paris to London and from rural Ardèche to rural Essex, ideas and words have been shared and debated – sometimes with passion, always with benevolence. This is truly a work of two minds.

Finally, an immense debt of gratitude is due to our friends and families for such generous forbearance and understanding. Barbara thanks especially Be, Catherine, Charlie, Louise, Rob and Theo, for coping so well with the book over the long haul and latterly for their practical contributions. Ariane thanks Jaqueline, Mathias, Poka and Kyra for their support. Sadly, Michel never saw the finished book. Calliopé and Galite have lived the whole of their young lives with this book, hopefully not too much in its shadow. May life bring them many treasures to collect in their pockets. Ariane thanks Tony for his steadfast support and love. His unique, down-to-earth attitude has been an anchor in the sometimes choppy waters of writing a book. It is a privilege to live with such a caring father and partner. Barbara thanks her dear Tom for his bountiful support and sustenance, his patience, good cheer and encouragement throughout, quite simply no author could wish for a better champion and companion.

ABBREVIATIONS

AAGM	Aberdeen Art Gallery and Museums		NAL	National Art Library, Victoria and Albert Museum, London
ABING	Abingdon County Hall Museum		NAM	National Army Museum, London
AC–NMW	Amgueddfa Cymru–National Museum Wales		NCMG	Nottingham City Museums and Galleries
AHML	Abbey House Museum, Leeds		NM	Norfolk Museums Service, Norwich Costume and Textile Collections
BARS	Bedfordshire Archives and Record Service			
BCG	Burrell Collection, Glasgow		NMS	National Museums Scotland
BCHM	Blaise Castle House Museum, Bristol		NoA	Northumberland Archives
BL	British Library, London		NYCRO	North Yorkshire County Record Office
BM	British Museum, London		OA	Ordinary of Newgate's Accounts (online)
BMBC	Bowes Museum, Barnard Castle, County Durham		OBP	The Proceedings of the Old Bailey (online)
			OX	Oxfordshire County Council Museum Service
BMGA	Bolton Museums, Art Gallery and Aquarium		PUL	Princeton University Library
BMH	Bankfield Museum, Halifax		RAMM	Royal Albert Memorial Museum and Art Gallery, Exeter
CAM	Museum of Cambridge			
CARM	Carmarthenshire County Museum		RSN	Royal School of Needlework
CBS	Centre for Buckinghamshire Studies		SHC	Surrey History Centre, Woking
CoW	City of Westminster Archives Centre		SHD	School of Historical Dress, London
CPW	Charles Paget Wade Collection, Berrington Hall, Herefordshire, National Trust		SSWM	Salisbury and South Wiltshire Museum
			TNA	The National Archives, Kew
CRL	Cadbury Research Library, University of Birmingham		TWL	The Women's Library, London School of Economics
CRO	Cornwall Record Office		UStA	University of St Andrews, Special Collections
DRO	Dorset Record Office		V&A	Victoria and Albert Museum, London
FITZ	Fitzwilliam Museum, Cambridge		VAMA	Victoria and Albert Museum Archive, Blythe House, London
FMB	Fashion Museum Bath			
HCT	Hampshire Cultural Trust		VDM	Vale and Downland Museum, Wantage
HL	Huntington Library, San Marino		WAAS	Worcestershire Archive and Archaeology Service, Worcester
HMA	Horsham Museum and Art Gallery			
HMS	Hereford Museum Service		WILS	Wilson Art Gallery and Museum, Cheltenham
HRO	Hampshire Archives and Local Studies (formerly Hampshire Record Office)		WORTH	Worthing Museum and Art Gallery
			WSA	Wiltshire and Swindon Archives
KHLC	Kent History and Library Centre		WYAS	West Yorkshire Archive Service, Wakefield
LACMA	Los Angeles County Museum of Art		YCA	York City Archives
LL	London Lives		YCM	York Castle Museum
LMA	London Metropolitan Archives, City of London			
MAG	Manchester Art Gallery			
MFA	Museum of Fine Arts, Boston			
MoL	Museum of London			

'small things forgotten'

It is terribly important that the 'small things forgotten' be remembered.
For in the seemingly little and insignificant things that accumulate to create
 a lifetime, the essence of our existence is captured. We must remember
these bits and pieces, and we must use them in new and imaginative ways
so that a different appreciation for what life is today, and was in the past,
can be achieved.

James Deetz, *In Small Things Forgotten*, 1977, 161

The nineteenth-century nursery rhyme in which Lucy Locket lost her pocket
is perhaps the only shared memory of the object at the heart of this book.[1] Yet
every day between the late seventeenth and the late nineteenth centuries, British
women and girls of all social classes wore detachable pockets like Lucy Locket's
(fig. 2). They tied them round their waists independently of their clothing,
reached them through openings in their petticoats and dresses, and put them on
and off at will (fig. 3). Pockets may seem obscure now, but when restored to our
attention they open up a nexus of historical questions, ranging from women's
domesticity and work to agency, from possession to financial independence and
from consumer practices to privacy. Far from being insignificant, they offer a
disconcertingly fruitful insight into women's lives in the past.

In the early summer of 1725, an advertisement for a lost pair of pockets
appeared in a London newspaper:

D[r]opp'd between St. Sepulchres church and Salisbury court in fleet-
street, going down fleet-lane, and crossing the bridge, a pair of white
fustian pockets, in which was a silver purse, work'd with scarlet and green
S.S. In the purse there was 5 or 6 shillings in money; a ring with a death at
length in black enamell'd, wrapp'd in a piece of paper; a silver tooth pick
case; 2 cambrick handkerchiefs, one mark'd E.M. the other E5D; a small
knife; a key and pair of gloves, and a steel thimble. &c. If the person who
took them up will bring them to mr. peachy's at the black boy in the o'd
baily, he shall receive a guinea reward, ann no questions ask'd.[2]

The woman who lost her pockets that day is unknown to us, but the
advertisement alerts us to the fact that detachable pockets could on occasion
come undone and slip off. At the same time it offers an intimate view into her
life: it takes us inside the private gendered space of her pockets, and reveals
an assemblage of small articles and tools with different purposes. Apart from
money, the pockets contained some objects intricately made in valuable
materials and recalled in detail – 'a silver purse', an enamelled ring, 'a silver
tooth pick case' – and some utilitarian goods – 'a small knife', 'a steel thimble'
and 'a key' – and the '&c.' indicates that there was more. The advertisement
provides considerable factual detail about what the woman carried in her
pockets, but also hints at what she valued and how material practices could
express and confer value. The purse with the initials 'S.S.' and the mourning
ring carefully wrapped in paper inside the pocket give a glimpse of things of
sentimental value and the woman's strategies to protect them. It is easy to see
how the wearer might feel bereft and exposed at the thought of a stranger in
the busy metropolis finding and fingering through this assortment of personal
possessions that she had thought safe at her side, and why she was keen to get
her pockets back with 'no questions ask'd'. Advertisements of this kind, like the
more numerous records of court cases involving the theft of pockets or their
contents, bring the historian close to women's material possessions, revealing
otherwise unsuspected aspects of their relationship to things, at a time when
women's rights to property were legally constrained.

Extant pockets of the period are equally evocative. Their materiality
embodies women's everyday practices of consumption and possession, and,
intriguingly, facets of value, sentiment and identity. Some are decoratively
embroidered but, while the dense iconography found on them is enticing,
their embroidery is certainly not the only thing to be 'read' in them.[3] Even a
seemingly unremarkable pocket, when closely observed, begins to divulge
a number of details, each fragmentary but collectively building a more
rounded picture of the pocket's significance than its plain appearance might
at first suggest. The apparently unassuming material of which a late Victorian

LEFT TO RIGHT
3 Dressed doll, mid-18th century (L 30 cm). Victoria and Albert Museum, London, W.42:1-1922.

3a With her gown in place, showing the opening for her pocket.
3b With her gown raised, showing her pocket.

pocket is made is, in fact, the direct result of Britain's empire and industrial development. Made in cotton, the first global fibre, the cloth is a complex compound weave, popularly known as 'marcella' and probably woven on a powered jacquard loom in the nineteenth century (fig. 4a).[4] It disrupts the generally accepted view that tie-on pockets of this kind disappeared in the early 1800s when waistlines rose and silhouettes became slimmer. An inscription of '1892' written in ink on the top back of the pocket confirms the late date (fig. 4b). By this time domestic sewing machines had been available for over thirty years, but the maker elected to pick up her needle to make this pocket by hand (fig. 4c). Paying attention to these details on the pocket shows that the adoption of new technologies was never uniform and consumption practices never predictable, and that within sweeping industrial changes, individual women retained choice and control over their everyday habits and practices.[5] The maker in this instance has created a wider than usual opening and carefully reinforced it, deploying skill and effort in order to limit wear and damage to what was one of the most vulnerable parts of the pocket. The inked marks – the date 1892, preceded by now illegible initials – evidence further efforts on the part of whoever cared for this pocket. Deliberate naming or marking of this kind was a constant concern and labour for women as prudent makers, keepers and managers of household and body linen all through the period. This work was part of what owning things meant in reality, but there are few traces of it in the traditional archive. If one seeks to retrieve 'the necessary intimacy that always subsists between social relationships and things', it soon becomes apparent that object-attentive scholarship can unearth evidence that may have no exact parallel in textual or visual sources.[6] No longer unremarkable, the 1892 surviving pocket now asks questions about chronology, technology, empire, consumption and women's domestic stewardship of things.

Object-centred scholarship with a connoisseurial tendency has been traditionally separated from more social historical approaches that focus on practices and their meanings but pay little or no attention to materiality.[7] Archaeologists and anthropologists have long been alert to how things, including cloth, carry meaning and shape human relationships and practices.[8] Yet it is only fairly recently that the surge in interest in material culture has brought historians to expand their traditional sources to encompass objects.[9] Tara Hamling and Catherine Richardson note the challenges: 'The study of an environment of materiality which connects individuals to wider social and cultural forces in many ways sits awkwardly within traditional academic disciplines, and within divisions between academia and the museum sector.'[10] With a few limited exceptions, what literature exists on tie-on pockets has not bridged the disciplinary divide.[11] It is the intention of our book to demonstrate that object-attentive scholarship can combine with the more established methods and sources of history to reveal pockets as socially and culturally embedded artefacts, makers and carriers of meaning and memory, and

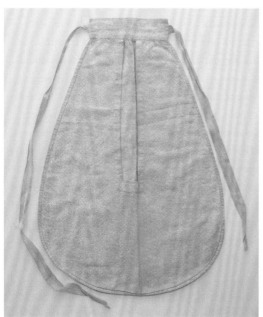

to show how social and cultural practices are materially embodied within artefacts themselves.

So this is not simply a book about tie-on pockets. It is a social and cultural history of women's lives in the long eighteenth and nineteenth centuries in Britain through the examination of this small object. It recognises that there is more to pockets than meets the hasty eye, and that, mundane as they may appear, they engage us with wider issues and open new and arresting ways of looking at women's lives in the past. As Laurel Thatcher Ulrich noted in the context of early America:

> Much better than a spinning wheel, this homely object [the pocket] symbolizes the obscurity, the versatility, and the personal nature of the housekeeping role. A woman sat at a wheel, but she carried her pocket with her from room to room, from house to yard, from yard to street [. . .]. Whether it contained cellar keys or a paper of pins, a packet of seeds or a baby's bib, a hank of yarn or a Testament, it characterized the social complexity as well as the demanding diversity of women's work.[12]

The heuristic value of smallness has been the topic of scholarly interest.[13] For us William Blake's 'world in a grain of sand' is both a metaphor and a way of looking.[14] Many historians have widened the scope of their enquiry by thinking of material culture in our period as shaped by global circulations.[15] Our small object, while in part a product of those worldwide transactions, invites us to zoom in. By refocusing our gaze on what is small and apparently tangential, we see more not less. The pocket merits a close-up study in itself because what is small can recalibrate our vision of the large.

Our commitment to objects as sources for the writing of social and cultural history is based on an unparalleled body of primary source material, established through extensive field work in more than thirty museums and private collections in the UK.[16] The documentation of nearly 390 extant pockets forms a central plank of the book, offering the accumulation of a 'critical mass' of a kind usually beyond the scope of studies in social and cultural history. The study and interpretation of surviving objects in museums pose specific challenges, not least the increasing pressures faced by curators, whose role is vital to object-attentive study. Fragile historic textiles present their own particular constraints.[17] Accidents of survival mean we cannot fully know the degree to which the pockets in our survey are representative of their class. Fibre testing and dye analysis (costly and intrusive) for the identification and dating of cloths were omitted from the survey; instead we relied on observation and existing museum documentation.[18] The relatively marginal status of pockets in museum collections, however, meant that, with some exceptions, most had no recorded provenance, and in collections with limited resources some were still awaiting full accession records at the time of our research. Nevertheless, many surviving pockets compensate for paucity of documentation and provenance by the richness of the physical evidence embodied in them, and the democratic nature of the object means that it is sometimes the only historical trace left by less privileged owners.

As Deetz argues, while written documents are important, 'there is also a time when we should set aside our perusal' of them 'and listen to another voice'.[19] It is in the nature of cloth that it readily absorbs and retains the evidence of its various uses and abuses; over time, its patina becomes a kind of document, requiring historians to bring to bear on it the same awareness of the specificities of its production and consumption, its materiality, artifice and biography, as they do on texts or images. The cloth itself, its wear and tear, repairs, degradation, accidental and intentional marks, construction with fine or botched stitches all contribute to the physical, historical record constituted by these objects. The very materiality of extant pockets has its own language and brings into close focus the lived everyday practices of women in the past.

Committed to grounding our approach in social practices *and* materiality, we use the findings of our survey of extant pockets to form a dialogue with other types of sources because, over time, tie-on pockets have also left a paper trail of their own, though a variable one. With no particular name to distinguish them from other types of pockets simply because no other name was required, the detached pockets at the centre of this book were just called 'pockets'.[20] The term 'tie-on pocket', which we use to differentiate this pocket type, is modern, not one used at the time. When a text reads 'pockets' or 'a pocket', only the context can clarify if what is meant was a discrete element of dress or not. For the historian, another challenge lies in the fact that such pockets appear only infrequently in some of the traditional sources of social history. For example, any presence they may have in probate inventories among an individual's worldly goods is usually, though not always, masked by the generic term 'wearing apparel'. So probate records do not allow us to carry out the kind of systematic, large-scale study others have undertaken for different possessions.[21] Tie-on pockets surface in other written sources, including newspapers, trade cards, advertisements, essays, novels and books of instruction, as well as private papers such as personal account books, bills, informal domestic inventories, diaries and letters. But here too their sporadic appearance means it is difficult to carry out systematic analyses. Nevertheless, the glimpses of pockets in these various sources accumulate to provide helpful clues about usage, value and social environment as we excavate their history. They enrich our understanding of the social practices in which pockets were instrumental by providing a context for their use, at least among the women represented in such written sources. Plebeian women have rarely left

5 Paul Sandby RA (1731–1809), *A Wine Seller*, *c*.1760, pen and ink, watercolour (18.3 × 13 cm). Ashmolean Museum, University of Oxford, WA1963.89.69.

inventories, account books and diaries – or if they did, few have survived. Their experience and the uses they made of their pockets must be gleaned from other sources.

Strikingly, it is often plebeian rather than elite pockets we see represented in visual art, such as Paul Sandby's depiction of a woman selling wine (fig. 5).[22] With a certain relaxed impudence, as she leans against the fence, resting her heavy load of wine – itself an invitation to refreshment and pleasure – the woman appears as free and easy as her clothes, and faces the viewer unapologetically, her pocket worn outside her other garments in plain sight.

The unabashed attitude of the woman may suggest too much sampling of her own stock, but it also signals her independence, moving at will in the city, raising her voice to call her wares, and dealing with cash, her pocket ready to receive it.[23] The woman's unsettling presence points to how pockets could be an instrument of female empowerment, granting them mobility, autonomy and agency. The woman may be poor, but her pocket is a complex index of freedom and risk, inviting but potentially unruly, putting her far outside the bounds of polite femininity.

The Proceedings of London's Old Bailey criminal court run from 1674 to 1913, a close parallel with the extended period in which the tie-on pocket was in use, and they form an invaluable resource for our book. We undertook a detailed analysis of 572 cases that shed light on tie-on pockets over the time span of the source.[24] Tie-on pockets, on or off the person, appear in these cases in a range of offences, including thefts such as pickpocketing, highway robbery, shoplifting, burglary, larceny, housebreaking and theft with violence, as well in some cases of murder, infanticide and coining. A small minority of cases concern women of higher status but most feature women lower down the social scale, either as victims or as perpetrators of crime. *The Proceedings* shed light on particular episodes in the lives of metropolitan women who otherwise leave little or no mark in the archive, such as the charwoman and washerwoman, servants in and out of place, prostitutes, the basket carrier and street seller, and those in more settled circumstances, such as the butcher's wife, the cow-keeper, the publican and the haberdasher. The indictments, together with the testimonies, give precious information about value and materials but also about practices. They contribute substantially to our understanding of why pockets – and the things inside them – mattered to women. The limitations and editorial selectivity of *The Proceedings*, coupled with the potential for mistakes and untruths on the part of defendants, victims and witnesses, are serious caveats.[25] Nevertheless, our findings, though provisional, are densely suggestive and present a uniquely intimate view of women's lives.

Accumulated shards of evidence are intrinsic to the excavation of lost or marginal objects, and our brief encounters with the women in *The Proceedings* form an essential stratum running through the book, but we also meet a number of other, more elite, women several times in different contexts. The written papers they left behind allow a closer view of where, when and how their pockets fitted into their particular lives. Alert to the interconnected social hierarchies where the consumption of one woman relied on the labour of another, our approach means that we also value an elite woman's bill for her pockets as an insight into the handiwork of the anonymous needlewomen who made them. Reading the pockets as things that connect the rich to the humble and nameless ensures we keep sight of the toil and output of women behind the scenes.

The diversity of our sources reveals the pocket's pervasive presence in vastly different social and cultural realities. The social versatility of the pocket meant that fashionable aristocrats as well as servants, publicans and market-stall keepers had tie-on pockets, which they put to different uses. The pockets of the latter group might have been made in rough denim, jean or leather instead of silk and damask, and contained less precious possessions than the pockets of aristocratic women, but, despite obvious disparities in their owners' circumstances, they still functioned in equally important ways for them.[26] Sharing the experience of wearing and using tie-on pockets, these women had a common language of gestures, haptic knowledge and organising strategies, and they could devise similar tactics to keep the contents of their pockets secure from prying eyes or the nimble fingers of thieves. In this respect, through the use of their pockets, a duchess and a pea seller can be said to have shared 'a community of practice', having a common experience linked by 'a shared repertoire of skills, discourses and artefacts'.[27] At a time when material literacy was more widespread than textual literacy, extant pockets are an irreplaceable source for the investigation of women's experience and practices across social rank.

This specific form of pocket for women in Britain was in use by the mid-seventeenth century and probably before. It remains open to question when and where detachable pockets first made their appearance in women's clothing before that point, and what their antecedents were, though evidence in paintings suggests they may have come to England from continental Europe.[28] Despite sporadic archival evidence for what might be tie-on pockets for women in the early seventeenth century, the low survival rate of garments from this period makes it difficult to establish a firm 'date of birth'.[29] By the later seventeenth century the evidence increases, and gives our book its starting point. The end of tie-on pockets is similarly serpentine and imprecise, belying the wishful narrative of their neat replacement by handbags and male-style pockets.[30] The pocket's vernacular elements, its commonplace usage by young and old alike, its resilience over generations and its particular capacity to accommodate change and continuity together also constitute a corrective to dominant narratives of fashion history.

The pocket's arrival, take-up, evolution and eventual disappearance from common use at the end of the nineteenth century cannot be explained adequately in terms of responses to the commercial production of fashionable novelties. Analysis of the pocket's manufacture, usage and meanings reveals a particularised picture of female consumers' actions, and suggests that their choices fitted into more grounded, commonplace customs and practices.

6 Dressed doll, mid-18th century, pocket opening (detail). Hampshire Cultural Trust, HMCMS:ACM.1949.97.

Women shaped their consumption of pockets more by the ways they worked and circulated within and between private and public spheres than by desires or dreams of fashion. Part of body linen, but migrating often ambiguously between dress and undress, the pocket is also a means of interrogating the categorisation of dress, fashion and accessory as well as the relationship between them (fig. 6).

Undoubtedly, the pocket's extended period of use gives our study a challenge. The world changed, sources changed, the sartorial context changed and our study crosses from the early modern to the modern, a period often associated with discontinuity, disruption and dramatic change. If we think of the pocket as a lens through which to look at the past, a tool to think with, its exceptional resilience for 250 years reveals patterns of continuity remaining alongside great changes over the period. It points to a coherence in the life of the object, which maintained its relevance and usefulness and carried ideological resonance all through what was a long and transformative period for Britain. It does not collapse time but it offers a slower view of time, in which women shared practices across generations and social classes. But the extended lifespan of pockets and their persistence are not manifestations of stasis. The tie-on pocket's materiality gives us a close-up view of the economic transformations Britain underwent in the course of the eighteenth and nineteenth centuries, a period that witnessed unparalleled developments in manufacturing, consumption and global trade.[31] In this object we see the spread of cottons, advances in industrial weaving, the advent of the sewing machine. We observe evolutions in spinning and new textile printing and dyeing technologies. Yet surviving pockets show that none of these developments or innovations ever totally obliterated older technologies. Pockets require us to recognise slower currents of consumer practices below or even against the mainstream. This long period also saw major change in women's social, legal and political status and corresponds to the development of women's rights. It might be tempting to think that the disappearance of the pocket can be explained by the gradual but ever firmer grasp women had of new forms of power and rights and their abandonment of old social and domestic practices. Yet our examination of what things women kept in their pockets, and the practices involved, shows that the earlier, more restricted legal capacity to hold property in their own right did not deprive women of a strong sense of possession – or dispossession when their pockets were rifled.[32] So the pocket can prompt different questions and disrupt established narratives.[33]

In our attempt to reconstruct the complex lives of women through 'small things forgotten', we draw on a wide, interconnected range of material, visual and documentary sources, and endeavour to accommodate different scholarly methodologies from social and economic history to the history of emotions, sociology, archaeology and anthropology.[34] To tell the story of the pocket 'in the round' we combine evidence of all kinds, from surviving artefacts to visual and written satire, we read needlework manuals together with private correspondence and journals, we analyse account books alongside coroners' reports, and utilise court testimonies as well as laundry bills. In each of these sources, the pocket is often marginal, a detail rather than the main focus. But once excavated out of its seemingly insignificant position and once the variety of our evidence is brought together, this small but attractive object forms an intimate viewpoint. It offers a fresh way of thinking about women's lives. It sheds light on their role as consumers and makers of textiles, dress and fashion, and takes us close to their work as custodians of a household's possessions. Looking inside women's pockets, we explore their variable relations to the things they carried in them. Pockets also invite our thoughts to radiate outwards as much as inwards. Portable and flexible, they adapted to different uses, facilitating women's sociability and mobility – indeed their participation in socio-economic life, high or low. Relatively protected, the small space of the pocket was also an index of women's experience of privacy – indeed, of their sense of self.

CHAPTER ONE

'Oh, pockets – pockets – pockets!'

Revealing Pockets: Practice and Polemics

'No. Not one pocket. Yards and yards of material. Pleats, frills, bows, scallops, fancy loops. But not one pocket.'[1] In *Bill's New Frock*, a children's book of 1989, a boy laments his predicament when made to wear a girl's dress for a day. The gendered politics of pockets has a long history. By the end of the seventeenth century, men already enjoyed a well-established tradition for integrated, firmly sewn-in pockets in their lined, stiffened and warmly padded sets of garments.[2] In 1721 a victim of pickpocketing admitted to the court that he was not entirely sober at the time of the crime; nonetheless, he defended the orderly use he had made of his many pockets, saying that 'his Watch was in his Fob, his Letter-Case in his Wastcoat Pocket, his Snuff Box in the other Wastcoat Pocket, and his Money in his Breeches Pocket, and that he did not fall down as he went home'.[3] While men's numerous, specialised and stable pockets indicated structured relations to possessions, women's apparel had fewer purpose-made berths to stow possessions, and the detachability of their pockets may seem characteristic of more uncertain, elastic relationships to things. However, women did not live in a more limited material world than men and were not short of options for carrying things about their persons. As well as their tie-on pockets, women also had pockets within some of their accessories, and others were contrived out of the folds and cavities of their apparel – objects could be tucked down inside their stays, or shawls and aprons could be turned into improvised bundles.

PAGE 22
7 Paul Sandby RA (1731–1809), 'Rare Mackarel Three a Groat or Four for Sixpence', *Cries of London*, 1760, plate 8, etching (H 24 cm). London Metropolitan Archives, City of London, p7515144.

Tie-on pockets may have been less specialised than men's integrated pockets, but they nevertheless offered women an effective opportunity to carry their things, sometimes in great quantity. They could be made as roomy as required without causing unwelcome pull or strain on the dress. This adaptability accounts in part for why they outlived or coexisted with some of the other containers traditionally thought to have replaced them, such as the reticule bag of the Regency period or later sewn-in pockets. The premature obituaries of the tie-on pocket written by fashion journalists who waxed lyrical over the appearance of the reticule *c*.1800 have been taken at face value, a mistake compounded by the tendency of fashion and dress history to consider garments and accessories in isolation from one another. In fact, tie-on pockets continued to be worn over time with dramatically different fashionable styles of dress and despite the competition of alternative carriers, such as reticules or male-style integrated pockets. Their resilience reveals a more intricate chronology, in which an essentially unfashionable accessory outlives supposedly more desirable novelties.

A garment and a container, visible and invisible, dress and undress, public and private, the clearly gendered but still puzzling pocket existed not only in the material world but also in the mind. Loaded with meanings as much as with portable possessions, pockets have had a powerful presence in discourses and representations of gender throughout the period. In her short story of 1914, 'If I Were a Man', Charlotte Perkins Gilman alerts us to the gendered politics of pockets. Written at a time when feminists were demanding both dress and political equality, the short story portrays its heroine, a 'true woman' who nevertheless wished 'heart and soul she was a man', suddenly turning into her own husband and spending the day as him. Pockets are among the numerous revelations and 'new views, strange feelings' she encounters on that day. On the way to (his) work in an office, she explores the many pockets of his outfit:

> Of course she had known they were there, had counted them, made fun of them, mended them, even envied them; but she never had dreamed of how it felt to have pockets.
>
> Behind her newspaper she let [. . .] that odd mingled consciousness rove from pocket to pocket, realizing the armored assurance of having all those things at hand, instantly get-at-able, ready to meet emergencies. The cigar case [. . .] the firmly held fountain pen, [. . .] the keys, pencils, letters, documents, notebook, checkbook, bill folder – all at once, with a deep rushing sense of power and pride, she felt what she had never felt before in all her life – the possession of money, of her own earned money – hers to give or to withhold; not to beg for, tease for, wheedle for – hers.[4]

8 Paul Sandby RA (1731–1809), *Asylum for the Deaf*, late 18th century, watercolour (34.9 × 53.7 cm). Victoria and Albert Museum, London, 1694-1871.

The chapter bridges the material and the immaterial, the descriptive and the interpretative, and explores how readily, and often dramatically, the pocket accommodated gendered ideology. Its material, formal and practical characteristics gave rise to metaphorical and polemical interpretations that made it alternately domestic and erotic – a reminder that pockets have always been political.

Sartorial practices

The male cloak, doublet and hose of the sixteenth and early seventeenth centuries became reorganised as the coat, waistcoat and breeches of the mid-seventeenth century onwards, and continued the benefits of plural pockets, as the garb of the raggle-taggle band in Paul Sandby's *Asylum for the Deaf* clearly shows (fig. 8). All through the period from the late seventeenth to the early twentieth centuries, the staple items of the suit remained in place, though constantly subject to fashionable changes in cut, materials and decoration, most notably in the early nineteenth century, when close-fitting trousers, sleeker jackets and coats came to dominate. Yet for the whole of that period, whatever the style or social class, men's fashions were united by a fraternity of pockets.[5] For men of all ranks, their pockets were finely attuned to their possessions, their work, pastimes and interests, and provided

numerous places in which to stow the gear and necessities of everyday life. Tailors created additional pockets to keep abreast of developments in the implements a man might think essential to his place in the world. The fob pocket was such a purpose-designed pocket, which appeared in the breeches with the spread of the personal timepiece, combining protection, security and ready access. In contrast, women often wore their watches un-pocketed, on a chain or chatelaine hanging from their waists, doing without fob pockets until the second half of the nineteenth century. A man's privilege, the fob pocket entailed a specifically masculine relationship to time, embodied in the particular gestures of pulling the watch out of the pocket and opening its different casings before reading the time.[6]

Eighteenth-century breeches allowed for numerous other pockets besides the fob: they usually had two front pockets, with sometimes another two in the sides. Supplementing this ample provision, the male eighteenth-century coat and sometimes waistcoat also had pockets, whose large, ornate flaps loudly signalled access to capacious interiors. The greatcoat, a long heavy garment worn by men for travel between the second half of the eighteenth century and about the mid-nineteenth century, added even more to men's stowing capacity.[7] In June 1783, as he journeyed back from a shopping expedition to Norwich, Parson Woodforde, despite the warm weather, was 'obliged to wear [his] great Coat, the Pockets of which also were loaded with two Pounds of Pins &c' that he had bought for his niece Nancy.[8] In December 1798 a 'Gentleman' advertised in a London newspaper the loss of a drab-coloured waterproof and double-caped greatcoat, demonstrating the benefits of these garments by how much he had stashed in its pockets:

> in the upper pocket a small black pocketbook with Trowting tackle; a pair of Shoes with strings, wrapt up in paper in one of the side pockets; and a pair of double kersey-wove Breeches in the other side pocket, with a change of Linen, &c. – A reward of One Guinea and a Half will be given for the recovery of the same.[9]

The cost of advertising and a reward made economic sense for the owner, given the inconvenience occasioned by the loss, midwinter, of such a pantechnicon of a garment. When the greatcoat fell from use, making way for slimmer over-garments, probably encouraged by the change from horse power to rail travel, the pocket superiority enjoyed by men took a serious setback. Essayist George Sala (1828–1896) wrote mid-century of 'Things Departed', mourning the greatcoat as yet another loss alongside numerous services, trades and everyday objects no longer to be found in the expanding, restless metropolis. Central to his description of the greatcoat as a male institution sacrificed to the fashionable foibles of modern life are the copious, ample pockets it contained: 'But where is the great-coat – the long, voluminous, wide-skirted garment of brown or drab broadcloth, reaching to the ankle, possessing unnumbered pockets; pockets for bottles, pockets for sandwiches, secret pouches for cash, and side-pockets for bank-notes?'[10] But even after the greatcoat was abandoned and their suits had lost the skirted amplitude of the eighteenth century, Victorian men continued to enjoy the security of multiple pockets. The nineteenth-century gentleman's suit of quality, marked by the sobriety of the new worsteds, turned a quieter face to the world, yet its smoother surfaces also accommodated numerous, if more discreet, pockets.[11] In 1899 a tailor, interviewed about the vast superiority of men's pockets over women's, counted no fewer than 'say twenty to twenty-four all told'.[12]

In contrast to such plentiful masculine pockets, women's tie-on pockets – detached and normally worn in ones or twos – may appear strikingly inferior. Because they were tied round the waist, the strain on the tapes caused by their load meant they could break or come undone. The testimonies of women at the Old Bailey register the vulnerability of women's pockets: 'pulled from her', 'torn off', 'snatched off', or 'cut off' are but a few of the descriptions of the ways in which pockets, worn hanging round the waist, could be taken from the body. Lost or stolen, pockets could be hard to trace; they could shift between individuals in lawful and unlawful ways and find themselves hidden, reappropriated or easily thrown away. When the widow Elizabeth Taylor was a patient at St Bartholomew's Hospital, London, in 1803, she stashed her pockets, containing her wages, under her pillow. A fellow patient saw the nurse

> put her hand under the pillow, and take out the pockets; she put them on a shelf behind the curtain, and put a bit of flannel over them; in a short time afterwards, I saw her go and take the pockets again, fling her apron over them, and take them to the privy; she staid there a short time; when she came back, she brought the pockets with her, and put them under the pillow again [empty of their contents].[13]

The loss and retrieval of stolen pockets illustrate how readily they were slipped out of their rightful place into improvised hideaways or were thrown away when they constituted incriminating evidence. Accused of stealing a pocket from under another woman's pillow in 1814, Maria Smith threw it down a well, while in 1835 Sandy Sutherland hid a stolen pocket with valuable contents in a nearby privy.[14]

Yet the versatility of tie-on pockets was also an asset, and not solely for thieves. Tie-on pockets could be adapted as circumstances required and, without disrobing, readily slipped on and off the body as many times as necessary during the day. It may have been a relief in the course of the day for women to take pockets off if they were full or heavy. This was particularly useful for trading women, whose pockets served as a portable store for their cash takings, to be removed at the end of the day, secured overnight, and put on again the next day. Elizabeth Stebbing explained how one morning in 1765 she set off to her tripe shop in Clare Market with her pocket in hand: 'I took and tied it up [. . .] and took it roll'd up in my arms to the market', intending to put it on only once there.[15] When unworn, the ties could be used to wind round the opening to secure the contents. At home, the tie-on pocket could be slung over a chair, and at night it was common practice for women to keep their pockets, with the contents still inside, close to their beds, or stow them under the pillow for increased security. Sometimes pockets acted as more permanent caches. In her will of 1639, Margaret Verney pointed her son to a series of containers with various sums of money, including a red box, an old glove and a white dish, but also 'ye black and white pocket' and 'ye Spanish pocket'.[16] These were not pockets in daily use but had become places of storage for precious possessions. Used as bags or purses, pockets could in turn be pocketed. In 1796 butcher Stephen Loosely said he had a pair of his wife's pockets in his own coat pocket in his bedroom, containing substantial sums of money and promissory notes.[17]

In these ways, tie-on pockets were functional both on and off the body. Their detachability also meant that they could be put to unexpected uses. In 1847 Mary Cullen explained in court how she had belted her light-fingered daughter round the head with her pocket. In her own defence, Mary said 'she took my pocket from under my pillow [. . .] I took the pocket out of her hand, and hit her with it, being in a passion; she is constantly plundering'.[18]

In use, tie-on pockets were capacious and usually reliable companions that offered undeniable advantages and functioned well with the rest of women's clothing. Separate from it, they were not contingent on the fabric or cut of the gown, giving women considerable latitude in how, where or whether they wore pockets. Women could wear one or two – either as an attached pair or as two singles. They could wear several pairs at the same time, or a pair and a single, or else could choose not to wear them at all. Frances Frances wore two separate linen pockets when she was assaulted in London in 1773, while Susannah Schooler, the wife of a publican, said in 1793 she was accustomed to wearing four pockets.[19] Regardless of how many pockets a woman wore, she could adjust where they went on her waist. On the side was the common habit, but for safety reasons the pockets themselves could be drawn more towards the centre and away from the pocket openings in the clothing, which gave

10 Laurie & Whittle, Fleet Street, *Beauty and Fashion* (London, 1797), mezzotint (41 × 29 cm). Lewis Walpole Library, Yale University, 797.01.24.01+.

access to them. Female offenders using pockets to hide stolen goods sometimes wore theirs in unusual places to avoid detection when searched. Frances Costelow, who had stolen a silver watch in 1796, hung hers between her thighs, and Mary Williams, suspected of using a false key to steal from Mary Wood in 1783, was found to wear her pocket not 'in the regular place' but 'hung behind'.[20]

Women had a choice about where their pocket was worn in relation to the rest of their clothing (fig. 9). All through the period, women's clothing was made of multiple layers: a chemise was worn next to the body, over which stays, stomacher or corset were laced, and for most of the period one or several petticoats were tied under or over a supporting structure, such as a hoop, panniers or a crinoline. Even if no under-structure was worn around the waist, bulk was created by one or more thick petticoats and skirts, with additional layers consisting of apron and cloak. Pockets could be worn at different levels within this stratified ensemble, petticoats and gowns having openings in their sides for the hand to reach the pocket beneath (see fig. 6). In turn, these openings could be used to loop up the sides of the gown out of the way (fig. 10). Depending on practicality, security and personal preference, women could choose to wear their pockets buried deep under the layers of their various clothes or closer to the surface, sometimes even visible (see fig. 7). Women employed in trade or service often wore theirs on the surface of their clothing. Although the practice made their pockets prone to assault, it was a customary choice for women handling money all day long (fig. 11; see also fig. 128). Eleanor Bird, a publican and victim of crime in 1766, was asked in court: 'Was your pocket on the outside of your cloaths?' The implication was that she was careless but was following a common practice for a woman in her trade.[21] The detachability of pockets, the fact that they were tied on, might seem to add to their vulnerability, but it also made them an important instrument in women's agency.

Complementing these versatile tie-on pockets were several other options for women to carry their things. Women's generous layers of garments offered many possibilities for devising makeshift or quasi-pockets, hidden or otherwise. Side hoops or pocket hoops – cage-like structures, often shaped with cane and covered with strong cloth, designed to hold skirts away from the sides of the body – could be made with a base and so act as containers that

11 Paul Sandby RA (1731–1809), *London Cries: 'Black Heart Cherries'*, *c.*1759, watercolour and graphite on paper (17.8 × 14.3 cm). Yale Center for British Art, Paul Mellon Collection, B1975.3.206.

could be reached through a simple opening at the top.[22] Women's stays were easily accessible because they were normally worn as semi-outerwear, creating a firm layer on top of the under-linen and leaving slim spaces between, with opportunities for stowing small belongings. Introduced early in life, they were a staple of women's clothing.[23] Eighteenth- and early nineteenth-century stays were less restrictive than the corsets of the mid- and later nineteenth century, but they were nevertheless very stoutly constructed.[24] The delicate balance between tightness and ease – stays had to be tight to provide support but at the same time had to allow movement and breathing – made them the perfect place to carry or hide things. A woman told the court in 1742 in London that she 'generally' put her money in her bosom, explaining that her purse was 'a little way down' her stays, for she wore them 'pretty loose and cannot go strait-laced'.[25] In a very different context, Sarah Hurst of Horsham, entrusted by her father with a large sum of money to take to London for him, put the gold in her stays the day before she set out in the coach: 'Put several hundred pound

12 Woman's stays with internal front pocket, 18th century. Museum of London, Z690.

of my father's in my stays to buy in the Stocks, am afraid I shall find it a great weight.'[26] To add further security, some pockets were inset between the layers of the stays by the staymaker during construction, while more makeshift patch pockets were fitted to the inside lining, probably at a later stage by the owner (fig. 12).[27] Such pockets could also be put to criminal uses, offenders using their stays or bosoms to stow illicit goods. 'I put my hand down her bosom and between her skin and her stays, I found a private pocket', said the officer who searched Elizabeth Green in 1798.[28] Mary Chandler, a prostitute accused by one of her clients in 1831 of taking more than her due, was found to have put his money 'in a concealed pocket, under her stays'.[29] Female criminals prosecuted at the Old Bailey hoarded some surprisingly uncomfortable items in their 'bosoms' – whether in a purpose-made stays pocket or not – such as keys, pocketbooks, buckles, tea, spoons, pepper pots, sugar tongs, spectacles and soap.

Women's muffs or aprons, when made with pockets of their own, could also accommodate small objects. For elite women, dress aprons were formal and highly ornate, part of fashionable rather than utilitarian dress. They represented a decorative highlight, and the capacity to carry things in these fancy aprons was secondary.[30] More serviceable and versatile, the common apron was a key element of working women's dress (fig. 13). It protected clothing and could be used to wipe the hands or face, but sometimes also

13 Marcellus Laroon (1653–1702), 'A Merry New Song', *The Cryes of the City of London Drawne after the Life* (London: Pierce Tempest, *c.*1690), fol. 35, engraving (22 × 33 cm). Lilly Library, Indiana University, Bloomington, GT3450.L331 C9 1690.

added to women's stowing capacity, either because it had pockets or could be turned into one itself. In 1734 Mary Rhodes of West Yorkshire put on an apron 'under her gown in the form of a pocket' to steal linen from a clothes line 'and [brought] the same away in the said apron so foulded up'.[31]

The 'handkerchief' was a generous wrap in almost universal use, covering the neck and upper chest, and added to the layering of women's dress. Easily detached from the body, it could then form a temporary bag or bundle when required. 'Bundles', so often mentioned in Old Bailey trial accounts, constituted a cheap, light and convenient means of carrying effects, typical of both a mobile society and of a flexible relationship to the material world. Women could improvise them out of handkerchiefs, shawls or virtually any piece of material. The stolen haul of Ann Vickers in 1834 was packed into a 'shawl [. . .] which was tied up in a bundle'; it contained, among other things, a glass salt holder, a chocolate stirrer, spoons, a tablecloth, wax candles, curtains, a china milk jug, a duster, three pieces of chintz and a powder box.[32] In practice, almost any piece of clothing could make an improvised berth. Catherine Roach, convicted in 1811 of trying to pass counterfeit money, kept her forged sixpence coins in what 'appeared to be a bag', which was made of 'part of a glove tied up'.[33] Adding to the versatility of female dress, the pins used in the eighteenth century to secure the several parts of a woman's attire could also be used to improvise yet more pockets, if necessary. When Jane Jonas was apprehended in 1779, 'three guineas, two half guineas and a shilling' were found 'all pinned up in the cuff of her sleeve'.[34] More precariously, Jane Hammond, charged with stealing a china dish in 1811, was found to have secured it to her dress by wrapping it 'in a child's frock, pinned under her petticoats'.[35] The sartorial inventiveness of female criminals evokes the myriad options available to women to supplement their tie-on pockets. Detached pockets fitted in well with this array of other carriers, which complemented one another to give a woman agency to choose where and how to carry her things. When Farmer Embling's wife's pocket was cut off in 1736 on her return journey from market in Bristol, most of her money was saved because she had split it between 'her Bosom pocket' and her tie-on pocket.[36]

LEFT TO RIGHT
14 Doll known as 'Lady Clapham', 1690s (L 56 cm). Victoria and Albert Museum, London, T.846.1974.

14a Dressed doll.
14b Doll with outer garments removed.

Resilience and continuity

At either end of our period, two very different sources complexify the chronology of tie-on pockets and show their persistence alongside other carriers. Little seems to link the 1690s wooden doll known as 'Lady Clapham' and, almost two centuries later, the disembowelled body of one of Jack the Ripper's victims. They could not be further apart: the fashion doll, a finely crafted object, has the demure poise of late Stuart respectability, with her fashionable clothing and well-coordinated accessories (fig. 14).[37] By contrast, Catherine Eddowes, who died so cruelly in Mitre Square on 30 September 1888, was the opposite of Victorian respectability. Living a life of squalor and destitution, rather than the life of opulent decency that the doll represents, her clothing was anything but matching or fashionable. It was instead a random assemblage of uncoordinated garments piled on top of each other to create warmth and possibly to protect them from theft in the notoriously unsafe, shared accommodation that was Catherine's lot. However, despite obvious chronological, social, cultural and even ontological differences between them, both of them combined tie-on pockets with other types of pocket and

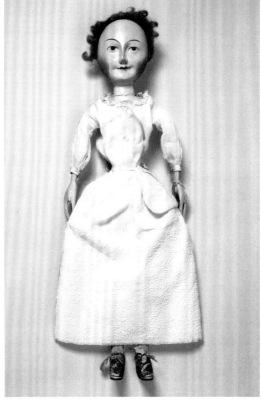

carrier. As part of her ingeniously crafted outfit, Lady Clapham has a single, linen, tie-on pocket, as well as a quilted petticoat with two sewn-in pockets, and a draw-string purse (fig. 14). On Catherine Eddowes's body were found three tie-on pockets – a pair of 'unbleached calico pockets' and a single 'blue stripe bedticking pocket' – worn in combination with a black cloth jacket with '2 outside pockets', a 'man's white vest' with another '2 outside pockets', and 'two small blue bed ticking bags' (see fig. 139).[38] In both these cases, the tie-on pockets were not worn in isolation but in combination with other pocket types and bags, illustrating how the tie-on pocket was only one of a range of containers, and functioned within a specific repertoire of clothing practices defined by choice and adaptation. A woman could combine tie-on pockets with integral pockets, as well as with hand-held bags. Chronology thus appears rather more complex and less linear than is sometimes implied by over neat fashion narratives where one novelty supersedes older styles. Sartorial practice was, in reality, much more fluid.

The male-style, sewn-in pocket, frequently thought to have appeared in women's attire in the second half of the nineteenth century, when it supposedly superseded the tie-on pocket, was present in female clothing as early as 1690 and had not totally eradicated the tie-on pocket by 1888, at the time of Catherine Eddowes's death.[39] Nor was the coexistence in a woman's wardrobe of tie-on pockets with other types of pockets exceptional. Borrowed from the male wardrobe, female riding habits had male-style pockets. They were the work not of mantua- or dressmakers, but of tailors, used to inserting pockets in men's jackets and waistcoats, who transferred the techniques to

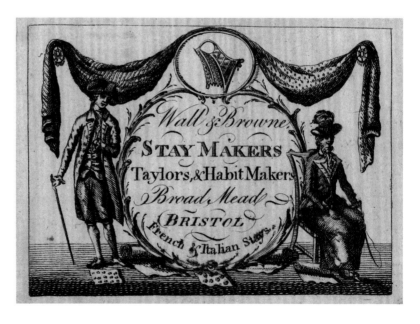

THE POCKET

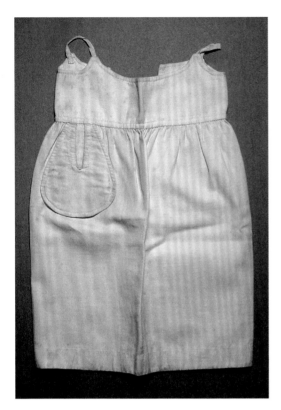

16 Doll's undergarment with attached pocket, early 19th century (L 31.5 cm, garment). Salisbury and South Wiltshire Museum, SBYWM.1943.4.

female outfits. However, riding habits occupied a territory of their own, uniquely combining modified skirts with a tightly fitted and seductively curved jacket, accentuating the female form (fig. 15).[40] The appealing cut of the habit was designed to thrill. Its dash and flattering fit meant that women wore riding habits on many occasions when they were not on horseback: for walking and travelling, but also for informal occasions. Part of their popularity may have lain in the many opportunities they afforded women of fashion to have male-style pockets.[41] A bill for a sumptuous riding habit for a Miss Pomier in 1778 itemises the pockets – 'To making, lining and backs for ye waistcoat, sleeve lining and pockets for ye jacket' – as part of the £1 10s. 0d. bill charged for the garment.[42] The bills of Georgiana Spencer and her sister Harriet Spencer similarly show riding habits routinely made with pockets. Between 1772 and 1774, the year of Georgiana's marriage to the Duke of Devonshire, she had no fewer than eight suits, complete with pockets, made by the metropolitan tailor William Hagelston, in different cloths and colour combinations.[43] Nevertheless, owning these pocketed suits did not keep the flamboyant future duchess from having six pairs of tie-on pockets made as part of her trousseau.[44]

Integrated pockets could feature in women's clothing throughout the period. Lady Clapham's quilted petticoat, with pockets inserted into its sides, is one such example, while a fine silver-lace dress of *c*.1660, made up of skirt and bodice, with one integral pocket, is evidence that such pockets existed earlier.[45] Alongside these early survivors can be found scattered written references to 'petticoats with pockets', a term often difficult to interpret but which might have described integrated pockets;[46] another possibility is demonstrated by the method given in *The Workwoman's Guide* for attaching pockets to the waistband of under-petticoats, an approach well illustrated by an early nineteenth-century doll's undergarment (fig. 16).[47]

Before the 1850s, the simple term 'pocket' was widely used in indictments, advertisements or inventories, in which its detachable form is amply evidenced. But by the mid-nineteenth century there was a need in common parlance to distinguish it from other types. The Old Bailey court proceedings are a rich source of everyday, colloquial speech. They show a shift in nomenclature at about the halfway mark of the century. Several cases make

A "NEW WOMAN."

The Vicar's Wife. "AND HAVE YOU HAD GOOD SPORT, MISS GOLDENBERG!"
Miss G. "OH, 'RIPPIN'! I ONLY SHOT ONE RABBIT, BUT I MANAGED TO INJURE QUITE A DOZEN MORE!"

17 George du Maurier (1834–1896), 'A "New Woman"', *Punch*, 8 September 1894. Punch Magazine Cartoon Archive, 1894.09.08.111.

use of compound terms such as 'dress pocket' or 'gown pocket' in an attempt to describe an element of dress different from the old-established tie-on pocket. In 1852 Ellen Bennett explained how, suspicious of the intentions of Charlotte Fielder, she removed her purse from her 'dress-pocket' and put it into 'a pocket under [her] dress', adding that this was 'not the same pocket' as the first mentioned.[48] In such cases, these pockets were contrasted with the 'old-fashioned' pockets. In 1860 Mary Hudson specifically explained to the court that 'the entrance to my pocket is a side slit in the skirt – it is not one of the old-fashioned pockets that tie round the waist.'[49]

Despite this perception of tie-on pockets as old-fashioned by the mid-nineteenth century, they nevertheless proved surprisingly resilient, whereas the status of integral pockets remained deeply equivocal. Except in rare cases, the sewn-in pocket was usually an isolated phenomenon. From the 1850s, a small patch pocket started to appear on garments such as cloaks or jackets, while a watch pocket, rather like a man's fob pocket, began regularly to be inserted into women's dress, dropped inside the side front waistband.[50] The more robust skirted suits of the 1880s and 1890s, so beloved of historians as symbolic of the 'new woman', sometimes had outer patch pockets on the jacket, as did the coats that accompanied them.[51] These were often the focus of satire because of the masculine behaviour and gestures they occasioned in the wearers (fig. 17).[52] Outfits with some kind of integral pocket certainly became more common from the second half of the nineteenth century.[53] In less tailored outfits of the period, a pocket could sometimes be awkwardly integrated into the skirts of the dress or the petticoat, or inserted into the back of the garment, in the bustle, or even in the hem of the skirt.[54] Moving waywardly around the dress, the sewn-in pocket, usually solitary, never seems to have found a settled place in women's outfits. Its erratic location, sometimes impossibly inaccessible, attracted the criticism of late nineteenth-century fashion journalists: 'Her greatest difficulty is her pocket. Dressmakers take a weird delight in concealing it, and you have to search for it as long and fruitlessly as for hidden treasure. The indiscreet person who, without first extracting her purse, hires a hansom, writhes about it inside in search of her pocket'.[55] The awkward positioning of the dress pocket stood in sharp contrast with the practical tie-on, which could be worn where and how a woman wished, with ready access through purpose-made side openings in petticoats and gowns. The practicality and adaptability of tie-on pockets were also factors in their resilience in the face of competition from the new reticule bags that had appeared at the end of the eighteenth century.

Small bags for women were nothing new. Knotting bags, sweet bags, gaming bags, purses and work-bags had been used for generations. In its humblest form the bag was a simple bundle, in its most expensive elite expression, it could be a highly decorative accessory. In the last decade of the eighteenth century, such bags – called 'reticules', sometimes 'ridicules' or 'indispensibles' – appeared. They were usually small and were carried in full view in the hand. A high-fashion item, the reticule could be ornate and made of luxury materials, such as silk and velvet, while fine leather ones also made an appearance. Repeatedly promoted in fashion magazines when they first appeared, reticules remained nevertheless marginal in practice, particularly for humbler women. Showy and fashionable, they were the polar opposite of the often invisible tie-on pocket. Reticule bags could be delicately dangled and their workmanship displayed (fig. 18). Their visibility meant that some were even used for campaigning, as when a female abolitionist society produced reticules to circulate their anti-slavery message (fig. 19).[56] But despite their attractions, reticules failed to dent the popularity of the versatile tie-on pocket. When, concomitantly with the reticule, figure-hugging muslin dresses

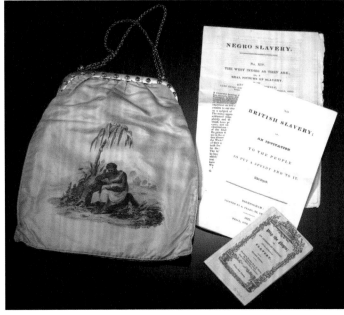

appeared in the early 1800s, pockets did not disappear. Instead they morphed: they lost the surface decoration that would make them visible underneath the gauzy fabrics and were more usually made of white, smooth-faced linens and cottons. A surviving doll wears a stout dimity tie-on pocket beneath her delicate muslin dress (fig. 20). Their shape also adapted to the fashionable, high-waisted styles by becoming longer, and they were tied higher up the body, under the bust (fig. 21; see also fig. 28). So the appearance of the fragile muslin gown was not the death-knell for tie-on pockets, as is commonly thought. On occasions, detachable pockets could be temporarily discarded – to achieve a smoother silhouette, for instance – but this did not mean that they were altogether abandoned. In 1801, at the height of the fashion for the muslin gown, Elizabeth Ham recalls taking off her pocket one evening when a visitor came, 'the perfection of fashion being then for the drapery to be as scanty and adhesive as possible'.[57] But temporary conformity to the dictates of fashion did not condemn the pocket to sartorial oblivion.

Tie-on pockets were decidedly not a fashion accessory, but an *unfashionable* accessory.[58] The choice to wear this form of pocket was not governed by a desire to shine or emulate, as it was largely invisible, being worn under the dress. But

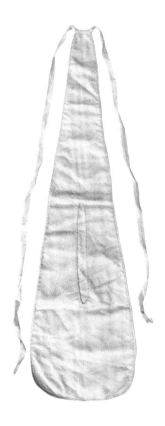

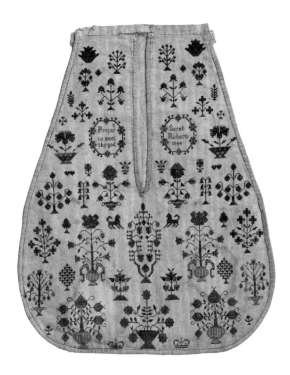

ABOVE, LEFT TO RIGHT
22a Sarah Roberts, sampler-style pocket, 1844 (L 26.5 cm). Fitzwilliam Museum, Cambridge, T.67-1938.
22b Sarah Roberts, sampler-style bag, 1845 (L 19.75 cm). Fitzwilliam Museum, Cambridge, T.68-1938.

despite the many efforts of the fashion press to cast the tie-on pocket as the old-fashioned accessory of doddery old women and the reticule as the prime accessory of the modern woman, use of the pocket persisted. It outlasted the reticule and, as we have seen, continued in use until the end of the nineteenth century, and even beyond. Sarah Roberts is assumed to be the maker of both a tie-on pocket and a draw-string bag, embroidered in 1844–5 with similar motifs, her name and the date. Sarah's work illustrates that these two pieces were not thought of as rivals but coexisted as part of a range of equally useful carriers (fig. 22). Dated extant pockets such as Sarah Roberts's, and the use of datable technologies such as press studs and machine stitching amply evidence of the enduring popularity of pockets through the second half of the nineteenth century (figs 23–4; see also fig. 4).[59] Dramatic changes in fashionable styles – neoclassical muslin dresses, the crinoline and the bustle – came and went, leaving the resilient tie-on pocket virtually unchanged.

The common narrative of dress history wrongly suggests that the tie-on pocket was abandoned in the early nineteenth century with the appearance of the reticule, or that it was later replaced by the sewn-in pocket when this became more widespread. Our study of actual practice and surviving objects concludes that the tie-on pocket continued in use despite these changes. The die-hard tie-on pocket compels us to reconsider some of the more simplistic narratives employed in histories of clothing consumption. It alerts us to the

difference between a fashion-led history of dress and one that focuses instead on sartorial practices.

Revealing pockets

Tie-on pockets eluded strict definition. Physically detached from the dress, they were also unfixed in terms of categorisation. Sometimes aligned with undergarments, at other times they were worn outside the clothing. In one of the earliest technical compendia describing the trade, Frenchman François-Alexandre de Garsault puts pockets within the remit of the *lingère*, who specialised in the making of body linen, listing them as part of the necessary pieces of a woman's trousseau, alongside her caps, smocks, petticoats and handkerchiefs.[60] In the bills that record the purchase of Georgiana Spencer's trousseau in 1774, '6 pr Pockits' appear together with quilted petticoats, caps and 'Irish cloth drawers' on a merchant's bill (fig. 67).[61] When pockets are mentioned in women's inventories, they often feature together with undergarments. In the 1747 inventory of the Duchess of Montagu's apparel, her pockets are thus to be found among her stockings, hoods and caps.[62] The same classification prevailed in the nineteenth century.[63] Yet, at other times, pockets seem to have belonged to a set of matching clothes or accessories that situated them within a regime of visibility and display.

A letter to Glasgow tradesman Robert Burn ordering the wedding ensemble of a bride and her groom in 1775 specifically cites the matching of the tie-on pockets to the fabric of a light-blue poplin wedding dress, specifying 'strings for a woman's pockets and waltening [*sic*] for same all according to the colour before mentioned'.[64] The same matching of outer dress and the tie-on pocket characterises an eighteenth-century doll wearing a pocket made in the same printed cotton fabric as her gown, establishing a visual link between different layers of garments that is not normally made (see fig. 40).[65] A pair of yellow silk quilted pockets that match a lightly boned waistcoat further complicates our understanding of the status of pockets (fig. 25). As part of a matching set, and made in a highly fashionable, vibrant colour, the pockets seem to belong to an aesthetic of visibility, on a par with the practice of matching the various parts of fashionable dress at the time.[66] On the other hand, the quilting, together with the light boning of the waistcoat, show similarities with maternity clothing, which would not be worn in public but might be worn as undress in the privacy of the home.[67]

These connections between clothing that otherwise belongs to different sartorial regimes illustrate the inherently unstable status of tie-on pockets. Having a fixed identity neither as a garment nor as an accessory, sometimes underwear, sometimes outerwear, neither dress nor quite undress, the pocket was in between. The ambiguous pockets do not settle easily into the categories

RIGHT AND BELOW
25 Woman's matching waistcoat and pockets, mid-18th century. Victoria and Albert Museum, London.

25a Quilted silk waistcoat (L 56 cm). V&A, T.87-1978.
25b Pair of quilted silk pockets (L 38.9 cm and 39.8 cm). V&A, T.87.A-1978, T.87.B-1978.

traditionally used to think about dress, and – beyond the question of whether or not pockets were meant to be seen – their liminal and shifting status invites us to rethink our own categories. They were an unsettled and unsettling presence in the traditional sartorial order of things.

When worn, the position of the pocket might shift from invisible to visible, but the act of revealing one's pocket could have vastly different meanings depending on context, age and circumstances. In George Eliot's *Adam Bede* (1859), Totty is 'a little sunny-haired girl between three and four', whose cousin Hetty will be seduced by the young local squire Captain Donnithorne. In a scene near the beginning of the novel, when the squire visits the family, Eliot turns the innocent child's tie-on pocket into an ominous signal anticipating the future sexual corruption of her cousin:

> 'Has [Totty] got a pocket on?' said the Captain, feeling in his own waistcoat pockets.
> Totty immediately with great gravity lifted up her frock, and showed a tiny pink pocket at present in a state of collapse.
> 'It dot notin in it,' she said, as she looked down at it very earnestly.
> 'No! what a pity! such a pretty pocket. Well, I think I've got some things in mine that will make a pretty jingle in it. Yes; I declare I've got five little round silver things, and hear what a pretty noise they make in Totty's pink pocket.'[68]

Totty's empty 'tiny pink pocket' speaks of her innocence, and the coins given by the rich squire are an omen of gifts that will soon seduce her cousin. Totty's empty pocket, about to be filled, foreshadows Hetty's desecrated innocence that will lead to her downfall. Worn under the dress, the pocket is revealed by the gesture of 'lift[ing] up her frock' – a gesture that is innocent enough when made by toddler Totty but has dramatic consequences for Hetty. The pocket signals both the candour of a child but at the same time an impending loss of innocence for a young woman. Just as their status in sartorial practice was unfixed, the metaphorical meaning of pockets was also fluid, and, throughout the period, the dynamic and shifting functions of pockets were harnessed in various discourses and visual representations.

Pockets and polemics

The war of words generated by the thriving fashion press at the end of the eighteenth century and the beginning of the nineteenth century, which set up reticules in opposition to tie-on pockets, was as much an attempt by the fashion trades to push a new commodity onto the market as a story about a revolution in the material and political world of women. The published accounts were divided into two clearly distinct groups: the 'pocketists' on one side and the 'anti pocketists' on the other.[69] For the latter, pockets were antiquated and irredeemably old-fashioned, while reticules were elegant and delightfully modern. 'Pocketists', on the other hand, derided reticules as vain and impractical, and aligned pockets with benevolence, good housewifery and orderliness.

The pro-pocket argument was grounded in a notion of self-sufficiency for women, related partly to the degree to which they were good household managers and could act charitably on their own behalf. A degree of self-sufficiency (though not full-blown independence) in such matters was associated with pockets. This connection is shown in Sir William Beechey's painting of Sir Francis Ford's daughter reaching for her pocket to give alms (fig. 26). The painting is both a portrait of Ford's children and an almost allegorical representation of benevolence, conveyed by the girl's passing a coin, evidently

27 Daniel Maclise RA (1806–1870), *Portrait of Mrs. Anna Maria Hall* (1800–1881), 1833, pencil and watercolour on paper (23 × 16.5 cm). Chertsey Museum, Surrey.

taken from the pocket under her apron, to the needy boy. In the anonymous novel *Celia in Search of a Husband* of 1809, the heroine is shown to be morally superior to her sister, who has abandoned pockets in the name of fashion, whereas Celia's pockets give her '*power* to be *charitable*'.[70] Benevolence by women was matched by their role as prudent housewives, and here too pockets were recruited into service. 'Never sally forth from your own room in the morning without that old-fashioned article of dress – a pocket: discard for ever that modern invention called a ridicule (properly reticule)'.[71] In Theresa Tidy's *Eighteen Maxims of Neatness and Order* (1817) the pocket is presented as the necessary accessory of the neat housewife, enabling her to have to hand 'a thimble, a pincushion, a pencil, a knife and a pair of scissars'.[72]

The same link between tie-on pockets and effective housekeeping promoted as a paramount feminine virtue appears over 20 years later in a full-length children's novel by Anna Maria Hall (1800–1881; fig. 27), *Grandmamma's Pockets* (1849).[73] Writing her didactic novel for girls at the mid-point of the century, Hall utilises the tie-on pocket as a symbol of the good housewifery of yore, now threatened by modernity. It is an expository novel in which close observation of material objects extends the significance of the older woman's pockets and what she keeps in them, contrasting them with modern equivalents:

> Let no modern lady housekeeper, who has a bag-like slip of silk inserted in the skirt of her dress – let no *demoiselle* with a three-inch pocket stitched into her pretty little apron [. . .] imagine that they understand a tithe [. . .] of the utility or comprehensiveness of GRANDMAMMA'S POCKETS![74]

Of note among the useful contents is a 'very large housewife', or 'huswif' – a container for sewing sundries: 'not a slip of silk ribbon, with a miniature roll at the end, capable of holding a few needlefulls of delicate silk and cambric thread, but a substantial housewife, containing every description of needle, from the Brobdignag "packing" to the graceful "darner"'.[75] Together with the keys, the knives, spoons and forks in cases, the scissors, corkscrews and 'solid, determined industry' thimbles 'with deep indentations', Grandmamma's pockets hold a nutmeg grater, needle-book, bodkins, silver bon-bon box 'with a puzzle top to it', cup and ball, snuffbox, files, 'a most perfect, tiny, hard-headed brass hammer', tin tacks 'in a little bag', recipe-book, nutcracker, spectacles, sticking-plaster case, pincushion, buttons and tweezers. This array of useful things underscores the different tasks assumed by a proper housewife. Hall's book sits firmly in the tradition of literature extolling the virtues of the

28 Edward Francis Burney (1760–1848), *The Waltz*, *c.*1810, watercolour (47.78 × 68.58 cm). Victoria and Albert Museum, London, P.129-1931.

work ethic in the private sphere of domestic life, and nothing articulates the proper duties of female domestic labour as well as the grandmother's pockets. Hall associates tie-on pockets with a highly formulated ideology, in which women were expected to develop – and reproduce – themselves as managers of their domestic economies. The quasi-mystical pockets are used to appropriate and organise the world in a regulated way, where different things are allocated different places, a well-regulated cosmos, presided over by the wise grandmother and her majestic pockets.

At the exact opposite end of the moral spectrum, pockets could become vehicles to expose women's duplicity and secret immorality. A large-scale watercolour of *c.*1810 by Edward Francis Burney, entitled *The Waltz*, pictures the new scandalous dance, which leads to moral and physical disarray: women are fainting and dishevelled, pockets are showing or have been torn away, discharging their immodest contents all over the dance floor (fig. 28). The erotic nature of the dance that brought male and female bodies into close contact is foregrounded by the general 'undressing' of the dancers, with shoes coming off, stockings slipping down and breeches splitting apart at the seams. The revealed tie-on pockets are part of the prevailing grotesque erotics of topsy-turvy. The cosmetics, billet-doux and even a romantic song sheet spilling

out of the pockets add to the sexual undertones of the scene, evoking as they do women's secret liaisons. In one of her *Moral Tales* (1821), Maria Edgeworth suggestively put 'one of the very worst books in the French language' in Lady Augusta's pocket – 'a book which could never have been found in the possession of any woman of delicacy – of decency', the narrator adds.[76] The physical position of pockets below the waist brought them closer to the reality of animal appetites and carnal desires that moved beneath the surface of civility. In satirical representations, the pocket was used to reveal women's vice and lust, a dark underbelly of polite, fashionable society. This is illustrated in a pornographic poem by the Earl of Rochester, which features a man spying on a woman undressing and pulling out of her pocket 'a bawdy Book' as well as 'a Tool, / Much like that with which Men Women rule; / She it apply'd where I'm asham'd to tell, / And acted what I could have done as well.'[77]

The tie-on pocket's proximity to the skin when worn under clothing contributed to its sexual associations. Joseph Bridges's *Adventures of a Bank-Note* (1770), which pictures the (male) banknote slipping down inside the woman's loose stays, also describes residing in 'the fusty warmth of a [woman's] greasy pocket'. In 'the heat of the old lady's thigh', the narrator inhabits what it lecherously calls 'the torrid zone'.[78] The proxemic association of pockets with the pelvic area heightened their potential sexual overtones.[79] Drawers were not in common use until the 1840s and the persistence of an open-legged form of undergarment until the emergence of leg seams in the 1880s meant that pockets were physically – and suggestively – close to women's genitals.[80] Pear-shaped and open down the front, pockets themselves were

30 James Gillray (1757–1815), *The Man of Feeling, in Search of Indispensibles; a Scene at the Little French Milleners*, 1800, hand-coloured etching (26 × 36 cm). Library of Congress, Washington, DC, PC 1-9577 (B size) [P&P].

strongly evocative of female genitalia. Literary and visual representations enthusiastically harnessed their formal similarities. Thomas Rowlandson's aquatint *A Sudden Squall in Hyde Park* (1791) plays on the wanton connotations of pockets (fig. 29). In the forefront of the fashionable crowd, thrown into disarray by a sudden gust of wind, stands a woman whose flimsy dress is sent flying, while a libidinous old man, holding in his hand a phallic lens, is ogling her gaping pocket, here a visual trope to signal the woman's promiscuity.[81]

In a similar vein, James Gillray's 1800 etching entitled *The Man of Feeling, in Search of Indispensibles* combines the sexually suggestive pocket with another frequent motif of female promiscuity, the milliner – and a French one, to boot (fig. 30).[82] The scene shows the exiled Prince of Orange feeling up women's skirts for their pockets. He is allegedly trying to settle a contemporary debate about 'whether they were placed at the Ancle, or in a more eligible situation'. Punning on the word 'indispensible', sometimes used to refer to a reticule, the print suggests women's muslin dresses were now so indecently transparent that a pocket acting as fig leaf was indispensable.[83] Gillray, playing on the formal association of the pocket with female genitalia, has the pocket both hide and yet suggestively reveal the milliners' genitalia, with the porcine man's groping hands acting out proxy penetration.

Tie-on pockets were in use at a time when gender was becoming increasingly defined by bodily difference, women's reproductive organs – vagina and uterus – being the sites where femininity was encoded.[84] What was at stake in these representations, therefore, was not merely male pornographic fantasies about what might be concealed under women's petticoats. Nor were

31 J. Barrow (fl. 1782–5), *Parliment Security, or A Borrough in Reserve*, 1784, etching with stipple (28 × 46 cm). Lewis Walpole Library, Yale University, 784.04.28.02+.

such depictions simply a commentary on how fashionable appearances might disguise questionable morals, or on women's supposedly unbounded sexual appetites. By aligning women with their bodies, these images were taking part in constructions of femininity while also acting as indicators of male anxieties over women's potential enfranchisement from patriarchal control.

The association of pockets with women's participation in politics was already an old one when the question of female suffrage came into view. Among the many graphic satires of the Duchess of Devonshire, one shows her holding the pocket opening in her petticoat from which the head of a fox appears (fig. 31). The image and its caption play on the double entendre of borough/burrow and on the name of the radical Charles Fox, linking the political campaigning of the duchess to her supposed affair with him. She is financing his campaign from her own pocket, and he is represented, in animal form, being literally in her pocket, while his tail lewdly sticking out from under her petticoat and his open panting mouth and lolling tongue complete the bawdy insinuation. The widely circulated motif of the duchess's promiscuity – many satirical prints depict her notoriously 'trading kisses for votes' – meets criticism of her involvement in politics.[85] A similar alignment of politics, women and sex is present in *Under Petticoat Government*, a print issued at the time of the 1832 Reform Act. Queen Adelaide, who was known for her opposition to the bill and was criticised for allegedly influencing her husband's policies behind the scenes, is shown, broom in hand, the meek face of her husband poking through her pocket opening (fig. 32). Her foot on the

THE POCKET

bill and her submissive husband crouching on the floor under her skirts, she is flanked by two men, one of whom, Lord Howe, was rumoured to be her lover. Castigating female political influence, the print associates the pocket with both pillow politics and suspicions of sexual promiscuity.

At the end of our period, when women were starting to abandon tie-on pockets, the lack of properly practical pockets in female dress was repeatedly lamented. In an essay of 1895, entitled 'The Pocket Problem' and opening with the words 'Oh, pockets – pockets – pockets!', American suffragist Elizabeth Cady Stanton tells of the impossible negotiation with a dressmaker to insert male-style pockets into a dress.[86] In another article, published in 1901, she explains the various predicaments of pocketless women, describing a woman seen hurrying onto a boat who had 'her train in one hand, her umbrella and handkerchief in the other, and her purse held in her teeth!', all problems that would be solved if 'part of the dress that trails on the floor' was cut off to 'make a generous pocket'.[87] In Cady Stanton's view, the physical impediment of the lack of pockets underlines the social inferiority of women, hampering their mobility and independence. When male-style pockets asserted themselves as part of the 'new woman's' dress, their role as sites of subversion and female enfranchisement was underscored both in print and visual form in the British press (fig. 33). This link was summed up in *The Graphic* in 1907 with the sweeping statement: 'The Woman's Question [. . .] began in the pocket'.[88] The 'emphatic call for pockets' was picked up by the *Draper's Record* in 1916 in a series of articles stressing the need to insert 'really useful pockets' into women's dress now that they were increasingly involved in the professions: 'a safe method for a lady to carry the office keys' had to be invented and it was 'a crass absurdity to pretend that this want is solved by a bag which has in turn to be carried in the hand', the articles claimed.[89]

In June 1914, at the height of British women's campaign for suffrage, the link between the absence of women's political representation and their lack of pockets was made clearly in an article entitled 'The Unwomanly Pocket', which asked 'Why should women be permitted to have pockets?'[90] This was inspired by a piece by the American suffragist Alice Duer Miller, her tongue-in-cheek 'Why We Oppose Pockets for Women', which ridiculed traditional anti-suffrage arguments by listing spurious reasons such as 'Because pockets are not a natural right' and 'Because pockets have been used by men to carry tobacco, pipes, whiskey flasks, chewing gums and compromising letters, and there is no reason to

33 Wallis Mills, 'Suffragettes at Home', *Punch*, 14 March 1909. Punch Magazine Cartoon Archive, 1909.04.14.269.

SUFFRAGETTES AT HOME.

He. "I SAY, THAT LADY OVER THERE LOOKS RATHER OUT OF IT."
She. "YES, YOU SEE, MOST OF US HERE HAVE BEEN IN PRISON TWO OR THREE TIMES, AND SHE, POOR DEAR, HAS ONLY BEEN BOUND OVER!"

suppose that women would use them more wisely.'[91] While it underscores the empowering potential of pockets in terms of individual liberty, Duer Miller's piece firmly situates pockets within a gender opposition that is inherently political. Initially published in the USA, it was reprinted and circulated in Britain, showing how similar pocket rhetoric could link women's political activism across the Atlantic.

These articles were appearing at a time when British suffragists sometimes used their pockets as part of their campaign. Emily Wilding Davison tells of her militant acts of arson involving her pocket:

> I took out of my pocket a packet of the same size as an ordinary letter. It was of grease proof paper tied with cotton. Inside was coarse linen well soaked in kerosene [. . .] I calmly applied a match [. . .] held it for a second [. . .] I let the packet, now well alight go down the receptacle, & threw the matches in afterwards.[92]

Conversely, it is the contents of Davison's pockets on 4 June 1913, the day she ran onto the Epsom racecourse, that have fuelled historians' debates about whether or not she intended to die a martyr for the suffrage cause. The police report on her death established that she had on her a small purse with a return railway ticket to Victoria station, as well as money, a notebook and stamps. As no handbag is listed in the police report or visible on the footage of the event, these items must have been carried in pockets, whether tie-on or sewn-in. The intense debate among historians about the list of her possessions and the quasi-relic status of the small leather purse show the continued polemical charge of the pocket as a locus of women's power and autonomy (fig. 34).[93] By the time the suffrage campaigning yielded its first results for British women in 1918, tie-on pockets had been mostly abandoned. Yet the loss of their unparalleled capacity was sometimes regretted. Remembering the dress of her childhood in late nineteenth-century Cambridge, artist Gwen Raverat (1885–1957) exclaims: 'We had *Pockets*' – the emphasis is hers.

> What lovely hoards I kept in them: always pencils and India-rubbers and a small sketch-book and a very large pocket-knife; beside string, nails, horse-chestnuts, lumps of sugar, bits of bread-and-butter, a pair of scissors, and many other useful objects. Sometimes even a handkerchief. For a year or two I also carried about a small book of Rembrandt's etchings, for purposes of worship. Why mayn't we have Pockets? Who forbids it? We have got Woman's Suffrage, but why must we still always be inferior to Men?[94]

* * *

The place of tie-on pockets within sartorial practices from the second half of the seventeenth to the end of the nineteenth centuries and within the discourses that appropriated them in text and visual form shows this apparently mundane thing to be far more complex and rich than its humble appearance and status in the dress hierarchy would suggest. Its chronology is not only longer than commonly assumed but also more complex, because other forms, such as the integral pocket and the small bag, both pre-existed and coexisted with them. Functional and capacious, the tie-on pocket trumped both so-called competitors by its independence of clothing. Because of its discrete nature, its form and appearance were not determined or compromised by the construction or fabric of the dress it was worn with, allowing it to continue in use through many a revolution in the structure and shape of dress. Its propensity all through the period to be charged with lively meaning and metaphor, appearing as alternately erotic and virtuous, reveals links to gender constructions as well as to sexual politics more generally. Its relationship to women's political power – or lack of it – appears ambiguous and contradictory, illustrating the continuing power of the pocket to trigger polemics.

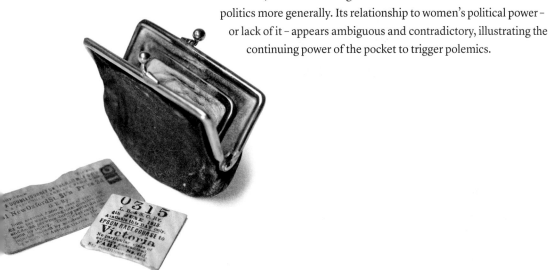

CHAPTER TWO

'work'd pocketts to my intire sattisfaction'

Making and Getting Pockets

In 1832 an elderly street seller, Caroline Walsh, went missing in east London in mysterious circumstances. At the ensuing court case, her two granddaughters identified some of her clothing. Both recognised her pocket, made by one of them, Ann Buton, a pedlar's wife, for her grandmother some time before. Ann's sister, Lydia Basey, the wife of a 'boot-closer', testified: 'This was my grandmother's pocket – it is the one I saw on her, and had seen my sister make'. Ann further testified to caring for her grandmother, and attending to her washing and lodgings. She made her a cap, knitted her stockings, 'quite different from what are sold in the shops', and made her the pocket, 'entirely my own work'. Ann also had detailed recall of all her grandmother's clothes: 'the flowers on the petticoat went of a turn; it was a kind of flower pattern, which went down not exactly in stripes, but it was a much lighter colour than the ground'. Accustomed to touching apparel to value it, a second-hand clothes dealer involved in the case was hampered in her identification of a bonnet: 'I cannot tell what it was made of, for I did not take it in my hand'.[1]

These testimonies of Ann, Lydia and the dealer reveal how experienced hands and eyes could form a tacit understanding of materiality in an age of handmade clothes, which persisted despite the industrialising of textile manufacture and global trade.[2] When Ann made her grandmother's pocket, she also demonstrated how making, central to household economy, could constitute a form of caring within social and familial relations, binding generations of women together. Lydia's observation of her grandmother's pocket being made and worn highlighted the informal transmission of methods of making and the commonplace presence and visibility of pockets in certain settings. Finally, the second-hand market, where Caroline's pocket and other apparel were sold, alerts us to the life of pockets as both personalised objects and commodities that could be bought new, ready-made or second-hand. The making and getting of pockets are treated separately here, but at a time when *making* was commonly how a woman went about *getting*, as practices they are not so easily disentangled.

Making pockets: the materials

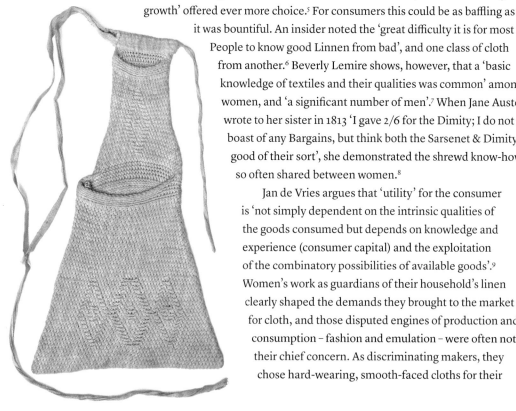

Cloth is inherently social in its manufacture and consumption, and merits being 'read' like any other type of evidence.[3] Tie-on pockets were prevalent when textile manufacturing in Britain saw complex changes that brought consumers an impressive variety of goods from around the globe. In Cumberland in 1683, thanks to networks of itinerant traders, as Margaret Spufford shows, 'the local purchaser could buy hollands and cambric from the Low Countries, Bengals, calicoes and muslins from India, silks, linens which were probably dyed in England, Scotch cloth as a cheap alternative to calico for the new-fangled window curtains'.[4] As time went on, cotton's 'amazing growth' offered ever more choice.[5] For consumers this could be as baffling as it was bountiful. An insider noted the 'great difficulty it is for most People to know good Linnen from bad', and one class of cloth from another.[6] Beverly Lemire shows, however, that a 'basic knowledge of textiles and their qualities was common' among women, and 'a significant number of men'.[7] When Jane Austen wrote to her sister in 1813 'I gave 2/6 for the Dimity; I do not boast of any Bargains, but think both the Sarsenet & Dimity good of their sort', she demonstrated the shrewd know-how so often shared between women.[8]

Jan de Vries argues that 'utility' for the consumer is 'not simply dependent on the intrinsic qualities of the goods consumed but depends on knowledge and experience (consumer capital) and the exploitation of the combinatory possibilities of available goods'.[9] Women's work as guardians of their household's linen clearly shaped the demands they brought to the market for cloth, and those disputed engines of production and consumption – fashion and emulation – were often not their chief concern. As discriminating makers, they chose hard-wearing, smooth-faced cloths for their pockets so that they hung freely without chafing against other garments. Cloths with prominent pile or metal thread, which caused friction or abrasion, and flimsy cloths were avoided.[10] Few knitted or crocheted pockets survive, despite the huge popularity of these crafts; their rarity reflects a design dead-end – they were too stretchy and prone to snag (exceptions are seen in figs 36 and 148). Otherwise the diversity of cloths evident in surviving pockets and other sources confirm that women took advantage of abundance but made knowing choices.

The alluring woven silks of the period were celebrated yet are rare among surviving pockets. However, some sources show that silk pockets featured in the wardrobes of elite women. Lady Arabella Furnese, accustomed to pearls and diamonds, was also fond of silk, as is shown by her purchase of eight yards of blue silk to hang over her dressing table in 1719. Later that year, in keeping with her shopping habits, she bought 'two Yards of Silk for pockets – 7s'.[11] A surviving pair of silk taffeta pockets from the 1740s, made to match a bravura canary-yellow waistcoat, shows how silk could promote the pocket to a co-starring role within a luxurious ensemble (see fig. 25). For women of more moderate means, silk was usually kept for more commonly visible items of clothing.[12] The scarcity of silk for pockets in women's Old Bailey testimonies underlines that it was too costly or unfitted for a labouring life, though silk ribbons were always a favourite.[13] Silk appeared at the Old Bailey probably as 'damask', an impressive cloth made of worsted, silk or a mix of both (see fig. 112). A workman thought its appeal sufficient to entice servant Sarah Breary to have sex with him. William Williams accused her of stealing money from him, but, in her successful self-defence, she countered by saying he had tried to lure her into bed, 'offer'd her Snuff, then a Snuff Box; afterwards to present her with a pair of Damask Pockets', all of which escalating temptations she refused.[14]

By contrast, leather was better fitted for purpose, but although sources confirm the presence of leather pockets all through the period, the two made wholly of leather found by our survey are even rarer survivors than pockets made of silk. One belonged to Ann Beynon (1803–1885), a farmer's wife from Pembrokeshire, Wales. Its value to her is plain from its extensive repairs (fig. 37). Her leather pocket was worked almost to death, perhaps explaining why so few have survived.[15] A milkwoman and a potato seller, among others who cited leather pockets at the Old Bailey, did similar work to Ann, underlining the merits of leather for heavy labour or holding the day's takings from trade.[16] It is notable that in both trials and inventories leather pockets were given low monetary values despite their stout utility.[17]

Cotton, *the* global product of the age, became available in many different cloths as time went on, and this expansion of the industry is amply apparent in surviving pockets.[18] Unlike leather, strong cottons were easily washed and mended. Old Bailey evidence mentioning pockets made of ticking and canvas underlines a taste for robust weaves.[19] *The Workwoman's Guide* advised making pockets out of 'dimity, calico, jean, twilled muslin', or 'nankeen or brown jean', and by 1840 these were probably all-cotton cloths.[20] The versatile cloth known as 'dimity' was widely adopted for pockets by women of all ranks.[21] By 1696 English dimity was already highlighted as 'of great use in our Nation'.[22] Martha Dodson (1684–1765), a merchant's widow, on each of two occasions (in 1749 and 1753) bought two yards of 'strip'd dimity' for pockets, at a mid-range price, reserving other more expensive dimities for a waistcoat, a petticoat and stomachers.[23] Many households bought large amounts in various forms: between 1765 and 1770, dimities purchased on behalf of young Lady Louisa Fitzpatrick included 'Dutch corded', 'superfine India Dimity' and 18½ yards of corded dimity.[24] The Old Bailey trial accounts reveal dimity pockets often in use by poorer women. Newspaper advertisements for lost or stolen pockets most often cite dimity as their cloth, and references to different types of

THE POCKET

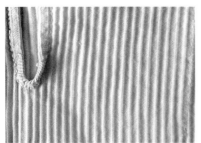 

dimity, such as 'corded' or 'striped', indicate familiarity with the material's varied forms.[25] The many dimity survivors in our survey (figs 38, 54, 66a, 72, 79, 80b) echo Abraham Rees's 1819 observations that 'striped dimities' were the most common because they were quicker to weave, therefore cheaper, and were 'commonly bleached of a pure white'.[26] These dazzling dimities resulted from advances in chemical bleaching and soaps of the late eighteenth and early nineteenth centuries (see fig. 86). Dimities for pockets, excelling in use and fitting most budgets, demonstrate the transformations in science, industry and technology benefiting consumers across all social ranks.

But cloth could look backwards as well as forwards. Marcella, technically advanced but aesthetically conservative, was one such example. It emerged first in the later eighteenth century in the form of skilful woven imitations of the prized hand-quilted goods thought to originate in Marseilles.[27] Sturdy, with figured patterns, and in common use for household linen and apparel for both sexes, its substance lent itself well to pockets. In 1782 Elizabeth Morris, a servant, stole 'a Marcella Jacket and Coat, trimmed with striped Muslin', a 'Marcella Petticoat' and 'a Pair of Marcella quilted Pockets'.[28] Then in the 1840s the newly improved, steam-powered looms introduced in Bolton in Lancashire produced a form of patterned marcella pocket front specially woven to shape, which played a particular role in the commercial life of pockets.[29] The motifs used in these mechanised approximations of hand-quilting recalled those seen on older embroidered pockets, but their bleached, washable, sturdy cotton cloth resonated with the domestic economy of cleanliness and moderation, making these distinctive pocket fronts sentimental yet also conveniently modern (see fig. 69).

Decorative floral prints were a transformative part of cotton's success and were well loved for their bright, fast colours, but a more differentiated narrative of consumption emerges from the survey and other sources, which indicates that these cottons were not much used for making pockets until the 1800s.[30] While David Wilkie's painting *The Jew's Harp* of *c.*1808 shows a young girl's modish printed cotton pocket in use (fig. 39), other sources tell a different story. In 1757 wealthy Elizabeth Jervis chose hardwearing fustian for her pockets

over the flowered cotton she earmarked for other purposes.[31] London servant Elizabeth Kirby had three pairs of pockets in 1786, none of printed cotton though she had a printed cotton gown and petticoat and 13 yards of the cloth not made up.[32] In surviving pockets, printed cottons were used selectively: for example, in a pocket of the early nineteenth century the front was made of an exotic printed cotton but the back of plain cotton (fig. 41). Similarly selective was the use of small scraps of printed cotton for patchwork pockets.[33] Women wore their clothing in layers of different cloths, as seen clearly in a dressed doll of c.1760, which shows bold use of a fashionable glazed-cotton floral print for its gown and pocket. Under the unusual pocket is a green ruched-silk petticoat and white cotton under-petticoat over a cotton-linen chemise (fig. 40). Here the pocket, mutable as ever, adjoins the fashionable printed cotton surfaces, while plain cotton and linen, the old favourites, are preferred for wearing closer to the body.

Likewise, from the later seventeenth century onwards the British linen industry strove to match the allure of imported Asian cottons by producing a 'new Fangle' of gay 'painted Linnen', in 1729 said by Daniel Defoe to be worn by a 'vast multitude' of country people and the poor.[34] However, such linens are not in evidence among surviving pockets, the example of a doll's silk pocket backed with striped linen being rare.[35] Linen pockets, very well represented in the survey, are, by contrast, mostly plain, and testify to the popularity of this long-established, reliable cloth, a staple despite cotton's dominant presence from the late 1760s onwards.[36] 'Linen' was the most common descriptor of pockets in the Old Bailey. John Styles argues that in the period up to 1800 linen remained popular for certain basic goods such as sheeting, shirts, shifts and other body linen, even as cotton took over for more glamorous uses. 'When appearance was crucial, cotton succeeded. Where utilitarian durability counted, cotton sometimes lagged behind.'[37] If consumers were selective about their use of cottons for pockets, the same applied to linens. A 'wave of linens' imported into Britain from numerous places in central and Western Europe offered diversity.[38] High-quality linens called Hollands were much prized; Lady Arabella Furnese, in addition to luxury silk pockets, also chose 'an Ell of Holland for Pockets' in 1726.[39] Those who opted for linen pockets were favouring something deeply familiar, a fibre worn by many generations next to the body.

Wool and wool-mix pockets are more evidence that consumers trod their own paths. 'If cotton was the first industry with a global reach, this was achieved alongside wool and not primarily, or significantly, at the expense of the older-established sector.'[40] Woollen pockets are poorly represented in the survey, but we know they were in use when, at the Old Bailey, women described a variety of woollen cloths for their pockets.[41] 'Callimancoe', often used for gowns, was a canny choice for pockets since this lovely cloth's sturdy and smooth surface, produced using heated rollers, was ideal.[42] 'Stuff', 'camblet', 'cloth', 'plaid' or 'plod', and 'hair shag' are other woollen cloths named in the Old Bailey for pockets. The pair of pockets with 'flower'd Plod

42 Jane Thomas's checked wool pocket, one of a pair, mid- to late 19th century (L 38.5 cm). Amgueddfa Cymru–National Museum Wales, 31.31.2.

one side and Camblet the other', lost in the street in London in 1730, showed distinctive choices.[43]

The use of woollen pockets appears to decrease after the 1760s, at least in the metropolitan life represented by the Old Bailey. However, two pairs of surviving pockets from Wales tell a different story about significant regional variations in the production and use of woollen cloth. They came from Jane Thomas, a farmer's wife born about 1833 and living not far from her birthplace in Cardigan. By the time of Jane's birth, cotton was a common choice for pockets, but Jane's were made of wool from their farm's own sheep, spun and woven nearby (fig. 42), and show the persistence of old production practices rooted in local communities.[44] Her red, black and white checked pockets, unique in the pocket survey, belong within the regional debate about Welsh national identity and economics. Checked patterns of this kind were regarded as properly Welsh, and were promoted as such by nationalist landowners in their own woollen mills, which makes Jane's checked pockets a material embodiment of contemporary cultural tensions between continuity and change.[45] Jane's other pockets, of wool flannel, embroidered sampler-style, are akin to some other surviving Welsh pockets dating from the mid-century, indicating that she was not alone in continuing to favour local cloth over more industrialised production (see fig. 132).[46]

The habitual stashing of cloth as future assets over long periods of time further shaped women's consumption practices. In 1790 Elizabeth Woodley, though a servant, had squirrelled away a yard and a half of muslin, two yards of lace, two yards of calico and several other pieces of cloth, in total valued at 28s.[47] Hoarded used or unused cloth retained value, and was part of cautious economy by women of all classes that curbed new purchases even in a period that saw prolific innovations in textile production.[48] On the death of Eliza Jervoise (1770–1821), a member of the Hampshire landed gentry, almost 20 per cent of her wardrobe comprised pieces of new and old cloth or parts of garments, pointing to the recycling that was so common in domestic and institutional settings alike.[49] In the 1740s at St Sepulchre's workhouse in Holborn, London, a gown was made of '2 old Gowns', and five undercoats were made from 'old Curtains'.[50] Affluent Mary Young (c.1790–1876), wife of MP George Young in the metropolis, in 1830 made 16 baby sheets 'out of old things' for the poor.[51] Well-off families also recycled for their own use.[52] Several surviving pockets cut from dress and furnishing pieces belong within

THE POCKET

this well-rooted culture of recycling. Extra strength for the pocket fronts of
an eighteenth-century pair came from pieces probably cut from an older
bedcover made with corded quilting (fig. 43). The printed cotton back of a
mid-nineteenth-century pocket still has needle holes from an earlier line of
pleating, perhaps originally part of a sleeve or skirt (fig. 44). A maker in the late
1700s designed a handsome pocket by mixing 22 pieces of printed, woven and
embroidered cloth from her hoard spanning a 30-year period (see fig. 151).[53]
Patchwork, which was thrifty but relied on imagination and labour, explains
why a publican's wife, Elizabeth Hordes, was adamant in 1794 that she could
identify her stolen dimity pockets, saying they were 'patch work of my own
doing'.[54] Not all patchwork was recycled within the home, as Thomas Williams,
working in the London cotton trade, remarked in 1807. Small pieces of new
printed calico were obtainable 'in all the markets' and 'sold as remnants to
make patchwork', so it could involve purchases.[55] Patchwork was sometimes
undertaken as a fashionable activity in prosperous households, but it lost status
over time until it became a sign of the deserving poor – a reputational change
captured in George Smith's 1850 painting *Temptation* (see fig. 1).[56]

In many homes, rich or poor, the ragbag served the purpose of virtuous
self-sufficiency (see fig. 142):

> A rag bag is a desirable thing to have hung up in some conspicuous part of
> the house, into which all odd bits, and even shreds, of calico, print, linen,
> muslin, &c should be put; as they are useful to come in when a gusset or
> chin stay, or some other small article is wanting. Those bits too small for
> this purpose may still be used by school children, for practising stitches
> of needle-work upon; or at all events, may be disposed of to the rag
> merchants, and thus prove of some value at last.[57]

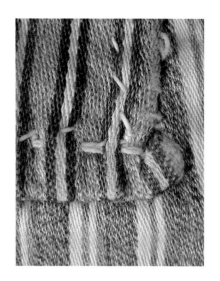

There are surviving pockets that testify to the ragbag habit (fig. 45). One distinctive patchwork example has a back resourcefully contrived from two otherwise unusable pieces: an excise frame mark, dated 1796, and two other indelible stamps, identifying the cotton as spun and woven in Britain, show a clever maker conjuring something useful out of 'odd bits' and appropriating the imprint of officialdom for a private object (fig. 46).[58] Another shows how snippets of printed cotton for appliqué could produce a cheap and cheerful front (fig. 47). Such objects enrich our understanding of how women used their productive labour to regulate their own personal consumption practices. Our sources, including the surviving pockets, show that a culture of preservation formed a powerful undertow to the consumption of novelty and fashion.

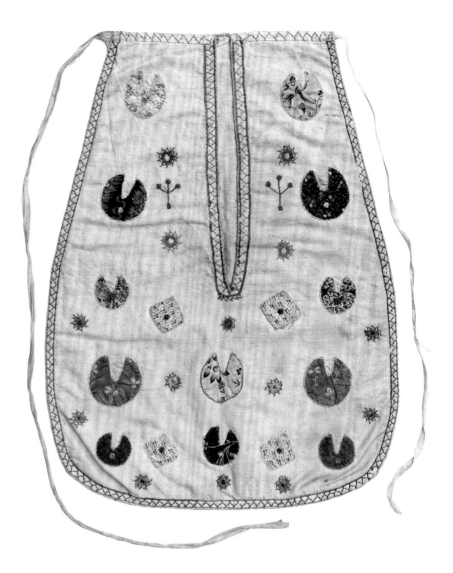

Making pockets: women and needlework

Gertrude Savile (1697–1758), sister of a baronet, chronicled in her diary a way of working that was familiar to many of her contemporaries when, in the summer of 1727 at home in London, she began to make herself some pockets. On 20 July she spent half an hour cutting them out. On 2 August the project moved on when, in the late morning, she had 'pleasure and agreeable imployment in the summer house which has a charming prospect [...] making pocketts', joined by her mother. She returned later in the day for another hour and a half when she 'drank coffee and work'd pocketts to my intire sattisfaction'. 'Cutting', 'making' and 'working' (embroidery) indicate the range of skills she brought to her 'agreeable' task. In 'hott dry weather', Gertrude was back in the summer house again on 10 August, reading, writing, interrupted by an unwelcome caller, but spending a further hour and a half on the pockets. On 18 August she was back again for a similar period. By 16 October, when she moved on to cutting out shifts with her mother and aunt, it seems that Gertrude's pockets were finished.[59]

The commercial production of ready-made clothing, though extensive by the start of our period, did not empty homes of the labour or satisfaction of making garments, as Gertrude Savile knew – a practice that continued into the era of the sewing machine, when domestic hand and machine sewing coexisted. The domestic needlewoman's output included shifts, caps, aprons, bed gowns, and lying-in, baby and infant clothes, and shirts for men and boys. Elite and gentry women and girls picked up their needles for utilitarian work for themselves and their families, in addition to the needlework done by their

49 Single pocket strongly constructed of satin weave black cotton, late 19th century (L 54.8 cm). Nottingham City Museums and Galleries, NCM.1983.728.

servants.[60] Mary Howit (1799–1888), daughter of a businessman and surveyor, recalled that, when she was at boarding school aged 10 in 1809 with her sister, her Quaker mother required them, instead of fancy-work, 'to make in our leisure moments half-a-dozen linen shirts for our father, with all their back-stitching and button-holes complete'.[61] Making pockets conformed to this plain needlework, and used the same tools, materials and stitches; pockets had similar tapes to petticoats and aprons, their openings echoed those of petticoats. Pocket construction was simple. Whole or pieced front and back sections were cut to shape, sewn right sides together, turned right sides out and bound together with back stitch to make a strong double seam. Extra binding or ribbon was often used to reinforce the edge and opening (see the frontispiece). *The Workwoman's Guide* (1840), which gives the most detailed instructions for making pockets we have for the period, noted that some examples have a straight side worn to the front, a choice seen in many surviving pockets and 'preferred by some persons, as it sets better to the figure than the others' (fig. 48). For the waist tie, the *Guide* recommended a broad tape on the top of the pocket or pair of pockets and emphasised stitching pockets 'firmly' – not surprisingly, given the tough treatment and abrasion suffered by the pocket both in use and in the wash (fig. 49).[62]

Linda Baumgarten notes different purposes for stitches in eighteenth-century clothing; gowns made in expectation of unpicking later for re-dyeing, cleaning, modification or recycling had long, easily removed stitches and little internal finish. By contrast, body linen had to withstand brutal washing methods and, in anticipation of this, such garments 'are almost universally sewn with small, tight stitches, and all raw edges of the fabric turned inside'.[63] Surviving pockets show stitches intended to last, which aligns them with other washable body linen, such as shirts, chemises and caps (fig. 50). The continuing popularity of the tie-on pocket took it well into the age of the sewing machine from the 1860s. Mechanised sewing is seen on 10 per cent of surviving pockets in the survey, giving evidence of consumer adaptation to changing technology, and underlining the resilience of the pocket's form. Although sewing machines greatly accelerated the construction of long straight seams, some surviving pockets illustrate difficulties encountered in steering the mechanically driven needle round their curves, and the early chain-stitch machine employed only a single thread, making weak seams, unsuited to the pocket's hard use (figs 51–2).

Endless modifications arose within the established template of construction. Individual women knew what worked best for them, and surviving pockets show many different widths and lengths (fig. 49; see also figs 21, 94): some are rectangular or triangular, most are more curvaceously pear-shaped. Openings are normally vertical, but sometimes horizontal. Some makers inserted eyelet holes, inside or outside, an instance of which enabled Mary Wakefield to identify her employer's stolen apparel in court in 1784: 'I know the pockets to be Mrs. Jones's, there is an oilet hole to tye them by'.[64] Eyelets could perhaps be used to attach the pocket to stays, as *The Workwoman's Guide* suggested, or to carry additional waist tapes, or to secure scissors or watches. The weakest part of the structure, when the pocket was filled or pulled, was where the tapes met the top; one surviving pocket tackled the problem of load-bearing stress with double tapes for tying round the waist and interior compartments with unusual buttoned closures, creating a secure and durable pocket (fig. 53). Others had a strong single loop (see fig. 46) at the top or combined tapes and buttonholes (fig. 54). Many women liked their pockets made in pairs.[65] The sewing machine was probably instrumental in an evolution of the pocket form in the late nineteenth century.[66] Made of very tough materials, forbiddingly difficult to sew by hand, numerous examples survive in museums to suggest batch or mass production of pockets, which successfully exploited the sewing machine's capabilities (see figs 124–6).

The making of a pocket – a piece of plain household needlework – was a labour that could also afford women private satisfaction and provide networks of sociability, as did more celebrated female accomplishments in handicrafts.[67] Jane Austen's nephew recalled 'some of her merriest talk was over clothes which she and her companions were making, sometimes for themselves, and sometimes for the poor'.[68] Utilitarian needlework could connect women to

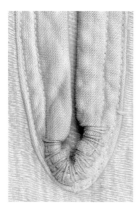

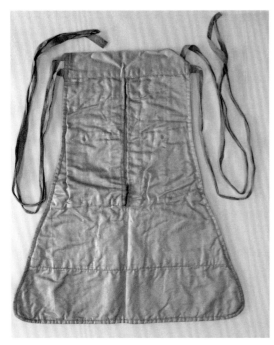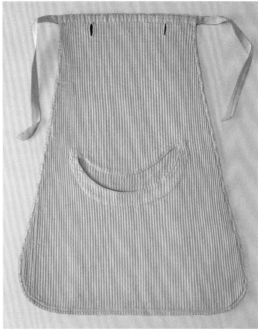

ABOVE
53 Pocket with double ties, mid-19th century (L 49 cm). Wilson Art Gallery and Museum, Cheltenham, CMAG.1951.83.10.

ABOVE RIGHT
54 Curved horizontal opening on a pocket with eyelets, early to mid-19th century (L 39.5 cm). Wilson Art Gallery and Museum, Cheltenham, CMAG.1965.19.10.

others outside their family or even their social class. Sarah Hurst (1736–1808), daughter of a tailor and businessman in Horsham, Sussex, was an indefatigable needleworker. Her cutting out and sewing of her own clothes led to frequent requests to do the same for customers in her father's shop, who often lingered to talk. In 1760 when a gentrified customer arrived to order a new silk gown, Sarah noted: 'I cut her out several things, very chatty.'[69] Pockets, discrete and portable, were well suited to picking up in odd moments, alone or in company, and fitting around other activities or disruptions, as Gertrude Savile did in her summer house. But some partly made pockets, surviving in museums or cited as stolen, indicate that delays and interruptions might get the better of women's plans (see fig. 59).[70]

Women who made pockets at home, for themselves or others, probably learned to do so at an early age. In 1786 Charlotte Papendiek (1765–1839), a companion to Queen Charlotte, recalled proudly the development of her 4-year-old daughter. 'She could stitch a pocket, she read prettily, and now began to write.'[71] Elite and gentry girls were often part of an industrious and visible culture of needlework among their mothers and other relatives, who also employed their servants to undertake sewing on a regular basis and even extra occasional hands as needed. In *Grandmamma's Pockets*, Anna Maria Hall depicts little Annie, the granddaughter at the centre of the plot, 'intrusted with the task of stitching a pair of little watch-pockets to go inside' her

BELOW
55a Child's embroidered
pocket, mid-18th century.
Nottingham City Museums
and Galleries, NCM 1977-497.

BELOW RIGHT
55b Crudely stitched pair
of doll's chamois leather
pockets, 18th century (L 9.5
and 10 cm). Hereford Museum
Service, HSS 3670.

grandmother's larger pair of pockets.[72] Like their mothers, girls soon learned the interplay between work and social networks. Harriet Martineau (1802–1876), daughter of a Unitarian textile manufacturer and 'excessively fond of sewing', made light of her plain sewing in girlhood as it was accompanied by 'the amusement of either gossiping, or learning poetry by heart, from a book, lying open under my work'.[73] Easily taken along when paying or receiving visits, work on pockets could be neatly accommodated within drawing-room sociability, and fitted in well with the role of handmade gifts to materialise affectionate relationships.[74] In 1782 in London, Esther Duché recorded how her younger sister sewed pockets and wrote a letter for her grandmother in Philadelphia.[75] Completing a letter and making pockets required some dedication by the child but also initiated her into a female social network, in this case linking different generations across the Atlantic. For girls of all social classes, learning needle skills in making a pocket was part of the progression from girlhood to adulthood, reinforcing an understanding of the construction and use of something long associated with female life and work. Some surviving pockets that are too small for adult use and display irregular work may have been made by children for their own or their dolls' use (fig. 55). It was common practice to teach girls to make scaled-down whole and part garments as samplers of basic techniques for full-size garments, as well as clothes for their dolls; surviving sets of dolls' clothes often include pockets (figs 55b, 56).[76]

In 1780 the author Dorothy Kilner (1755–1836) promoted the practice of making and using pockets as a basis for good behaviour for young girls. She approved of a child who chose to 'sit still and work' rather than play, 'which she did very diligently, till she had finished her pocket; and then, when she had made it up, she fetched [the] doll and tied it on'.[77] For Kilner, use of a pocket signified tidiness and good domestic practice for girls and women, while making it was a selfless act, and play with dolls anticipated motherhood. In *Celia in Search of a Husband* (1809), a novel critical of the beau monde, the heroine promises to

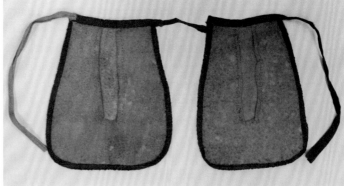

56 A doll with miniature clothing, including a pocket, early 19th century (doll, L 45 cm, pocket, L 11 cm). Hereford Museum Service, HSS 3744.

teach her young niece to make a pocket to help her distinguish between useful and frivolous behaviour.[78] For poor girls, making their pocket and learning their plain sewing was part of their schooling in housework of all kinds. *The Workwoman's Guide* observed in 1840 that 'home and school' should contribute to the education of girls in 'domestic arts and economy', arguing that cutting out was particularly 'fitted to be taught in schools' because it equated to 'a sort of unassuming household mathematics' (fig. 57).[79]

The remarkable and comprehensive *Workwoman's Guide* covered dozens of projects for domestic needlework, including pockets (see fig. 48). Its author was concerned that women were becoming 'mere novices in [the] unostentatious attainments' of plain sewing and household management.[80] To address a perceived decline in needlework skill among those thought to need it most, instructions codifying the construction of apparel had appeared in print from the late eighteenth century but did not cover pockets.[81] Surviving pockets, however, show that precisely the same methods set out in the *The Workwoman's Guide* were in use for more than 150 years before the book appeared, and more than 50 years afterwards, confirming the pocket's slow tempo and providing a corrective to many contemporary complaints about the race for novelty fuelled by the fashion trades. This begs the question as to how these methods were transmitted before such books were available. Women followed a handed-down way of doing things, and the assimilation of needlework within networks of sociability meant that women and girls often saw pockets being made. These informal means of transmission, where a girl learned at her mother's knee, underpinned the consistency of construction methods across the many generations who made pockets (fig. 58).

Within this continuity of form, women's agency and choice were clearly present in the diversity of techniques – sometimes beautifully achieved, such as appliqué, embroidery, quilting, crochet or patchwork – that they used to personalise their pockets. However, decorated pockets were not objects apart: even the most richly worked surviving pockets bear the same signs of wear as undecorated ones. Diaper quilting or monochrome patterns were unassuming, but any quilting, like embroidery, reinforced pockets (see fig. 25b). In *Grandmamma's Pockets*, Hall describes a pair 'quilted into a stiff border of vine erect leaves, with a still stiffer flowerpot in the middle'.[82] Embroidered survivors date predominantly from the eighteenth century, but dated examples of 1832 and 1844 confirm that such pockets had not been entirely displaced by then (see fig. 22a).[83] Like men's caps and women's stomachers, pockets were 'sufficiently small in scale for the less ambitious embroiderer to tackle'.[84] Limited space nevertheless allowed charming or distinctive results. In some pairs, the maker, with double the available surface, created a visual interplay between them. A surviving pair of unfinished pockets shows the processes involved: a floral pattern is marked out in ink on rectangular ground pieces backed by linen, then embroidered, probably in a frame, before being cut to shape and made up (fig. 59).

Embroidered motifs are predominantly floral, sometimes with birds and animals. Larger motifs, such as a vase, basket or outgrowth of flowers, were commonly placed below the opening in an echo of the ancient 'tree of life' (fig. 60); other motifs illustrating horticultural knowledge were used, as was the exotic palampore motif of Asian textiles, already well established on clothing and furnishings in the seventeenth century.[85] On many embroidered pockets, stems, leaves and flowers entwine themselves round the opening, like guardians of the space and contents within (fig. 61).[86] Depiction of the human form is rare on surviving pockets.[87] In one case a cleric with dishevelled hair and a cherub above, accompanied by a leaping deer and exotic bird, appear on a pair of pockets (see fig. 150). The deer and bird resemble those found in seventeenth-century sources,[88] so although the cloth and style of embroidery place the pockets in the early to mid-eighteenth century, the decoration was clearly rooted in an older tradition, exemplifying how pockets can conflate different histories. If the maker associated these motifs in some personal cosmology, sadly it is now lost to us.[89] Some embroiderers added a date and initials to the front of their pockets, an enduring practice seen in surviving specimens from 1718 onwards and akin to the habit of dating and signing samplers as a commemoration or celebration of good work (see frontispiece and fig. 22).

Embroidered pockets show different levels of needle skills, but indicate that, as in the construction of the pocket, women shared ideas (see fig. 60).

Let sloth adorned with splendid arts,
Another's labour own,
That Virgin doubly strikes our hearts,
Whose finery's all her own.

London, Printed for ROBERT SAYER, Map & Printseller, N.º 53 Fleet Street, as the Act directs 13 June 1777.

BELOW, CLOCKWISE
FROM TOP LEFT

60a Embroidered vase on
a pocket, early to mid-18th
century. Nottingham City
Museums and Galleries,
NCM 1964-35.

60b Embroidered vase on
a pocket, early 18th century.
Victoria and Albert Museum,
London, CIRC.86-1938.

60c Embroidered vase
on a pocket, mid-18th
century. Charles Paget Wade
Collection, Berrington Hall,
SNO 1452.

60d Embroidered vase on
a pocket, early to mid-
18th century. Worthing
Museum and Art Gallery,
WMAG.1966.389.

In practice, women often exchanged patterns, reinforcing their familial and neighbourly networks. In 1792 Nancy Woodforde records how, on a morning visit, 'Lady Bacon brought me a Pattern to worke my Muslin Petticoat by it from Lady Ca Hobart who has worked one like it. I drew of the Pattern and return'd it to Lady B this Evening.'[90] In colonial America, c.1760, Hannah C. Sansom noted in her journal that her cousin Sarah Smith Pemberton had drawn embroidery patterns for her, including two patterns for silk-embroidered pockets.[91] The frequent circulation of commercial patterns added to the possibilities. Subscribers to *Wheble's Lady's Magazine* in 1772 opened their July issue to find free inside an 'exceeding pretty Pattern of a Lady's Pocket'. In October 1786 the *New Lady's Magazine* included a pattern depicting the astounding ascent of the Italian aeronaut Vincenzo Lunardi in a hot air balloon, complete with cat and dog, made in London in 1784. In September 1786 Lunardi had again been in the English news when one of his assistants died during a flight. The following year, Mary Hibberd (or Hebbert) used the pattern in her own way on her named pocket (figs 62–3).[92] An amateur domestic embroiderer could get her pocket pattern drawn by a professional pattern drawer, a service often offered by haberdashers (fig. 64). Motifs could also circulate through peripatetic teachers of embroidery.[93] So there was no shortage

of help for the domestic embroiderer wanting to adorn the front of her pocket. Some surviving pockets suggest that women thought of their pocket front as a place to improvise from memory or from amateur drawing. More generally, the motifs used by women on their pockets show an active engagement with nature, exotica, technology, current events and the wider world (see figs 59, 62, 119, 120).

In *Grandmamma's Pockets*, little Annie regrets that her grandmother's wonderfully embroidered 'state pockets' could not be seen. It is still commonly

BELOW
62 Pattern for a pocket front, 1786. Huntington Library, San Marino, California, Box 1, Folder 25b.

BELOW LEFT
63 Embroidered pocket made by Mary Hibberd (or Hebbert), 1787 (L 40 cm). Museum of Fine Arts, Boston, 40.80.

asked today whether decorated pockets were meant to be seen when worn; in wear or in making, all kinds of pockets *were* on occasion visible and the link between decoration and display was more complex than the question implies. Grandmamma's answer to Annie – that 'it was the fitness of things and not the show of them, that young women ought to think of!' – beyond its moral lesson, also draws attention to the personal satisfaction derived from a woman's sense of appropriately matching her pockets to particular occasions.[94] The 'state' pockets might not have been seen, but they were selected to be worn on birthdays and festivals, and articulated the private and the public in intricate ways.

Embroidery is not the only expressive needlework visible on pockets. The pocket form was stable over the period, but standards of needlework were not, and surviving pockets show that plain structural sewing could be distinctive. It reveals many differences in the skill, resources and even the mood or temperament of makers. Some pockets are assembled with botched, wild, unkempt stabs of the needle, marks of an impatient, unschooled or unwilling maker who perhaps found the task disagreeable or daunting (see fig. 45). Others appear to have been made by an expert but hurried hand. Some show a disciplined, steady execution, with stitches of impeccable regularity (see fig. 73). Even stitching with the newfangled sewing machines was not uniform (see figs 51–2). Women commonly recognised their own work when they saw it, and often stated that it was theirs under oath in court during the identification of stolen goods. In 1800 Sarah Huguenin, identifying her pair of pockets in court,

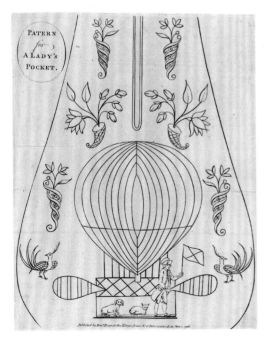

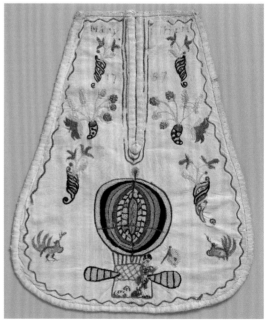

64 London haberdasher's trade card, advertising 'drawn' and 'ticken' pockets, second half of the 18th century. Victoria and Albert Museum, London, 12863.12.

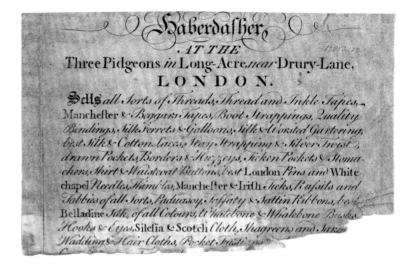

said: 'These are my property, they are my own work.'[95] A surviving pocket on which horizontal openings were securely edged with neat decorative stitches (fig. 65), and another showing individual stitches misaligned as the needle was worked through the seams in the back both manifest the *work* in the needle*work* that would be recognisable to their makers. Books of instruction provided ideals, but needlewomen's actual labour practices can be retrieved only from surviving objects. They constitute a unique material archive of a history that would otherwise remain largely silent.

The commerce of pockets

When the Sussex rector Giles Moore paid 2*d*. and 3*d*. for ready-made pockets for his young niece in 1667 and 1668 from two different suppliers, and Ann Brockman, a Kent gentlewoman, purchased a pair of ready-made pockets in 1703 for 6*d*., it was not exceptional.[96] Pockets were commonly available for sale throughout the period, purchased by or for girls and women of all ranks, in town or country, including those already engaged in productive domestic needlework of their own. In 1802 Sarah Hurst, despite being an accomplished needlewoman, also bought ready-made pockets for herself, at a cost of 2*s*. 6*d*., an example of the concurrent practices of buying and making.[97]

Pockets were simple commodities widely distributed. During a period when shops in the modern sense were developing, more traditional circuits of distribution still persisted, and pockets were sold in all manner of outlets from the humblest petty traders to upmarket haberdashers and milliners.[98] In Mary Hoare's London shop in 1709, pockets and shirts lay together on view.[99] Far away from the metropolis in 1721, Stephen Lawrence's shop in Tregony, Cornwall, also stocked pairs of pockets, among other ready-mades such as

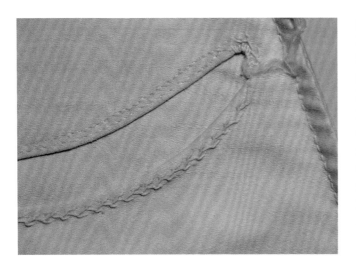

65 Decorative stitching on a pocket with two horizontal openings, mid-19th century (detail). Fashion Museum Bath, BATMC VI.14.4.

gloves and hosiery, and other goods likely to meet most local needs, including consumables, spectacles, mousetraps, paper, tools, harness, lanterns and locks.[100] In 1789 Robert Blunt advertised pockets with shirts, shifts and dimity petticoats for sale from his warehouse in Charing Cross.[101] Outside the capital's fashionable areas, Eliza Sinclair had seven pockets among 'a great quantity of goods' at her clothes shop in White Cross Street in the East End of London in 1810.[102]

Ready-made pockets were on the move among small portable goods carried by itinerant sellers on their rounds. In 1750 widow Ann White would seem to have been carrying her goods for sale when she was allegedly attacked and robbed of '2 baskets, value 1s., 29 dimitty caps, 14 stomachers, 4 pair of ticken pockets, 13 pair of scissars, 4 pair of silver buttons set with stones and other things'.[103] Margot Finn notes that pedlars and hawkers had been 'essential cogs in the distributive process since at least the seventeenth century [. . .] traversing both the unstable dividing line that distinguished traders from consumers and the artificial boundary that separated the market from the home'.[104] An early nineteenth-century pedlar doll survives with a pocket on her tray of goods. The 'List of articles sold by Sarah Thrifty, Licensed Hawker' situates pockets as modest necessities, akin to other simple ready-mades and to haberdashery needed to sew and knit at home (fig. 66; see also fig. 135).[105] By this means, ready-made pockets were available on the doorsteps of consumers almost everywhere.

New ready-made pockets were acquired in other ways. Poor girls in the kind of schools addressed by *The Workwoman's Guide* often made pockets and garments destined for sale. Women living near a school that sold articles sewn by its pupils could buy pockets or other simple garments there. Sarah Trimmer had laid the ground for this approach to self-financing schools and the teaching of 'industry' in her 1787 *Oeconomy of Charity* – principles followed by elite women like Mrs Larpent when she established a school in Surrey.[106] In the 1830s a school in London offered plain garments such as shirts and pinafores but also pockets at *6d.* a pair; in Wales the Bangor National School advertised different articles 'done by the Scholars', including pairs of pockets for *3d.*[107]

In keeping with prices in schools and shops, the pockets cited in Old Bailey indictments were worth between *2d.* and *6d.*, with a few more valuable exceptions, though their age and condition are often unspecified. Trade cards rarely advertised prices. Inventories of shop stock can reveal the value assigned by appraisers, if not the final cost to the shopper. In 1783 an inventory taken of stock belonging to two York milliners, Sarah and Ann Haighton, included ten pairs of pockets at 4d. each and eleven pairs at 6d., giving some choice, and these were stocked alongside a tempting profusion of cloth from which the customer could have goods made up and finished to order.[108] Among substantial stock valued at £789 5s. 9¾d., most of the 930 different sorts of goods were for millinery and light dressmaking. Finished bespoke hats valued at 16s. and 18s. awaiting collection and Brussels lace valued at 14s. 6d. per yard signal some stylish customers. The shop also offered ready-mades, including sleeves, stays, handkerchiefs, aprons, gloves and fans, as well as pockets. Although 96 per cent of all types of stock were worth more than the pockets, the Haightons, in their comfortable shop, characteristic of the new urban retail culture, evidently reckoned that it was worth keeping unpretentious pockets conveniently on hand for customers in search of their higher-quality goods.

Over 60 years later in Bristol, the same low value for ready-made pockets was evident in John Mabyn's aggressively promoted 'Cheap Linen-Drapery Establishment', where he proclaimed the sale of £6,000 worth of new spring stock in 1844.[109] The stock included a massive 525 dozen 'Ladies' Quilted Pockets, 2½d. each', probably of woven 'quilting'. Mabyn's practice of buying insolvency or fire-damaged stock, even shipwreck cargos, would keep his prices low.[110] Their modest price, the same as a lady's cambric handkerchief, ranked the pockets at the bottom of the pile in this bargain bonanza; only a spray of 'French Flowers' cost less. The 'bargains' were also offered at a 'very liberal allowance' to 'country shopkeepers', an established distribution practice in which an urban outlet acted as wholesaler to petty rural shops, so some of the quilted pockets may have been destined for shopkeepers or pedlars and their rural customers. The availability of very large quantities of cheap ready-made pockets for sale suggests their continuing use on some scale in the mid-nineteenth century and also points to bulk production.

Plentiful, cheap pockets such as those sold by the Haightons and Mabyn would have been turned out by low-skilled labour as part of the production of ready-made everyday clothing throughout our period. As Beverly Lemire establishes, the skill for such basic work was available 'in abundance'.[111] In 1755 Anne Philip testified at the Old Bailey: 'I work with my needle; I quilt; I make-leather pockets, and so', an indication that she could turn her hand to different and demanding labour.[112] But Anne and her like are mostly lost to history, 'obscured' as Lemire notes, in a 'workforce and its products at once commonplace and concealed', making apparel that was 'unremarkable and ephemeral in duration, neither fashionable nor noteworthy to the casual contemporary observer'.[113] While surviving pockets often record evidence that

other sources cannot, they too remain mostly silent about their makers. Among
the simple undecorated pockets that survive, it is impossible to distinguish
those made at home for the maker's own use from those made for sale by
this 'concealed' workforce. The same is true of embroidered pockets, some
of which show momentary lapses or imperfections, seemingly caused by
inattention or haste as likely to result from a competent needlewoman working
at speed for money as from an amateur's needle plied for private satisfaction.

In contrast with an anonymous workforce churning out 'slops',[114] better
needleworkers served women of means, who could afford to have their pockets
made bespoke with their other body linen. This gave them, if they wished,
complete control over materials and design. In 1774, just weeks before her
marriage to the Duke of Devonshire, Lady Georgiana Spencer, born and married
into extreme wealth, had six pairs of pockets made at 2s. a pair at a high-end
business in London's fashionable Covent Garden (fig. 67). Orton and Stow
specialised in basics such as petticoats and childbed articles, emphasising again
the relatively low status of pockets – even those for a duchess-to-be.[115] The bill
for the pockets, which were far inferior in price to the 'fine large quilted Caps'
or the 'fine Irish Cloth Drawers' bought for the trousseau, illustrates their lowly
position even within the realm of undergarments.

Other women preferred to turn to trusted servants to make their pockets. In 1784 a nursery maid, Mary Wakefield, made for her employer, Mrs Jones, a pair of dimity pockets with distinctive 'oilet hole to tye them by', which, as we have seen, she later identified in court.[116] Eliza Jervoise, like many women of her landed class, divided her clothing purchases between London and suppliers closer to home in the country. For many years Eliza charged Mrs Killick in London's West End with the making of her more elaborate garments, often in luxury materials, sometimes paying bills in excess of £40. However, in Hampshire she kept her costs to a minimum by employing Sarah Randell (sometimes spelled 'Randall'), a trusted servant to her throughout her marriage. Over the years, Sarah turned her hand to different tasks for Eliza, including ironing, so she was no stranger to heavy work either. In 1807 Sarah charged Eliza 4d. each for twelve pockets made into pairs, and Eliza can hardly have expected fancy work at that price (fig. 68).[117] Eliza's choices show her to be a knowing consumer, operating within a varied network of producers and suppliers, and her judgement that the making of her pockets was safe in Sarah's provincial hands underlines the homely status of these objects within a gentrified hierarchy of appearances.

A single pocket could simultaneously carry the imprint of domesticity and commerce, as when it was embroidered at home from a pattern sold by a haberdasher or a magazine. An equivalent mapping of different spheres onto the tie-on pocket is evident in 20 surviving marcella pockets whose similarities were identified for the first time by our survey.[118] They extend our understanding of how women could embrace new ready-made products but retain agency through familiar needlework techniques. Buying and making are fused together in the creation of the pockets in this group. With even the openings and edges ready defined in basket weave, the pocket fronts were woven precisely to shape on technically advanced jacquard looms associated with the Lancashire town of Bolton. Seven in the group, found in diverse museum collections, have identical fronts, underlining the practice of batch or mass production, but at the same time were assembled in different ways. Using these ready-made fronts, the makers cut longer or shorter openings, made single pockets or attached two to make a pair, used different cloths to form the backs and made identification marks in different ways (fig. 69). These identical pocket fronts were woven commercially, but makers adapted them to suit their own taste and needlework practice, an expression of women's labour and resourcefulness that embraced industrial output while individualising it.

Used pockets were equally easily obtained by various means. They were part of a recirculation of goods at second hand, third hand and beyond that played a major role in the clothing strategies of large numbers of people.[119]

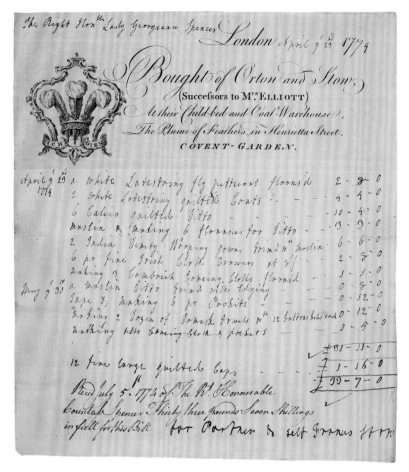

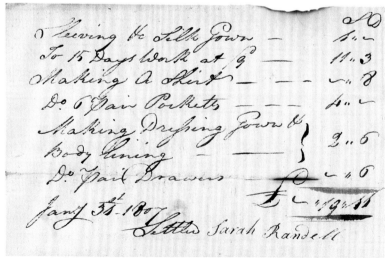

'Consumption was a multifarious process, rarely the final act in the social and economic retail interplay [. . .] where material goods retained many of the functional features of money, as mediums of exchange and repositories of practical value.'[120] In the early 1770s Elizabeth Shackleton passed a number of items of new and old clothing to a young servant, including an old pair of dimity pockets.[121] A parcel of clothing and 'old things', including a pocket, was sent in 1870 to an orphanage in Bristol, to be sold or used 'for the benefit of the orphans'.[122] Outside private networks of circulation such as these, buying old pockets and other old clothes was easy for consumers in towns and cities. In Derbyshire in 1755, a pair of ticken pockets and three others were in a mix of new and used female apparel and household goods being sold by Richard Shooter but said to have been stolen; he tried to pass the sale off as due to the death of his wife.[123] There were large numbers of dealers with fixed shops selling old clothes in London and the provinces, and markets such as east London's Rag Fair in Rosemary Lane were a well-established part of the scene (fig. 70). It was common enough for stolen goods to find their way to such markets.[124] When elderly Caroline Walsh went missing in 1832, as we saw at the start of the chapter, several women traders of Rag Fair gave evidence at the trial, probably unwitting participants in the dispersal of her stolen clothing. Mary Sable snapped up the distinctive stockings Ann Buton had made for her grandmother, and sold them on the same day. Sarah Cotton, who traded next to Mary Sable, bought the shawl Ann's sister Lydia Basey had given Caroline, and Hannah Channel, another dealer, bought the pocket and sold it on to Celia Burke. The dispersal of Caroline's clothes demonstrates how a pocket could

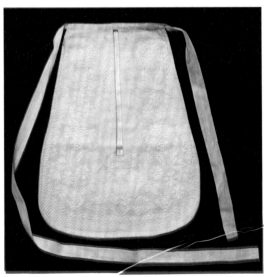
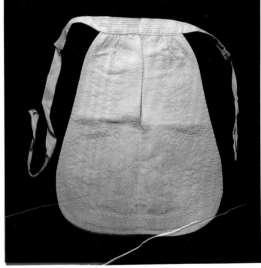

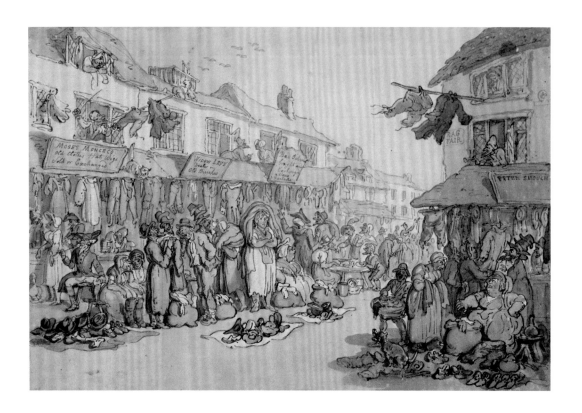

70 Thomas Rowlandson (1757–1827), *Rag Fair*, c.1800, pen and ink, watercolour (18.4 × 27.1 cm). Royal Collection Trust, RCIN 913692.

swiftly change hands as the city's thriving used-clothing networks rapidly swallowed up and dispersed a person's material belongings.

Clothing also formed a considerable portion of goods pledged at pawnbrokers.[125] A pocket was not a high-value item but was still a useful part of an individual's or family's credit-worthy apparel when times were hard. Because women frequently owned more than one pocket at a time, they had some flexibility if they wished to turn one into cash at the pawnbroker. The ledger of York-based pawnbroker George Fettes records in 1778 a woman repeatedly pledging her pocket along with other garments.[126] In 1802 the pawnbroker James Cromp Lowe came across his new young servant, Sarah Chard, helping herself to a pair of pockets from the racks in his warehouse.[127] By these alternative routes of donation, sale, theft and pawning, a used pocket continued, despite the cheapness of many new ones, to hold value and utility on the margins of domestic economy.

* * *

In miniature form, surviving pockets register continuity and change. They record women's engagement with an expanding and globalising material world and illustrate slow undercurrents of consumption that happened across the social spectrum. Duchesses and servants had pockets of dimity, old and new cloth was hoarded by gentry and working women alike, recycling happened in mansions and workhouses. Pockets also embody a remarkably constant form, transmitted across time, space and social class, at a mother's knee, in schools and in informal interactions between women inside and outside the home. There were significant changes in women's lives over the period from the late seventeenth to the late nineteenth century, but the pocket points to individuals retaining what was familiar and useful in habitual practices that counterbalanced the rise of commercial fashion.

While ready-made pockets, old or new, were commonly available on the market from at least the late 1660s, when women made their own pockets they implemented many personalised adaptations and only selectively adopted technical innovations. At the same time, their needlework, plain or decorative, was a peculiarly feminine form of communication, by which women and girls participated in the public sphere of global trade, design and aesthetics. On their own modest scale, pockets register the evolutions and revolutions in industry, trade and commerce witnessed by Britain in the course of two transformative centuries. They also disclose how women carved their own particular paths as consumers and makers of textiles, dress and fashion. While cloth and its uses could serve to display and reckon a person's place in the world and reinforce social distinctions, our evidence suggests that in practice matters were less fixed. The convergence of the many material elements within a pocket constituted for their makers both inner and outer worlds.

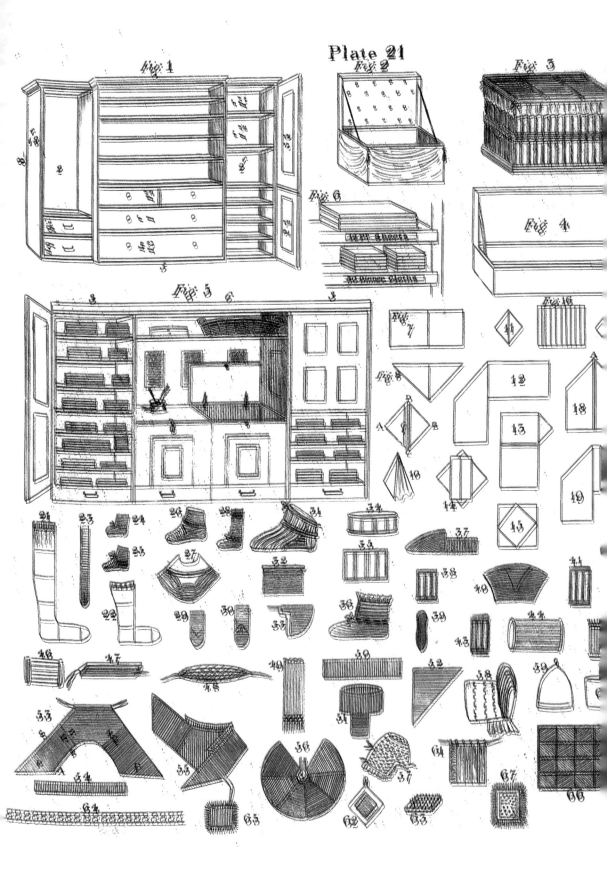

Plate 21

CHAPTER THREE

'So many things'

Pockets and the Labours of Consumption

Prudent consumption relied on the upkeep and preservation of things long after their initial acquisition, and Anna Larpent kept a sharp eye on such matters. She noted in 1796: 'I employed the morning in looking over my clothes &c for mending, altering buying new &c I do this every quarter & find much order & economy arises from the habit.'[1] Anna's regular assessment of her stock and the jobs it generated were vital for diligent management of household resources. From the perspective of those who did the heavier work: 'So many things for our Attendance call, / Had we ten hands, we could employ them all.'[2] These comments remind us of what Lorna Weatherill calls the 'numerous, time-consuming and arduous activities necessarily undertaken in all households', arguing that they repay our attention by helping us to understand 'household organization' and thus the realities of consumption itself.[3] These labours of consumption come into closer focus in this chapter, where we examine the material traces of pockets and the practices they required when they were detached from their wearers.

When separate from the body, pockets were far from adrift. They were part of a household's resources, requiring storage and protection, given identification numbers and marks, circulated between people and places, mended, washed, dried and ironed. These cycles of 'time-consuming and arduous' practices and the specificities of women's everyday tasks, skills and concerns constituted the long continuum of consumption and the 'order &

economy' so beloved of Anna Larpent and her like. They also correspond with the dynamics of women's use and control of particular household spaces.[4] However, though a potent trope and aspiration of 'industrious consumption' throughout the period, neither order nor economy could be taken for granted, and through the specific lens of the pockets this chapter charts some of the challenges involved.

The labours of prudent consumption in general have a somewhat ghostly presence within conventional sources and historical accounts.[5] Elusive and overlooked, these labours, however, remain physically embodied in extant pockets. Many pockets testify eloquently to the work done *by* them and the toll it took on them, while at the same time also revealing the work done *to* them and the efforts entailed in maintaining them in use; in both respects the labour involved is well preserved, not lost. No longer in mint condition, their imprints of wear and tear, washing, ironing, mending and marking trace their sociality, making them embodiments of the continuum of consumption and ownership itself.[6] Such traces could also situate pockets within a wider narrative of female attachments. Maxine Berg finds that women of urban middling class, when bequeathing apparel and household linen, 'to a far higher degree than men noticed their possessions, attached value and emotional significance to these and integrated them into the web of their familial and community relationships'.[7] Arguably the labour involved in the preservation of possessions played a part in how they were 'noticed' and accrued significance.

The period covered by our study saw 'a remorselessly creeping change toward greater material abundance'.[8] From the late eighteenth century, pockets came to belong more firmly within the proliferating quantities of body linen, a category of clothing constituting an important driver in the accumulation of linen stocks. Daniel Roche identifies the inflation of linen consumption with 'the triumph of cleanliness'.[9] We argue in this chapter that cleanliness was inextricably dependent on cycles of labour beyond washing, such as the organisation, supervision, preservation and circulation of the linen stock. A well-managed linen stock materialised the virtues of restraint and order, and cleanliness was seen as next to godliness.[10] But consumers had their work cut out, not least in coping with the inescapable descent of linen from new to old. Including pockets, everything slipped from best to second best and eventually to rags, requiring what Roche calls 'another form of technical intelligence', 'in which the old new and the new old were constantly manipulated and re-employed. Nothing was wasted and anything could be created in the transmutation of textiles' (see fig. 160).[11] Balancing acts of this kind were taking place in British households and institutions of all kinds throughout the period. In the flourishing literature on domestic economy, it became a common refrain that, one way or another, articles of clothing formed 'so essential a part of the expenditure, and require so much the care and attention of a superintendent of the family' that anyone wanting the convenience of a sound economy must address their 'proper management'.[12]

Abundance and necessity

Owning multiples of pockets was widespread across all social ranks, urban and rural, and especially so from the late eighteenth century.[13] Mary Waller (1765–1829), widow of a schooner trader on the Hampshire coast, owned seven pairs of pockets.[14] Her much wealthier near contemporary in the same county, Eliza Jervoise, already an heiress before she married into the landed gentry, had a dozen pairs.[15] Mary Young, living in the metropolis, had 18 pockets in 1823.[16] These three women, in common with many others, had still bigger quantities of shifts or caps. Many extant pockets have a number marked on them, identifying them as part of a set; across our survey the numbers range from 1 to 9, corresponding to the quantity of pockets often found in inventories of women's possessions (fig. 72).[17] Owning pockets in multiples was a long-standing habit even among working women; Jane Reynolds, a former servant, had four pockets in 1744.[18] The practice continued for as long as pockets were in common use; when Sarah Bagg of Birmingham died in 1847, four pairs of dimity pockets featured in her inventory.[19]

Something of the dynamics of abundance and necessity and what these meant in practice to different consumers can be seen in multiples of pockets. Countess North had recently moved house in London three times when, in 1804, she testified that she had gradually 'lost things' at each address. She accused two of her servants of stealing linen worth over £9, including 20 shirts,

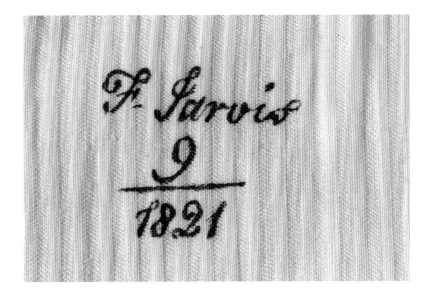

40 handkerchiefs and 16 napkins. When asked who had 'the care of the linen', she replied like a model housekeeper: 'Myself; I had the key in my pocket; it was kept in a closet in our bed-room [. . .] if any one went to fetch linen for use, I went with them'.[20] Her story was a common one. Those with servants to assist them might keep their linen locked up and counted out like tea and sugar, but could still regard the servants themselves as one of the challenges in conserving an abundance of portable things in a mobile society. There was also abundance in lesser households. Hester Clifford died in 1775 in Marlborough, leaving 23 different sorts of clothing. Almost half of these came in washable multiples, including two pairs of pockets and 14 'plain capps'.[21] With 47 per cent of her stock described as 'old' and 'plain', Hester had evidently put thrift and utility before profligacy or pursuit of novelty. Multiples of body linen, like pockets, shifts and caps, account for a significant proportion of clothing generally during the period, driven by the frequent washing deemed necessary for items worn closest to the body and head. Hester and her pockets were part of the pronounced trend towards cotton and whiteness in the body linen of all but the poorest women.

Apart from the tradition of matching decorated pairs, it seems multiple pockets seldom exactly matched. What Mimi Hellman calls the 'laboriously achieved sameness' of matching sets of luxury goods in the period and the 'aesthetic of surplus' often seen in expensive outerwear are not characteristics of extant pockets.[22] However, four pockets survive with other items of the 1820s apparel of Fanny Jarvis to show how individual items could share structural needlework traits without being identical (fig. 73; see also fig. 86). This quartet is striking evidence of the investment of material and labour in the multiples necessitated by cleanliness. They belong to a group of apparel with exceptionally high levels of needle skills that have 'to be seen to be believed'.[23] A dozen each of Fanny's numbered caps and collar frills, a chemise numbered 9, a nightgown numbered 14, and a pocket numbered 9 record their places in sets (fig. 72), testifying to a meticulous household where first-rate needlework, able to withstand the roughest of washing, was matched by careful organisation of stock. Fanny's surviving apparel demonstrates that the practices urged by contemporary literature on domestic economy had equivalence in everyday life.[24]

However, just as linen of all kinds was subject to dirt, wear and tear when in use, when laid aside for long periods of time it was vulnerable to degradation, discolouration and damage or even theft, as Countess North believed; advice literature therefore treated over-abundance with caution, counselling, for example, only an amount that was 'absolutely needful'.[25] What comprised 'absolutely needful' for their stock was determined for individual women by many factors. For pockets, in addition to allowing for lengthy cycles of washing, drying and ironing, other matters such as broken ties, loss and other mishaps

CLOCKWISE FROM TOP LEFT
73a Opening on Fanny Jarvis's pocket no. 9, 1821 (detail). Manchester Art Gallery, MCAG.1947.1252.

73b Opening on one of a pair of Fanny Jarvis's pockets, 1824 (detail). Manchester Art Gallery, MCAG.1947.1253/2.

73c Opening on one of Fanny Jarvis's pockets, 1820s (detail). Manchester Art Gallery, MCAG.1947.1254.

73d Opening on one of a pair of Fanny Jarvis's pockets, 1824 (detail). Manchester Art Gallery, MCAG.1947.1253.

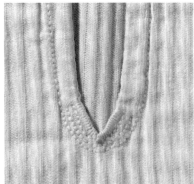
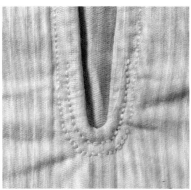
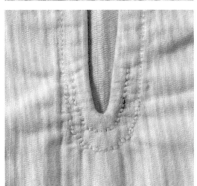

meant that replacement ones were 'needful'. Eliza Haywood made a joke of this in her tale of a lady who habitually kept a little pet dog in her pocket. In company, when the inevitable accident happened, she was helped to remove her smelly and 'offensive burthen', and issued the order to 'send my servant home with these filthy pockets, and let him bring me a pair of clean ones'.[26]

Daniel Roche argues that the 'struggle to maintain an appearance which conformed to social requirements was a stimulus to accumulation'.[27] But accumulation of linen was also a stimulus to labour – a limited resource – so abundance was finely tuned. It was not the result of superfluous or showy consumption, but was shaped by rational habits of consumption based on notions of cleanliness and household economy. Women were occupied with extending the life of individual items within their stock by means of orderly rotation through cycles of care and upkeep and a managed transition from new to old. They might also look on parts of their stock as potential cash or credit in hard times. Multiple pockets fitted within this necessary kind of abundance.

Storage and circulation

In a theft from their house in London in 1781, a gentleman's family lost ten pairs of pockets and their servants six pairs.[28] A single pocket was a slight thing, easy to store or move, but women's tendency to own several at any time meant pockets could proliferate in households with daughters and female servants or lodgers, becoming another call on space. In the flow of daily life and work under her roof, like many women before and after her, Lady Grisell Baillie (1665–1746), living in Scotland, understood the stagecraft that kept the show on the road, as she spelled out in her copy of her own mother's 'Derections for the House Keeper' in 1743. 'See that every one keeps what is their charge in there [sic] proper stated places, then nothing will be out of order, or to seek when wanted, nor any hurry.'[29] She advocated 'proper stated places' to facilitate control of labour as well as things. Daniel Roche expands on the significance of where we keep things. 'All methods and procedures of storage deserve our interest, because they throw light on the rhythms of life, the ordering of possibilities, the strategies of the circulation of goods, their hierarchical organisation between the intrusions of the functional and those of the aesthetic.'[30] But what was the proper place for a pocket?

Mary Churchill (1689–1751), Duchess of Montagu, split her four pairs of stored pockets in 1747, two alongside some of her stockings, shoes and caps and two elsewhere with flannel petticoats and more caps. In her capacious 'Wallnut Tree Cabinet', 'India Drawers' and 'Press No.1', the duchess stowed almost 500 items of apparel that matched her glamorous former life at court.[31] Despite a less glittering life among the landed gentry of Hampshire in 1821, Eliza Jervoise had even more to her name. Six pairs of her pockets lay in a drawer in her wardrobe with 150 other items, *all* identified as 'old', mostly consisting of night and day shifts, 'under Shirts', napkins, pocket handkerchiefs and stockings. This was below a drawer of 'good' things of the same type, in which were another six pairs of pockets, all part of a total stock of over 1,100 individual items.[32] The storage habits of Mary Churchill and Eliza Jervoise, separated by three-quarters of a century, underline the long-standing association of pockets with informal, low-status apparel and items for bodily extremities such as stockings and caps – another reminder of how pockets inhabited the sartorial edge.

Mary Young devised written systems to monitor and control her stock of linen regularly, echoing advice in contemporary literature on household management; this methodical approach was entirely in keeping with her other efforts to spell out the precise tasks of her servants and the education and behaviour of her children.[33] Within this regime, she divided her stock of pockets into six 'in wear' and 12 'laid by', as she did her larger stock of shifts, cotton and silk stockings, nightcaps and under-caps.[34] Reserves on this scale, combined with body linen for her husband and seven children and all the requisite household linen, called for generous amounts of storage. Specialist linen presses with internal divisions allowed things to be kept in their 'stated places'. Good storage was a priority in a culture of preservation beset by hazards such as mildew, insects, fugitive dyes and damage from light (see fig. 71).[35] Eliza Jervoise, like many women, took the extra precaution of using boxes, paper and 'net' to protect some of her things stored inside her furniture.[36]

Women of lesser means would keep their more limited stocks together in chests of drawers and boxes that may have held the majority, if not all, of their possessions. Their cramped and insecure settings often jeopardised their best efforts at prudent management. In 1744 Jane Reynolds stored her pockets in her 'drawer and trunk', mingled with a large quantity of clothing, including shoes, clogs and a silver salver, and lost them in a break-in.[37] As for many other women in precarious circumstances, her things could be for immediate use but were also worth storing carefully under lock and key because they had longer-term exchange potential, in addition to any sentimental value they might have held. Women might also store other women's pockets and other belongings if they were helping out in a crisis or if they took them in for needlework or washing. Compromises were necessary in many poorer households. Ann Morgan took lodgers in 1719 'and let them have the use of a Chest of Drawers, all but one Drawer, which she reserv'd to her self'.[38] Servants often kept their pockets with their other things locked in their boxes, which accompanied them from home to places of service; but it offered limited space and no guarantee of security or privacy – many servants lost their boxes moving between places, and suspicious employers could insist on opening them (see fig. 136).

Pockets, when put temporarily into baskets and bundles to await washing or ironing, might be in the kitchen or back parts of a house instead of in bedrooms or garrets. Detached pockets were also on the move, in the luggage of women travelling on visits. When Sarah Hurst went from Chichester to stay with old friends in Rochester in 1806 she took what seems to have been a reduced stock of clothing but still packed three pairs of pockets.[39] On a longer journey in 1774 six pairs of pockets were en route for Calais, with a dozen each of shifts, aprons, pocket handkerchiefs and stockings, petticoats, gowns and towels, in a trunk that was cut off and stolen from the Dover coach; the vulnerability of luggage in transit is suggested by an engraving after Robert Dighton's *Return from Margate*, which depicts the mode of coach travel in the late eighteenth century (fig. 74).[40] In different circumstances, temporary storage was available when women pawned their clothing. Pawnbrokers offered relatively secure storage for clothing awaiting collection during periods of economic difficulty, often better than the damp or insecure storage available in the homes of the poor.[41] In York in 1778, Mrs Green's pair of pockets went in and out of George Fettes's nearby pawnshop, pledged and redeemed three times in as many months. It seems there was no time during the year in which she did not have some of her clothing in his shop.[42] Women most often pawned

Printed for & Sold by BOWLES & CARVER.   The RETURN from MARGATE.   Nº 69 in S.ᵗ Paul's Church Yard, LONDON.

74 After Robert Dighton
(1752–1814), *The Return from
Margate*, 1793, hand-coloured
etching and engraving
(17.2 × 27.5 cm, plate mark).
Lewis Walpole Library, Yale
University, 793.00.00.177.

aprons, stays, shifts, petticoats or gowns, but Mrs Green's pockets gave her extra
flexibility as she repeatedly juggled goods and cash. The storage and circulation
of pockets, whether resting in grand cabinets or precariously itinerant like Mrs
Green's, show how women used particular spaces to preserve their things,
endeavouring to maintain control, though with varying degrees of success.[43]

Marking and reckoning

Pockets were used in an age of marks, when marking goods of all kinds
guaranteed origin, authenticity or ownership, and was crucial in many contexts,
including marks imposed by makers of ceramics, clocks and watches, and
hallmarks on precious metals. Cloth could carry a manufacturer's mark or even
an official stamp to record excise duties, or a so-called 'private mark' added
by a shopkeeper to keep a tally of stock (see fig. 46b).[44] At home, consumers
commonly added their own personal identification marks to their household
linen and to body linen for both sexes in what Beverly Lemire calls the 'victory
of quantification' and the domestic adoption of practices drawn from counting-
houses, shops and warehouses.[45] Many pockets were marked painstakingly
in cross-stitch or ink with a name, number and year. These inscriptions were
designed to fuse text and textile permanently (figs 75–7).[46] Marking goods at
home foregrounds specific practices and basic skills in literacy and numeracy
that women needed to manage their linen and keep it in 'proper stated places'.[47]

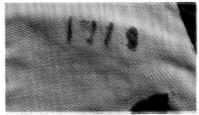

Marking linen was an embodiment of possession and order within the domestic economy of households or institutions and a means of making intelligible the status of things and the tasks associated with them. The inscriptions functioned in three concentric domains. The first domain was a set, the year or numeral on each item within the set allowing the owner to track rotation in use, methodical demotion and replacement. The second was the household as a whole, showing where and to whom things belonged. Thirdly, outside the household, marking allowed identification when items were transported, sent out for washing or were lost or stolen. At its most efficient, a household marking system would tally with written records kept by the owner or responsible servant.

Identification marks on pockets, like other apparel, were normally tiny, and more than half the marks found in our survey are on the back, invisible when the pocket was worn, though some embroidered pockets have initials and dates on the front alongside the decorative work. Marks consist of various combinations of initial or first name, surname, number and year, the most minimal being simple initials such as 'ET' or 'P' and the fullest inscription being 'Mary Crosby No' 4 1836' (fig. 77).[48] Not surprisingly, extant pockets show that ink, so much quicker to execute than cross-stitch, was used for

77 Mary Crosby's named, numbered and dated pocket front, 1836 (detail). Abbey House Museum, Leeds, LEEDM.E.1968.0061. 0020.A.

longer inscriptions like Mary's. Marking ink was widely available throughout the period, and its legibility could be improved by first applying sizing to the area to be inscribed. Despite widespread use of Coventry blue marking thread on apparel of the period, twice as many of the survey pockets are marked in red thread as in blue.[49] Within a single household, habits of marking could vary. A description given in court of a large quantity of linen stolen in London in 1777, including a pair of pockets, showed differences in the methods used; some of the lost linen 'is marked S, and a coronet over it in black liquid, some is marked MS in needlework, and some has both sorts of marks on it'.[50] However, the four pockets belonging to Fanny Jarvis were marked in a way that was consistent with the marking of her other apparel.

The painstaking job of marking household and body linen gave the women in charge a working intimacy with their stock that paid dividends, as the testimony of servant Elizabeth Bridgen in 1784 indicates. Elizabeth's expertise was crucial in identifying apparel stolen from the house where she had worked for over two years. She said 'these are a pair of stockings of my mistress's which I have mended for her several times; they are marked No.3. with new black silk; my mistress has many of these clouts, this is one, this stock is new [. . .] they are marked 1 and a dot'.[51] It was a fortunate employer that had a servant like Elizabeth who knew exactly what was what. In complex households with families, lodgers or live-in servants, marks differentiated between their possessions. When a London house was robbed of nearly 130 items of apparel and household linen in 1769, more than three-quarters bore marks with six different sets of initials, including 'CG' on a pair of pockets; the feat of recalling all these items with their particular marks for a detailed advertisement underlines their significance.[52] The marking of linen helped to preserve the boundaries between the living bodies of servants and their employers, but, *in extremis*, marked garments could also assist in the identification of corpses.[53]

The household records of Eliza Jervoise of Herriard, Hampshire, demonstrate a marking system in action. Eliza spent at least a third of each year about 40 miles away at Britford, Wiltshire. Handwritten lists of her clothing kept track of its whereabouts and fitness over time, an impossible task without marks. An annotated list of 1814 showed which of her many silk stockings were where (fig. 78). Their marks were transcribed: 'marked in Blue ♦ ∴ Numbered – 1.2–3.7.8.11.12', and their division between her two houses was noted: '– should be 6 gone to B. 4.5.6.9.10.13'. Also on the move were four

78 'A List of Mrs Jervoises Cloathes committed to the care of Elizabeth Thompson November 1814'. Hampshire Record Office, Jervoise of Herriard Family Papers, 44M69/F10/88/49.

of '6 pairs of Pocketts', which had gone 'to Britford'.[54] A list of 1816 identified some items as 'old' or 'not now in wear' and six of her handkerchiefs allocated 'For parcels or odd purposes – 4 to Britford'.[55] The work of all the marking is underlined by numerous purchases Eliza made of 'marking thread'.[56] Eliza's lists illustrate the benefits of a marking system for specific circumstances, revealing the scale of the intricate industry required and the numeracy and literacy needed to make it work. They are akin to Eliza's own diligent account books of personal, household and estate expenditure.[57]

So ingrained was the practice of marking that even dolls had marked linen (fig. 79).[58] Routine marking had a material culture of its own. *The Workwoman's Guide* detailed how to keep the linen-press 'in the most perfect order', including having an inkstand at the ready, as illustrated in a plate showing the interior of such a cupboard (see fig. 71). The author also included two recipes for making permanent marking ink and one for removing ink when 'linen is erroneously marked or spotted with marking ink'.[59] The ever meticulous Mary Young already had her own 'most perfect order' in hand when she annotated her 1830s household inventory: 'Every Pr of Sheets and Pillow Cases is marked with a letter to denote the bed they belong to and particulars of the date when they were purchased kept in a small red book – in the linen press'.[60] Sometimes the precise meaning of surviving marks can be unclear. Even the systems used in a household as well regulated as Queen Victoria's can remain opaque. Kay Staniland notes that the 'Queen's cipher was always worked on each [under]garment; the numbering system associated with the ciphers is not understood

70 Doll's pocket and marked handkerchief, mid-19th century (L 7.5 cm). York Castle Museum, YORCM: BA4530.

today but it is likely that the garments were ordered in quantities and then worn in rotation.'61

The centrality of marks and marking to careful consumption is underlined by the focus it received in needlework lessons for non-elite girls destined for domestic service, despite the commercial efforts of inventors of gadgets for automatic marking.62 The Countess of Salisbury's school at Hatfield was founded in 1732 for 40 poor girls, who were taught 'to Read, Sew, Knit and Mark in order to fit them for Service'.63 A century and a half later little had changed for workmen's daughters attending the Park School at Wilton House: 'needlework was their craft and the making and marking of the Wilton house linen was their duty'.64 Schools often used the products of needlework lessons to help fund themselves and this could include marking: for example, Bangor National School charged 4d. per dozen letters of marking in 1833.65 Instruction literature cast needlework in general, and marking in particular, as embodying virtuous neatness, and a child would be taught 'to make her stitches exactly the same size, and to set them at a regular distance from each other'.66 There were no short cuts to good marking. 'The thread must not be passed from one letter to another, but must be neatly fastened on the wrong side, and cut off. Each letter is to be begun as at first. Every capital letter has seven stitches in height' (fig. 80a–b).67 Marking in cross-stitch remained embedded in needlework lessons for girls up to the mid-twentieth century, despite the ready availability of laundry marking ink and the arrival of pre-woven name tapes from the 1870s.68 The evidence of the surviving pockets shows that, in practice, skills varied. A surviving pocket carries the mark 'SS 1841' in uneven, bungled cross-stitch – a signal, if one was needed, that not everyone did as teacher said (fig. 80c).

Ready-made or bespoke pockets were available from suppliers who also did the marking to order: for example, Georgiana Spencer's six pairs of pockets from Orton and Stow came ready marked in 1774 for her trousseau (see fig. 67).69 Many women did their own marking, for themselves or others. In 1799 Jane Austen wrote to thank her sister Cassandra for marking her silk stockings.70 However, a woman's own mark could have particular potency for her. In *The Mill on the Floss* (1860) George Eliot pictures Mrs Tulliver, fearing that her stock of prized linen will be sold, weeping 'over the mark "Elizabeth Dodson" on the corner of some table cloths she held in her lap'. She recalls the day, before she thought of marriage, when the weaver delivered the cloth, woven from yarn she had spun herself. 'And the pattern as I chose myself – and

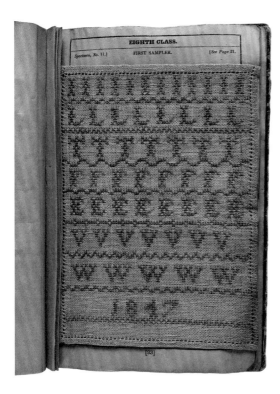

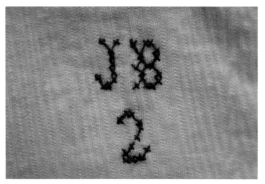

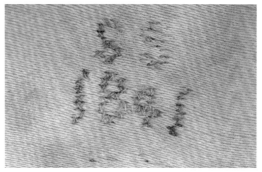

80a Marking stitches demonstrated in *Simple Directions in Needlework and Cutting Out Intended for the Use of the National Female Schools of Ireland* (Dublin: Hibernia Press, 1835). Victoria and Albert Museum, London, T.2 to C-1942.

80b Exemplary cross-stitch marking on the back of one of a pair of pockets, early to mid-19th century (detail). Norfolk Museums Service, Norwich Costume and Textile Collections, NWHCM:1935.53.107.

80c Cross-stitch marking on one of a pair of pockets, 1841 (detail). Hereford Museum Service, HSS 5449.

bleached so beautiful – and I marked 'em so as nobody ever saw such marking – they must cut the cloth to get it out, for it's a particular stitch.'[71] Eliot alerts us to a woman's continuous physical and mental involvement with material things – in this case from spinning to marking – and how even a small stitched name could carry meaning and memory.

The marks of orderly consumption were never entirely secure. Oliver Twist spent 'eight or ten days' learning to unpick identification marks on stolen handkerchiefs early in his career with Fagin, a reminder that, although marks were intended to last, some came to grief.[72] Oliver's real-life contemporary, servant Lucy Jackson, described thieves in London in 1838 removing her marked initials from her new caps and handkerchief: 'the mark has been picked out – here are the traces where they have been – it was marked in red marking thread'.[73] Alterations to marks (for reasons unknown) are visible on surviving pockets, such as inked marks thoroughly struck through and replaced; one retains an 'F P' in ink, but an inked name on its waistband is snipped out (fig. 81). Repeated wear and rough washing practices have made several inked and stitched marks illegible on surviving pockets, evidently a familiar problem. Jenkin Jones, testifying in 1784 about his 'great quantity' of lost linen, had to admit that his household's marking was imperfect: trying to identify a shirt, the jury could not 'judge of that mark, because it is washed

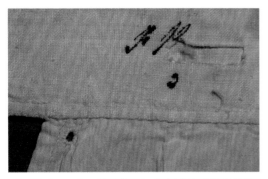

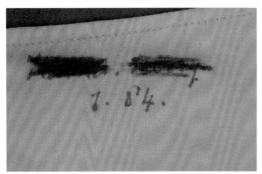

out'.[74] So, despite the labour spent marking pockets, without continuing care the marks could be lost in the course of the pockets' working lives, and when 'servants frequently forget to look at the marks', then even the best efforts at order were in vain.[75]

The marked pockets in our survey highlight the once common place of marking in everyday life, a practice that continued throughout the nineteenth century. The surviving unmarked pockets suggest households where it was neglected or thought unnecessary. By contrast, a named and numbered pocket asserted its place within virtuous and orderly stewardship of resources, and points to increased work in the wake of increased consumption. Marks on extant pockets may be the only traces left of the girls and women who made them but their tiny inscriptions are not obscure marginalia, rather a detailed record of their labour.

Mending and minding

Mending was another core reality of consumption, a part of life that contrasts sharply with recent times.[76] It aimed to preserve possessions rather than replace them at the first sign of wear, but it was only one element within extensive practices intended to prolong the useful life of clothing, including alterations, dyeing, re-lining garments or turning them inside out to get more wear.[77]

Mending decelerated the consumption of new goods, and for poorer women it was an absolute necessity. In 1787 the Revd David Davies recorded the income and expenditure of six labouring families in his Berkshire parish, and noted that they all bought mending thread on a weekly basis. He reflected later that 'the women spend as much time in tacking their tatters together, as would serve for manufacturing new clothing, had they the skill to do it, and materials to do it with'.[78] Poorer households had to eke out small stocks, a task made more difficult by badly made or second-hand goods. But mending apparel and household linen was not confined to this level of society: upkeep could also be relentless in middling and elite households. Lady Arabella Furnese enjoyed luxurious bespoke clothing but her things were also mended and turned on a regular basis.[79]

81a Inked name cut away on the back of a pocket, leaving the letters 'F P', early to mid-19th century. Royal Albert Memorial Museum, Exeter, EXEMS 567/2006.

81b Marking replaced and unpicked on the back of a pocket, early to mid-19th century (detail). Museum of London, 39.119/10.

81c Pocket front with name struck out, 1884 (detail). Royal Albert Memorial Museum, Exeter, EXEMS 74/1964/4.

Like plain sewing and marking, mending was taught in schools because many saw these skills as necessary for poorer girls, to make them 'good servants, and useful mothers to families of their own'. In a scheme of 1789 entitled *Instructions for Cutting Out Apparel for the Poor*, designed to be taught to poorer children, girls mended linen for their families, an early introduction to the work that awaited them in their own homes or in service.[80] One writer on domestic economy thought a live-in housemaid with a modicum of skill could keep on top of a household's mending: 'it is her business to make whatever repairs may be required, and to inform you when so worn out as to be past mending, that new articles may be procured, and the stock kept up'.[81] With her considerable stock, Mary Young divided the labour between at least two servants. Her nursery maid mended the children's clothes. Her 'Upper Servant or Needle Woman' superintended the mending not only of the household linen but also of Mr Young's shirts and silk stockings, and did any needlework 'I may give her', in addition to her other duties. An indication of the onerous scale of mending in the Young household occurs in a note of 1830, when 16 of Mr Young's shirts were 'put in complete repair', bringing his total stock of used and new shirts to 32.[82] As a measure of the economic impact of mending in general, Mary often had enough work on hand to justify the employment of outside needlewomen, some of whom, such as 'Sophy', she employed on and off for years.[83] However, the novelist Catherine Hutton (1756–1846), by her own account a prolific producer of decorative needlework, thought nothing of turning her hand to her own mending, even after dinner and away from home: 'Darned my pocket and a muslin apron.'[84]

In *Amos Barton* (1857), George Eliot's Milly Barton, the impoverished clergyman's wife, eked out meagre funds to clothe her family. She 'put patches on patches, and redarned darns', and rose early in the morning to 'renew her attack on the heap of undarned stockings'.[85] Was there love in the darning? Harriet Martineau first realised she was valued as a child when a friend asked why her mother 'sat up at night to mend my stockings, if she did not care for me'.[86] Remedial needlework was not without its satisfactions. For Nancy Woodforde, it was part of social and kinship networks; in 1792 she told female friends how 'to make Tuckers out of their old fashion double Ruffles', and, when her brother Samuel came to stay, she 'Work'd hard all Day for Br Sam mending Shirts &c.'[87] The erudite Anna Larpent found a mending session in 1797 gave relief from anxiety about her sister: 'fulfilling my female duties warms my heart as much as Mental pursuits delights it [*sic*]'.[88] A year before, she had portrayed herself 'eagerly patching up work', and she regularly noted how she mended shirts for herself and her family.[89]

Mending methods ranged from simple patches to complex darning, from fine work to botched or hasty, and pockets were no exception; those in the survey

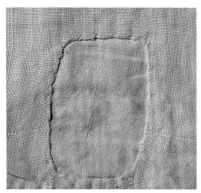
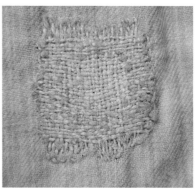

register the realities of keeping pockets in active use (fig. 82). Anyone making a hash of it could at least hope their pockets stayed hidden under their petticoats. The pockets show the stress exerted by the weight and friction of the contents, the motion of the body and the action of the hand reaching in and out. In some cases, stretched and abraded cloth still bears the 'memory' of its load (fig. 84; see also fig. 93a–b). Even leather was damaged by hard use (see fig. 37). A pair of embroidered pockets from the mid-1700s exhibit many of the commonest problems; abrasion has worn off areas of embroidery; one pocket has a hole on the lower back and a heavily worn area opposite the opening, the other has a rough patch to reinforce the binding of the opening (fig. 84). Patching was a good remedy for damaged pockets, and mending went on top of mending (see fig. 132b). This could often be done in habitual and personal ways, as shown by five surviving pockets that came from the same household (fig. 85).[90] The speediest of all repairs happened when broken ties were knotted together, an easy remedy for women on the go (fig. 83; see also fig. 93d). In court, Ann Buton identified the pocket she had made for her grandmother in 1832, adding: 'but I did not sew these strings on it; it has different strings now', probably because her grandmother, a vendor of tapes, laces and darning cotton, had the wherewithal to replace the strings herself.[91] In 1743 Sarah Heath pointed up how vulnerable pocket ties or strings could be when she accused David Todd of stealing her pocket from her in the street: 'my Pocket was pulled off my Side, the String was broke, and left about my Waist'.[92]

The mending of pockets allows a close-up view of women's practices in a period often associated with increased consumption of fashion-led goods. Jan de Vries argues that with 'small, incremental purchases, people of modest means could still participate in a broad societal engagement with fashion and experience a new sense of change'. He also suggests this had 'the effect of shortening the fashion life cycle of a wide range of semi-durables. In both ways – physical and stylistic – the depreciation of goods was speeded, and the user necessarily became more of a consumer and less an heir.'[93] Pockets complicate

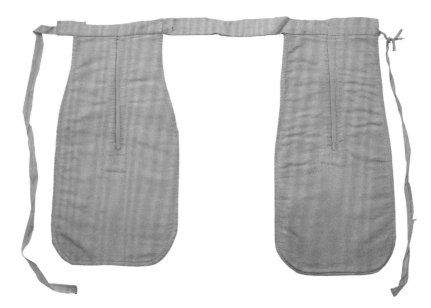

83 Knotted tie on a pair of pockets, mid-19th century (L 41.5 cm). Nottingham City Museums and Galleries, NCM 1965-92.

84 Pair of embroidered pockets, showing all types of wear and repair, mid-18th century (L 36 and 35.2 cm). Museum of London, 49.91/2.

RIGHT
85a Machine-sewn pocket (from the same household as the examples below), with heavy hand-stitched repairs and patches, mid- to late 19th century (L 35.5 cm). Amgueddfa Cymru–National Museum Wales, 59.285.9.

BELOW, LEFT TO RIGHT
85b–c Hand mending on two machine-sewn pockets, mid- to late 19th century. Amgueddfa Cymru–National Museum Wales, 59.245.30, 59.285.7.

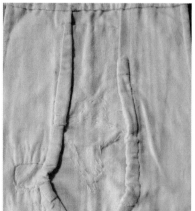

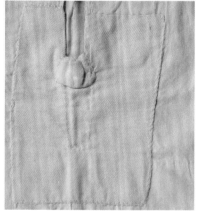

this picture. They resisted change, though they coexisted with it. In contrast to the obsolescence of more fashion-centred goods, mended pockets represent a deeply rooted culture of preservation.

Washing and cleanliness

Wash-days made prior investment in marking worthwhile. In 1800 Mary Harrison, a London publican, reclaiming her five pockets and other belongings stolen from her washing line, said: 'I know these to be mine; there are the initials of my own name and my daughter's upon them.'[94] Doing the laundry was a major task and expense in households of all kinds across the period.[95] It came into particular focus within a growing literature on domestic economy, with advice aimed at the relief of poverty but also at middling readers concerned to keep their own families afloat and respectable at a time when cleanliness was widely associated with restraint and decency in both domestic and institutional life. But whiteness was a pleasure as well as a virtue, particularly when, in new cloth, it was at its most luminous. In 1779 Elizabeth Shackleton wrote: 'I am on this day 54 or 55 years old [. . .] I put on my new white long lawn Pocket Handchief mark'd E.2. red in Honour of this Good day.'[96] In such ways, cleanliness was a matter of private gratification as much as of public display.

The same inventories that open women's cupboards and allow us to see their storage methods also reveal the extensive influence of cleanliness in the form of washable materials. While not all commonly used cloths were safely washable – wool and silk were vulnerable – nevertheless, washable items formed over 88 per cent of Hester Clifford's apparel in an inventory of 1775 taken after her death, a proportion similar to Mary Waller's larger posthumous stock in 1835.[97] Mary's household linen encompassed many washable items besides bedlinen, such as dimity curtains and muslin blinds. The 'triumph of cleanliness' spanned social ranks; at least two-thirds of Eliza Jervoise's apparel was washable.[98] Cotton especially embodied ideas about cleanliness because of its capacity to cope with new industrial bleaching methods; the brightly patterned printed cottons could withstand recurrent washing, giving 'a new and fresh appearance after every wash', which made them immensely popular.[99] Where cleanliness was valued, even pockets were worth the expense of washing, bleaching and starching. Our survey includes many pockets of cotton dimity, made dazzling white by chemical bleaching processes, like the pockets of Fanny Jarvis (fig. 86).[100] Victoria Kelley characterises cleanliness as 'a richly material concept', one that 'accorded status to things, signalling their importance'; 'clean things', she observes, 'could in turn be used to articulate relationships between people'.[101] According to their resources, householders commonly distinguished between themselves and their servants, not only in the allocation of domestic spaces but also in the quality of food and other items designated for them. Doing the laundry was part of this intricate dance of social difference when servants' and employers' things were kept separate. In 1828 Ann Fox, wife of a London cheesemonger, regretted allowing her servant to wash her clothes mixed in with her own when she realised her pockets

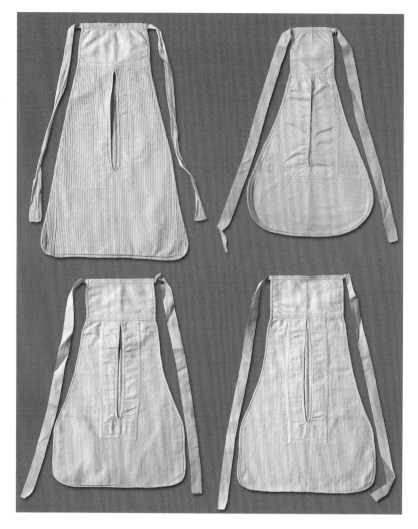

and pinafores were missing. Ann admitted 'they might have been mixed up in the drying'.[102] Ann Fox would have been better off had she used a washing record book. One such, published in 1845, was organised in three sections, for 'Family', 'Nursery' and 'Servants', and divided pockets between those belonging to the family and those belonging to their servants (fig. 87). With seven children in her care and a quantity of servants to manage, ever tidy Mary Young surely found the purchase she made of a 'washing book' in June 1820 very useful. [103]

The author of *The Workwoman's Guide* was in no doubt about the potential magnitude of laundry labour and its recurrent cost in the houses of the gentry. She listed 43 separate categories of articles that might go to wash from the nursery, a further 27, including pockets, from the lady of the house and 17 from

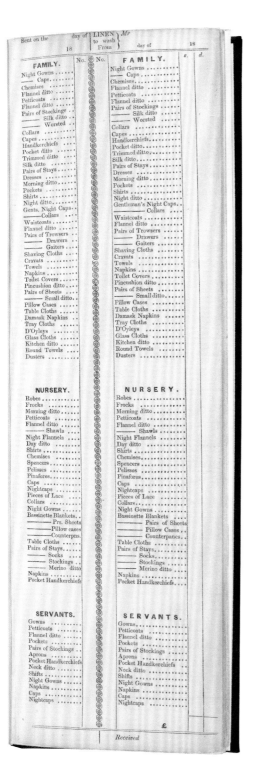

the gentleman, and 15 categories of house linen.[104] The last comprised 'bed-room linen, table and pantry linen, housemaid's linen, and kitchen linen, to which may be added stable linen', and bedroom linen was further subdivided into 'best', 'family' and 'Servant's'.[105] With six to twelve towels for every washing stand, two covers to every pillow and most categories of body linen coming in multiples, small wonder that the scale of the work drew the advice that it was 'the best economy to wash by the year, or by the quarter, in places where it can be done, and by the score or dozen in preference to the piece'.[106] Articles for washing had to be gathered from their place, separated – everyday from best, servants' things from the family's – and in careful households all the items individually tallied. Clean things returning from the laundry had to be checked again and reallocated to their places. 'The Laundry-maid ought to be very correct in counting, and setting down the various articles she receives, and to return whatever has been delivered to her.'[107] Household stock could outgrow domestic washing facilities and necessitate putting it out. Done at home or away on this scale, any 'triumph of cleanliness' was also a laborious triumph of organisation.

In 1803 Ann Green washed a pair of white pockets for her near neighbour Prudence Pearson who wore them the next day, though in many cases matters were not so speedy.[108] In 1819 the Listers of Louth in Lincolnshire lost 'the whole of the linen of a three weeks' washing. Even the baskets were taken'. The scale of three weeks' linen led them to suppose the thieves must have used a cart for 'carrying off the booty'.[109] The frequency of wash-days was determined by the capacity of the wash-house, the availability of labour and the amount of stock available for rotation. Drying clothes in winter was a slow business, another reason for households owning numerous sets.[110] Ann Brockman's arrangements between 1700 and 1704 for weekly and fortnightly washes of clothes,

with delicate items – such as gloves, or 'mending & washing my french lace head' – done separately as needed, echo common practice in dividing the work.[111] Many householders chose to alternate washes for household and body linen.[112] Capable and trustworthy washerwomen were to be valued in these major operations. Servants trusted with repairs were often the same people involved in the washing. Elizabeth Batchelor, Mary Waller's loyal local needlewoman, also undertook washing for the family, and continued to do so after Mary's death (fig. 88).[113] London servant Mary Evans claimed length of service in 1786 to support her identification of stolen things, including pockets: 'I know Mrs. Whitnell's things [. . .] I have washed for her these ten years; here are two petticoats; I know them by the bindings.'[114] Mrs Randell worked for Eliza Jervoise for nearly 23 years, mending and dressmaking – including making her pockets – but also washing and ironing.[115] Mary Hardy, a yeoman's wife in Norfolk, must have wished for such dependable washerwomen when she faced frequent uncertainties in marshalling adequate labour to supplement her own maids. She recorded with some relief in April 1791: 'We borrowed Mr Davy's Washing Mill & washed 3 weeks linen without a work woman'..[116]

88 Elizabeth Batchelor, bill for washing, 1830. Hampshire Record Office, 29M67/43.

Even the pleasures of travel could be disrupted by getting the laundry done in distant places. Lady Grisell Baillie's accounts of a continental trip contain regular entries for washing in the cities visited.[117] *The Workwoman's Guide* warns its readers that 'very indifferent washerwomen are usually met with at watering or sea-bathing places', and advised travellers to take cheaper sheets with them.[118] Practical advice offered by Mariana Starke to travellers for over a decade in successive editions of her *Letters from Italy* details the price for washing pockets in different Italian cities and regions. So important was the task of getting the laundry done well that she even recommends individual washerwomen by name.[119] We do not know whether Mary Godwin had an edition of Mrs Starke's travel advice with her when she eloped with Percy Bysshe Shelley to the continent. But the journal she kept during their continental travels contains lists of clothing that probably correspond to washing lists, in which we see pockets being washed among shifts, shirts, stockings, pillow cases and even 'Shelley's cap'.[120]

Washing used costly resources and turned the search for domestic order on its head. A household could be disrupted for days on end by all the demanding

89 Julius Caesar Ibbetson
(1759–1817), *Washing with
Ashes*, undated, pen and ink
and watercolour on paper
(6 × 7.6 cm). Yale Center
for British Art, Paul Mellon
Collection, B2001.2.955.

processes of cleanliness.[121] Getting piles of soiled linen ready and mended if necessary was the easy bit. Water was pumped and carried for cold soaks, fires were fuelled at daybreak to heat water for the main wash, there was scouring, washing with wood-ash-based lye or soaps, rinsing, starching, mangling, drying, folding, ironing and 'getting up' the finished articles, and returning them all to their allotted places in the house (fig. 89). Garments were turned inside out, dirt exposed to view. Laundry checklists might envisage the separation of servants' and employers' linen, but female servants handled their male and female employers' intimate things; what touched the skin when worn was laid out in plain sight, and sartorial compromises made for appearance's sake were all too evident to everyone in the wash-house.[122] The ferocious methods used for washing linen always risked damaging it, as one writer recalled in detail:

> It will be unnecessary to caution an honest servant against being wasteful of soap, tearing the linen, &c. either in washing, or drying it upon hedges and fruit trees; or stirring the linen in the copper with sticks that are splintered or have nails in them; or to suffer it to mildew by laying too long undried or unironed.[123]

In April 1761 Sarah Hurst lost her temper with it all: 'Very busy all day washing & ironing, out of temper because it is wet weather, oh how absurd & ridiculous is this, & what is still worse angry with Mamma for not contriving it better, NB to beware of such behaviour for the future.'[124] Despite her resolution, Sarah's angry ironing continued next day. In her own household, Dorothy Wordsworth helped out in 1800 with ironing at the 'great washes about once in 5 weeks', but was pleased that the weekly ironing of smaller things happened 'in a place apart from the house and we know so little about it as makes it very comfortable'.[125]

At home or away, the upheaval of washing brought the additional risk of theft. Rebecca Pearcy told how a fellow servant helped herself to pockets and a substantial quantity of other linen in 1786 from the kitchen of a dwelling house, after Rebecca herself had 'packed up the linen to go to be mangled, and left it upon the dresser'.[126] With clothes drying out on lines or hedges

90 Henry Taunt, *Washing on Hedge in Front of a Cottage, Surrey*, late 19th century, photograph. Historic England Archive, DD62/00008.

in the open, linen was at risk at every step of the way (fig. 90). When the linen was sent out to a neighbourhood washerwoman, it could pass through several hands if the washerwoman sent another person, sometimes a child, to fetch or return it, and the containers were carried or trundled on carts through the streets. Once at the washerwoman's place, the linen might be less well supervised than at home. Mary Rowland, a weary washerwoman, reported in 1782 that she lay down to rest; she had a number of valuable things in her room 'folded for ironing', and woke to find them stolen, including a pair of dimity pockets.[127] Linen was also sent considerable distances if wealthier Londoners wanted their washing done in the country. Jenkin Jones's laundry went by road and river to his country house every week, and a pair of dimity pockets was on one occasion stowed with a substantial quantity of other linen in 'a very large trunk', all stolen near the start of its journey.[128] The licit and illicit bundles, baskets and boxes that criss-crossed rivers, roads, lanes and alleys on their way to and from washing often contained a combination of linen belonging to different individuals, jumbled together into new social configurations and embodying tensions between order and disorder, thrift and profligacy.

The wash-house itself was often no better, a site of potential damage, disruption and disorder. Not only was the linen out of its own place and at risk, but the women who washed it could themselves be disorderly and the wash-house was often seen as anarchic territory.[129] Eleanor King was indicted for theft in 1743 after she visited another servant and they got 'prodigious fuddled'. The constable said 'he never saw two People more in Liquor in his Life; they both lay drunk in the Wash house against the Door'.[130] In Lincolnshire in 1844, Mary Nadin, a temporary charwoman, drew suspicion when her pocket seemed 'very bulky'. She had stolen a pound of soap and a bottle of currant wine. The house servant Eleanor Bowman, described by Mary as 'very tipsy', confessed to giving her a piece of soap 'to wash a cap for her', and the wine was concealed in the wash-house.[131] Such misdemeanours fuelled householders' anxieties about the potential chaos of wash-day: they feared the invasion of the wash-house by untrustworthy occasional workers, the opportunities for regular servants to stray, and the wash-house as a place of gossip and subversion outside the scope of normal supervision.[132] Mary Collier (*c.*1688–1762), poet and washerwoman, gave a rare insider's view of the wash-house in 'The Woman's Labour' in 1739. She wrote vividly of the drudgery faced by washerwomen before a cold dawn, giving no quarter to the mean, carping mistress, who 'Lays her Commands upon us' while harbouring suspicions about damage, waste and theft.[133]

Wash-days were one of the greatest challenges to domestic economy and order in households of all kinds. However carefully a pocket was mended, marked and stored, when sent to the wash it was in an entirely different domain. For the beneficiaries, from the noise and sweat came the intimate pleasures of crisp clean linen next to their skin, but the wash-house was also a kind of nether world of decency in which cleanliness was achieved at great cost and commotion and consumption demanded relentless cycles of heavy toil.

* * *

Women's consumption and custodianship of linen was a long continuum. It was dependent on particular labour practices and knowledge, which though faintly represented in written records remain clearly visible in surviving pockets. Often shabby and threadbare, these are valuable evidence of women's past labours, which otherwise might be lost. Detachable pockets were assets within household economies, showing the valorisation of accumulated stock, its preservation, cleanliness and order. They retained sociability, they were a *presence* rather than an absence in the dynamics between consumers, their things and wider social practices including the demarcation of people and spaces. Their treatment shows that advice literature on household economy could reflect actual practice, but also that efforts to preserve possessions and stem the potential chaos of consumption could meet with less than satisfactory results when thwarted by damage, loss or theft. They embody a consumption that was industrious rather than conspicuous, underpinned by unrelenting labour to order, keep clean, mend and prolong usefulness.

RIGGING OUT A SMUGGLER.

'they say there is no bottom to them?'

Pockets, Possession and Promise

One evening in 1754 on Barnes Common near London, a highway robber struck lucky. He took a gold watch and a pair of white dimity pockets from a 'Lady in a Coach'. Inside the pockets he would discover a veritable world of goods, valuable enough for the owner to offer an exceptional reward for their return. He made off on horseback with the watch and the pockets,

> containing among other Things, a small round Tortoiseshell Snuff box, lined with Metal, and a Pinchbeck Hinge; a London Almanack, in a black Shagreen Case, with a silver Rim and Hinge; an Ivory Carv'd Toothpick Case, with a Gold Rim; a Silver sliding Pencil; a white Cornelian Seal (engraved with Minerva's Head) set in Pinchbeck; a Tortoiseshell Comb in a Case; a Silver Thimble and Bodkin; a Bunch of Keys, a red Leather Pocket-book; a green knit Purse, containing Half a Guinea, a Crown Piece of William and Mary, and about Five Shillings, with two Glass Smelling Bottles.[1]

The roll call of 13 finely wrought and valuable goods in these pockets contrasts with a pocket taken the year before in London from 'gentlewoman' Jane King: 'One ticking pocket, value one penny, one iron key, value two-pence, one penknife, value one penny; one brass thimble, value one halfpenny'.[2] A hundred years later, in her novel *Adam Bede*, George Eliot assembled, in desperate Hetty Sorrel's pocket, a collection of small things with heavy narrative punch. The juxtaposition of her seducer's gifts of jewels, the words

PAGE 110
91 Thomas Rowlandson
(1757–1827), *Rigging out a
Smuggler*, 1810, etching with
stipple (35.1 × 25 cm, plate
mark). Lewis Walpole Library,
Yale University, 810.09.25.01+.

on honest Bede's gift and the paltry contents of Hetty's purse and case lay bare
her predicament.

It was then she thought of her locket and earrings, and seeing her pocket lie
near, she reached it, and spread the contents on the bed before her. There
were the locket and earrings in the little velvet-lined boxes, and with them
there was a beautiful silver thimble which Adam had bought her, the words
'Remember me' making the ornament of the border; a steel purse, with
her one shilling in it, and a small red-leather case . . . [containing] nothing
but common needles and pins, and dried tulip-petals between the paper
leaves where she had written down her little money-accounts.[3]

The things in the pockets of these three women point to extensive
differences in how they enjoyed the material world. The distinctive possessions
of the 'Lady in a Coach' in 1754 record exotic raw materials imported by
an imperialising global trading nation. With the ingenuity and invention in
fashionable goods for which England was then famed, they were carved,
engraved, set, lined and rimmed into little things that spoke of their owners'
participation in polite society.[4] The iron key, the penny penknife and the brass
thimble of 1753 denote a more modest life (or a more prudent traveller), but the
potential of these objects could make them more important to their owners than
their monetary value conveys. A century later, Hetty's possessions embodied
sentiment, promise and loss. The things inside women's pockets may be a
yardstick of plenty or want, but they also offer a more suggestive account of the
material past. Once glimpsed, they point to how women could own and think
about material things and use them to inhabit and negotiate the social world.

There are obvious challenges to our focus on the contents of women's
pockets. Given that pockets were intended as personal and secure domains,
they would seem outside the historical record, like much else in women's lives.[5]
How is the historian to know what lay inside a pocket when even a woman
who wore one in 1780 said: 'I don't know exactly what I had in my pocket'?[6] To
address this question, we foreground our findings from accounts of trials in the
Old Bailey spanning the years 1676 to 1904 that involved the contents of tie-on
pockets.[7] We use the indictments as a form of inventory of what women had in
their pockets at the time, and analyse the associated testimonies representing
the individual voices of women, men and children, as victims, witnesses or
defendants. The attraction of these individual voices and their stories must be
set against the obvious limitations of the source.[8] However, indictments and
testimonies together constitute a rich resource, revealing everyday practices of
possession and ownership, otherwise hard to access.

In this chapter, we explore the intricacy of relations between people
and things that is at the heart of Igor Kopytoff's argument that the 'cultural

Patent French Improver

ah' that's just the thing

A SKETCH for the LADIES ALLBUM !!!

92 William Heath (1795–1840), *A Sketch for the Ladies Allbum!!!*, 1831, hand-coloured etching (36 × 25 cm, sheet). Lewis Walpole Library, Yale University, 831.05.08.01+.

biography' of an object takes place in a shifting 'world of categories'. 'As with persons, the drama here lies in the uncertainties of valuation and identity.'[9] The same thing may be seen as a commodity at one time but not another, or be seen differently at the same time by different people, revealing 'a moral economy that stands behind the objective economy of visible transactions'.[10] In Kopytoff's contrast between the process of commoditisation and establishment of exchange value and the process by which singular or private value is generated by individuals, he observes the 'drive' of the individual to 'discriminate, classify, compare, and sacralise'.[11] He notes that there are situations where 'the forces of commoditization and singularization are intertwined' in subtle ways, not entirely 'insulated' from each other, and that things can 'shuffle' between them over time.[12] Like Hetty Sorrel, in this chapter we spread out the contents of women's pockets and think about their value and significance. Borrowing from Michel de Certeau, we also think of the inside of a pocket not as merely a physical space but as 'a *practiced place*', a site in which habits of use shape and are shaped by women's relations to the material world.[13] To do this, we join our findings from the Old Bailey with other sources to explore, through the contents of women's pockets, the nature, promise and variants of possession, organised as aspects of order, agency, promise and ownership.

Order

Inside their pockets, women could practise an intimate order for their things, often at odds with representations in print and visual culture of their pockets as sites of disorder and excessive consumption. In 1759 Adam Smith argued that his contemporaries were wasting their money 'on trinkets'. 'All their pockets are stuffed with little conveniences. They contrive new pockets, unknown in the clothes of other people, in order to carry a greater number.' These misguided 'lovers of toys', who 'loaded' their pockets, would find that 'the whole utility is certainly not worth the fatigue of bearing the burden'.[14] Smith's arguments mirror an array of anxieties voiced by various authors in the period about unbridled consumption, with women often being the target of criticism.[15] Elsewhere the interiors of women's pockets were imagined as uncharted sites of duplicity, profligacy or crime (figs 91–2). In a period

93a Strained tie of a pocket, mid- to late 19th century (detail). Norfolk Museums, Service, Norwich Costume and Textile Collections, NWHCM.1968.873.9.

93b Abrasion on the bottom of a pocket, mid- to late 19th century (detail). Amgueddfa Cymru–National Museum Wales, 59.285.9.

93c Pocket tie, knotted to mend, 18th century (detail). Abingdon County Hall Museum, OXCMS:1997.7.1.

93d Pocket tie mended on one of a pair of pockets, mid-18th century (detail). Victoria and Albert Museum, London, T.697.B-1913, T.697.C-1913.

of expanding consumption, the spectral disorderly pocket resembled the 'new unfamiliar' London that emerged after the Great Fire, 'grown beyond individual comprehension'.[16] As the city swelled, so associated fears about over-consumption and its criminal opportunities were fuelled by the voluminous pockets found on female offenders in Old Bailey trial accounts: 'a pair of pockets that hung to her ancles', or 'two pockets almost as big as sacks' used by convicted thieves Sarah Taylor, Hannah Stevens and their like.[17] Popular accounts of criminal trials, and what John Beattie calls the 'message of the gallows' to the crowds who watched punishment meted out, created a cautionary tale of crime and may have reminded women to secure their possessions deep in their pockets.[18]

Although the Old Bailey heard many cases of stolen pockets with frugal contents, the court remained a place in which excessive stuff inside the *terra incognita* of women's pockets loomed darkly in the imagination. The examining lawyer who suggested to Margaret Jones, whose pocket was picked in 1794, that 'ladies pockets are generally pretty full, they say there is no bottom to them?' was swiftly rebuffed when Jones replied: 'I am very careful that I do not lumber my pockets with a parcel of litter.' Nevertheless, she had detected the moment when the accused, John Mitchell, took her belongings,

THE POCKET

because she 'missed some weight' from her pocket.[19] Inside and outside the court, it was often thought that women's pockets were so bloated and jumbled inside that the owners might not even recall what was in them. Even the meticulous advertisement prompted by the Barnes Common highway robbery in 1754, cited above, omitted details of additional 'other Things' contained in the stolen pockets. Weighty pockets entered criminal lore; the notorious thief John Jones was said to 'whipp off' a woman's pocket 'tollerably well' in a collaborative strike, but declined to trust it to his 'Comrade' when he had 'felt it very weighty'.[20] Newspaper advertisements for lost pockets, and surviving examples, evidence how they could slip off accidentally or ties could fail, possibly because of heavy contents (fig. 93).

A shadowy feature of women's consumption emerges in Old Bailey testimonies describing the loss of their pockets. In 1722, when thieves violently snatched the pocket of Elizabeth Knowles, they made off with her watch and chain valued at £5 5s., her snuffbox valued at 13s. and 'other things'. One of her convicted assailants, John James, alias Eaton, alias John the Grinder, allegedly said before he was hanged that his crime was 'a very slight and trivial Fault'. He was said to believe 'that No Body bore their All about them, nor could be much detrimented by so small a Loss, as that of a few odd things they carried in their Pockets'.[21] Teenager John's perception of his 'very slight and trivial' crime was at odds with many victims' testimonies spelling out to the court the gravity of their loss as well as the shock and fear it caused. Sarah Wood complained in 1724 that having her pocket and its valuable contents violently pulled from her 'put her into a Fright, and such Disorder, that she did not recover her self in two Months'.[22]

In fiction, writers relished an unruly, over-brimming pocket. In 1795 *The Observant Pedestrian* revelled in an imagined foul-up inside a fat lady's 'loaded dirty pockets' which magnified her corpulence: 'the soft pomatum has melted and ran all over the cold tongue, and the dried sprats, and here's your roll of brimstone, for the cramp, grinded all to powder; Lud a mussy, what a mess!'[23] In often censorious imagery, women's fathomless pockets were choked with stuff or were elided with unsettling bodily intimacy. Full pockets attracted criticism in polite circles if they led to rummaging with awkward gestures, and in 1802 novelist Susan Ferrier joked to her sister about the *noise* of things in the pockets of a woman she encountered at a concert. 'She came bobbing along, sticking out at all points and places, keys and *coppers* jingling in her pockets [. . .] I thought I should have swooned with shame when she stopped and stared at me.'[24]

The largest pockets in our survey are an astounding 61.5 cm long and 43.5 cm wide, and many are around 50 cm long and 30 cm wide, so extant pockets could certainly hold considerable cargo (fig. 94). Their distended shapes and strained tapes prove that many did (see figs 84, 93).[25] Their size resonates with the perception of weighty or seemingly bottomless pockets, but the chaos in

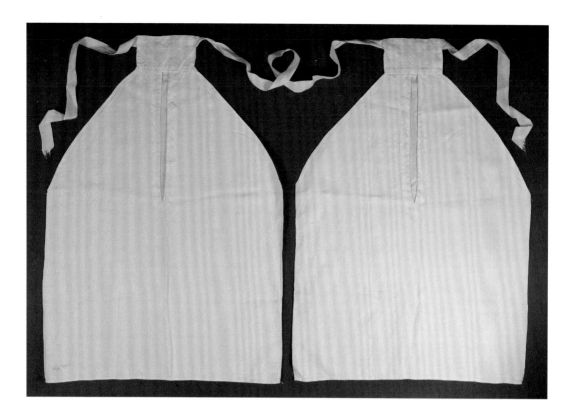

the fat lady's pockets and other imagined disarray are in marked contrast to reality. Many women's pockets were far from full and a 'loaded' or partially loaded pocket was not of necessity disorderly. There is plentiful evidence of women adopting various organising strategies, both in constructing their pockets and managing the contents, making their pockets effective places to carry and protect possessions. Numerous surviving pockets have extra single or double interior compartments (fig. 95; see also figs 36, 53, 69a, 112). When hung from the waist under layers of clothing, the pocket's contents were invisible to the wearer, identifiable initially only by touch, so internal divisions were helpful.[26] Without such care, things could easily be pulled out accidentally and lost. Olivia Harrington in 1777 wisely kept her keys and coins in her pocket 'loose in a little inside pocket'.[27] Extra compartments of this sort remained popular over the period; in 1831 the pocket used to help identify murder victim Fanny Pighorn had a 'secret inner' pocket.[28] An eyelet neatly bound on the inner section of Mary Crosby's pocket of 1836 meant she could tie or button things inside (fig. 95a). Other pockets were made with two main compartments, one in front of the other, with horizontal openings. Pins were another way to organise contents (fig. 96).[29] Keeping the inside of a pocket sorted in these ways was an obvious antidote to disorder and the risk of loss, theft or damage.

95a Interior compartment in Mary Crosby's pocket, 1836 (detail). Abbey House Museum, Leeds, LEEDM.E.1968.0061. 0020.A.

95b Internal compartment in a pocket, mid-19th century (detail). Worthing Museum and Art Gallery, WMAG.1962.1949.

95c Interior purse in an evolved form of pocket, sometimes called a 'railway pocket', late 19th or early 20th century (detail). Manchester Art Gallery, MCAG.1947.845.

95d Pocket with double horizontal openings, mid-19th century. Nottingham City Museums and Galleries, NCM 1976-195.

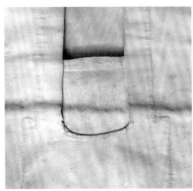
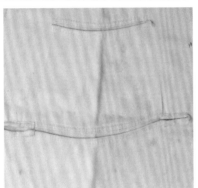

There could be no clearer material expression of the values attached by women to their small possessions and their assiduous protection of them than a handsome eighteenth-century pocket with a rich pink silk damask front and yellow silk back. The fashionable exterior hides an ingeniously constructed interior skilfully lined in chamois leather (fig. 97; see also fig. 112). The smooth, soft and resilient leather was particularly suitable for holding metal objects, and was therefore routinely used in men's fob pockets. This woman of means could slip her precious keepsakes, such as miniatures, a watch or a snuffbox into any of four inner chamois compartments, each neatly bound in silk stitching (fig. 97b), trusting they would not be lost or suffer damage from the more mundane contents like keys or coins.

There are many attached pairs of pockets in our survey and wearing more than one pocket in this way, or two or even three singles, was another effective organising strategy. In 1789 Mary Digman organised all her rent 'but two shillings' into two pockets, knowing precisely what was where: 'I had nine shillings and sixpence in one side, and two shillings and sixpence, in halfpence, in the other'.[30] Novelist Anna Maria Hall elevated the division and organisation of women's tie-on pockets to a moral realm:

96 Patchwork pocket with an attached safety pin, 19th century (detail). Private collection.

[Annie's] grandmamma made a decided distinction between these larger receptacles. The right-hand pocket might be considered an active member of society – a positive fountain, pouring forth what was wanted: the left-hand pocket, on the contrary, was a reservoir wherein everything was preserved. One typified the spirit of activity, the other that of carefulness. 'I should be in a state of confusion without my two pockets,' the old lady would say. 'What I wanted to preserve, would get confused with what I wanted to use; [. . .] and no matter how we *realise*; unless we *preserve*, we shall neither be useful nor rich.'[31]

Grandmamma's pockets held numerous little containers to augment her 'decided distinction' between 'activity' and 'carefulness', or giving and preserving. Here Hall was reiterating women's everyday practice of dividing and further enclosing the things inside their pockets to protect, apportion or earmark them.

Various types of containers, purpose-made or improvised, gave women further opportunities to organise and safeguard their possessions. The description by Oliver Goldsmith (1728–1774) of the 'plumb cake' that was 'all squeezed into crumbs' in his wife's pocket after she had walked through a crowd reminds us that protection and segregation made practical sense. Less messy contents could still require specific containment inside the pocket.[32] The popular long or 'stocking' purse, used by men and women alike, held coins or other small articles in both ends of its stretchy, mesh structure, each end separated and sealed off by a sliding ring (fig. 98). Eleanor Bird, keeper of a public house,

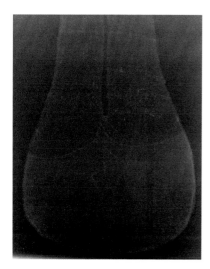

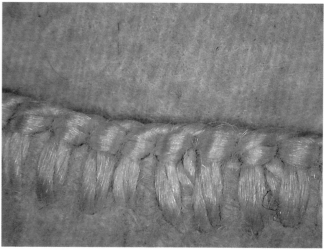

OPPOSITE, BELOW LEFT
97a X-ray of a damask and leather pocket with four interior compartments, early to mid-18th century (L 44 cm). School of Historical Dress, London, TSHD-2014-44.

OPPOSITE, BELOW RIGHT
97b Detail of silk thread binding on the edge of the interior compartments of a damask and leather pocket, early to mid-18th century. School of Historical Dress, London, TSHD-2014-44.

BELOW RIGHT
98 Stocking purse, beaded knitting, 19th century (L 40.5 cm). Victoria and Albert Museum, London, T.1443-1913.

in 1766 kept in hers 'one 13 s. and 6 d. piece, twenty-six guineas, and four quarter guineas' and 'two gold rings for mourning, value 20 s'.[33] However, purses constituted only a third of the containers cited in the Old Bailey trials, and money was not all they contained. The 'huswif', designed to hold small needlework sundries, also made an improvised purse (fig. 99). Judith Smith, faced with an assailant demanding money in 1735, said 'I took out my Huswife and gave him a Shilling'.[34] The pocketbook was another multi-purpose holder easily slipped in and out of the pocket. 'Pocketbook' is an umbrella term, including what Samuel Johnson defined as a 'paper book carried in the pocket for hasty notes';[35] more generally it could refer to a wallet purse, sometimes with compartments. In 1720 Mary Baldwin carried a pocketbook inside her pocket to protect a 'Note of 31 l. 5 s.'.[36] Pocketbooks could accommodate bulkier items: in 1793 Elizabeth Caldcleugh put small tools in her 'red morocco leather pocket book, with a silver lock'.[37]

The 13 itemised things inside the pair of pockets stolen on Barnes Common in 1754 included nine different encased or boxed things, in turn mirroring evidence from the Old Bailey, where small containers are the second most numerous class of objects after coins in pockets. Small boxes of various materials offered an easily accessed rigid structure to separate and protect things, as Sarah Satcher explained in 1784. When her pocket was taken in a distressing armed burglary it contained a 'china box I kept my money in, what little I had'. She said she used the box even though it did 'not shut very well' because 'I always liked to keep six-pence under my thumb'.[38] In 1761 Elizabeth Chalkley, a 'milk-woman', kept her 'two guineas and a half guinea' in a wooden screw box, valued at a farthing, inside her pocket.[39] However small, the rigid

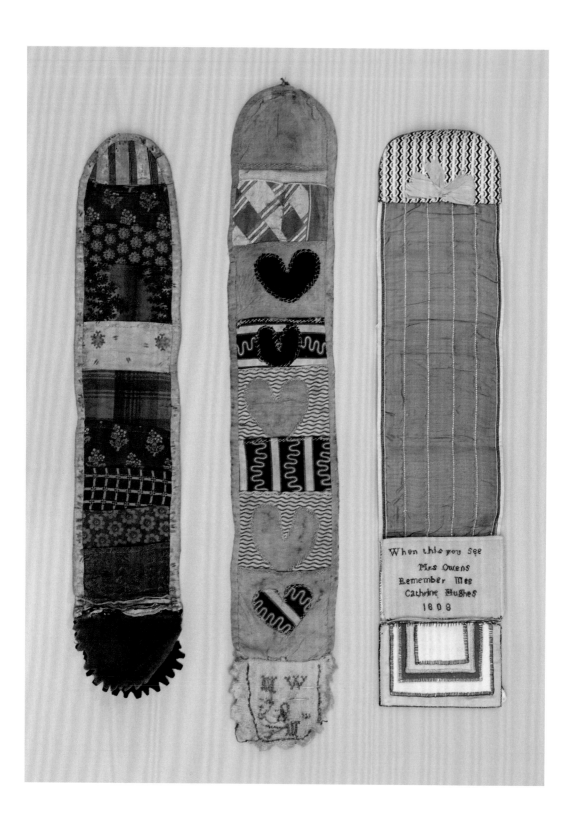

OPPOSITE
99 Huswifs or needle-cases
(rolled out), early 19th century
(left to right, L 43.5 cm, 51 cm,
45 cm). Amgueddfa Cymru–
National Museum Wales, (left
to right) 29.321, 13.99, F69.134.

BELOW LEFT
100a Samuel Pemberton
(maker), snuffbox, 1803, silver
(L 2.5 cm). Metropolitan
Museum of Art, New York,
1983.575.14.

BELOW RIGHT
100b Miniature nutmeg
grater in three parts, *c*.1698–9,
silver (L 7 cm). Metropolitan
Museum of Art, New York,
63.53.229a–d.

form of a box structured space within the pocket, perhaps amplifying a sense of security, differentiating forms of money and physically and mentally earmarking them.[40] When Elizabeth Bevan went out dancing with her husband in 1767, she snuggled her 'two 5 s. 3 d pieces' inside her iron snuffbox along with the snuff itself.[41] Women with valuable possessions also used the potential order provided by their pocketed boxes to separate and protect their things. In 1730, as Jane Kidd travelled by coach, she carried rings set with precious jewels worth £22 15*s.* in her snuffbox (fig. 100a).[42]

These habits of protecting or 'nesting' possessions in containers were evidently a commonplace way of organising things inside a pocket. 'Nesting' (our term) describes securing small valuables in a suite or progression of containers, frequently improvised, for the carrying of which the tie-on pocket was particularly well suited. Inside the pocket of Elizabeth Adams in 1784 were 'two nutmeg graters, one was full of receipts and duplicates, and the other had a guinea wrapped up in a piece of paper', indicating how she separated her quasi-money from actual money. She also testified to 'some few insurance papers' in the graters (fig. 100b). Many Old Bailey testimonies evoke nesting as a deliberate routine, perhaps a ritual – as in 1794, when Catharine Norton, a basket carrier, put her exceptional sum of 14 guineas in a silk purse, then put the purse into her tin snuffbox 'and put it all into my pocket afterwards', when she went to work.[43]

Random combinations of things inside a pocket might seem chaotic, but wrapping, like nesting, helped to organise the interior, suggesting other mental structures at work. Eleanor Hunter, a London servant, wrapped her wages up in a handkerchief before putting them in her pocket in 1753; and in 1772 Richard Boulton said he saw a fellow labourer pick out of a woman's

pocket 'a Woman's Cap wherein was contained [. . .] about four shillings'.[44] When Frances Gardner, 'lunatick and distracted', drowned herself in London in 1766, inside her pocket was found 'in the Corner of a Handkerchief, tied up; [. . .] half a Guinea, half a Crown and three Shillings, and a Sleave Button [. . .] a House Wife, a pair of Spectacles in a Case, a Scissars, a pair of Worsted Gloves, and a Hankerchief' (fig. 101). Her assorted cache, 'tied up', and her containers show Frances exercising at some point a personal sense of order.[45] The use of caps or handkerchiefs to wrap things may partly explain their presence inside pockets, in the Old Bailey proceedings and elsewhere. There is also the remarkable case of a deliberately concealed pocket containing a cap, which we see below. Nesting and wrapping things inside the pocket were in keeping with similar practices outside the pocket. Men and women used their clothing and accessories to organise and protect their valuables, as in 1736, when Ann Branson 'wrapped [money] up in a blue Apron, and laid it up in a Cupboard'.[46]

These practices show that order, beyond simple practicality, could express values of guardianship and the creation of a personal cosmos in miniature. Pockets constructed with interior compartments, and the nesting and wrapping of possessions before they were buried deep inside the pocket, indicate order, convenience and security. Adapting snuffboxes or caps to different purposes through improvisation extended their uses, and also underlines the fluidity of the pocket's work. The mix of contents might seem incongruous but there could be an intimate discipline of things shaped by an individual for herself.

THE POCKET

Agency

If women created spatial or mental order with and for things inside their pockets, the same small possessions could give them agency outside their pockets. Women's testimonies about their keys give specific insight into this. Trial accounts describe women carrying keys for the street door and garden gate, for all the rooms in their houses and for furniture, and the tiny keys that wound a watch or secured a pocketbook. Most of these women had more than one key in their pockets, often four or five, or 'bunches'.[47] But just one key could control other keys. Part of the case against Elizabeth Nichollus, accused in 1765 of theft from her employer, was that 'she had a key that opened a closet door, where Mrs. Taylor's bunch of keys were', giving her access to well-stocked locked drawers.[48] But an absence of keys in a woman's pocket may not indicate an absence of responsibilities, merely that she had left her keys with trusted kin or neighbours, or that she carried them elsewhere on her person.[49] In 1790 Mary Maxwell left hers behind: 'I was going to walk, and I thought they would be heavy.'[50] Not surprisingly, however, many women preferred the encumbrance of keys to being burgled.

A woman's custody of keys in her pocket allowed her control of both things and people, in her own right, or on behalf of others. The pocket carried keys around the clock, was taken off only at night, when it was stowed under the pillow, and was instrumental in women's cycle of work as guardians of resources, meagre or ample. Susannah Satcher, the wife of a publican, testified in 1784 that it was her 'business', not her husband's, to check all the night-time household security.[51] For women like Susannah, running households or in trade, the responsibility for security and control of resources, such as linen or consumables, meant carrying keys at all times, indoors and outdoors. In 1777 Olivia Harrington was a widow with significant household and commercial interests, having 'Twelve or fourteen' in her household, running a hotel, taverns, and her late husband's 'Haddock's bagnio at Charing-cross' with 25 rooms.[52] To control her businesses, she carried a 'great number of keys' in her pocket, which she wore at all times of day and night, even when she was 'very ill' with breast cancer and being treated with 'a plaister of hemlock' in her bedroom late at night. She liked to unlock things herself when they were needed. Her servant testified: 'I never had my mistress's bunch of keys except when she was present.'[53] Keys also had particular significance when multiple occupancy of houses was common. Locking the house was not only to secure it against external threat, but to control the movements of people already in the house, as lodgers, apprentices and servants did not normally have free passage. Ann Taylor, already suspicious of her servant Elizabeth Nichollus's early-morning movements, kept the street door locked to prevent her leaving the house and took the key into her own room as a precaution.[54]

As we have seen, pocketbooks could be used to organise the inside of the pocket, but they also helped to order life outside it. Amanda Vickery argues that the pocket memorandum book was a crucial tool in household management, being 'both the means and the emblem of female mastery of information, without which the upper hand was lost and prudent economy obliterated'.[55] Pocketbooks were printed as portable 'companions', and could provide important dates, ready reckoners, rates for transport and extended practical knowledge beyond the household into the outside world (fig. 102).[56] With handy pages to jot down expenses, they were used to keep track of economic activities and material goods, whether plentiful or scant. In 1778 Margaret Griffiths, found hanged in her lodgings, had used her pocketbook to stow a letter and keep track of her pawnbroking activities with 'an Accot. of things Pledged at different Places'.[57] Although uncommon in women's pockets in our Old Bailey cases, when pocketbooks did appear it was often in association with trade. Probably little got past Olivia Harrington, despite her being charged with keeping a disorderly house, but in 1777, among many other valuables stolen by a male servant was her well-worn pocketbook with a silver clasp. 'I have had it in my possession seventeen years [. . .] having it so long in my possession, I need no marks to swear to it.' Its importance was clear. Her personal servant was asked: 'Do you know your mistress's pocket-book?' 'Yes', she replied, 'by seeing it a great many times'.[58] Running a bagnio doubtless meant her pocketbook was best minded securely at her side. Women used pocketbooks in their own singular ways, sometimes at odds with the use intended by the manufacturers. When Sarah Gatehouse, from a family of minor gentry and farmers in Hampshire, acquired a printed pocketbook for the year 1771, she took no notice of the publisher's intentions (fig. 103). She continued to scribble her expenditure in it for several years afterwards, eventually pinning a piece of paper inside dated 1790. A thrifty woman, she recycled another one, made in 1757, and kept it long enough to record in it the prices of cheese between 1805 and 1808.[59] She employed these little books for her own singular ends at her own slow tempo, showing Kopytoff's entwined 'forces of commoditization and singularization' at work, and complicating how agency might be reckoned.

A MARKETING TABLE.
By the STONE.

Beef, Mutton, Veal, Lamb, Pork, &c. at per lb.	1 Stone or 14 lb. is	2 Stone or 28 lb. is	3 Stone or 42 lb. is	4 Stone or 56 lb, is
d.	s. d.	s. d.	l. s. d.	l. s. d.
1	1 2	2 4	3 6	0 4 8
1¼	1 5½	2 11	4 4½	0 5 10
1½	1 9	3 6	5 3	0 7 0
1¾	2 0½	4 1	6 1½	0 8 2
2	2 4	4 8	7 0	0 9 4
2¼	2 7½	5 3	7 10½	0 10 6
2½	2 11	5 10	8 9	0 11 8
2¾	3 2½	6 5	9 7½	0 12 10
3	3 6	7 0	10 6	0 14 0
3¼	3 9½	7 7	11 4½	0 15 2
3½	4 1	8 2	12 3	0 16 4
3¾	4 4½	8 9	13 1½	0 17 6
4	4 8	9 4	14 0	0 18 8
4¼	4 11½	9 11	14 10½	0 19 10
4½	5 3	10 6	15 9	1 1 0
4¾	5 6½	11 1	16 7½	1 2 2
5	5 10	11 8	17 6	1 3 4
5¼	6 1½	12 3	18 4½	1 4 6
5½	6 5	12 10	19 3	1 5 8
5¾	6 8½	13 5	1 0 1½	1 6 10
6	7 0	14 0	1 1 0	1 8 0

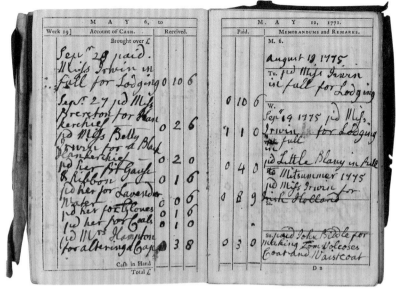

103 Lady's Pocket Book for 1771, with notes by Sarah Gatehouse, 1771–92 (L 12 cm). Hampshire Archives and Local Studies, 35M63/67.

Only a small number of women in the trials reported keeping a watch in their pockets, though it was an iconic item for men, sometimes linked by historians to men's increased engagement with the more precisely measured pace of business.[60] But the relative absence of female watches in our Old Bailey cases does not show limited agency on the part of women, who were time-conscious in other ways. It has been noted that, owing to the omnipresence of clocks in public places, 'in London at least, even those without watches could easily tell the time to within one hour'.[61] Watches were expensive though often unreliable, and came more slowly into use by women than men. For a woman, a watch was a wandering possession, without a fixed position on the body – sometimes in the main pocket, sometimes worn outside her clothing. In 1778 Elizabeth Ironmonger made a clear distinction between the latter practice and her own habit of pocketing her watch; valued at £3, it was worth protecting. 'I keep it usually in my pocket; I don't wear it hanging loose by my side.'[62] While the watch was readily accommodated within men's generously pocketed clothing, it sat uneasily with women's established pocket form, making it one of the very few things for which the tie-on pocket was not best suited, unless provided with extra internal compartments or eyelets to which it could be securely attached.[63]

Even with striking changes in fashion over a period of more than 200 years, sartorial practices continued to involve numerous detachable items, such as hats, caps, gloves, stomachers, neckerchiefs, cuffs, lappets and aprons, all of which had to be attached, detached, tidied and adjusted, often with pins (fig. 104). In Dorothy Kilner's view, a young girl should learn early that a pin, as well as 'some silk, thread, tape, ribbon', must always be to hand in 'her huswife and pincushion, which are ever in her pocket' – a reflection of the well-regulated life that she and those within her sphere of influence should lead. To fail in her regulation of such things was to pay a price in her 'appearance, behaviour and expence'.[64] Even the butcher's wife needed to hitch her skirt out of the mud, change her cap or adjust her neckerchief. These daily concerns help to explain why many women stowed clothing and accessories in their pockets, though garments might also be used – as we have seen – to wrap up small items for safekeeping there. The large handkerchief worn around the neck and shoulders, easily removed, was the most common item, making up over 30 per cent of the total of this class of goods in our cases. Mary Rutherford carried '2 Muslin Aprons, a Handkerchief, a pair of silk Gloves' in her pocket in 1716.[65] Jewellery was also often tucked into the pocket. In 1717 Elizabeth Clark, 'as she was passing along Holborn', had in her pocket 'three Gold Rings, value 40 s.'.[66] Stowing these items inside her pocket may have stemmed from caution against crime, but more generally shows a woman's ability to regulate and vary her appearance according to circumstances.[67]

Pockets also gave women agency because they enabled them to carry a variety of tools and devices for needlework and other purposes. Tools such as toothpicks, tweezers or mirrors gave a woman control of her personal appearance, though they feature only infrequently in our cases, despite evidence from elsewhere that they were in common use. This may result

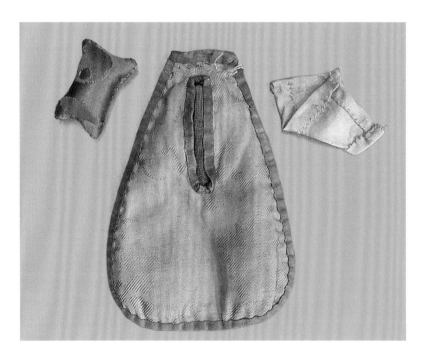

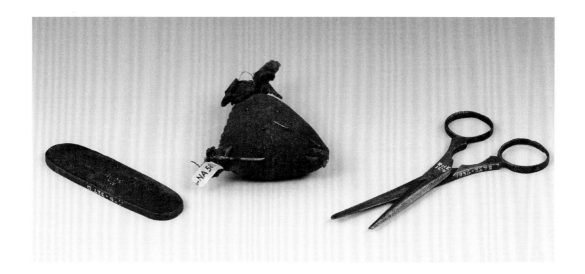

105 Some of the contents found in a pocket: a fleerish, a pincushion with pins, and scissors, 18th century. National Museums Scotland, H.RHE 10.

from many falling below values of interest to the court rather than an actual absence of such possessions. Thimbles, ranging in value from a halfpenny to 5*s*., outnumber other tools, such as scissors and knives, in our findings.[68] In 1760 Susanna Morgan had 'a Silver Thimble a Corkscrew and a pencil', as well as a 'purse of money' in her pocket, pointing to different activities she could undertake during the course of her day.[69] Unusually, an eighteenth-century pocket survives with its contents still intact, showing that the owner had to hand various things, including a pincushion with wire headed pins, a pair of scissors and a steel or 'fleerish'[70] – a mix of practical items that explains the wear and tear seen on many pockets (fig. 105).[71] The self-sufficiency expounded in the conduct books addressed to better-off women was equally prized by metropolitan working women such as Elizabeth Caldcleugh, who had more such tools in her pocket than most in 1793: a pair of steel scissors, a double-bladed knife and two pairs of steel nippers all inside her red morocco pocketbook.[72] Some women kept their tools to hand so habitually that they became familir to others. In 1794 Richard Bullen was confident he knew an old green knife 'of no value' when questioned in court:

> With respect to this green handled knife I take it for granted that you are only able to speak to it by its being green? – No, it is not; it is by knowing it a long time [. . .] Mrs. Bullen used to have it in her pocket; she had it when first I was married to her.[73]

Sometimes pocketed tools linked up with stated occupations. Ann O'Dell had in her pocket in 1832 a 'bit of stone-blue' that tallied with her work as a washerwoman.[74] In many cases, however, the contents of pockets cannot be correlated with one particular trade because tools such as thimbles or knives could be applied to so many tasks. Small instruments in a pocket may represent the frequently overlapping activities of paid and unpaid work in a woman's life. A paper of 'pins' in a pocket does not disclose their precise purpose because different forms were made for different trades, such as lace-making, upholstery and wig-making, as well as plain and fancy sewing, and for keeping clothes and accessories neatly fixed.[75]

Promise

Agency for women was not always immediate or linear: it could lie in the future promise of her things – a characteristic of possession exemplified by a bodkin belonging to Sarah Childish in 1718. Haggling with a man she solicited at Southwark Fair over the bill at a tavern, to show she had no money she turned out her pocket revealing that 'there was nothing in it but an Ivory Bodkin, some Farthings and two Crusts of Bread'.[76] Although her gesture of turning out her pocket to show its scant contents might indicate a woman down on her luck, her ivory bodkin was a possession invested with multiple potential values. It could be sold or pawned, it was an aid to dressing decently (threading ribbons and lacing bodices), or, in its sharper form, it might become an awl or even a weapon. Beyond its obvious exchange value and utility for personal or waged tasks, a bodkin, as Mary C. Beaudry shows, was 'far more than a type of needle', being often prized and marked with its owner's name, as a gift, a bequest or a souvenir, and playing a role 'in the construction of personal identity'.[77] So the promise inherent in the mutability of material possessions such as Sarah's bodkin tells us that pockets like hers were not entirely cheerless places. In her critique of neo-classical economics, Victoria de Grazia calls for more attention to be paid to 'the promise of goods to the purchasers'. She argues that calculations of their value 'often depend on the effort needed to use goods, which in turn involves some combination of time, skill, physical capacity, knowledge, and motivation', and that these pivoted around gendered differences of power.[78] Here we argue that 'the promise of goods', even very small ones, is not only present in their instrumentality but in their investment with private meaning and in their potential to be 'shuffled' between private and market values.

The constantly mutable value of things meant small pocketed possessions held different promises. In 1750 Bridget Bourne had her pockets stolen, containing 'four gold rings, a little pair of ear rings, a pair of silver buttons, a pair of silver buckles, a stock buckle, a guinea and half, a piece of queen Anne's gold, fourteen shillings in silver'.[79] Her assortment of accessories gave Bridget options to adjust her appearance, while they may also have held sentimental value for her. At the same time, the precious metal of her rings, buttons and buckles suggests they were not entirely dissimilar to the coins she carried in her pocket as objects with widely recognised exchange value. When hard times hit, pocketed goods could deputise for cash or promise bargaining power. After Hetty Sorrel laid out her possessions on her bed, *in extremis* she unlocked one of the promises of her earrings and locket by leaving them with the innkeeper, who advanced her 3 guineas on the understanding he would keep them if they were unclaimed after two months.[80]

Nowhere is the mutability of possessions more visible than in money. It was the most common and flexible means of agency, though not without constraints and caveats for women of all ranks. Money could draw a woman into what Ann Smart-Martin calls 'the dramatic tensions between authority, ownership, choice, and decision that were present within households'. She notes that there is still much to learn about women's 'acquisition of things through their own agency [. . .] The question, who decides? leaves little written trail for study.'[81] Money was cited in 54 per cent of our cases, more often than any other class of legitimate property in tie-on pockets, and provides one kind of 'trail' of metropolitan women using money and revealing variants of agency and control. There is well-established evidence for the centrality of credit in the lives of working people, and in the economy generally.[82] Margot Finn argues that 'the English economy was fundamentally structured by credit relations', and 'Immersion in the world of goods clearly co-existed with limited familiarity with coinage, paper money and monetary calculation in English market culture.'[83] However, our evidence from *The Proceedings* highlights another story, in which there was a plentiful presence of coins in everyday circulation throughout our period, at least in the pockets of these metropolitan women. Our findings also show the coexistence of coins with credit from pawning, a paucity of trade tokens and the 'limited' reach of paper money for women.

With ready money to hand in their pockets, it would seem that purchases by credit were not always necessary for these women. Mary Cock went to buy meat one night in 1718 at Newgate Market with a guinea and 9*s.* in her pocket.[84] Cash allowed discretionary spending, for oneself or others (fig. 106). Elizabeth Macdonald, an Irish 'servant of all work' who had money in her pocket in 1799, said: 'I wanted to buy something for the children, who were with me'.[85] Amounts varied hugely. Half of the women in our cases carried money worth over £1 in their pockets. It was not unusual for women to carry money that amounted to less than the value of other contents and their pocket combined, while a few testified to carrying big sums in the form of wages, rent due, takings from trade or funds drawn from a bank, illustrative of various spheres of women's activities. Mary Garrat, facing the death sentence in 1784 for taking 'twenty guineas [. . .] eighteen half guineas [. . .] one half crown [. . .] and two shillings and sixpence' from Elizabeth East's pocket, could only say: 'I did not imagine the money belonged to her, or that she could have so much.' Elizabeth testified that she had 'sold out 100 *l.* bank stock last Friday week, out of the

3 per cents'. Her 'right hand pocket', containing her money, was a tool of her autonomy, enabling her to move around and spend her day settling bills and buying clothes, until Mary picked it.[86]

Copper, silver and gold were habitual ways to classify coins, registering their base material in addition to their face value, copper coins being perhaps more disposable and less iconic than silver or gold. In our period, there were long-standing problems caused by the poor quality and uncertain supply of coinage, despite successive efforts by the authorities to regulate and improve it.[87] This led to men and women questioning both the conferred and the intrinsic value of the coins in their pockets, and paying attention to the physical changes to coins caused by wear and defacement. Nicholas Mayhew argues that in England 'practical experience showed that all but the most grotesquely butchered money in fact passed at its face value'.[88] In this context, foreign coins were sometimes kept in women's pockets as an asset alongside coins of the realm. So common were they that in 1783, in a case concerning Spanish silver coins called 'bits' in a woman's purse, it was argued that there were in circulation 'about five millions of these pieces of bits, especially since the war'.[89]

The power and spell of money is evident as much in its form as in the longer-term promise it could hold. As a child, Harriet Martineau, unaccustomed to handling money, was fascinated by it. 'The very sight of silver and copper was transporting to me, without any thought of its use. I stood and looked long at money, as it lay in my hand.'[90] New coins of the realm seemed notable, even by the end of the eighteenth century. Daniel Wade testified to the numerous coins in his wife's pockets under her pillow in April 1799; he singled out *9s. 6d.* of this as 'money that my son made my wife a present of at Christmas'. It seems they both took repeated pleasure in her possession of this gift over the intervening months. Daniel said: 'I have seen it a dozen times,' and he stressed it was new money: 'There is some of both new and old silver; I can speak particularly to the new money [. . .] my wife had it in her pocket [. . .] it is in this King's reign'.[91] For some women, the different coins they carried were familiar and distinctive, perhaps because of chronic coinage problems. Elizabeth Pristow, robbed in 1726, said she had 'a particular Half-penny which I knew to be mine, by a Cut across the Face'.[92] This familiarity also came from stashing coins in pockets for a long time, sometimes coins of considerable age. As well as her marked thimble in her pocket, in 1760 Susanna Morgan had several coins, including three crowns from the reign of Charles II, so memorable that she recalled 'one had the date 1679, another 1671, the other 1673'.[93] In 1743 Sarah Heath lost 'a Queen Elizabeth Shilling' worth 10*d.* when her pocket was snatched.[94] Susanna's and Sarah's old coins suggest a subjective valuation, fusing time and promise in money, making it worth more than everyday spending or giving. When Margaret Bastin testified in 1778 that she had one of her two old crowns

in her pocket 'a number of years', it was at least 64 years old, but she mixed these old coins with her shillings and her weekly baker's bill, showing her to be conversant with complementary value systems and timescales.[95]

Conventional economic analysis of money 'fails to capture the very complex range of characteristics of money as a social medium'.[96] We argue that in women's pockets the intricate interplay between money, agency and the more immaterial promises held by both money and goods becomes apparent. With the old, the new, the defaced, the familiar, the foreign and the transient coins in their pockets, and the potential of jewellery or other goods, women were fluent users of all kinds of currency, all invested with latent promise unfolding over time. During a period when 'the translation of goods from one commodity to another and from material form to credit or cash, [was] a significant feature of the plebeian economy', pockets enabled women to exercise skills in reckoning and deploying the value of their possessions across various forms.[97] Elizabeth Anderson, typically, participated simultaneously in two different economic systems, each with its own inexorable timetable of demands. Her pocketbook, stolen from her pocket in 1804, contained 'a great many duplicates', or pawnbrokers' tickets. She had pawned 'a great many things of different descriptions', including 'eight yards of silk lace I had pledged for 8 s.', left at the pawnbroker eight months before, and 'some of gowns and other things'. The court recognised the economic importance of the duplicates to her, noting that they were 'as valuable as money to the owners of them'. But unless she could meet or extend the pledge deadline, she would forfeit the goods and any further promise they might hold for her in the future. At the same time, her pocket was also a kind of bank, containing 'A 2 l. note, a 1 l. note, and three 7 s. pieces'. In answer to the observation 'This was a good deal of money for you to have about you?' she said: 'It was money we had saved up to pay our rent.'[98] Ready cash earmarked for her rent stored alongside tickets of extended credit with the pawnbroker made Elizabeth's pocket a hybrid tool for juggling her domestic economy. Alannah Tomkins argues that 'individual people exploited the essential flexibility of pawning to cover routine expenses, regain their financial equilibrium following a crisis, or stave off deeper destitution for so long as their material wealth would allow', underlining inextricable links between money and time.[99]

Treasured companion coins in pockets show women electing to take them out of circulation entirely, exchanging the promise of spending for a more immaterial promise inherent in sentiment and memory. A burglar took a large quantity of goods, including a silver Spanish dollar, from Esther Maclode in 1781. Esther 'always' carried the coin loose in her pocket. 'The dollar I had had above forty years: my husband gave it me before I was married'.[100] Coins, in theory, denoted the promise of fixed values physically stamped with the authority of the state, but testimony about coins in our Old Bailey cases reveals, in practice, habits consonant with Kopytoff's idea of fluidity between exchange value and private value, showing how coins could carry individual and intimate *unfixed* values, with their own particular temporality. It seems that women's pockets were reservoirs for hoarding or safeguarding money as much as for dispensing it.

Contrasting with coins, paper in various forms was often kept in women's pockets. Some papers, such as banknotes or pawnbrokers' duplicates, acted as money or quasi-money, while others had seemingly no intrinsic or agreed value. Not part of any exchange system, these papers nevertheless could be promissory in their own right. Letters, pocketbooks, 'a direction, that I was to find out my aunt by', books and paper and prayer books record women's literacy and numeracy and engagement in print culture as well as variants within it.[101] Their presence in women's pockets gives glimpses of their owners' participation in social and economic life, sometimes even their spiritual life – as when Mary Ferguson had her prayer book, worth *6d.*, stolen from her pocket.[102] In an exceptional case, a book proved life-saving. Catherine Peterson, identified as a 'Gentlewoman', accused Richard Jackson of highway robbery in Chelsea in 1738, and explained how he 'thrust at me with his knife – I thought he had run it into my Guts but I happened to have this book [in] my pocket and the knife run against that'.[103] More fragmentary and ephemeral papers could still hold immense value for their owner. Elizabeth MacDonald's 'written' character references and Susannah Andrews's 'Copy of her Indictment', given to her at her request by the court on her acquittal of a crime, would be of lasting importance in their lives.[104] Such ephemera may be under-represented in court cases, ostensibly valueless and thus probably falling below the scope of indictments, but it is clear that by preserving these fragile but potentially vital documents in their pockets women conferred on them values of their own. In this context, who is to fathom the motives of Elizabeth Anderson for keeping 'a song' in her pocket or the value of its promise to her?[105]

Women used their pockets as a *sanctum sanctorum* or long-term refuge for things that could be meaningless outside but represented private ways of negotiating the world. Some things inside the pocket derived from sympathetic magic, a legacy of earlier belief systems still present despite the powerful presence of the Church and the apparent march of science and enlightenment.[106] As observed in 1869, 'An old woman [. . .] always carried in her pocket a dried toad, as a preservative from small-pox.'[107] Almost anything might be transformed into an amulet to keep in the pocket. Touch-pieces were common and it is possible that old or marked coins encountered in our cases were regarded as lucky or protective. Perhaps prayer books took on this role for some. Bridget Bourne explained in 1750 that a 'sciatica bone' was among

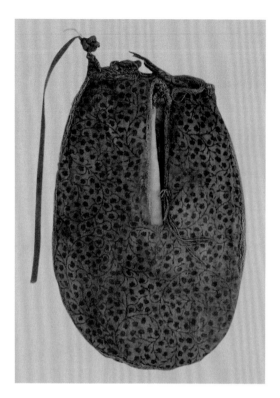

the 'few things of no value, which I had in my pockets before they were lost'.[108] When Bridget said her bone had 'no value', she was referring to the official indictment process, not to her belief in the bone's capacity to relieve her aches and pains. Mary Marshall, found drowned in 1796, had in 'her right hand Pocket [. . .] a large Key a Silver Thimble a Farthing and a Cramp-bone and a gold ring upon her finger'.[109] Such bones, named after the condition they were thought to alleviate, stayed close to the body, making the pocket a natural place to put anything that promised personal protection.

The things inside women's pockets could be transitory, or preserved with the patina of habit; they could have high or negligible value; they were sometimes contemporary, but sometimes rooted in custom and resistant to external authority or modernity; they might be mnemonic. Their complexity is evident in one of the most startling pockets to survive, discovered in 1994 concealed intentionally within the fabric of an old house in Abingdon, Oxfordshire. The pocket dates from the mid-1700s. It contained a baby's cap, an assortment of coins, metal trade tokens and fragments of business receipts, and possibly the cover of a letter; it contained dried hops, which also surrounded the pocket in the attic wall cavity (figs 107–8). If the earliest date of concealment was 1797 – the date of one of the coins – the pocket itself and some of its contents were already old by this date: paper fragments date from the 1670s, the oldest coin from 1573-7, representing a long reach of time and memory, even before the pocket was hidden within the house for two more centuries. In keeping with other deliberately concealed objects in old houses, the pocket and its contents are thought to have been put in place to provide protection for the house and its inhabitants, the hops giving additional healing benefits. Like bones carried in pockets because they promised relief or protection, so this pocketful of things was believed to perform a similar function for an entire building and its occupants.[110] While it is extraordinary, the concealed pocket resonates with everyday practices in which women used their pockets to contain items of special promise over long periods of time. Agency and promise came in multiple and elusive forms and could make women's pockets hopeful and valued places, suggesting hidden intricacies of possession largely beyond the radar of contemporaries and historians alike.

108 Contents of a pocket, 16th–18th centuries, found concealed in the wall of a house in Abingdon. Abingdon County Hall Museum, OXCMS.1997.7.2–19.

Ownership

Susanna Morgan testified in 1760 that her silver thimble in her pocket was marked 'S.M.', and in 1803 the pocketbook in shopkeeper Prudence Pearson's pocket had her name on it – unequivocal signs of their sense of ownership.[111] Being in possession of something did not automatically confer absolute ownership, and the inside of a pocket discloses intricate relationships between women and property. As Amy L. Erickson argues, women in early modern England 'lived and died with an awareness of overlapping economic and emotional influences on their property which historians can only hope to approximate'.[112] She notes that women could differ from men in their 'perceptions of self-interest', and could have 'different ideas about moral desert, about who was in need and about what was important – if these did not constitute a different culture, they were certainly distinct economic values, and deserve to be further investigated'.[113] Trial accounts in *The Proceedings* can point to some of these 'overlapping economic and emotional influences' in the microcosm of everyday practices involving small possessions. They show poor and middling women's experience of possession and ownership of small things as fluid, shaped by economic circumstances and social relations. The duplicates so often encountered in women's pockets illuminate further complexities of possession. Precisely what ownership did a duplicate grant? Although duplicates were equivalents of the goods left at the pawnshop, they also embodied more 'tenuous' modes of possession if we ask, with Vivienne Richmond, to what extent 'can a person be said to "own" something when it spends five days a week in the pawnshop'?[114]

The legal concept of 'coverture', which curtailed the independent ownership of property by married women, apart from a limited range of necessities, made many small things in their pockets – in theory, at least – proxy possessions.[115] However, as Susan Staves argues, in practice 'very complex' variables prevailed, and 'the legal rules of married women's separate property in and of themselves could not determine women's experience'.[116] While the contents of a married woman's pocket were formally cited in indictments as the property of her husband, possession and ownership of small pocketed things were negotiated at an informal level in daily life, and signalled multiple realities of possession. When Thomas Porter, publican, prosecuted a man in 1784 for burglary, one 'silk huswif, value 4d.' appeared in the indictment as his property, but it was clear that in practice it belonged to his wife, who testified, 'it is very remarkable, it has some writing in it, Greek, or Latin, or something that I do not understand; I had it given me, and I value it'.[117] At the everyday level, women seemed ready and able to hold different or complementary concepts of property in mind at the same time. In 1797 Margaret Ley, when identifying goods that had been stolen from the house she occupied with her husband, could say in a single breath: 'These pockets are mine, the two pair of cotton stockings are mine, the two muslin half handkerchiefs, the blanket, and every article here is mine; I can swear to every thing that is here to be my husband's property.'[118]

The traffic of things *between* people's pockets was a common variable of ownership, and could consolidate social relations and signal intimacy or trust. The traffic could flow from women's to men's pockets, as when a gentleman's wife, in a crowded place in 1764, pulled off her delicate 'Double Ruffles, Sheir Lawn' and put them in his pocket.[119] The traffic also flowed the other way. Agnes Torrent's pocket solved a family problem when she was trusted enough to 'take money' from customers during her publican father's period of illness in 1767. When some of it then went missing, she testified: 'I told my father of it; he marked some money, and I put it in my pocket, and when I went to bed I put it under my head as usual'. This father–daughter team effort, making her pocket a shared arena of responsibility, succeeded in catching the thief, who was found in possession of the marked money.[120] Shopping as a commission for others was a long-established practice and might involve a woman pocketing goods that were en route to someone else or carrying another's cash in order to shop for them. The Old Bailey testimonies show how this traffic of things frequently involved women using their pockets to hold their husbands' personal belongings in trust, often over time. This augmented the male pocket and made the female pocket a joint as well as an individual domain. The testimonies show how plebeian women could steward common and often transient resources in their pockets, echoing in miniature the stewardship by women of the middling or elite sort of larger, more permanent resources.

The pocket equated to a common purse for certain work or expenditure within a relationship. In 1693 Henry Wilkinson, a soldier charged with housebreaking, elided a common purse with a pocket when claiming that he lived with his accuser, Dorcas Essington, as 'Man and Wife, and lay together, and kept one Pocket and one Bed'.[121] Despite the risks of loss or theft, in practice the pocket remained close to a woman's side, giving her immediate guardianship of any belongings her husband entrusted to her. When a husband made his wife's pocket an extension of his own, or a safer alternative to it, it was often for items of significant value. Watches, for example, migrated from men's to women's pockets for safekeeping. In 1781 William Turner identified his silver watch in court as having been kept in his wife's pocket at their bedside overnight.[122] A woman working in trade alongside her husband could act as custodian of their takings, as when, in 1731, Elizabeth Tinsley had come to London from Greenwich with her husband, Daniel, a gardener, and her son, bringing their produce to market. Taking responsibility for the cash they earned, she afterwards 'put the Money in her Pocket, which was about 4 l.'.[123] When Mary Orris alleged in 1767 that she was the victim of highway robbery, her husband, a labourer, was asked in court 'What was your wife's stock in her pocket that day?' He answered 'I can't tell; what I got I always gave her'. In this case, for all practical purposes, Mary took control of what he passed to her and merged it with her own meagre money, which she had received as alms.[124]

Proxy possession could involve close collaboration, and turn a woman's pocket into a shared resource, as when Matilda Lewis had money stolen from her pocket in 1814. Her husband identified it, explaining, '*we* counted it before we went to bed' (our italics).[125] Mothers kept things in their pockets on behalf of their children. Lucy Alloway, in 1827, had in hers 'a small knife, belonging to my little boy'.[126] In 1810 Ann Sippel, a sailor's wife, left Wales for London with her husband, Samuel, and their three children to collect his substantial 'prize money' of 'forty-seven pounds four shillings and sixpence', due after an extended time at sea. Samuel testified that he was already minded how to allocate some of it. 'The three ten pound notes were to put my children out apprentice with.' At his request, Ann pocketed it, acting as guardian of the money during an unsettling period away from home. It was stolen and the loss of so much money threatened serious repercussions for all their lives and aspirations. But Samuel's trust in his wife was justified. As he left London for Bristol armed with identification numbers for three of the notes, hoping to catch the thief, Ann 'catched him' in London.[127] The testimonies indicate that it was unexceptional for the female pocket to serve, like Ann's, as a portable bank or safe for money intended for the use or benefit of a husband or family, and thus to become a place where the interests of men, women and their dependants converged. Pocketing a key on behalf of another person was also a form of proxy possession that entailed trust. For domestic servants, it was an unmistakable sign of confidence in them to be asked to carry their employer's keys and undertake household matters on their behalf. In Elizabeth Barker's case, she loyally managed resources over a long period. Successfully defending herself in 1735 against an accusation of theft, she said: 'I lived twelve Years with my Old Lady Madam Freer. I kept all the Keys, and was entrusted with every thing that was of Value in the House.'[128]

A woman's place in the world was underpinned by the things of her own that she carried in her pockets, but when possessions were held in trust for others, sometimes earmarked for particular purposes, they highlighted her role in kinship or social networks. Possession by proxy shows the pocket at work in ways that exemplify what T. H. Breen calls 'the creative possibilities of possession'.[129] However, to have what belonged to another person lingering too long in a pocket, particularly within master–servant relations, was an invitation to trouble, as Eliza Haywood warned female servants in the sternest terms:

> When you have Money of another's in your Pocket, have kept it for some Days, and find it is totally forgotten, may not the Devil, who is watchful for such Opportunities of seducing the unwary Mind, suggest to you, that as you want a thousand Necessaries, which the Smallness of your Wages will not supply you with, there is no Harm in making use of a Trifle, which the Owner can very well spare, and will do you so great a Service.[130]

In 1767 Anne Brewer, servant to a publican's family, did exactly what Eliza Haywood advised against when she claimed she found money on her employer's bed. 'I took up this two shillings and six-pence from off the quilt, and put it in my pocket, and forgot to deliver it.' She was found guilty of theft and sentenced to transportation.[131] Her case underlined that pocketing what belonged to others in such circumstances had few convincing alternative explanations. The difference between proxy possession and thieving could be fuzzy. Accused of stealing from her mistress in 1765, Frances Burk claimed she had only temporarily put Ann's belongings in her pocket; but her defence was unsuccessful, and the court deemed that she had appropriated rather than protected Ann's possessions.[132] Chance could also play a part in cycles of possession and ownership. In 1758 a sixpenny gold earring was found in Margaret Taylor's alehouse. She told her servant, 'if any body owned it, they were to have it, if not it was her own; and she put it into her pocket'. Nobody claimed it and a month later she testified it was her own property when, in another twist, it turned up in a former servant's pocket: 'the things that were in my pocket on the Saturday night, were in his pocket on the Sunday morning'.[133]

The obvious benefits of tie-on pockets for women – portability, invisibility, capaciousness, and the ease with which they could be removed, stowed or hidden – made them particularly good companions for women who stole or committed other crimes requiring concealment or removal of evidence. Women were most likely to commit petty theft as prostitutes, as servants stealing from their place of work, as shoplifters or as receivers of stolen goods, and the pocket served them well in all these situations. The testimony of female victims and offenders in our cases indicates a distinctive role for the tie-on pocket when the lure of other people's possessions became irresistible; there was sufficient association between the pocket and crime for the cry 'I have no pockets about me' to be worth trying when an offender faced her accuser.[134] Tie-on pockets were used to assist crimes by women in 10 per cent of our Old Bailey cases. Theft was the fleeting and opportunistic flipside of ownership, and Lynn MacKay finds that female thieves in the decade 1779–89, compared to males, were 'disproportionately' likely to target clothes and household goods, as well as cloth, money, watches and jewellery.[135] These findings echo the patterns in our Old Bailey cases, in which 37 per cent of the women in our group who used their tie-on pockets for criminal purposes stole money and 33 per cent stole clothing, cloth or accessories, the latter category of goods being favoured by all of the women who used their pockets to steal from shops (fig. 109).[136] In 1807 Hannah Stevens was accused of using 'two pockets almost as big as sacks' to steal 17 pairs of gloves and three pairs of stockings from a shop.[137] In 1849 *The Times* reported a case involving a female shoplifter, Lydia Dixon, who, when caught, tried to get rid of 'a capacious pocket, capable of containing at least half a dozen dresses and in it, at that time, were a cashmere dress and six lace collars'. Her case was made worse by the discovery in her apartment of incriminating evidence that she was a well-prepared thief. Not only was it full of stolen clothing, but in it 'several disguises were observed', in particular different-coloured wigs, a 'shawl, with one side woolen and the other silk, and a cardinal cloak fitted with capacious pockets'.[138] Even when tie-on pockets had all but disappeared from everyday use, habitual shoplifters continued to use them. In 1911 *The Times* featured 'Shoplifting at the sales', and explained how a female thief was caught with 'the usual pocket worn by shoplifters under her skirt, in which there was a slit through which she could drop articles into the pocket'.[139] So effective at swiftly swallowing stolen

109 After John Collett (1725–1780), *Shop-Lifter Detected*, 1787 (35.2 × 25 cm, plate mark). Lewis Walpole Library, Yale University, 787.08.10.01+.

89

SHOP-LIFTER DETECTED.

From an Original Picture Painted by M.ʳ John Collett.

London, *Printed for* ROBERT SAYER, *Map & Printseller N.º 53 Fleet Street, as the Act directs Aug.ᵗ 10.1787.*

goods, thieves' pockets shifted possessions from rightful to aspiring owner. They were a place in which ownership might be contested or even eventually transferred from one person to another, a *boîte noire* of ownership.

* * *

While contemporary concerns about order and disorder, luxury and the display of possessions presupposed a degree of choice, the pocket gives a view outside polite society of the more numerous lives lived without much choice. There were times when a woman's pocket could be custodian of all her worldly possessions with the exception of the clothes she stood up in. In these makeshift lives, what was inside a pocket could be an instrument of survival. Our findings also point to an exchange of pocketed things between men and women based on a willingness to improvise notions of property in a shared practice of a particular familial or affective 'common good'.

For the historian, possessions in a pocket cannot easily be reckoned up or taken at face value, despite the efforts of legal indictments to do so, because their role and significance can be recalibrated according to circumstances. However, in a pocket we see portable possessions in action over different timescales, and otherwise disparate small belongings in relation to each other circulating in value systems that are untraceable in formal documentation of property such as wills or inventories. The exchange value of small possessions could also complement the possession of goods whose value became symbolic – things 'shuffled', to use Kopytoff's word, from the market place to a sphere of entirely private meaning and promise, or back again. For many women, what was inside their pockets constituted an important, perhaps fundamental, element in their maintenance of their place or reputation in the world.

In their capacity to hold and to keep, pockets illuminate the ambiguities of ownership. They express women's competency in appreciating the mutability of their possessions, the coexistence of different currencies and the more elusive promises their things held. Without wishing to overload these private caches with more significance than they should bear, we nevertheless glimpse, in all their various uses, the subjectivities and fluid dynamics of women's relationship to things.

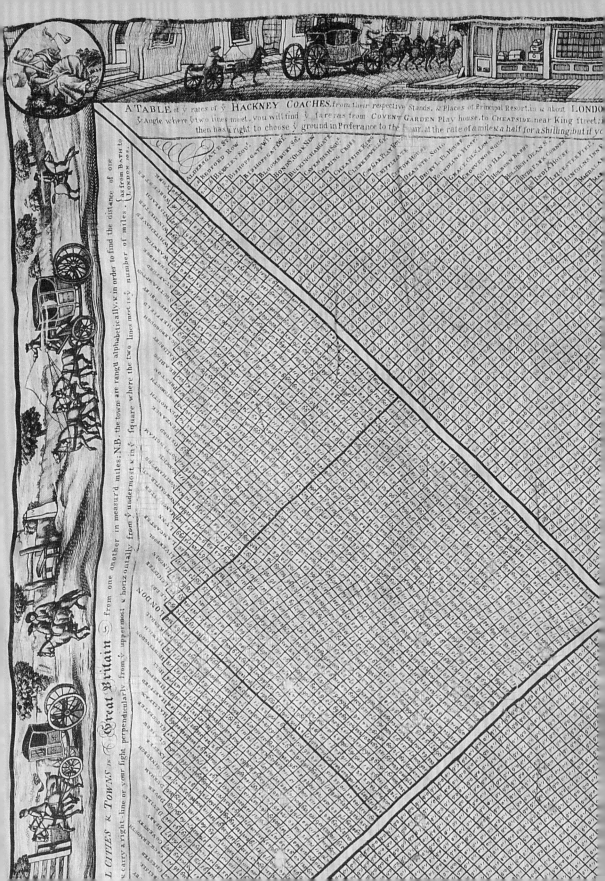

A TABLE of ye rates of ye HACKNEY COACHES, from their respective Stands, & Places of Principal Resort, in & about LONDO

ye Angle where ye two lines meet, you will find ye fare; as from COVENT GARDEN Play house, to CHEAPSIDE, near King ftreet, r
then has ye right to choose ye ground in Preferance to the hour, at the rate of a mile & a half for a Shilling; but if yo

L CITIES & TOWNS in Great Britain from one another in measur'd miles; N.B. the towns are rang'd alphabetically, & in order to find the distance of one
carry a right line or your right perpendicularly from ye uppermost & horizontally from ye undermost & in ye square where the two lines meet is ye number of miles. as from BATH to
(LONDON 105.

'for the play and coach'

Pockets, Mobility and Sociability

In 1745 Eliza Haywood ridiculed fashionable women by drawing attention to the role of their pockets in negotiating fashionable sociability.

> The snuffbox and smelling bottle are pretty trinkets in a lady's pocket, and are frequently necessary to supply a pause in conversation and on some other occasions, but whatever virtues they are possess'd of, they are all lost by a too constant and familiar use and nothing can be more pernicious to the brain or render one more ridiculous in company than to have either of them perpetually in one's hand.[1]

Castigating the follies of fashion, Haywood accurately observed that pockets allowed women to carry around the props and accessories they needed to play their parts in the theatre of sociable occasions, with fans, opera glasses, boxes for snuff, patches and bonbons, or clever novelties.[2] Intricate etuis, exquisite scent bottles, seals, snuffboxes and other pocket accessories were made in a variety of finely crafted precious and often exotic materials, with both male and female consumers in mind.[3] At a time when women were increasingly trespassing into male territories, both indoors and outdoors, the mobility made possible by pockets turned them into significant instruments for women's appropriation of space.[4] Armed with their pockets, women could navigate a variety of social spaces from the assembly or the opera to fashionable shops or pleasure gardens. Pockets allowed a woman to carry cash for private coach or chair hire, turnpikes, omnibus fares, refreshments or guidebooks and other necessities for social outings and travel. Their portability allowed her to move unencumbered and with a degree of self-sufficiency, making pockets essential to her participation in various commercial, cultural and intellectual activities.

Elite women's account books and private papers record their everyday use of their pockets to make purchases and small disbursements throughout the day, while they also register what pocket accessories they would have carried with them when out and about. Useful contrivances, shrunk in size by the engineering spirit of a commercial and industrial age, were marketed to such women. These portable, pocket-sized objects 'for the ladies' were predicated on their active lifestyles, supporting not only social interactions but also leisure pursuits that took women out of doors. The period from the end of the seventeenth century to the end of the nineteenth witnessed great changes in both men's and women's relationship to space and mobility with the development – for instance – of tourism and the railway, and the expansion of empire. These changes deeply transformed British society, affecting its relationship to the landscape, space and the lived environment in general.[5] The uses and designs of women's pockets capably accommodated these transformations and equipped women to embrace them.

Pockets and fashionable sociability

Small ingenious pocket accessories were produced in the eighteenth century in great numbers for both male and female consumers. In an age of expanding consumption, the small space of the pocket was the focus of ever encroaching production and advertising of innumerable accessories.[6] These cunning little devices enabled women to carry and keep at hand the miniature wherewithal of polite sociability (fig. 110). Natty, fashionable 'conversation cards' provided them with appropriate cues in both French and English for drawing-room chit-chat.[7] Also endowed with the 'power of portability', small memorandum books and almanacs, sometimes in strikingly tiny format, were published in huge numbers.[8] They were compendia of useful information on anything from 'marketing tables' and pages for personal accounts to fashion plates showing the latest styles or the rules of 'precedency among ladies' that helped to avert any social faux pas (fig 111; see also figs 102–3).[9] Promoted for female consumers, such pocket aids to polite sociability were ridiculed in literature. Portability could be a mixed blessing. In the anonymous novel *Pin Money* (1831), Mrs Lucretia dives into her 'cavernous' pocket to retrieve 'a small morocco note-case, containing sundry bonmot, scraps, sketches, epigrams,

A Lady & Children in the Dress of 1770.

Twelve of the Newest Head Dresses 177.

and lampoons'; she affects 'to turn over the leaves with an air of uncertainty, although they were worn to a diaphanous slightness by incessant reference; and [. . .] as familiarly known to its proprietress as a breviary to a priest'.[10]

Miniaturisation was made possible by developments in engineering and technology: tiny hinges and sliding and screwing mechanisms allowed the manufacture of portable sets such as etuis and *necessaires* convenient for tucking into a pocket.[11] Size, though a matter of real advantage, was also part of the very performance of these objects. The delicate gestures required to open the diminutive screw tops of smelling bottles, to open and close snuffboxes and manipulate the various parts of pocket accessories, leaf through miniature almanacs or write on the tiny ivory tablets of a *necessaire* turned these objects into social props (fig. 113). They were conspicuous for their luxury and clever mechanisms but also engaged the user in a choreography of graceful gestures. Pockets enabled women to take these objects onto the various social stages where their tasteful performative pleasures came into their own.[12] A surviving pocket shows how a woman of means could slip watch, snuffbox, scent bottle or opera glass into its four inner chamois leather compartments, trusting that each could be easily located and retrieved when desired (fig. 112; see also fig. 97).

Equally important was the way in which pockets allowed women to negotiate *between* different spaces. With 'upwards of thirty thousand hackney coach fares', the *London Companion* of 1773, a comprehensive listing of all the fares of hackney coaches, watermen and chairmen in the city, was intended as a practical item to be kept in the pocket while out and about.[13] Many almanacs or pocketbooks intended for women had similar information in condensed

ABOVE
112 Damask pocket with
internal compartments of
chamois leather, early to mid-
18th century (L 44 cm). School
of Historical Dress, London,
TSHD-2014-044.

RIGHT
113 Etui, mid-18th century,
enamel, metal, glass and ivory
(H 6.9 cm, W 7 cm, D 2.5 cm).
Museum of London, A9792.

form, together with other useful facts and figures, while some printers even produced linen handkerchiefs with shorthand guides to fares and distances (fig. 114).[14]

Relatively absent from our survey of trials at the Old Bailey, these objects were often advertised on trade cards, and their survival in numbers in museum collections manifests their popularity. Etuis and scent bottles were luxury items sold by jewellers and toymen, and almanacs, pocket companions and novelty handkerchiefs were equally beyond the means of most prosecutrixes at the Old Bailey. The objects elite women kept in their pockets and how they used them to facilitate their sociable lifestyles can better be gauged by looking at account books and diaries. Here we foreground three elite metropolitan women, through whose private papers we explore the symbiotic relation of pockets to mobile lifestyles over the period.

In the 1780s young Ann Heatley was sent to London to finish her education. Keeping her own horse in the city, taking dancing and music lessons, regularly hiring books from the library and receiving love letters from different suitors, Ann was a modern young woman about town. She was modish without being particularly extravagant: she could spend a modest 3*d.* on 'India Cotton', but also lavished close to £4 on her own 'birthday treat'. Her

regular purchases of shoes, gloves and hats, alongside her dimity pockets, show that her wardrobe fitted her for an active, mobile lifestyle.[15] Her frequent shoe repairs, and the purchase, washing and altering of riding stays, riding shirt and riding dress underline the demands of such energetic activities. Her pockets were clearly a space where she nurtured her sense of fashion and self-adornment. Over the years, we see her spend the 'pocket money' she received every month on 'pocket handkerchiefs' in various materials as well as, among other things, 'a small glass', 'a fan', 'a smelling bottle', 'a letter and card case', 'a green and silver purse' and various pocketbooks and almanacs, while in January 1786 she became a monthly purchaser of the *Lady's Magazine*. Her pockets allowed her enthusiastic enjoyment of fashionable London. Her accounts show regular out-of-pocket expenses to get to different venues and participate in the host of pleasures offered by the city – she spent money 'for the play and coach', to hire a 'chaise and driver' and buy an 'assembly ticket' on St Valentine's day in 1786, to go to Vauxhall, purchase 'a song and silk', 'rasberries', 'macaroons' and 'cherries', as well as 'Toys at the fair', and she also lost money 'at cards'.[16]

Gambling was a common fashionable activity that involved pockets. In January 1715 Lady Arabella Furnese from Kent, also a London socialite, with pockets of silk and Holland rather than dimity like Ann's, noted in her accounts 'Taken out for Card money – £10:15s', and in December 1721, she wrote 'lost at Cards since 9th June £14:16s'.[17] That pockets were instrumental in female gambling is illustrated by a notation in the letters of Georgiana, Duchess of Devonshire, a notorious gambler. On her marriage, Georgiana, like many of her set, started on a path of reckless gambling. With an allowance of £4,000 pin money to spend a year, she had the use of her own private pocket to indulge her taste for risk and excitement. If her mother's anxious plea to her is anything to go by, Georgiana seems to have employed her pockets as money bags on gambling evenings. 'Pray take care if you play to carry money in your pocket as much as you care to lose and never go beyond it.'[18] Given the huge debts she accrued over her lifetime, the advice seems to have gone unheeded. Although not as uncontrolled as Georgiana in her gambling habits, Arabella Furnese's regular references to losing money at cards on her various jaunts illustrates how her pockets aided her participation in this and other fashionable activities. For less elite women, another way to gamble money was to take part in lotteries, for which carrying money in a pocket was also necessary (fig. 115).

Living in early-nineteenth century London, Mary Young was a savvy consumer and indefatigable social visitor – two other activities that took elite women out and about with their pockets. Buying for herself and her children, Mary Young patronised numerous traders and craftsmen across the capital. Her papers give a rare insight into the geographical scope of an early nineteenth-

century female consumer. If some of the traders sent their goods on approval, or came to her, the precision with which she noted addresses and the comments she made on the elegance of some shops point to actual visits. She notes that Calder, who sold bonnets, was '7 Market Street, 7 doors from Oxford Street', for instance, or that one shop was a 'very fashionable linen warehouse'. She lists eight different dressmakers in different parts of London, some close to the family home in Limehouse, others further afield in St James's Square, Bond Street, Goodge Street and Pentonville. The ten different drapers she used were similarly scattered across the city from the East End to the newly developing West End. Her cash book indicates a highly mobile woman. It lists repeated omnibus and carriage fares, and her housekeeping accounts list 'coach hire' as one of the staple headings, alongside victuallers, washing, clothes and furniture.[19] Armed with one of her 18 pockets, Mary Young would have been well equipped to make disbursements or carry the smaller goods on these shopping trips.[20]

115 Robert Dighton (*c.*1752–1814), *The Lottery Contrast*, 1760, mezzotint (H 35 cm). Guildhall Library, City of London, P5435033.

Her papers also record the further fashionable activity of visiting, which had become more formalised by the beginning of the nineteenth century. A compulsive archivist of her own life, Mary Young drew yearly lists of families she visited, breaking it down by month and day, showing how fully she had embraced visiting as the lynchpin of female sociability.[21] The practice of paying and returning visits, which had its own codes and rules, was crucial to women's social identities over the whole period of the eighteenth and nineteenth centuries, and formed part of an individual woman's social and personal reputation. When paying a visit, tipping the host's servants was a prerequisite for which pockets again came into their own. It was out of her personal cash, her 'pocket money', that Lady Arabella's married daughter Catherine tipped the servants of friends and relatives.[22] Another use for ladies' pockets when visiting would have been to carry pen and paper to write notes or visiting cards left at the addresses called on. Visiting cards – part of the commodification of pocket contents – developed in the course of the eighteenth century. Some calling cards were fairly simple, while others were more elaborate, with a small formulaic printed text and blanks to be filled in with the names of the caller and the intended host.[23]

Similarly representative both of the increasing importance of visiting and of publishers' attempts to create fashionable pocket companions for women, were books such as *The Ladies' Complete Visiting Guide* (1800), which presented 'at one view, to the Lady of Fashion, and those honored with her visits [. . .] an accurate arrangement of visits paid and received, which never could be furnished by the most retentive memory' (fig. 116).[24] The book, which 'reduced to a system the first acknowledged felicity of polished society [i.e. visiting]', is neatly divided into four geographical parts of the West End, and enabled its owner to note down the street number and name of the person visited, the number of cards delivered and the number of cards received, as well as the number of letters received and answered.[25] This precise accountancy of card dropping was part of the increasing number of rules and rituals that came to regulate visiting: visits had to be announced and accepted, spatial access carefully monitored and conversation and behaviour closely guarded.[26] The ever more complex practices of visiting were riddled with possible faux pas, and the 'Lady of Fashion' with such a book in her pocket could stay on top of the social game.

Part of the agency given by their pockets to Ann Heatley, Lady Arabella Furnese and Mary Young lay in the way they enabled spontaneous charitable acts, as when Ann 'gave a poor man' or 'gave a poor woman'.[27] Pockets were empowering tools for women, giving them latitude to act independently (see fig. 26). The personal accounts of Lady Arabella abound in examples of day-to-day charity, as when, in June 1719, she recorded: 'Given to ye woman yt opens our seat in ye Chappell 5s'. Lady Arabella also gave money to beggars and poor people whom she encountered on the streets of the capital. On the same day she made a donation to the pew opener, she also gave 5s. to 'a poor woman that lives at the end of Dover Street'.[28] A sign of these women's independent use of their own money or allowances, their spontaneous acts of charity accompanied their participation in various philanthropic events. Lady Arabella's accounts show how philanthropy and fashionable sociability often went hand in hand. She records many instances of theatre benefit nights and raffles. These evenings combined socialising, spectacle and charity in what Sarah Lloyd has described as a specific manifestation of benevolence that appeared in the eighteenth century and which 'linked charity, religious practice, fashion, and politics'.[29] Such events contributed to the new

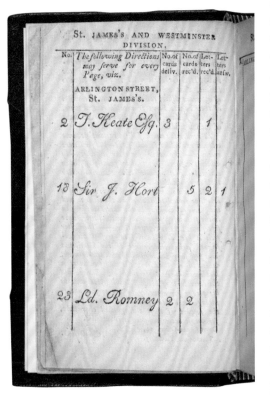

urban culture of English towns at the time.[30] One of the consequences of the interconnectedness of charity extending 'beyond churches, alms and sermons to the theatre' was that it 'opened a space for philanthropic ladies'.[31] Whereas the homosocial spaces of the club, the corporation and the tavern were usually closed to elite women, those of the theatre, the raffle, and the assembly were not, and they provided an arena in which female authority and agency could be asserted.[32] Women like Lady Arabella who were conspicuous participants in these events thus had a share in the complex social networks and spaces that constituted the eighteenth-century public sphere. If it is clear that theatre-going, gambling, shopping and visiting were modes of female participation in the social fabric and the public sphere, charity was no less empowering. The pockets that held the cash spent on entry or raffles, refreshments or alms given along the way were tools for women's active access to these social spaces and for the performance of their codes and rituals.

Ann Heatley, Lady Arabella and Mary Young were characteristic of their respective circumstances. Arabella's gambling and theatre-going were typical of eighteenth-century elite sociability, Ann's youthful enjoyments were those of a young woman of taste come to London to meet eligible young men. By the time Mary Young married, the growth and spread of stylish West End shops had expanded the discerning shopper's hunting ground for spotting the best goods and suppliers, increasing choice but also the time and effort involved, and thus raising the stakes of fashionable consumption and sociability. Visiting had developed into a ritualised process of dos and don'ts, specialist stationery and double-entry accountancy systems. Our three metropolitan women's pockets supported their participation in the sociability characteristic of their different times. Their adaptable pockets allowed elite women to equip themselves for the changing demands of sociability but also furnished them with the wherewithal for more rustic outings, in which the pocket visiting guide or list of hackney coach fares could be swapped for the pocket book of botany.

Pockets, botany and the outdoors

In 1795 *The Lady's New Elegant Pocket Magazine* was advertised, promoted 'solely to the use and amusement of the fair sex'. Unlike others of its kind, noted for 'the inconvenience of [their] unwieldy larger sizes', this new magazine was 'the most convenient publication of the kind for the Pocket; forming a most agreeable companion [. . .] on a walk when nature and the weather call us abroad'.[33] By the end of the eighteenth century, walking had become a favourite pastime for elite and middling women. Books were also common companions for the pocket on such occasions. Small format books could easily be tucked in the pocket and taken out when resting under a tree or on a bench to while away an hour in a wood or a garden (fig. 117). Making

117 Nicholas von Heideloff (1761–1837), *Gallery of Fashion* 7, 1 July 1800, Figs 267, 268, hand-coloured engraving. Yale Center for British Art, Paul Mellon Collection, L 218 (4to).

for easy one-handed reading, duodecimo books were portable – indeed, they invited wandering.[34] Eighteenth-century printers produced small-format editions of novels in a bid to attract the female readership.[35] The space of the female pocket became commodified, a territory to fill with consumer goods, whether they were pocket editions of novels, pocket ink horns, or pocket microscopes for the keen botanist (fig. 118). Some pockets were so capacious that several books could be carried at once by the more literary minded when going for walks. In 1818, recalling Sarah Sophia Banks, sister and assistant of Joseph, the famous naturalist, a contemporary commentator remembered how she carried books in her pockets on her walks:

118 Folding pocket microscope in a case, *c.*1800, glass, ivory and metal, made by W. & S. Jones, England (box, L 6 cm). National Museums Scotland, T.1938.103.

her [. . .] quilted petticoat had a hole on either side for the convenience of rummaging two immense pockets, stuffed with books of all sizes. This petticoat was covered with a deep stomachered gown sometimes drawn through the pocket holes [. . .]. In this dress I have frequently seen her walk followed by a six-foot servant, with a cane almost as tall as himself.[36]

Some botany books were specifically made as field guides to be taken on walks. At 6½ × 4 inches, *Germany's Flora, or A Botanical Pocket-Companion for the Year 1791* (in English translation) was presented to 'lovers of botany' as a 'botanical pocket-companion' whose 'commodious pocket-size' solved the 'incommodity of being obliged to carry in the pocket one or more octavo volumes' on 'botanical walks'.[37] *Flora Diaetetica* (1783) similarly notes the practicality of its small size: 'for it being portable in the pocket [. . .], it must become directly useful to those who travel, as they will be hereby enabled to satisfy themselves in regard to the [. . .] plants they may meet with abroad'.[38] The absence of such a guide is precisely what Dorothy Wordsworth laments in 1800 at the beginning of her *Grasmere Journal*: 'Oh! That we had a book of botany.'[39] Her wishes were answered shortly afterwards, as the Wordsworths acquired a copy of William Withering's *Arrangement of British Plants* (1796). They also purchased from the publisher two botanical pocket microscopes.[40] The improved design of these microscopes meant they were 'now in a form more convenient for the pocket'.[41] Dorothy annotated the copy of Withering with observations she made during her frequent walks around Grasmere, while her journal is full of descriptions of the flora encountered on her walks, often reading like field notes.[42] Some books, like *The Lady's and Gentleman's Botanical Pocket Book* of 1800, contained space for the owner to note down their own observations and were clearly meant to be used on the move.[43] Pockets, whose embroidery often expressed women's botanical interest and knowledge, were well fitted for the carriage of such botanising aids. The motifs used on eighteenth-century embroidered pockets testify to women's lively engagement with natural sciences. Some floral motifs are fantastical or exotic, while others are loving renditions of common plants the owners would have encountered on their walks – forget-me-nots, wild strawberries or clover (figs 119, 120).[44]

ABOVE
119 Embroidered carnations, reminiscent of Turkisch decorative art, on a pair of pocket fronts, early to mid-18th century (L 35.1 cm and 34.5 cm). Worthing Museum and Art Gallery, WMAG.1966.389.

RIGHT, CLOCKWISE FROM TOP LEFT
120a–d Details of embroidered flowers and fruit on pockets. Victoria and Albert Museum, London, T.730.B.1913; Victoria and Albert Museum, T.1411-1900; Swaledale Museum, SM.T.1; Victoria and Albert Museum, T.1411-1900.

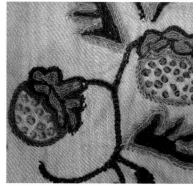

Women also took to nomadic practices of writing, their pockets the place where the necessaries for writing would be kept.[45] Richardson's character Pamela is described as carrying pen and ink in her pockets, but the ink spots on some surviving pockets document the practice beyond novels (fig. 122).[46] Ink horns that were specifically made to fit into a lady's pocket were common.[47] In 1783, together with 'one of the ladies pocket books', Nancy Woodforde was given by her uncle 'a pretty pocket leather inkhorn'.[48] Portable containers to store quills complemented the pocket ink horn for the writer on the move, and enabled her to carry them safely in her pocket. Throughout the period, these portable writing instruments became increasingly common, with some stationers advertising 'pens, more portable than ever, and on a principle entirely new [. . .] cut to suit the various hands of writing both for ladies and gentlemen's use'.[49] Some 'penners' or portable writing sets had a little phial of ink integrated into them (fig. 121).

Eliza Jervoise was directly involved in redesigning the grounds of her home in Herriard, Hampshire, and was a keen gardener, who bought botanical

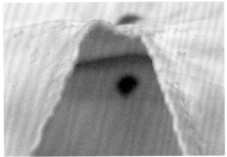

magazines and plants out of her own funds. Her accounts for the spring and summer of 1812 feature 'a pair of galoshes', 'a parasol', 'gloves', 'a small book' and 'a quarter of hundred portable pens' at precisely the time when she had some 'Pocketts' made; all would have been extremely useful on her frequent walks on the estate.[50] The portability of writing grew hand in hand with the popularity of gardening and walking and the idealisation of nature as a place of inner truth (fig. 123). Fanny Burney (1752–1840) tells of being able to steal a private moment away from her official obligations at court as Keeper of the Robes to Queen Charlotte to write to her sister from her favourite wood, thanks to a portable fountain pen: 'This day the Royals were at the grand naval review, I spent the time very serenely in my favourite wood, which abounds in seats of all sorts and there took a fountain pen and wrote in my rough journal for copying to my dear Sorelle'.[51] Even youngsters found uses for their pockets as they set off for their various rural adventures. Gwen Raverat, Charles Darwin's granddaughter, fondly remembers 'What lovely hoards' she kept in hers. Keeping her sketchbook, pencils and erasers at hand for whatever might present itself to be sketched, the young girl had snacks to stave off hunger, and she also 'carried about a small book of Rembrandt's etchings, for purposes of worship'.[52]

From walking and botanising, to gardening, reading, writing or drawing, women's generous pockets equipped them for the newly discovered pleasures of the outdoors, which had taken on new cultural weight with the increasing interest in nature that had developed during the course of the eighteenth century. With microscopes, field guides, journals, pens and books in their pockets, elite women went out of doors to practise their various educated interests. In the process, they enjoyed relative freedom to roam, observe, record and explore nature – itself a ready invitation to introspection and self-expression.

Pockets and tourism

As tourism developed, women adapted the contents of their pockets. Holding money for fares, timetables, tickets and travel guides, pockets facilitated travel and provided refreshments when on the go. With more people enjoying the pleasures of discretionary travel, satirical images of non-elite travellers emerged as a counterpart to the wider unease about social mobility and the loosening of fixed social markers. Henry Seymour Conway wrote to his cousin Horace Walpole in 1737 to tell him of a trip in a post-chaise he had shared with two women: 'I was comfortably jumbled cheek by jowl with an immense, fat, loquacious, brandy-faced female and she had a dear coz with her.' The two women seem to have kept all kinds of refreshments for the trip in their bottomless pockets. On top of cherry brandy and a dram bottle,

> one of the ladies, fainting took out a bottle of vivifying asafoetida [. . .] as well as a bottle of hartshorn [. . .] And what I took for a simple pocket [was] a cornucopia, for it disembogued itself successively of 20 different stores as raisins, almonds, apples, oranges etc. etc.[53]

The same correlation between coach travel, fat, garrulous women and full pockets appeared in the mock travel narrative *The Observant Pedestrian* of 1795. Arriving at an inn, a woman finds it impossible to get off the coach, 'for being very corpulent, and her pockets well filled with packages, it was impossible to pass thro' the door'. The woman's protestations that she is 'an Alderman's *only* daughter', that her husband has 'made a fine *fortin* in the pawnbroking line' and that therefore she should be treated with decorum and respect are belied by the dirty bulging pockets she is forced to remove in order to alight.[54] Written by members of the elite, these satirical descriptions are redolent with social snobbery. Such critics of the spread to the lower classes of travelling by coach are quick to ridicule the over-preparation of these keen but inexperienced travellers (see fig. 74).

Travelling to the continent was another significant way to contribute to the display and maintenance of rank. Exporting her housekeeping skills to foreign countries, Lady Grisell Baillie in 1731 set off on a 'Foreign Tour' with her family, a two-year trip taking in Holland, Germany, France and Italy.[55] Not merely in charge of keeping accounts, Lady Grisell also dealt with tradesmen, thanks to her gift for languages.[56] Having been an exile in Holland as a child, her Dutch came flowing back, allowing her 'to do all the business necessary'.[57] Once in Italy, she taught herself the language quickly, and again 'did the whole business of her family with her Italian servants, went to shops, bought everything she had occasion for' and was even asked by friends to transact *their* business.[58] The detailed expenditure accounts she kept during the trip show the constant use Lady Grisell made of her pockets, including perhaps those she bought on this tour. Hiring coaches, paying carriers, tipping hosts' servants, and paying for excursions and sightseeing entailed specific pocket disbursements.[59] In Rome she noted the round of palaces and villas they went to visit: 'For seeing mosaickwork 0 1 7 [. . .] villa Borghese 0 2 1, Borhese palice 0 1 7, Farnesi Palic 0 1 7'.[60] Later family 'memorandums', a compendium of information for travellers on the continent, advise travellers on when and how much to tip their way into various places, indicating yet another way pockets came in handy when travelling.[61] The document also points to a more unexpected use for pockets, advising Protestant travellers: 'Put your Bibles or Prayer book in your pocket or hide them in the seat of the chaise which is seldome searched or they will certainly take them from you or any English books they think heretical.'[62]

Pockets could equip women for all kinds of adventures far and wide. One female traveller to Syria thus advised her friend, 'do not forget always to have your slippers in your pocket', so that she could change out of her shoes when visiting mosques.[63] Pockets were used to carry other essential aids to travel, such as guidebooks or letters of introduction. In her immensely popular travel guide, *Letters from Italy*, first published in 1800, Mariana Starke stresses the importance of those letters when travelling to avoid being imposed on.[64] Marianne North, the Victorian artist and traveller, writes that when in Java in 1872 she carried 'a big letter in [her] pocket from the Governor General to all officials, [. . .] asking them to feed and lodge me, and pass me on wherever I wished to go'.[65] Guidebooks such as Mariana Starke's also facilitated travel, giving the English on the continent ready tips on accommodation, the price to be paid for just about everything, including getting your pockets washed, and, indeed, what to keep handy in your pocket when travelling.[66]

In the last decades of the nineteenth century, as tie-on pockets were starting to fade from common use, they were revived as a specialised accessory for travelling. In 1880 *The Queen* featured 'pockets for travelling'. 'When travelling a pocket for money is convenient', the paper explained (fig. 124).[67] Almost thirty years later, in 1909, the same convenience of travelling with a detachable pocket was noted in *Fashions for All*: such a pocket was 'a real boon in which to carry your ticket, small cash, handkerchief, pocket comb and glass, stylo pen and a wee box of some good face cream or lotion with which to cleanse the face after a long journey'. The anonymous author also advised a woman to keep the bulk of her money 'in a safety pocket under [her] skirt'.[68] A leading Oxford department store, Elliston & Cavell, in 1908 advertised 'underskirt bags' alongside travelling requisites such as trunks

No. 4. WASH-LEATHER AND TICKING POCKETS FOR TRAVELLING.

No. 6. SHOI COSTUME.

ELLISTON & CAVELL, Ltd., OXFORD.

Japanese Rush Hampers,
No. 35.
1/11½, 2/6, 2/11, 3/6, 3/11, 4/11, 5/11

No. 36.

Holdalls,
in fancy check and plain brown, mail canvas, 24, 27, 30, 33-in., ranging from 4/11 to 25/-

Metal Trunks,
No. 34.
In a range of sizes, from 8/6 to 23/6 Either Black or Oak colour.

No. 38.

Hat Boxes,
Basil, lined stripe, with lock, 5/11
Do. do., with inside fittings, 7/6
Do., do., lined velvet, 10/6
Do., do., Hide, lined quilted sateen, 21/-

Underskirt Bag,
No. 37.
lined leather, fitted with purse, 7/6

School or Play Boxes,
No. 40.
16   18   20   22   24-in.
5/11 6/11 7/11 8/11 9/11 each

Underskirt Bag,
No. 39.
very thin and useful suede leather, grey, black, tan, 3/6

5 PER CENT. DISCOUNT FOR CASH.

and hatboxes (fig. 125). These sturdy 'underskirt bags', though not called pockets in Elliston & Cavell's catalogue, precisely match in shape, material and construction several of such evolved pockets documented in our survey, which museum documentation sometimes associates with travel.[69] The numbers of almost identical extant examples indicate both their durability and popularity, as well as batch or mass production.[70] Available from department stores, advertised in wide-circulation middle-class newspapers and made on some scale, they were marketed as travelling aids to an expanding audience of potential female travellers, keen to be equipped with the best-suited gear for their adventures at a time when tourism had become decidedly more socially widespread.

In 1893 the New York newspaper *The World* explained the advantages of 'a useful travelling pocket':

> A very convenient travelling companion is a deep pocket made separate from the skirt and tied under it around the waist with tapes, to hold money, keys, jewelry, and other small valuables not immediately requisite in travelling. These pockets may be purchased ready made, having an inner purse-shaped receptacle of the same material, usually silicia, with a steel rim and secure clasp. An appreciable weight is removed from the mind of the average travelling woman in knowing that the contents of her pocket cannot be reached by thieves nor by any chance left in the cars or railroad station.[71]

With their interior metal-framed clasp purses and the use of stout webbing to attach them to buckled belts, these evolved pockets were, indeed, particularly safe against theft or loss at a time when the development of travel had also expanded the risks to belongings that it entailed, and some thieves had become specialised 'Railway pickpockets'.[72]

A surviving pocket closely resembling one of the models advertised by Elliston & Cavell's is made of suede with a brass-framed purse inserted into it and two compartments inside. Winifred Marian (née Gibbs), Lady Ponsonby, is known to have worn the pocket under her skirt during her travels in Africa and South America in the 1930s (fig. 126). Born in 1887, Winifred married Colonel Sir Charles Edward Ponsonby in 1912, later moving to the Ponsonby family home in Oxfordshire. The family's history is interwoven with Britain's imperial history, with various members fighting in colonial wars. Charles was involved in different parts of Africa, had interests in New Zealand and Australia and acted as chairman of the Royal Empire Society, later the Royal Commonwealth Society. In the 1920s he travelled extensively in Africa, leaving Winifred at home at a time when her five children were young; but in 1932 Winifred and her eldest daughter, Priscilla, accompanied Charles on a trip to Rio de Janeiro. In 1933–4, for reasons of her son's health and to make a family visit, she took her two eldest daughters and her son to South Africa, and to Southern Rhodesia, where her brother was a farmer. It was on these trips that Winifred is said to have worn the pocket.[73] Unfortunately, Winifred did not leave published memoirs as her husband did, but her pocket acts as a record of her travels. This provenanced example of a well-travelled pocket of this late period confirms the continuity and lasting social relevance of the pocket form. Lady Ponsonby's pocket shows how the tie-on pocket managed to adapt to the changing scope of travel at the height of Britain's colonial power. It confirms that the history of the pocket in the later part of our period was not simply that of a slow descent into solely plebeian use or oblivion, when up-to-date women had moved on

to adopt other forms of pockets or handbags. On the contrary, in this case, it was associated with the upper classes and the stakes they had in empire building.

* * *

Elite women's account books and private papers manifest how the pocket became commodified as a receptacle for portable knick-knacks in an age of expanding consumerism, but also how it constituted an aid to sociability. Not evidently an item of conspicuous consumption because it lay mostly hidden from view, the pocket and its uses nevertheless underpinned the performance of rank, cognate with a lifestyle that involved going shopping, attending fashionable entertainments, and mastering the rules and geography of visiting. Botanising, travelling to the continent or, with the development of empire, going 'wider still and wider', were similarly marks of fixing and securing boundaries of class and cultural capital. The ever mobile and adaptable tie-on pocket took the railway and exotic travel in its stride to accessorise these elite manifestations of rank and education. As it supported female mobility and agency, the pocket was an empowering tool for women, enabling them to explore the world.

126 Evolved pocket belonging to Lady Ponsonby, early 1900s (L 25 cm). Oxfordshire County Council Museum Service, OXCMS:1980.115.1.

Twelve Views
in North & South
WALES
Nᵒ D

CHAPTER SIX

'I turn my Hand to any Thing to get a Penny'

Pockets and Work

On the night of 10 April 1744, Mary Footman had left Milford Lane, where her husband ran the Black Boy public house, to go to a play. As she was coming out of the theatre at around 10.30, she was attacked and her pocket was cut off. It contained a penknife, 12 keys and a brass nutcracker, but also a ring, a cambric handkerchief, a fan and a snuffbox.[1] The mixture of objects in Mary's pocket is a reflection of her ability to negotiate different metropolitan situations. Her pockets accompanied and supported her as she moved from the workplace, where her set of keys, the penknife and the nutcracker would have been useful, to the theatre where her fan, snuffbox and cambric handkerchief were more decorous appendages. The incident, like many in the records of the Old Bailey, reveals that there were many sociable activities on offer in the capital for women like publican Mary Footman. As they moved relatively independently around the city at all times of the day and night, their pockets and contents enabled their actively sociable but hardworking lives. The activities of women who fell victim in the metropolis to pickpocketing, assault or highway robbery – three types of crime foregrounded in this chapter – are recorded in *The Proceedings of the Old Bailey*. In these crime cases, as in provincial newspaper stories, we see what women thought necessary to carry with them in their pockets when out of doors – an index of their industry and participation in various economic activities in the city and beyond, as market stallholders, servants, hawkers or basket women.

Paul Sandby RA (1731–1809),
'View of the Eagle Tower
at Caernarvon, &c.', *Twelve
Views in North & South Wales*,
1786, aquatint (24.2 × 31.7 cm)
(detail). Llyfrgell Genedlaethol
Cymru–National Library of
Wales, 99397554502419.

ABOVE
127 Pocket, front and back,
early 19th century (L 34.5
cm). Charles Paget Wade
Collection, Berrington Hall,
SNO 1748.

Alongside trial accounts and newspaper stories, the role pockets played in these women's lifestyles can be gauged by the rich testimony of surviving pockets, many of which manifest a life of toil and labour (fig. 127). Joined with other sources, this material archive manifests how tie-on pockets supported a lifestyle in which women often had to shift between different employments and roles, their pockets a vehicle for improvisation, multi-tasking and bricolage.[2] As suggested by Sara Mendelson and Patricia Crawford, reconstructing the realities of women's work in the past requires concentrating on 'tiny glimpses [. . .] and on a multitude of examples'.[3] Steven King argues that the nature of female work in the eighteenth and nineteenth centuries calls for historians to change their methodology if they are to catch something of the 'entrepreneurial wanderings' of basket women and their like and recalibrate their vision.[4] The humble pocket might offer a lens to do just that.

Hustle and bustle

A vivid picture of the busy lives of plebeian and middling women in the metropolis is revealed by Old Bailey testimonies, which shed light on the routes women took, their means of transport and the distances they covered. We see, for instance, women hiring hackney coaches, taking boats to cross the river or, later in the period, using the city omnibuses; but by far the most common means of transport for these women in the city all through the period was shanks's pony. In 1851 Mary Sweeney, who said she got her living from selling 'oranges, nuts, and lemons', was walking from Hampton Court to 'London to market'. Stopping at Brentford around midnight 'for half a pint of beer', she was enticed to take lodgings and halt her tramp across the city. The 15 miles represented by the journey were covered entirely on foot it seems, and there is no suggestion that this type of walking was out of the ordinary for Mary.[5]

The court cases evidence women's activity around the clock, many attacks on their pockets happening 'in the dark of the evening'.[6] Night and its blurring of categories, moral and otherwise, has a natural association with crime.[7] In a legal culture where visual identification was crucial to conviction, darkness was favourable to thieves.[8] Yet, because domestic servants could be sent on errands in the dead of night and markets were open late, women frequently criss-crossed the city at all times of the night. In 1769 Sarah Cook was attacked by two men 'at about 1 o'clock in the night as [she] was going for a pint of beer at the Angel in Islington', and in 1788 Elizabeth Cockburn crossed paths with Elizabeth Goldsmith in New Gravel Lane 'about half after one in the night' as she 'was going out on some family business for [her] master'.[9] This night-time activity was not the preserve of the metropolis, as Ann Hicks knew to her cost when she was attacked 'towards one o'clock in the morning as she was returning soberly and steadily [. . .] from Bristol Fair' in 1826.[10]

Like their wealthier counterparts, plebeian women, supported by their pockets, were involved in a variety of sociable activities, from going for a pint of beer to attending shows. In 1781 Eleanor Williams was assaulted as she was 'going, between ten and eleven o'clock, for a pot of beer, to the corner of Parrot-alley, East Smithfield', while Mary Orris's pocket was pulled off her side as she came out from 'the Castle' where she had gone 'for a pint of beer' on 'the day after new Christmas-day' in 1767. In her case, the liquor she drank probably did not help keep her money safe, though her husband, when asked whether his wife was sober when she got home that night, declared: 'I can't say she was quite sober; she went up stairs as well as ever she did in her life.'[11] Plebeian women in our Old Bailey cases of pickpocketing, assault and highway robbery were also engaged in a host of other consumer situations. Mrs Karrsone was 'buying some oranges on London-Bridge' in June 1695 when John Carter picked out of her pocket the silver box in which she kept her money.[12] It was in Rosemary Lane, as she was buying a second-hand 'pair of breeches' and 'a waistcoat', that Elizabeth Dyke had her pocketbook and the tin box where she kept her cash stolen in 1807.[13]

The court records show women frequently attending church or the meeting house, as well as plays, concerts and exhibitions.[14] In 1755 Margaret

Nelson was attending the 'rehearsal at St. Paul's', and after the music was over, as 'the coronation anthem was singing', she felt a hand in her pocket.[15] Anne Pearson's pocket was picked in 'the Passage going into the New Playhouse' of Drury Lane on 27 April 1728.[16] Ironically, she was on her way to see *The Beggars' Opera*, which features the thief-catcher Peachum and the corrupt jail keeper Lockit exhibiting on stage a booty of 'seven and twenty women's pockets complete; with the several things therein contain'd; all seal'd number'd and enter'd'.[17] It was in the same playhouse that Susanna Birtue's pocket was rifled as she made her way to 'the two shillings gallery' in 1770.[18] Those who could not afford 'the two shillings gallery' could still enjoy free forms of entertainment. In 1778 Margaret Bastin was part of the crowd come to pay tribute on the death of William Pitt the Elder when her pocket was picked.[19] It was when she was watching the Lord Mayor's procession in 1835 that Sarah Ann Morning had her pocket pulled right out of the pocket-hole in her dress and turned inside out.[20] Naturally because pickpockets 'haunted Churches, Fairs, Markets, and all publick Meetings, that they might work their Feats in the Throng', these locations feature large in our Old Bailey findings.[21] Nevertheless, looking at crimes perpetrated against women when out of doors allows us to glimpse something of the hustle and bustle of their lives. The court cases show that plebeian women were regular participants in the entire social fabric that animated eighteenth- and nineteenth-century civic spaces.

Pockets at work

However, it was waged and unwaged labour that consumed most time for plebeian women as they performed their roles as servants, street sellers, pedlars, hawkers or prostitutes. In these various occupations, pockets were put to regular and varied uses. Reading court testimonies with the pocket as our lens not only provides us with a convenient shorthand of the many activities they were involved in, it also gives unique access to the lived experience behind the harsh economic circumstances of many women during our 200-year period and the role their pockets played in their makeshift existence.

The continuing presence of coins in everyday practice meant that female market stallholders had to have a pocket, sometimes several, to trade with ready money. Katherine Redmane testified that Ann Faulkner, who bought eggs from her in the market in 1722, 'made her tell them over three times into her apron under which her pocket hung' and that once the customer left, she missed the 23*s.* that had been there.[22] In 1685 Mary Cooke, who sold mitts in the market in York on Thursdays, had her pocket picked of the '6s 1d. and one farthing' it contained.[23] *The Proceedings* often associate traders with a pocket referred to interchangeably as 'pocket apron' or 'apron pocket'.[24] The terms are usually mentioned in relation to women working in markets and at stalls,

Speech bubbles in image:
Kally you had better hould your tongue and dont make me speak out, for you know I can blow you up, becase I know what myself I know —

To the Devil I look you for a new years gift; whad do I regard you, or any varmint, like you; I know I am both a Wh....... and a thief, but worrng that, I defy you to say black is the white of my eye!!!

Ah by Jasus Kitty may say that; for keeping my poor Biddy, that was hung for only taking care of a gentlemans gould watch, how art thee sober fort in the Market!

SCANDAL REFUTED, or *Billinsgate Virtue* ..

128 Charles Williams (*fl.* 1797–1830), *Scandal Refuted, or Billingsgate Virtue,* 1818, hand-coloured etching (24 × 35 cm). Lewis Walpole Library, Yale University, 818.00.00.19+.

such as a butcher's wife keeping a stall in Honey Lane Market in the City of London, a woman 'selling pease and beans', a woman keeping a 'tripe shop in Clare Market', or yet another butcher's wife, Mary Hollingsworth, who clearly differentiated between her 'pocket apron', exclusively used to carry out business, and another pocket she wore simultaneously, a 'side pocket' holding her personal money and playing no part in her business dealings.[25] There were various ordering strategies for things inside pockets, and having a pocket for personal possessions and one for business was a means of reducing muddle and averting accusations of theft. Sarah Price, a substantial trader who ran a shop selling single and double gin, had 'two side Pocketts and nine pocket aprons', in addition to three aprons and three 'old check aprons' among the possessions listed in her 1743 probate inventory.[26] A satirical print showing traders wearing two distinct sorts of pockets tied round their waists – one with vertical openings, the other with horizontal ones – indicates the likely difference between pockets and apron pockets, a difference also visible in a surviving example (figs 128–9).

Street traders handled cash constantly, their hands passing in and out of their pockets all day long, so it made sense to have the pockets easily accessible. If female traders did not have a purpose built apron pocket, they could wear

129 Machine-sewn pocket, of the type sometimes known as an 'apron pocket' or 'pocket apron', late 19th century (L 39 cm). Bolton Museums, Art Gallery and Aquarium, INV.4326.

the customary pocket, but in a position that facilitated access (see figs 5, 8, 11). In 1766 Eleanor Bird, who kept a public house near Well Street, had just finished giving change to a client out of her green silk knitted purse near the bar in the drinking room. After she had put the purse in her left-side pocket, she was hustled by Ann White, who made off with more than 26 guineas. Cross-examined, Eleanor had to admit that she 'had only [her] gown over it'.[27] Visual representations bear out the practice. They show innkeepers, servants and traders keeping their pockets to hand by drawing their aprons or overskirts to the side. This made access to the contents easier but also kept skirts out of the way. In *Cobler's Hall* (1779), we see a cobbler and his wife working at home (fig. 130). The man is depicted making shoes next to the window and the woman, with a pan in hand, is cooking over the fire. Her pocket, revealed by the gown's gathered-up sides, is clearly visible and accessible. Protecting her gown from the fire in this way also allowed her convenient access to whatever she might need from her pocket. The pocket openings commonly set in the sides of gowns to allow access to pockets could also serve the extra purpose of enabling women to loop their unwieldy skirts out of the way when working. So pockets, skirts and pocket openings could all be made to work in combination when practicality required.

A portable pocket that left a woman's hands free was also essential to those with itinerant occupations (fig. 131). Basket women earned small sums of money fetching and carrying goods for people, often on market days. Constantly on the move, they took part in the 'culture of itinerancy', which characterised Britain all through our period.[28] For such women, the pocket was the only place to keep whatever valuables they might have. In 1794 Catharine Norton, a basket woman in Covent Garden, had her pocket picked of the substantial sum of 14 guineas, which she had 'earned honestly' probably over a significant amount of time: 'I went to Covent-garden between five and six in the morning, and I came home for another basket', at which point she met the defendant, who took her money from her pocket.[29] These women's livelihoods depended on having reliable pockets. Sturdy materials such as leather made their pockets more durable and also safer. One such surviving Welsh nineteenth-century pocket is known to have belonged to Ann Beynon, a farmer's wife, who used it when she went to market to sell eggs and milk (see fig. 37).[30] The work it did for Ann is evident in the many traces of wear

Printed for & Sold by BOWLES & CARVER.   C O B L E R 's   H A L L.   Nº69 in S.t Pauls Church Yard, LONDON.

ABOVE
131 Anon., Fish sellers of Llangwm, Pembrokeshire, wearing pockets under their aprons, late 19th century, photograph. Amgueddfa Cymru–National Museum Wales, digital image 359698.

OPPOSITE
132 Pair of sampler-style pockets, mid-19th century (L 34.5 cm and 34 cm). Amgueddfa Cymru–National Museum Wales, 31.31.3, 31.31.4.

132a Pocket fronts (above).
132b Pocket backs (below).

and repair it bears, but service of this kind did not necessarily exclude aesthetics, as the pockets of her fellow Welshwoman Jane Thomas demonstrate. Jane's two pairs of surviving pockets are decorative, but their signs of hard wear and extensive repair are nevertheless equally eloquent about their life of work (fig. 132; see also fig. 42). Jane lived with her husband, 'a farmer of 100 acres', and their two daughters at Pantybryn, Pontshaen, in Cardigan in the last decades of the nineteenth century.[31] Jane lived in the same rural parish where she had been born and married, and her pockets, made of wool from their own sheep and woven locally, show similar grounding in her native community. Yet at the same time, the pockets served a livelihood that was dependent on travelling on a routine basis. Like Ann Beynon, Jane wore her pockets to nearby fairs and markets to sell the farm's produce, in her case going regularly from the farm to Llandysul and elsewhere. How she travelled the 14 miles or so to Llandysul is unknown, but the whole family would have depended on her getting back safely, with her pockets guarding whatever takings she had made that day. Another contemporary and fellow Welshwoman, Mary Davis, who wore her pockets to trade in the local market, kept one pocket 'for silver, one pocket for copper' (see fig. 147a).[32]

Going to and from markets put women and their belongings at risk especially on the return journey when they were carrying the day's takings. The likelihood of a stash of cash was what the footpads counted on when, in 1736, they attacked 'Farmer Embling's Wife of Chew who keeps Bristol Market with Cheese and Butter' as she was travelling back home at the end of the day. She was knocked off her horse and her pocket containing 9*s*. 8*d*. was cut off.[33] Pockets stored cash, but in Wales, and elsewhere, it seems women also kept balls of wool and knitting needles in their pockets to knit stockings while on the move – a practice we see in Paul Sandby's depiction of Welsh market women (fig. 133). The barefoot woman Sandby places in the foreground not only knits and walks at the same time, she also carries a hefty child on her back (see detail, p. 162). Ahead on the road, a woman wearing a pocket and carrying a large basket looks out for her. The picture serves to illustrate pockets as places of multi-tasking, enabling women to alternate between different types of labour and to work, move and socialise at the same time.[34]

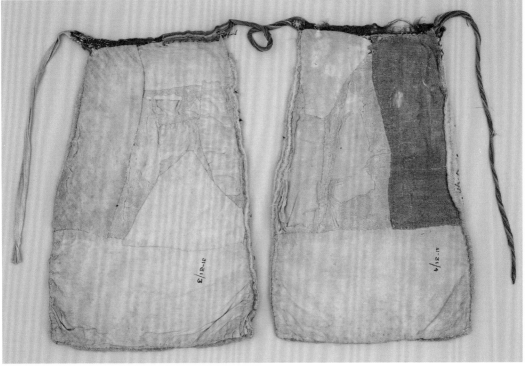

133 Paul Sandby RA (1731–1809), 'View of the Eagle Tower at Caernarvon, &c.', *Twelve Views in North & South Wales*, 1786, aquatint (24.2 × 31.7 cm). Llyfrgell Genedlaethol Cymru– National Library of Wales, 99397554502419.

View of the EAGLE TOWER at CAERNARVON &c

A similar vision of pockets as instruments for both toil and pleasure is conjured up by the accounts left by husbandman Richard Latham of Scarisbrick, Lancashire, in which he recorded purchases for the farm, himself and a largely female household. Married to Nancy Barton in 1723, he had seven children, of whom six were girls born between 1726 and 1741. The girls were actively involved in the farm and were part of a busy household with a wide range of activities manifested in the accounts. The pocket bought for Sara, aged 18, in 1747, cost 1*s*. 6*d*., but not all items purchased for the Latham womenfolk were so practical: the household's consumption reflects an interest in novelties, taste and culture.[35] The account books make evident that Nancy and her six girls were farm women who worked in the fields, but regular entries for seeds, calving and haymaking are interspersed with some luxuries and trinkets, such as 'licerice', '2 little books', a looking glass and an 'ivery comb'.[36] The Latham accounts exemplify how a lifestyle that was rural and hardworking was not necessarily divorced from concerns for taste and the satisfaction of small pleasures. Going regularly to 'Lirpole' (Liverpool) on shopping trips, or to 'Prescott Fair' to buy gloves, as Betty did in 1747, or buying treats such as gingerbread at the fair in 1748, the Latham girls would have used their pockets to keep the money to pay the tolls for their journey or to buy and carry the small items recorded in the accounts for those trips.[37]

The mixed contents of pockets of women in transit could prove life-saving. Elizabeth Woodcock survived eight days buried in a snowdrift in February 1799. The weather, it is known from contemporary sources, was particularly cold, with more snow than had been known 'for the last 10 years',

134a W. R. B., *Elizabeth Woodcock*, *c.*1799, engraving (24 × 21.5 cm, framed). Museum of Cambridge.

BOTTOM
134b Elizabeth Woodcock's nutcracker, late 18th century (L 10.5cm). Museum of Cambridge, 1143/37.

and 'the roads impassable'.[38] Elizabeth was caught in the snow as she was 'returning home' from Cambridge market, where she had gone to 'sell some poultry etc. and buy some necessaries for her family'. Travelling on horseback and equipped with a 'basket with some shop goods on her arm', she was thrown off her horse and buried alive in a snowdrift. After she lost her basket in the accident, it was the contents of her pocket that saved her life. Besides a nutcracker and a snuffbox, she also had a handkerchief and an almanac. The almanac told her 'there would be a new moon the next day' giving her hope that she might be found alive. When she attached her 'coloured handkerchief (which she with great difficulty took from her pocket)' to the end of a stick and thrust it out of the snowdrift, it was spotted by a local farmer (fig. 134).[39]

Female pedlars depended on a variety of containers to travel up and down the country for long periods with their packs. Baskets for the carriage and display of goods played an essential role in the itinerant economy. Nineteenth-century

pedlar dolls surviving in museum collections show the combination of portable containers on which these women depended.[40] Carrying their wares in boxes, bundles, trays or baskets, the dolls sometimes wear pockets as well. Just as such women needed sensible shoes and a thick cloak to protect themselves from the weather, a means of carrying their money and small possessions when on the road was also a necessity (fig. 135; see also fig. 66). Elizabeth Gatehouse, a 'travelling woman and a trader in lace', was walking between Sturminster Marshall and Wimborne Minster in Dorset in 1729 when she dropped dead. She had lodged the night before at an inn, an indication that she was some distance from home. Her sudden death resulted in the assembly of a coroner's court and thus a rare record of what she had about her person. She was walking with a pocket, a basket and a box. The 'Goods in the Pockett of Eliz. Gatehouse' consisted of two snuffboxes, a thimble and money – presumably her personal belongings – while her box contained all her lace goods and a napkin marked with the initials 'EL', and she carried in her basket 'one linen handkerchief and two caps', 'and a new blue apron'.[41]

Hawkers, pedlars and street sellers were choice victims for footpads and highwaymen as,

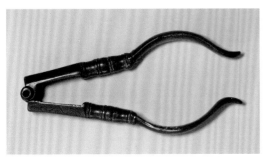

135 Pedlar doll 'Sarah Thrifty' with her tray of goods, early 19th century (L 20.3 cm, doll). Manchester Art Gallery, MCAG.1922.566.

often alone, they were sure to be carrying both a quantity of small, desirable objects and cash. In March 1752 the *London Evening Post* reported an attack on a travelling woman, Mary Carter of Buckinghamshire, that happened near Dartford in Kent. She was set upon in the evening on the road by two footpads. They took her clothes including her pockets in which was a 'large square silver snuffbox' engraved with her name, and 'also a square oaken box containing spoons, buckles, thimbles, studs, stayhooks &c all of silver, which were goods she sold'.[42] It was also probably the day's earnings that William Fisher hoped for when he attacked hawker Sarah Rowen in East Smithfield as she was returning home one night in 1853. She stopped in a doorway to lace up her boots when Fisher 'tore my apron clean from me; and from my pocket he took my money'.[43] The 5s. and half-crown that were stolen from Sarah Rowen were comparatively meagre compared to Sarah Plater's loss in 1796. She was a trader in lace who had come 'to town the 13th of November, with some lace, and on the 14th of November sold it to Mr. Wells, in Fleet-street, for which [she] received, in the evening, between seven and eight o'clock, eighty guineas in gold, and half-a-guinea'. She declared that she had put the money 'in a leather purse, and tied it up with a string, and put it in [her] left hand pocket'. After buying a pie for her dinner from a pastry shop, she was 'hustled' and the purse was taken from her pocket, and she was left to cry that she was 'ruined for ever'.[44]

Supporting another kind of nomadic life, pockets were key to women receiving charity. Travelling on the roads without a hawker's licence or a

pauper's pass could lead to a charge of vagrancy, and incur the traditional sentence of a week's confinement to a house of correction, a whipping and removal to the last parish of settlement. This is what happened to Ann Yeats, originally from Bishopsgate, London, who was arrested in Norwich for 'wandering abroad and begging' outside her parish in 1778. After questioning, she was sent on her way home with a pass warrant in her pocket.[45] A pass was a highly valued legal document that would have been carried safely deep in a pocket, ready to be produced for protection at every stage of the way.[46] Women who travelled with a pass could receive parish relief, seek casual alms, or move freely in search of seasonal work. Combining several strategies, they could go from one area to another and from one means of survival to another. Mary Saxby, a vagrant travelling without a pass, explained how she would sometimes get money from singing ballads, sometimes seek seasonal employment in the fields making hay or picking hops, or else sell small goods to villagers.[47] However, travelling with a pass in one's pocket was no guarantee of a safe journey. Sarah Griffin, a young girl from Worcestershire who had come to London to be a servant but found the air did not 'agree with her constitution', decided to make her way back home in 1740. Before she set out on her journey she had obtained a pass 'from a proper magistrate'. On the first night of her journey she asked for lodgings in Acton and was offered space in a barn. Despite her entreaties to keep her presence a secret, the 17-year-old boy who had shown her the barn told a group of five men. Her attempts at saving herself were vain. Beaten up and tortured, she was gang-raped by all six men. Afterwards, they wanted whatever money she had and 'cut off the Woman's Pocket, and took out of it Two-pence Three farthings, and a Pass, which she said, she had to travel with'.[48] The tragic story of this young homesick servant shows that though service was theoretically a fixed occupation, known as 'having a place', in practice it was often instead a story of displacement and homelessness, a 'female migration experience'.[49]

Young Susannah Blakeway had just arrived in London 'from Shropshire to get a place' in 1791 when all her clothes were taken from her, after she was enticed into lodgings by unscrupulous thieves. The indictment lists Susannah's total possessions, consisting of two gowns, a pair of stays, two aprons, a pair of stockings, three handkerchiefs, a shawl, a silk hat, a shirt, five caps and a pocket, while she was left with nothing but what she had on: 'my shift, and stockings, and cap, an handkerchief, and an old petticoat'.[50] The Old Bailey abounds in cases of this kind concerning servants who not only sometimes covered large distances to find employment but also often lived a life of short placements, sometimes staying in a position only a month at a time, sometimes even less.[51] The vulnerability of these women in search of employment in the city was so well known that it served as the starting point of William Hogarth's

modern moral satire in *A Harlot's Progress* (1732; fig. 136). Caroline Parker in 1837 told the court that her box was stolen after she left her employment with Mrs Wise. She explains: 'I was only a month with her – I only went a month on a trial – I have been to several situations'.[52] Moving from house to house was often the plight of women employed in domestic service. In 1736 Mary Hanson, a woman accused of theft by her master in Bedale, Yorkshire, had come from Ripon to look for a place, and though she was twice hired into families, she never stayed more than three weeks.[53]

Being able to pack and move their possessions around was crucial to these women. While the bulkier items of clothing were kept in the servant's box, the pocket served to carry small possessions or whatever money a woman had. Freshly arrived in London 'in the wagon' from Bedfordshire in June 1838, Lucy Jackson was looking for a place with a laundress when she was lured into lodgings with the promise of help. She was talked into taking off her pocket, which contained her money, and putting it into her box before going out, on pretence that it would be safer. She was then waylaid, her belongings were stolen from the lodgings and she was forced to return to her uncle in the country.[54]

For servants, pockets also played a special role in their career prospects, since it was in their pockets that they would keep 'the character' to recommend them to potential employers. This crucially important personal archive carried the symbolic authority and reach of the written word. Prized and preserved in their pockets by even the illiterate, the 'character' was kept so close to the

137 William Shayer Sr (1787–1879), *Outside the Royal Oak, c.*1840, oil on canvas (63.5 × 76.2 cm). Richard Green Gallery, London.

body itself that this fragile archive could be said to transfer some authority and reassurance to the woman who carried it.[55] In 1799 Elizabeth Macdonald, a servant of all work who had her pocket cut, was asked: 'You are an Irish woman, and travel about with your character in your pocket?' Although not listed in the indictment because of no monetary value, 'the written characters' which she kept in her pocketbook were of far greater value to her than the £1 note she had lost.[56] They represented the promise of future employment and stability. When in employment, the portable pocket was also necessary for servants working around the house or sent on errands: carrying messages, settling bills or fetching goods. A servant's pocket was central to performing her duties. In it she carried the keys with which her mistress might have entrusted her, or the simple needlework tools needed to mend and darn the household linen.

Pockets were so closely connected to the role of the female servant that in visual and literary representations, they could even be used as an insignia

Sophia, Honour, & the Chambermaid.

He told us Madam (tho' to be sure it's all a Lye) that your Ladyship was Dying for Love of the Young Squire, and that he was going to the Wars, to get rid of you.

Fielding's Tom Jones *Book X Chap. 5.*

of service (fig. 137). An illustration of 1780 depicts the scene in Henry Fielding's *Tom Jones* (1749) in which Sophia Western and Mrs Honour arrive in the middle of the night at the inn in Upton and are greeted by the chambermaid (fig. 138). The chambermaid wears a quilted petticoat on which hangs a pocket that has been crudely mended. Together with the quilted petticoat, the set of keys and the heavy leather shoes, the patched-up pocket identifies her as the innkeeper's servant. In literature, Peggotty's pocket in *David Copperfield* (1850), from which she produces cakes and money for the young hero when he is sent away from home, becomes symbolic of her role as a loving, caring servant.[57] These

THE POCKET

representations of pockets as the dedicated, almost iconic, tool of domestic service mask the fact that many women did not have a fixed trade all through their working life. In this context women often had to turn – with their pockets – to various lines of work as opportunity arose, legal or illegal.

Opportunistic pockets

Domestic servants were thought to be well placed to cheat their employers, having ample time to observe the household in which they lived and the opportunity to exploit their insider knowledge. Taking advantage of the relatively unrestricted circulation they enjoyed around the house, it was thought that servants used their pockets to steal food, clothes or money. Hidden as they were, pockets seemed perfectly adapted to thieving and petty pilfering, their invisibility and capaciousness fuelling the widespread anxiety over servants' theft.[58] In 1764 the author of *Low-Life* had servants stealing on Sunday mornings. 'Servant Maids, while the Families they live with are at Divine Service, are looking over their Mistresses Drawers and Boxes, and conveying away, with their pilfering Fingers, such Things as they think will not be missed.' By the evening, they were entertaining their friends on the proceeds.[59] Anxieties about the enemy within were such that when anything went missing, the servant's pockets, along with her box, were among the first places to be searched.

The charwoman, who was not attached to a household but was called in for an occasional day's work, seemed to represent a particular threat. In *Punch* in 1850, a portrait was made of the typical charwoman, Mrs Grimes, an 'out door drudge' presented as a rootless figure, prone to pilfering whatever she laid her hands on: 'The "Ladies" down stairs, [. . .] always lock up their tea caddies, Jeames counts his spoons, Cook hides her kitchen stuff and Missus makes a general clearance, whenever Mrs GRIMES comes to stop for a day. Whatever is missing, the Charwoman is sure to be the thief.' And it was her pockets that were supposedly instrumental in her pilfering habits: 'she wears large pockets which keep gradually swelling towards night time'.[60]

Court cases seem to confirm the use of pockets as tools of theft by servants.[61] In 1822 Sarah Shaw, who had 'been charring that day' at the Swan with Two Necks, was found to have 'three pockets on, containing victuals' – clearly incriminating evidence.[62] Women accused of 'theft from master', which became a category of crime in its own right in 1823, used their pockets in various ways: to smuggle goods out of the house, to store stolen goods or to keep a key that allowed repeated offences. In 1796 Eyston and Crooke, haberdashers and hosiers in Pall Mall, found they were the victims of recurring thefts by the housekeeper and cook Ann Kennedy, who kept in her pocket a key to the bookcase where the key to the shop was locked on Sundays.[63]

The normal daily circulation of servants around the house, armed with their pockets, enabled them to seize opportunities as they arose. In 1765 Frances Burk took a stash of things she would commonly handle on behalf of her employer. When 'her pocket appeared pretty bulky', Ann Clough, her mistress, asked to examine it. It contained a silk handkerchief, a pair of stays, a linen apron, a linen bib, three-quarters of a yard of flowered cotton and a linen napkin, all belonging to Ann. In her unsuccessful defence, Frances explained: 'I don't deny but that I had the things in my pocket: my mistress had the key of the room in her pocket, so that I could not carry them into the room as I intended.'[64] The ambiguities of a servant's position in a household were easily exploited and pockets were convenient for serendipitous theft.

Moving up and down the house, servants were also constantly in and out to run errands. If a theft was committed, the goods could easily be squirrelled away in the offender's pocket. In Mary Leadbeater's *Cottage Dialogues* (1811), a series of interviews with Irish servants, one servant named Nancy owned up to regular thieving:

> many's the good bit I bring home and the fine ends of candles and lumps of soap, and grease to dip my rushes, and sometimes a bit of tea and sugar [. . .] Mrs Nesbitt knows nothing about it; but such things are not missed out in a big house, and I may as well get them as another.[65]

This candid admission of routine pilfering fits into what Michel de Certeau defines as an 'art of the weak', the unselfconscious 'guileful ruse' of 'everyday tactics', 'always on the watch for opportunities that must be seized "on the wing"'. This unpremeditated theft could 'make use of the cracks that particular conjunctions open in the surveillance of the proprietary powers', to 'poach [. . .] in them'.[66] In 1777 Jane Griffiths was surely making the most of the opportunities given by her capacious pockets when she attempted to carry off in them two live ducks belonging to Thomas Wainwright.[67]

As more and more women were employed as day workers in manufactories turning out new goods, from textile workers in the north to metalworkers in the Midlands, they took their share – and sometimes more than their share – of the products of these industrial transformations. In 1792 Sarah Emmot, a cotton spinner, was accused of repeatedly stealing 'cotton twist on bobbins from the cotton works' where she was employed, using her pocket and her bosom to spirit them out of the workplace.[68] In 1818 Elizabeth Collett, who was 'employed in counting and papering needles', was charged with stealing some by putting them 'in her pocket and bosom'.[69] In 1846 in London, Mary Green had been employed for about three years by a horsehair manufacturer, for whom 'she did piece-work – working from eight o'clock in the morning till eight or nine at night'. The foreman spotted her 'take some hair off [a] pile, lift up her clothes and put it into a large pocket which she had tied around her'.[70] When she was searched, 15 ounces of horsehair were found in a 'pocket tied under her gown behind her'. In this case, it seems the theft was premeditated to some degree, since Mary had equipped herself with an extra pocket in addition to her normal pockets.

For 'girls of the town', as for other women who earned their living on the streets, a tie-on pocket was sometimes the only place they could call their own. Just like market women or street pedlars, a prostitute often had to carry her world about with her as she walked the streets. The cash transactions involved in sexual services entailed small sums that were pocketed on the spot. In 1831 Sarah Bottley who, in her own words, 'saw gentlemen' in her own home, was given four half-crowns to spend the night with a client. Despite her precautions when undressing – she explains 'I took off my pocket which had the purse in it, wrapped it in my stays and put them on the drawers' – she found her pocket empty and the client gone when she woke up.[71] Conversely, prostitutes were often accused of pocketing more than their due by making the most of their clients' slumber or drunkenness. In 1823 Michael King was thus robbed of his money by a prostitute, in whose pocket was found the sum of £12 that was his.[72] Inherently versatile, pockets adapted to an occupation that was itself somewhat blurred. Prostitution in eighteenth-century London has been described as 'an outpost of poverty' rather than a well-defined profession.[73] All through the period, the lines between prostitution, other types of street commerce, begging and opportunistic thieving were easily crossed.

Most plebeian women's lives were similarly shifting and improvised. As noted by Peter Earle, during the earlier part of our period few women were 'engaged in the same occupation throughout their working lives', and those who reached old age were likely to have had 'at least three occupations', going from 'service to needlework to washing clothes or some other combination'.[74] At a time when unskilled women rarely had fixed trades, and constantly turned their hands to whatever came their way, the 'everyday tactics' they used to make a living, moving from one place or occupation to another, were aided by their pockets. Tie-on pockets, themselves multi-purpose and adaptable, served well for a life defined by relentless adjustments to economic circumstances and opportunities. At the same time, the portable pocket was useful when so many women did their waged work while also raising and provisioning their families in a round of tasks indoors and out. Pockets were often places of resistance to the economic strictures women experienced. In a trial for theft in 1725, one of the witnesses described the constantly reinvented life of a market woman:

My Name is Mary Lee; [. . .] I turn my Hand to any Thing to get a Penny: Sometimes I sell Things in Leadenhall Market; and sometimes I do an odd

Char at one House, and sometimes at another. We Market-Women are
up early and late, and work hard for what we have. [. . .] I was never the
Woman that spared my Carcass.[75]

Mary's testimony sums up the makeshift economy that characterised women's
work in unstable occupations, changing with the seasons or the various
opportunities that arose.

The trajectory of the life of a 56-year-old blind violin player interviewed
by Henry Mayhew in his exploration of the London underworld exemplifies
the constant readjustments necessary to stay afloat. She started off as a servant
when a young woman but was 'left almost destitute' at the death of her husband,
so that she took to selling a 'few laces in the street' but hardly made enough
money from it. She was then taught how to play the violin but, not being a great
performer, the money she got was given to her 'in charity, not for my music'.

Some days I pick up 2s., some days only 6d. and on wet days nothing. I've
often had to pledge my fiddle for 2s. – I could never get more on it, and
sometimes not that. When my fiddle was in pledge, I used to sell matches
and laces in the streets and have had to borrow 1½d. to lay in a stock.[76]

Constantly moving from begging to hawking and back, the blind woman
navigated as best she could the tough terrain of London poverty, using
pledging as a form of credit. Pockets were central to these practices – places
where the 'web of resources deployed by individuals [. . .] to cope with
everyday hardship' interconnected.[77] The relentless efforts of women to adapt
and make a living could fail, as is evident from the contents of some pockets
found on the bodies of women who took their own lives. Despite her efforts to
hold her life together, if only in the account she kept in her pocket of the things
she had pledged, Margaret Griffiths hanged herself in 1778. In her pocket
were found 'a Letter and an Accot. of things Pledged at different Places'.[78] The
record of her scattered belongings reminds us of the role of pockets as sites of
resistance, hope and sometimes despair.[79]

In 1832 Caroline Walsh, an 84-year-old woman, went missing.[80] She
made a living from 'selling tapes, laces, &c. about the street, which she carried
in a basket, and she took alms, if they were given to her, and got sometimes
apparently more than she wanted'. Her pocket would have been put to heavy
use on the streets for carrying the proceeds of her sales or safeguarding the
alms she received, or, indeed, as a place where she could keep a biscuit.[81] The
ubiquitous pocket adapted well to the extemporised lifestyles of such women.
Equipped with tie-on pockets, women could hawk, beg, trade, pilfer, take cash
or food from clients or keep pawnbrokers' duplicates in the hope of better
times. Falling 10s. behind with her rent, a widowed needlewoman interviewed

139 Police constable's notebook listing Catherine Eddowes's clothing, her pockets and their contents, 1888. London Metropolitan Archives, City of London, CLA/041/IQ/03/065/135.

by Mayhew took to the streets in Shoreditch with her daughter to sell matches. 'I stood that night till my own and my child's pockets were full with the pence we received. At eleven o'clock, my child said her pocket string had broke, and she would lose her money if she did not go away. We therefore went home, and on counting our money, we had got no less than 6s. 3d., which we considered a good day's work.'[82] The numerous broken or hastily repaired ties on surviving pockets show that this was not an unusual plight, even when pockets were made of the hardwearing materials plebeian women favoured (see fig. 93c–d). When women's livelihoods depended on whatever they carried in their pockets, keeping them functional was a priority, even when women had limited resources to do so (see figs 37, 82, 85, 93).

The way tie-on pockets supported the makeshift lives of poor women in late Victorian London is dramatically revealed in the 1888 series of murders identified with Jack the Ripper. Often referred to as 'prostitutes', the victims were in reality women who moved between different occupations centred on the street. Selling sexual services to passers-by may have been an occupation for some of them, but only one of the various expedients to which they

resorted, including hawking, begging, pawning their possessions and scavenging things to sell to the tinman or rag-and-bone merchant. In six out of the nine cases usually linked to Jack the Ripper, detailed records exist of the clothing of the victims, showing several tie-on pockets in use. The meagre contents of the women's pockets listed in the records paint a chilling picture of the harshness of life for such women. Annie Chapman, who was found dead on 8 September, was wearing a tie-on pocket which had been 'torn down the front and also at the side' by the murderer. In a macabre symbolic disembowelment, the pocket had been slit open and its contents were found lying by the body: an envelope, pills, a small pocket hair comb and a piece of coarse muslin.[83]

Catherine Eddowes had three tie-on pockets on her when she was found murdered three weeks later. The list of possessions carried on her person by the 43-year-old, who 'used to go out hawking' – making a living by 'sell[ing] a few things about the street' – shows the material reality of her life.[84] She had a pair of 'Unbleached

No Drawers or Stays.
Pair of Mens lace up Boots, mohair laces, right boot has been repaired with red thread, 6 Blood marks on right boot.
1 piece of red gauze Silk, various cuts thereon found on neck.
1 large White Handkerchief, blood stained.
2 Unbleached Calico Pockets, tape strings, cut through also the left hand corners, cut off one.
1 Blue Stripe Bed ticking Pocket, waist band, and strings cut through, (all 3 Pockets) Blood stained.
1 White Cotton Pocket Handkerchief, red and white birds eye border.
1 pr Brown ribbed Stockings, feet mended with white.
12 pieces of white Rag, some slightly bloodstained.
1 piece of white Coarse Linen.
1 piece of Blue & White Shirting (3 cornered).
2 Small Blue Bed ticking Bags.
2 Short Clay Pipes (black).
1 Tin Box containing Tea.
1 do do do Sugar.
1 Piece of Flannel & 6 pieces of Soap.
1 Small Tooth Comb.
1 White Handle Table Knife & 1 metal Tea Spoon.
1 Red Leather Cigarette Case, white metal fittings.
1 Tin Match Box, empty.
1 piece of Red Flannel containing Pins & Needles.
1 Ball of Hemp.
1 piece of old White Apron.

Calico Pockets' described as 'large', as well as a single 'Blue Stripe Bed ticking Pocket' (fig. 139).[85] As in the previous case, the pocket strings were 'cut through, (all 3 Pockets) Blood stained'. The string linking the pair of calico pockets was severed. In one, Catherine had '1 White Handle Table Knife & 1 metal Tea Spoon', a 'Red Leather Cigarette Case, white metal fittings', one 'Tin Match Box. empty' and '2 Short Clay Pipes (black)'. In the second of the pair, she had '1 Small Tooth Comb', '1 piece of Red Flannel containing Pins & Needles' and a 'Ball of Hemp'. In her 'Blue Stripe Bed ticking Pocket' she had '1 Tin Box containing Tea', '1 d[itt]o do do Sugar', '1 Piece of Flannel & 6 pieces of Soap'. She also had with her '2 Small Blue Bed ticking Bags', '12 pieces of white Rag', '1 White Cotton Pocket Handkerchief, red and white birds eye border', '1 large White Handkerchief', '1 piece of white Coarse Linen' and '1 piece of old White Apron'. The officer noted that 'she had no money whatsoever on her'. Next to her body were also found 'three small black buttons of the kind generally used for women's boots, a small metal button, a common metal thimble, [and] a small mustard tin containing two pawn tickets', which led to her identification.[86] Made of unbleached calico and sturdy bed ticking, her three pockets were workaday and capacious, allowing her to carry her possessions about her person. Her portable material world reflected her nomadic life on the streets of east London. Like so many other women she eked out a living by selling bits and pieces to passers-by or to other indigent men and women, like the ragman for whom she might have collected 'the 12 pieces of White Rag' or the 'piece of old White Apron' she was carrying. She had small personal accessories to maintain her appearance on the move: a tooth comb, pins and needles, a piece of coarse linen and soap, as well as cutlery and even tobacco and the wherewithal to make tea to sustain herself as she went about her day in the city.

The investigation established that two days before the attack Catherine had returned with John Kelly, her partner, from Kent, where they had gone hop-picking; not having had much luck finding work there, they had come back to London penniless. Unable to return to the 'common lodging house' they normally used on Flower and Dean Street, they had sought shelter at the casual ward in Mile End and pawned Kelly's boots for 2s. 6d. to buy food and drink, some of which was found in her pocket in the form of tea and sugar.[87] After this particular expedient, which compromised Kelly's mobility and earning capacity, Catherine set off on another tramp across the river to Bermondsey, in an effort to find her daughter (in what would have been the first contact for more than two years) 'to get a trifle'. With her tenuous family relationships, unstable accommodation and sporadic earnings, we see the relentless daily efforts and compromises required of Catherine to keep body and soul together. As for many other women in similar circumstances, Catherine's pockets sheltered all her worldly goods, with the notable exception of the articles securely lodged with the pawnbroker. Both a reservoir of her meagre belongings and an instrument of her various labours, in the apparent jumble of her pockets, we see her multi-tasking resilience and resourcefulness in bleak circumstances.

* * *

A tool of the trade for the servant or street seller, the pocket epitomised some of women's traditional occupations. Being multi-purpose, pockets also adapted to the various tasks women took up in a single day and throughout a lifetime, whether at work or at play. In challenging economic circumstances, they were particularly suited to shifting between various expedients. While crime records offer a rich insight into plebeian women's working lives, giving us access to something of their struggles and resilience, the material evidence of the surviving pockets themselves is a unique testimony to the economy of makeshift in which these women lived. The heavy and sometimes improvised repairs to many surviving pockets show plebeian women's resourcefulness at work on their pockets. Almost an exact contemporary of Catherine Eddowes, but in very different circumstances, Jane Thomas, the Welsh farmer's wife, was rooted in her rural parish rather than adrift in the city, but the backs of her sampler-style pockets, like a palimpsest, embody her own preservation strategies for these utilitarian but companionate objects (see fig. 132). Worked to bits and patched to within an inch of their lives, her pockets, like many others in the survey, register women's unrelenting efforts to prolong usefulness.

Extending the life cycle of objects essential to them by clever or crude mending, plebeian women, like Lévi–Strauss's 'bricoleur', were resourceful and creative, using 'odds and ends' and 'making do' with whatever was at hand – the wear and tear, grime and makeshift repairs on pockets a close parallel to women's bricolaged lives.[88] Jane Thomas, Mary Davis and Ann Beynon might not have been able or inclined to leave a written record behind, but their patched-up pockets are an eloquent and intimate reminder of their existence, recording the hardship of their lives as well as the love and labour that they expended on preserving their well-used pockets (see figs 37, 42, 132, 147). If individuals can be said to speak 'through the medium of things', the material testimony of these damaged yet expressive objects is irreplaceable if one is to approach the lives of women whose voices are often otherwise absent from the written historical record.[89]

CHAPTER SEVEN

'I always have the last sheet of my journal in my pocket'

Pockets, Privacy and Memory

A domestic drama unfolded in August 1770 in a London lodging house. One of the lodgers, Elizabeth Warner, an unmarried former servant, was charged with killing her new-born baby daughter in the house. Mrs Smith, the midwife, was called to the house to investigate the goings-on, and when the case reached the Old Bailey courtroom two months later her testimony underlined how Elizabeth's pocket had a central role. The trial account reveals that, suspected by the landlady and other women in the house of having given birth, Elizabeth at first prevaricated, no doubt in dread of a possible charge of the capital crime of infanticide, but then confessed to an early miscarriage in the privy. After a doctor's examination, to which Elizabeth submitted unwillingly, confirmed a fuller-term birth had taken place, Mrs Smith described the search for the baby's body. 'There was a box locked; I asked her for the key; she would not let me have it till I threatened to break the box open. I opened the box, and found a parcel of dirty things. I found the after-birth in a leather pocket. I looked farther, and found the child wrapped up in one of the prisoner's shifts and petticoats, dead.'[1] Elizabeth's sad tale of loss and fear manifests patterns of power relations in gender and class enacted within domestic space and expressed in material things. The story also illuminates intimately how pockets were sites of illicit dreams, unfulfilled hopes and dark secrets. It was to her leather pocket that Elizabeth entrusted her safety and privacy when, *in extremis*, she bundled into it the evidence from her own body. Her story also demonstrates how, in the contested geography of domestic space, pockets were crucial yet vulnerable in their work of providing privacy for women and how, despite a woman's resistance, they were never inviolable to those with authority over her.

The enjoyment of private spaces in the domestic interior was never guaranteed for women. Even elite women with responsibility for the domestic sphere could not necessarily retreat to a room of their own or have a locked piece of furniture in which to keep personal objects or papers.[2] And poorer women often lived in multi-occupancy accommodation, where the very notion of withdrawing from other people's presence or keeping information hidden was incongruous (fig. 141). Against this background, pockets afforded every woman, elite or plebeian, a space she could hope to call her own and where she could enjoy a modicum of privacy. However, as Elizabeth Warner's tale shows, women's control over this small space was hard-won and fragile, and even the pocket could never guarantee women an undisputed experience of privacy.[3] The frailties of female privacy were nowhere better demonstrated than in institutional settings. Living in a regime of strict surveillance in such places as workhouses, schools or orphanages, women often had no pockets at all or pockets whose contents were closely supervised, a tacit acknowledgement of the power of pockets to subvert.

Although the security of pockets was never complete, the companionate intimacy they represented for women was crucial to their experience of the private, providing them with a place to keep records of their lives and

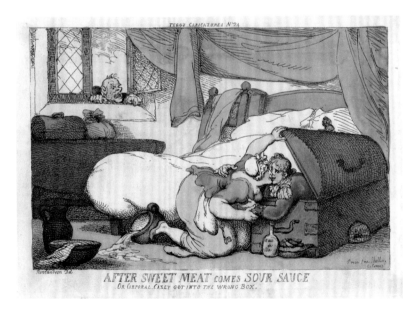

TEGG'S CARICATURES N° 24

AFTER SWEET MEAT COMES SOUR SAUCE
OR CORPORAL CASEY GOT INTO THE WRONG BOX.

THE POCKET

relationships in the shape of personal papers or sentimental mementos. In George Eliot's novel *Adam Bede* (1859), Hetty's pocket becomes a place through which the dairy maid wishfully constructs a new self, while also concealing the evidence of her guilt. Hetty stores candles, 'secretly bought', in a locked drawer in her bedroom, the key for which she keeps in a 'large pocket that hung outside her petticoat'. The night after her first private encounter in the woods with Captain Donnithorne, full of romantic ideas, she unlocks the drawer to perform 'her peculiar form of worship' – adorning herself with her fineries and admiring herself in the mirror, fancying herself married to him. As she looks approvingly at her reflection in the blotched looking-glass, she imagines herself riding in a coach and dressing 'for dinner in a brocaded silk, with feathers in her hair, and her dress sweeping the ground'. The key kept in her pocket not only unlocks the drawer where the candles and glass earrings are kept but also unlocks a world of inchoate fantasy, a deeply private place of her own where her innermost dreams – thoughts she 'could hardly bear to shape' – are played out.[4] Later in the novel it is in her pocket, close to her side, that she keeps the valuable locket and earrings given her by Donnithorne. Eliot underscores how the pocket could offer secrecy, but also how, by harbouring sentimental tokens, it became the site of fantasies, manifesting the power of its small space to represent the human psyche – a place where the immaterial invests the material. In novels, as in practice, pockets enshrined memory and embodied deeply personal yearnings – and some surviving ones still do. Bringing back to life the shapeless dreams and untold stories once entrusted by a real, rather than a fictional, woman to her pocket can be a challenge, but, as archaeologist Chris Gosden reminds us, if 'the movement from the material to the emotional is not easy', it is nonetheless 'vital if we are to grasp the true complexity of our involvement with the material and social worlds'.[5]

The geography of female privacy

In our period, the elite enjoyed architectural transformations that facilitated the rise of domestic privacy.[6] Most other families in urban areas lived crammed into a single rented room in a house in which lodgers and the landlord's family, servants and apprentices all lived. In such households there was little physical privacy. Mrs Kensington, who claimed she had been robbed of her rent money in 1786, lived in the kitchen of William Cato's house, while her husband and children lived in the milk cellar. Forced by dire economic circumstances to live in shared accommodation, the family protected their belongings as best they could by keeping the rent money 'in a little drawer at the top of the chest of drawers locked; I wrapped it very curious in a pair of black gloves', she told the court.[7] The Old Bailey *Proceedings* paint a vivid picture of how the multi-occupancy that was the norm in urban dwellings compromised the security of possessions and thwarted attempts to regulate domestic spaces. Well into the nineteenth century, servants continued to sleep in communal rooms or in passages, rather than having their own quarters.[8] Keys to rooms were seldom in their possession. If they were entrusted with them, it was only briefly to accomplish a particular task: the usual custody of keys remained with the mistress or the master of the house.[9] The same limited spatial control also applied to lodgers' rented rooms, which were routinely locked at night by the landlord or landlady, who could claim access to their rooms at all times.[10]

Even for elite women, territorial control over the domestic space was not guaranteed. If the managerial role of women in the household meant they were usually put in charge of the keys to the various rooms of the house, dependants such as spinster sisters or daughters, or, indeed, wives who lived under the thumb of abusive husbands, did not necessarily have the privilege of spatial control. Fierce territorial wars could be waged: the house could become a battlefield for gendered spatial politics, and women were sometimes subordinates in their own house.[11] For those fortunate enough to enjoy the privilege, having 'a room of one's own' was a source of infinite pleasure and enjoyment.[12] Jealously guarded against possible intrusions, access was carefully overseen by their owners. In the case of wealthy London MP's wife Mary Young in the 1820s, admission to what she calls her 'little cabin', with its shelves and books, was granted to the maidservant only in specific circumstances and for stipulated tasks, all under Mary's authority.[13] Despite not always having a room of her own, Jane Austen knew what such space might mean to its owner.[14] Fanny Price in *Mansfield Park* (1814) fondly refers to her room as 'her nest of comforts', replete with personal memories, where 'Everything was a friend, or bore her thoughts to a friend'.[15] The possession of such a place could play a seminal role in fostering subjectivity, as we see charted in Emily Shore's journal, started in 1831 when she was 11. Aged 17, she devotes a long passage of her journal to a description of her 'dear little room', her 'lion's den', which she describes as 'quite [her] property', calling it a 'true delight'. She relishes listing her possessions, among which are likenesses of relatives, a 'bronze-mounted thermometer which Anna gave me', locks of hair, a shelf full of letters and her cherished writing-desk.[16]

In the absence of a room of her own, containers of all sorts provided a woman with a sense of ownership, control and self. Locked furniture was probably the next best thing to a room of one's own. Jane Austen's portable writing-desk, given to her by her father for her 19th birthday in 1794, complete 'with a long drawer and glass ink stand', would have provided her with a space to call her own.[17] At a price of 12*s*., however, Jane's mahogany desk was a product of the luxury market, which few could afford.[18] More modest alternatives were boxes, trunks or even work-baskets or work-bags, spaces

142 David Wilkie RA (1785–1841), *The Refusal*, 1814, (after Robert Burns's song 'Duncan Grant', 1798), oil on panel (60.5 × 52.5 cm), showing a young woman with various containers around her. Victoria and Albert Museum, London, FA.226[O].

usually under the custody of women, which could act as temporary containers for personal possessions.

The work-box or -basket, holding needlework in progress and sewing implements, was a particularly female vessel (fig. 142). Although work-baskets are often used in conduct literature to instil notions of order, industry and productivity, their prescribed function could be subverted. An episode in George Eliot's novel *Felix Holt, the Radical* (1866) illustrates how such containers could be used to escape patriarchal control. During Felix's first visit to Esther and her father, he knocks a table, sending the contents of Esther's work-basket onto the floor. Amid the 'reels, thimble and muslin work' that spill onto the ground, a duodecimo volume of Byron's poetry that she reads in secret is revealed. Blushing, she picks it up, as she 'would not have wished [her father] to know anything about [it]'.[19] Portable within the house and often covered or closed, the work-basket could offer interim shelter to personal objects. Compared to the pocket worn on the body, the work-box or -basket represented an immediately more sociable space – its contents consisting of sewing sundries that could be shared or exchanged, and itself often a decorative item displaying the needlecraft of its owner. In this respect, the work-box was similar to the hand-held reticule that appeared around 1800 and seemed somewhat exposed and defenceless compared to pockets. *Le Ridicule et les poches*, an amusing piece published in French in 1815 at the height of the reticule vs the pocket polemic, reproduces the imaginary dialogue between a pair of pockets and a new-fashioned reticule. As each is trying to defend its pre-eminence over the other, the pockets draw attention to their superlative discretion: 'a woman [. . .] who entrusted us with some token of her confidence was completely safe: we never left her, constantly at her side in the day and under her head at night, and never would a searching hand have dared penetrate the folds in which we shrouded her secrets.'[20]

Pockets were not always as impenetrable as this portrayed, but nevertheless they held the potential for some privacy. Although small, they could play a role just as important as a private room in supporting a sense of self, as we read in the diary of Elizabeth Isham, the daughter of a seventeenth-century Northamptonshire gentry family. In what she herself terms her 'confessions' written in 1638, at the age of 29, where she tracks both her spiritual and emotional development, she tells of being allowed 'to keepe a closet to [her] selfe', where, as a child, she would retreat for prayer. Her pocket was no less instrumental than her closet (private chamber) in her spiritual well-being. She tells of keeping passages from the scriptures in her pocket to read at will: 'I finding a louse paper of the Epistles of Saint John [. . .] I folded it up and made mee a little booke of it and being very ioyent of it I keept it in my poket, reading it often to my selfe'.[21] It seems that Elizabeth's own mother, Judith, took similar spiritual solace from certain snippets of writing: 'I can no better express my mothers troubles then out of the nots of her owne handwriting, which she keept (carrying them about her) as remembrancess and instructions to her selfe.'[22] Both women's pockets played a role in preserving written matter that offered emotional and spiritual support, allowing Elizabeth to read the epistle 'often to [her] selfe', while Judith used hers to carry 'remembrancess and instructions to her selfe'. Scraps, snippets and fragments were frequent forms of early modern women's writing. The pocket's structure and capacity were well fitted to these small wisps of writing, whose 'intimate material form' heightened rather than diminished their significance.[23]

The pocket space might have been small, but sometimes small sufficed. In 1888, at the death of his wife, Frances, in mysterious circumstances, an astounded Charles Cole Wright learned that the 71-year-old was carrying a substantial sum in gold pinned inside her tie-on pockets, which he had never suspected. It was the investigating police officer who discovered the money hidden in one of her pockets:

> she had two pockets under her dress, and in one of them there was 17l. 10s. in gold, it was tied round the waist with a piece of tape and the money was carefully pinned in the corner with several pins; in the second pocket there was 12s. 4¾d. and some keys.

When cross-examined he was more specific: 'I believe I was the first person to see the pocket, containing the gold; all the pins were in it when I saw it, six or eight; it was done up in a way that until the pins were taken out no one could see the gold; I had to take out all the pins before I could see the gold, it was not in paper'.[24] While in one pocket Frances had ready money, in the other one she obviously kept money out of circulation, in a cache unknown to her husband. Secured by 'six or eight' pins, that corner of her pocket had been turned into a secret compartment quite separate from the rest of the pocket, and remained known only to herself until her mysterious death. What exactly she had earmarked this money for and where it came from is unknown, but evidently Frances had used her pocket to create a space that escaped the attention of her husband. This case highlights the potential role of tie-on pockets in securing some privacy for women. Small but theoretically easier to protect than other spaces in the domestic interior, in a context of overall scarcity of female spatial control, pockets offered women a place under their own jurisdiction, though this remained ambiguous, uncertain and often contested.

The contested terrain of pockets

A lock was worthless unless its key was kept safe. In order to avoid leaving keys lying around and running the risk of having them stolen or copied, men and women often kept their personal keys in their pockets. This was all the more important for less privileged women who had to live in close proximity with others in shared accommodation. In 1828 Ann Buckworth rented a room in Shoreditch and then took a lodger to share the room. She said she left the house after making sure she had 'left my drawers and door locked', adding 'I locked them myself'. She left the key to the room with a neighbour so her room-mate could let herself in, but kept the key to her personal drawers in her pocket.[25] In 1768 Dorothy Foulkes, a servant who had recently come to London with all her savings from 14 years in service in the country, kept her money carefully sewn in a little piece of new leather, itself sewn into a linen purse, which was 'put down in a nook of the box', the key of which she kept in her pocket.[26] The voices heard at the Old Bailey repeatedly show the embedded rituals of protection, in which pockets represented the last stratum

143 *Moss Alley, from Ladd's Court*, 1912, photograph. London Metropolitan Archives, City of London, 4578c.

of security, in a complex series of nesting practices that linked pockets with other containers, inside and outside.[27] The challenges of multi-occupancy to securing personal possessions remained a long-standing problem in urban Britain (fig. 143).

The ability to hide pockets at night and keep them in close bodily proximity was a definite advantage. In 1806 Sarah Chipperfield, a widow, knew as much as most people about multi-occupancy. She lived in the lower room of a house entirely 'let out in tenements', and had to hire a live-in nurse, who slept in the same room with her and her five children. She was well aware of the difficulty of protecting her property in such circumstances, and had adopted a strict security routine. 'I always made it a rule to carry my silver and gold, or whatever I had, in a purse, which I put in my bosom; when I go to bed I take it out of my bosom and put it in my pocket under my head.'[28] This practice continued throughout the period, women putting their pockets 'under the pillow', 'under the bolster' or 'under [their] head' at night when they went to bed. In 1850, in order to protect her possessions, Margaret Airburg explained that her habit was to lock the chest she owned, place the keys in her pocket and then place the pocket under her pillow to protect it.[29] As noted by Jane Hamlett, in the common lodging house or in insecure lodgings, 'often the only way to make sure goods were safe was to secure them close to the body, so that any movement would be detected during the night'.[30] Yet, clearly, even hidden under the pillow, pockets were still at risk as many women knew to their cost.

Even at the age of 66, Elizabeth Ham vividly recalled the humiliation she felt when she was about 17 because the contents of her pocket were emptied out by a stranger. In 1801, required to surrender her room to guests of her father's, she forgot her pocket under her pillow:

> when I was dressing and missed my pocket, I ran into the room to find it. What was my horror to see it lying on top of the bed, with every object it had contained spread about and the letters all lying open! Those letters that Misses in their teens write to each other! It was a cruel joke against me for a long time, though the gentleman at last assured me on his honour he had not seen a word of their contents.[31]

Experienced as desecration of her private space, the emptying out of her pocket by a stranger and the particular anguish caused by her letters 'all lying open' remind us that pockets were trusted by their owners as privileged receptacles for personal belongings, despite being never totally safe – sometimes through their own negligence.

In an early episode in her journal, 16-year-old Fanny Burney tells of losing a page from it out of her pocket – an illustration of the precarious command even elite women had over the private within the domestic interior, and the role that small containers such as pockets could play in attempting, even if not always successfully, to secure some level of seclusion:

> Last Monday I was in the little parlour, which room my Papa generally dresses in – and writing a letter to my Grand Mama Sleepe – you must know I always have the last sheet of my journal in my pocket, and when I have wrote it half full – I join it to the rest and take another sheet – and so on. Now I happened unluckily to take the last sheet out of my pocket with my letter – and laid it on the piano forte and there, negligent fool! I left it.[32]

Besides the risk of accidental disclosure or theft, when women lived in dependent situations – for example, when they were employed as servants, or rented accommodation – control of personal boxes and pockets was always contested, as we are reminded by Mr B's question to his servant Pamela in Richardson's novel of 1740. He suspects that she has been writing letters in secret: 'now tell me, where it is you hide your other written papers, your saucy journal? [. . .] Tell me, are they in your pocket?'[33] The pocket as well as the box was a space over which the employer had some jurisdiction or right of entry when suspicion fell on a servant. In 1851, when Amelia Moses, the wife of a China dealer, suspected her servant Mary Lynch of theft, she went up to her room and searched her box before searching her person and taking hold of her pocket.[34] As hard as servants tried to resist, deploying tactics to escape the inquisitive gaze and hand of their mistresses, their custody of the private space offered by a pocket was only ever, like the house keys, granted temporarily. As soon as mischief was suspected, the privilege could be suspended.

In institutional contexts, the lack of female privacy was manifest in the close control and rationing of access to containers, including their pockets, that women and girls were allowed. The Grey Coat charity school in York in the 1780s, like others, instituted a regime of tight surveillance. The 35 girls being prepared for lives of domestic service or trade were each issued with two pockets. These were part of a complete wardrobe supplied to them during their time in the institution. The regime encouraged a degree of individual accountability, but still closely monitored the girls' possessions and their potential access to secret storage. Borrowing 'anything of each other' was strictly forbidden on the grounds that it was 'always provocative of mischief', a veto that made explicit the very possibilities for informal or illicit circulation of goods, money, provisions and correspondence that it was intended to prevent. In addition to their two pockets, the girls were also issued with a pair of scissors, a thimble, a knitting sheath, a pincushion and four receptacles – a 'huswife', a work-box, a work-bag and a comb in a case.[35] This collection of containers was provided to facilitate orderly labour in the work rooms, but they also represented, with the pockets, the potential for a small but autonomous space. Each Easter, to aid the efficiency and productivity of the work rooms, there was a general overhaul of these items, suggesting a regime in which the girls had only temporary tenure of them between the annual inspections conducted by the matron. In some institutions, control over the potentially private space of pockets could be achieved by their being required to be worn by the inmates in full view. In *Jane Eyre* (1847), Lowood's uniform, with its visible pockets, materialises the school's oppressive regime:[36]

> the eighty girls sat motionless and erect: a quaint assemblage they appeared [. . .] in brown dresses, made high and surrounded by a narrow tucker about the throat, with little pockets of Holland [. . .] tied in front of their frocks, and destined to serve the purpose of a work-bag [. . .]. About twenty of those clad in this costume were full-grown girls, or rather young women; it suited them ill, and gave an air of oddity even to the prettiest.[37]

In the Magdalen House founded in London in 1758, the 'rules, orders and regulations' of 1759 made it clear that if each girl had a box to store linen and clothes, whose key she kept, the wards were nonetheless closely supervised by matrons, and, as in many other institutions, it seems that pockets were absent from uniforms.[38] One remarkably late exception was the tie-on pocket that was part of Christ's Hospital uniform for girls into the 1920s. In her memoirs of her time as a pupil between 1916 and 1925, Louie Angus recalls:

Under our tunics we wore pockets, and there was a slit under one of the pleats through which to put your hand. They were very useful. They were strong dark blue material and had a belt to go round your waist. They could be taken off for games or gymnastics, too. In those early days my pocket was my most treasured possession, my only secret hiding place. I was deep in the collector stage when I went to C.H. and on one occasion I forgot to take my pocket off for gym. Miss Langham stood its rattlings for a few moments and then told me to take it off. [...] As I put it on the platform beside her she eyed its bulges with suspicion and asked me to see the contents. Apart from my hanky and a pencil end and a letter from my mother, there were at least five Gallaher tobacco tins purloined from my father. In these were my current collections – stamps in one, crests in another, chrysalises awaiting their metamorphosis in another, regimental buttons in the fourth and bits of skeleton of a small bird in the fifth.[39]

By controlling or altogether denying girls' access to pockets of their own, these institutions acknowledged the potential role of pockets to provide private territory, their contested secrecy being both a focus of disciplinary control and a tool for potential emancipation. As Jane Hamlett notes 'while the material world was used to control inmates, it could also create opportunities for them. The agency of objects can work in more than one way.'[40]

Secrecy and companionship

'I writt about a weeke since to my daughter Jones, and forgott to send it soe writt another and finding it lye in the bottom of my pockett I inclose it heare that you may know some of the History of my life', wrote Mary Jepp Clarke in 1705.[41] Sometimes simple forgetfulness could lead to private papers making a prolonged stay in a woman's pocket. In other cases, personal papers were kept there for sentimental reasons. Sarah Hurst of Horsham, as a teenage girl, nourished a strong, and partially secret, sentimental attachment to a man named Captain Smith. She met Henry Smith in 1752 when she was only 16, and eventually married him in secret ten years later.[42] During the years preceding the secret marriage, she kept a journal where she recorded her feelings for Smith, whose family did not encourage the union.[43] The journal was kept in the pages of the *Ladies' Complete Pocket Book*, whose wrap-over leather binding made it particularly fit for pocket use. Sarah's pocket was a sheltered place for the secret nurturing of her relationship with Henry, as it contained not only her diary and letters but also the miniatures of the two lovers (fig. 144). Such portraits had been part of the currency of sentiment since the Renaissance.[44] In the eighteenth century, miniatures were exchanged within kinship circles as well as between friends and lovers.[45] Sometimes worn as jewellery, miniatures were also kept at hand in one's pocket. This offered relative security while also providing a more

144a An opening from Sarah Hurst's Diary, including the entry for 22 July 1759 (L 11.5 cm). Horsham Museum and Art Gallery, HMS 3542.

BELOW
144b Miniatures of Sarah Hurst and Captain Smith (L 13 cm and 13.5 cm, framed). Hurst Family collection, on loan to Horsham Museum and Art Gallery.

discreet place for them, especially, as in Sarah Hurst's case, when relationships were secret.[46] Kept in Sarah's pocket, the pictures could be pulled out when circumstances allowed to provide emotional support. Sarah Hurst had to endure long separations from her 'Dear Smith' who was sent to North America in the Seven Years War. Having a likeness of him was a great comfort to alleviate absence, and in her diary she records 'oft gaz[ing] on his lifeless image'. On 25 May 1759, after over four months without him, she writes: 'frequently view my Dear Smith's picture'.[47] Wishing him the same solace, she later sat to the same artist for her own miniature, thinking 'it woul'd give [Smith] pleasure' to have an image of her.[48] The diary does not say if Captain Smith ever received her miniature, but for a time, at least, it seems the couple, separated in real life by geography and family politics, was united in the intimate space of Sarah's pocket.

We know Sarah kept both the miniatures and her diary in her pocket from a passage in the journal that reads almost like an episode out of Henry Fielding's *Tom Jones* (1749), where Sophia Western is thrown off her horse and loses her pocketbook out of her pocket.[49] Riding with her father to Cuckfield on 22 July 1759, Sarah lost her pocket and its precious contents, her journal and the two miniatures. She writes in her diary of discovering her loss a few hours later: 'When I return home [. . .] to my great surprise find I have lost my pocket, Memorandum Book & Capn Smiths picture & my own, am like to faint' (fig. 144a).[50] Sarah's father, who knew of her sentiments for Smith while not actively supporting the marriage, set out the next day on the road 'at 4 in the morning, to recover my loss if possible'. She waited at home 'in dreadfull anxiety, fearing what hands this book might fall into, for tho' there is nothing criminal my whole heart is laid open'. When her father returned with the pocket, she wrote: 'I am thankfull', a likely understatement of her relief that her 'little treasure' was safe at her side again.[51] Not all love stories entrusted to a woman's pocket found such happy endings. In 1773 'a young woman' was found 'hanging in her garters in her chambers, occasioned by a disa pointment [*sic*] in love, her sweetheart having paid his addresses to another person, as appeared by a note which was found in her pocket'.[52]

The motifs on some pockets certainly confirm the emotional associations of the pocket as a repository of a woman's sentimental attachments, whether secret or not. The heart as a sentimental motif was popular in all settings and media.[53] In Edward Francis Burney's *The Waltz*, for example, a love letter pokes out of a young woman's pocket decorated with a heart (see fig. 28). A number of surviving pockets bear heart motifs.[54] The left-hand pocket of an eighteenth-century embroidered attached pair features a heart with flowers growing out of it (fig. 145a). Worn on the same side as the wearer's heart, the motif emphasises the identification of her pocket with the woman's emotional life (fig. 145b). When an unwelcome suitor found a way to smuggle 'a passionate declaration

ABOVE
145a One of a pair of embroidered pockets, 18th century (detail). Bankfield Museum, Halifax, 1935.122.

ABOVE RIGHT
145b Detail of a quilted heart decoration below the opening of a pocket, mid-19th century. Amgueddfa Cymru–National Museum Wales, 47.132.9.

of love' into Mary Delany's pocket, the resentment and 'detestation of him' she felt was undoubtedly increased by the sly intrusion of the unwanted note into such a private place.[55]

Pockets did more than provide secrecy, they provided intimate proximity and companionship. Christopher Wren wrote an exquisite love letter to his future wife, Faith Coghill, in 1669 to accompany her watch when he returned it to her after repairing it.

> I have sent the watch at last & envie the felicity of it, that it should be soe neer your side & soe often enjoy your Eye, & be consulted by you how your Time shall passe while you employ your hand in your excellent workes. But have a care of it, for I have put such a Spell into it; that every Beating of the Balance will tell you 'tis the pulse of my Heart, which labours as much to serve you and more trewly than the Watch.[56]

He voices a direct association between physical proximity, love and constancy in his extended metaphor, and, true to metaphysical tradition, fuses the material and the immaterial. The companionate intimacy of a material thing, endowed with 'such a Spell' by Wren, resonates with many other accounts of pocketed keepsakes.

Pincushions, handkerchiefs, locks of hair in lockets, purses, thimbles and huswifs were all small objects at the centre of an intense traffic of gifts that gave pockets a particular role in expressing women's attachments. In a tender letter to her close friend Jane Pollard in 1788, Dorothy Wordsworth writes about a series of pocketable tokens of friendship exchanged between the two women:

> I have sent you a lock of my hair, it will serve to remind you of poor Dolly whenever you see it [. . .] you will receive a thimble [. . .] which my Dear

Mary Delany's needlework pocketbook, a gift from Queen Charlotte, 1781, satin, coloured silks and enamelled gold, with contents displayed (H 14.5 cm, W 7.5 cm, D 2.7 cm). Royal Collection Trust, RCIN 45126.

Love, I hope you will accept. [. . .] I hope it will serve to remind you of my affection for you. I have got the handkerchief in my pocket that you made and marked for me, I have just this moment pull'd it out to admire the letters. Oh! Jane! It is a valuable handkerchief. [. . .] Adieu my love, do not forget to send me a piece of hair.[57]

The pocket was the chosen repository for the handkerchief that Jane made and marked for her friend. It is integral to a gift economy characterised by reciprocation, in which proximity of the material gifts became an important kind of companionship.[58]

A pocketbook with a series of delicate instruments inside, given by Queen Charlotte in 1781 to Mrs Delany, illustrates how small pocket accessories, cementing bonds of friendship, turned the pocket into a particularly female site for the expression and experience of sentiment. Described as 'a *most beautiful* pocket case, the outside satin work'd with gold and ornaments with gold spangles, the inside [. . .] is lined with pink sattin, and contains a knife, sizsars, pencle, rule, compas, bodkin, and more than I can say', it was sent by the queen as she knew she was about to spend the winter separated from her friend. Gifted to the accomplished needlewoman that Mrs Delany was,

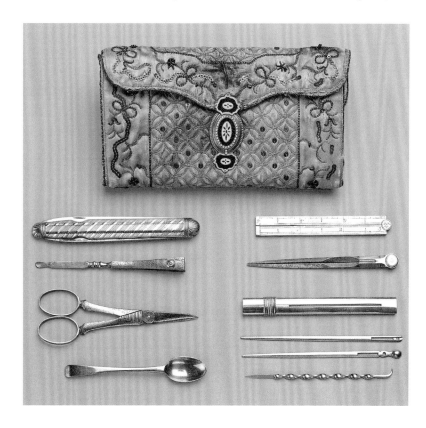

it contained small instruments that she could use for her needlework. It also contained a letter tucked inside one of its flaps instructing Mrs Delany to keep the gift in her pocket. 'I must therefore desire that Mrs Delany will wear this little Pocket-Book in order to remember at times, when no dearer Persons are present, a very sincere well wisher, Friend, and affectionate Queen, Charlotte' (fig. 146).[59] More modest but equally potent gifts were huswifs or needle-cases made with heart motifs or embroidered in messages for female friends (see fig. 99). Pockets were choice receptacles for mementos given by loved ones: worn close to the body, the gift mirrored the emotional closeness of donor and recipient. Such physical proximity is associated by anthropologists and sociologists with intimacy and intense sentimental investment.[60] At the same time, they were places of communication and exchange, a shared feminine space where friendship, bonding and female networking processes were expressed and materialised.

Eleanor Butler and Sarah Ponsonby, known by their contemporaries as the Ladies of Llangollen, were certainly no strangers to the power of making small pocketable gifts to express attachment, as in 1788, when they made an intricate gift for their patron and protector Frances, Lady Douglas.[61] Co-produced by the two women, one with her needle, the other with her pen, it was composed of a knitted purse, a pocket vellum booklet with hand-drawn illustrations and poem, and a silk portfolio embroidered with the recipient's initials, all three items intended for Frances's pocket. Something made with another woman in mind as recipient throughout the hand-making process, then pocketed by the recipient for a further period of time meant that the gift's potency could reach over a protracted time span and geographical distance.

If men's fixed pockets similarly harboured sentimental tokens, the fact that women's pockets themselves were often handmade and could be made for, and exchanged between, loved ones, lent them a particular place in fostering specifically female material expressions of sentiment and self. Mary Carryll, who lived with the Ladies of Llangollen for many years as a servant and is known to have had an affectionate relationship with them, made pockets for them, which were 'laid out for both at the bottom of their bed on New Year's day of 1790'.[62] Pockets were also made as gifts to family relatives. Little wonder that when they appeared in wills pockets were usually bequeathed to the immediate circle of female friends.[63] Mrs Mugge, who died in 1744, left Mrs Hesse Nugent of Westminster a substantial quantity of fine body linen, including her 'best pair of stays' and 'a pair of dimity pockets'.[64] As Maxine Berg notes, 'women bequeathed their clothes to their close female relations and female friends as a way of passing on something of themselves, a token and a memory'.[65] The circulation of a woman's pockets to her female friends was not the preserve only of those who wrote a will. The mysterious case of the missing Fanny Pighorn in 1831 reminds us that the practice cut across social ranks. When a bundle of clothing was found near 'a quantity of human flesh', the testimony of a witness was crucial to link the remains to Fanny. The witness came forward with a 'fellow pocket' that corresponded 'in the most minute particulars' to the one found in the bundle by the police, being 'exactly of the same size, the cloth [being] of the same quality and [both pockets being] evidently cut from the same piece'. Made for her own use by a Mrs Bell, the pockets were once a pair, separated when Mrs Bell died a few months before the case came to light, and given to two of her friends: 'one was given to Fanny Pighorn and the other came into the possession of the woman by whom it has now been produced'.[66]

Fanny and the witness had their pockets for only a few months, but gifted pockets could be kept over much longer periods. When 86-year-old Helen Craggs's room was broken into in 1808, among other things the burglar took away was a pair of pockets, which she told the court she had had for 50 years: 'they have been my property these fifty years; a lady left me them fifty years ago [. . .] I had them in the year fifty-three'. Although Helen did not state in court in what circumstances they were left to her, her precise memory of the year when they were given to her manifests how such gifts could create strong bonds of allegiance between individual women.[67] Not safeguarded in a box but put to heavy use by Jane Thomas in the last decades of the nineteenth century, another pair of pockets was embroidered with the name of Sali Jones, probably their maker (see fig. 132a).[68] How they were transferred from Sali Jones to Jane Thomas we do not know. Their much repaired backs (see fig. 132b) testify to use over an extended period of time and to the care and effort exerted to keep them in service – a possible indication of their importance to Jane.

Identity and memory

A significant number of pockets in our survey bear names and initials, as we saw in Chapter Three. Some stitched or inked initials on the pockets clearly have a utilitarian function as laundry marks (see figs 72, 75, 76b). Others display more personal marks of identity. Embroidering one's name on the front of a pocket in the manner of Sali Jones seems to have been customary in Wales. Among motifs common on samplers, such as hearts and flowers, women's names are blazoned across the fronts of five pockets surviving in different Welsh collections.[69] These strong assertions of identity and ownership are in one case elaborated: 'Anne Williams Her Po[c]ket Age [11?] Ye[a]rs old / DREW[?]DA 1845'.[70] The inscription of the names of their makers on these worked pockets situates them in the sampler tradition, indicating that they might have been made as part of the needlework training

ABOVE
147a Pair of sampler-style
pockets, mid-19th century
(L 41 cm and 40 cm).
Carmarthenshire County
Museum, CAASG.1976.3668.

of girls. If they bear strong marks of personal identity, they also highlight
how individuals worked within the particularities of a Welsh approach to
decoration that signalled a wider cultural and regional identity. At the same
time, while fitting exactly into the traditional form of the tie-on pocket seen
across the entire period, they also represent the only consistent regional
difference within Britain that has emerged from our survey (fig. 147). Such
pockets linked an expression of both individuality and communality,
connecting the individual to shared practices and visual references. They
articulate a message about the importance of community, lineage and
memory as ways of anchoring specifically female identity.

The Welsh group is distinctive but other women also inscribed their
names on their pockets. 'Elizabeth Reynolds' is dramatically placed in red and
green letters across the front of a single pocket dating from the mid-1800s
(fig. 148). Mary Hibberd's embroidered depiction of Vincenzo Lunardi's
balloon ascent on her pocket front of 1787 also conspicuously bears her full
name (see fig. 63). On a pair of embroidered linen pockets, stitched on the
front with 'G O 1774', the mark is more cryptic but nonetheless boldly places
its maker within the decorative scheme on the front rather than the back
(see frontispiece). These are significant examples of adult women validating

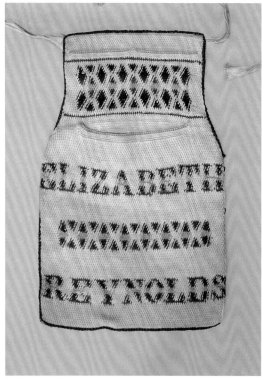

147b Sampler-style pocket, 1848 (L 40.5 cm). Amgueddfa Cymru–National Museum Wales, 59.357.

ABOVE RIGHT
148 Elizabeth Reynolds's knitted and embroidered pocket, mid-19th century (L 35 cm). York Castle Museum, YORCM: 1953.284.9.

their own work as creators with their names.[71] By stitching or inking their names onto their pockets, women claimed both authorship and ownership in powerful ways. The object might have been small but it was theirs.

Another way to personalise the pocket was through decoration. It is tempting to think that the inclusion of idiosyncratic motifs on some pockets, such as human figures, bore special meaning for their owners, though it is impossible to tell what these associations were (figs 149–50). Similarly pointing to both personal memory and permeability to the world around, recycling complexifies the small space of the pocket. A practice linked to thrift, it was also associated with sentiment, making it deeply evocative yet tantalisingly elusive.[72] Pieces of cloth associated with loved ones could be used to create fresh apparel or accessories.[73] Elizabeth Shackleton used the memorial power of recycled textiles when, in 1778, on the day of her absent son's birthday, she wrote in her diary: '[I] put on in honour of this good day [. . .] a new light brown fine cloth pincushion [made of] a piece of a coat belonging to my own Dear child, my own dear Tom, with a new blue string'.[74] Replacing absence by bodily proximity, the coat piece recycled into a pincushion became for Elizabeth a powerful material metonymy for the beloved son. Patchwork was a way in which scraps and offcuts, 'tangible fragments of the past', could be pieced

OPPOSITE, ABOVE
149 Pocket embroidered with a man and a woman, with floral motifs, mid-18th century (detail), Nottingham City Museums and Galleries, NCM 1964-35.

OPPOSITE BELOW, LEFT TO RIGHT
150 Two details on an embroidered pocket front, one of an unattached pair, early to mid-18th century. Private collection.

150a Head of a cleric.
150b Cherub.

RIGHT
151 Front of a patchwork pocket, late 18th century (L 40.5 cm). Manchester Art Gallery, MCAG.1947.1250.

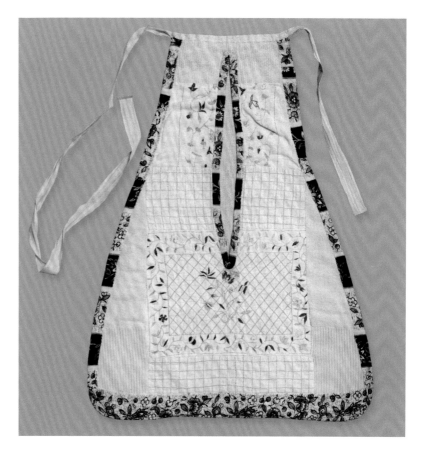

together in an object that potentially carried a whole life story or even family history over several generations.[75]

A late eighteenth-century pocket made in patchwork uses numerous pieces of cottons, linens and some older embroidered fragments accumulated over a 30-year period (fig. 151). It remains unknown what memories and histories, if any, these 22 pieces of cloth may have carried. But we do know that cloth and women's needlework were often transmitted as heirlooms in families, sometimes together with the stories associated with them (see fig. 96).[76] In a letter sent with a textile heirloom to her 9-year-old daughter Mary, who was being brought up by her father, Ellen Stock (née Weeton) explained:

> The green ribbon is part of a box-full my mother (your grandmother Weeton) once had; they were taken in a prize which my father captured during the American war [. . .] I am thus minute, my Mary, that you might know something of the history of your mother's family [. . .] the piece of patchwork is of an old quilt, I made it above 20 years ago [. . .] the Hexagon in the middle was a shred of our best bed hangings, they were chintz,

RIGHT
152 Woman's pocket made from a grenadier's cap, after 1768 (?) (L 45 cm). National Army Museum, London, NAM. 2006-08-53-1.

OPPOSITE, BELOW
153 David Morier (1705?–1770), *Grenadiers, 31st, 32nd and 33rd Regiments of Foot, 1751*, *c.*1751–60, oil on canvas (40.7 × 50.9 cm). Royal Collection Trust, RCIN 405590.

from the East Indies which my father brought home with him from one of his voyages.[77]

The heirloom is replete with family memories and tells a story of successive recycling taking place over time. This palimpsest of recycling endows each piece with a new layer of meaning. The story remains an open-ended one because we do not know what Mary Stock did with her piece of patchwork from her mother's quilt. She may herself have incorporated it into a new decorative project of her own. Recycling could be prompted by poverty and thrift, and shaped by aesthetic or practical considerations, but, at the same time, it might be grounded in the use of pieces endowed with memories of personal or family history.

The careful reassembly of the various parts of a drummer's mitre cap and regimental grey coat of the 70th Foot regiment into a functional, decorated tie-on pocket illustrates the extraordinary and ingenious efforts to which its eighteenth-century maker was committed (fig. 152). These caps were in common use across British regiments of the period (fig. 153). In this case, probably after 1768, the crown, drum and flags were removed from the front of the cap and then appliquéd to the grey coat cloth, cut to form the front of the pocket.[78] The regimental number would have been worn in battle on the reverse of the bonnet but was also removed to decorate the pocket front. It is believed that the cap belonged to drummer Daniel Shore.[79] But whoever cut and fitted this pocket together certainly lived up to the regimental Latin

motto it bears, meaning 'Hardship does not deter us'. It is difficult to imagine the undertaking of such time-consuming and dramatic reinvention of the military cap unless it carried special meaning for the maker who painstakingly reconfigured it into a functional pocket. In the process of such repurposing, a significant recontextualisation of the object has taken place – from military to civil, from male to female, from head to hips, from visible to invisible, from part of a regimental uniform to the deep idiosyncrasy of a unique object. The cap-turned-pocket, like Tom Shackleton's coat-turned-pincushion, offers an illustration of recycling bridging and subverting the gender divide. Like the pincushion worn by Elizabeth Shackleton to honour her son's absence, a woman's pocket made from a man's regimental cap may have held potent mnemonic, and even talismanic, associations. Even though its history was never committed to paper in the way Elizabeth recorded that of her pincushion, the pocket still registers something of its dense meanings. The fact that the woman might have been wearing, in the warmth of her body, the cap of a male relative adds to the possible resonance of such a rich object.

The pocket, the living and the dead

A pocket found deliberately concealed in the wall of an old house in Abingdon (Oxfordshire) draws attention to anthropological readings of pockets as the material expression of protection (see fig. 107). As we saw in Chapter Four, the hidden pocket contained a number of objects, including a baby's cap, and was itself embedded in the wall of another 'container' – namely, a house.[80] A second pocket, also containing a baby's cap and found in the walls of an Oxfordshire house, suggests a recurrent folklore practice.[81] Like many other deliberately concealed items, which were normally placed in strategic positions near openings – windows, doors or chimneys – the Abingdon pocket was placed near a threshold, in a position that articulated the inside and the outside, a point of potential penetration needing particular protection. The babies' caps found inside the walled-up pockets point to the womb-like pocket as a powerful expression of a specifically female form of containment, love and protection.

Anthropologists argue that societies and individuals give material expression to cultural and personal values by creating a space structured around an inside and an outside, and bringing some things into that space and excluding other things from it. From this viewpoint, the floral motifs embroidered on the fronts of eighteenth-century pockets flag up the openings and convey the idea of a protected space and the guardianship of this space and its contents by the wearer – who was often also the maker (figs 154–5). Pocket decorations, far from being superficial trifles, remind us that technologies of containment are always also linked to 'technologies of the self'.[82] Textile artefacts can often play a specific role in what could be termed

this anthropology of containment. Their soft but fragile feel, resembling that of skin, turns them into powerful symbols of the human body.[83]

When worn, pockets were experienced through and by the body of their wearer. It was through dynamic, embodied practices that the textures, weights and finishes of the different materials of pockets made themselves evident.[84] Leather felt different to the touch from silk, dimity or wool. Drawing on phenomenological notions of the body image that may incorporate inanimate objects, we can see that various aspects of the user's experience of the pocket meant pockets were part of the embodied experience of the wearer, in something of the same way as the blind person's cane becomes an extension of their sentient body. With their rounded uterine shapes, and feeling soft and warm when worn, they were almost organic extensions of the self – something reflected in the popular idioms used in our Old Bailey cases.[85] 'From her person', the wording of indictments describing possessions taken from the pocket, frames a host of expressions, such as 'taken from me', 'under my thumb', 'I had about me', 'under my head' which, in women's own words, seem to elide body, pocket and person into one.[86] The testimonies also record women's extended bodily awareness when they declared they 'felt the weight' of something in their pockets or the tug of somebody pulling at it, or else 'missed the weight' of the absent contents when their pockets had been picked.[87] Women's hands feeling their own pockets, clasping them, checking and touching their contents, were instinctive gestures that they had unwittingly integrated into everyday embodied routines.[88]

The interconnectedness between material things and bodily experience is sometimes manifest in surviving pockets. A very well-crafted damask pocket, lined in chamois leather, with four internal pockets, allows for the separation and protection of its contents and the ease and comfort of its user (see fig. 112). The maker deliberately put the smoother side of the leather where the most sensitive part of the hand, the palm and fingers, would touch. The pocket was strong but also soft and warm to the touch. Probably bespoke, it orchestrated the smooth interaction of the hand with the objects inside it, skin against skin. Putting one's hand into one's pocket was an intimate gesture that was wholly dependent on touch, a sense identified by some as bearing most heavily on the individual's sense of self.[89] As material extensions of the self, sheltering tokens of affection given by friends, relatives or lovers, pockets were sites where self and other met in intimate contact. They allowed the individual to keep cherished objects close at hand, and, more metaphorically, they were also places where the traditionally distinct categories of subjects and objects met, where inanimate keepsakes could become personified emblems of their donors, and pockets, in turn, could become embodiments of their owners.

'This Pocket was used in the year 1733 by Miss Rolland of Burnside by Dumferline C Anderson' can be read on a small card formerly stitched to a pocket front – a reminder that, as faithful companions to a woman's life over the years, as worn apparel, pockets readily accommodated memory (fig. 156). The pull or stretch of the cloth in some places, the wear and tear in others, as well as the traces of soiling where the hand rubbed, all register traces of the body of a pocket's wearer, just as the construction and repairs show the hand of the maker and mender. In the way an old shoe or a coat can bear the imprint of the user's body and movements, so too the sensory context of the use of pockets can help us further understand their emotionally charged functions. Relatives and friends, just like the person who wrote on a piece of paper and then stitched it to the front of Miss Rolland's pocket, might have preserved pockets to retain something of the memory of their former owner.

In 1805 William Cantell, a recently widowed carpenter, was ill in bed when his charwoman robbed him of his dead wife's apparel.[90] The testimony given in court reveals that, contrary to traditional practice, Cantell had not distributed his dead wife's clothing for sale or to the servants or their daughter. William had kept it, packed in two boxes and drawers, locked in 'a private room where [his] wife died'. Since her death, access to the 'private room' had been fiercely guarded by Cantell, who kept the key under his pillow and entrusted it to 'no person in the world', not even his own daughter 'except somebody went with her'. In the room were clothes he wanted 'to keep as long as [he] live[d]', among which were 'a cap, a pocket and two pairs of stockings and a handkerchief'. These items would have held only limited monetary value, but worn close to his late wife's body, for William they carried strong emotional value. From the warmth of the body, they would have retained her smell past her death, preserving something of her living presence within their fibres long after she was gone.[91] Another heart-broken widower, Edmund Harrold, took things even further. In the same diary that he used to record the particularities of his very active sex life with his wife, he noted at her death in 1712 how he had made for himself a mourning suit out of his late wife's 'black mantue and petticoat' which he would 'wear [. . .] for her sake'.[92] Recycled and reinhabited by Edmund, the clothes were brought back to life, the inherent sensuality of cloth a medium for sensory communion between the living and the dead.

One extraordinary extant pocket speaks powerfully of the mnemonic power of pockets. It was made by an inmate of the Duke Street Prison in Glasgow and given to Annie Stirling, the governor's wife, in 1851. The small linen pocket still contains locks of human hair, and human hair is used on

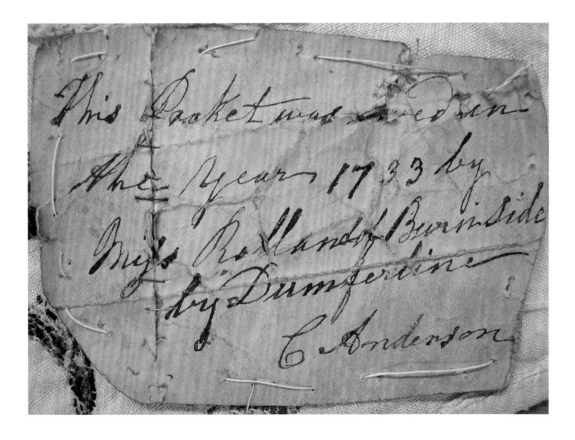

157 Miniature pocket, made by Margaret Deas, embroidered with and containing human hair, 1851 (detail). Private collection.

the front as embroidery thread (fig. 157; see also fig. 140). Embroidered with the full name of the maker, Margaret Deas, several hearts and the motto 'forGet Me not', this little object gives striking expression to personal identity and sentiment. The particular setting in which the pocket was made is also remarkable. Margaret was confined in a prison that implemented Jeremy Bentham's panoptical theory, with its 'rotunda for the governor's house' and its '120 cells so arranged as to be under the ad libitum view of the governor and to afford the means of complete classification and seclusion'.[93] The making of a pocket in such a system of oppressive scopic control would have been freighted with complex implications. A pocket, even small, represented a space secluded from the disciplinary regime of transparency in the prison. It embodied the possibility of an escape into a place of one's own.

This small item also fits into the specifically female sociability and networking practices that pockets articulated, both the contents of pockets and the pockets themselves being exchanged between female friends and relatives during their lifetime and at death. Hair worked into mottos and decorative motifs in jewellery and other accessories had long been part of the material practices of both mourning and sentiment when the pocket was made in 1851.[94] We do not know the exact circumstances in which this pocket was made and what motivated Margaret Deas's plea to be remembered by Annie Stirling. The use of a woman's actual hair to inscribe her full name onto

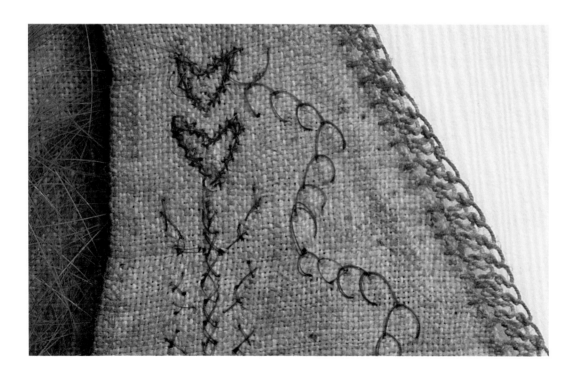

the front of the pocket makes the call to be remembered both evocative and compelling. Margaret Deas's name, stitched in hair, positions the pocket as both object and subject. A reliquary for Margaret's hair and skill, the pocket becomes almost a magical object, through which her ghostly presence is made palpable: 'Remember me', says her pocket. One of a kind in our survey, the pocket nonetheless sheds light on other less distinctive pockets and their role as embodiments of memory and identity. Any act of making an object that may potentially outlive the maker is also an act against oblivion.[95] The distinctiveness of a binding or shape, the particularity of a stitch or a darn, the unique creases and strains imprinted in cloth from wear – what tailors call 'memory' – the distinctive ability of textile to retain intimate sensory traces of the body, all these mean that any pocket could embody its maker or wearer, turning it into a unique material register of the self.[96]

* * *

There were many ways in which a woman invested meaning in her pocket and its contents. Through their associations with emotional attachments and personal memory, tie-on pockets provided a fecund space for the exploration of the owner's interiority and sense of privacy. At the intersection of personal and collective practices, they provided women with a means to situate themselves and anchor their identity in relation to loved ones, family and community. In a context that afforded women few such spaces, pockets were therefore powerful tools for women's experience of self. At the same time, because surviving pockets carry the marks of the bodies that wore and used them, they are a record of these women's lives and stories, sometimes the only one that has survived. These stories are rich and complex but often elusive, resisting definitive interpretation, keeping a share of their secrets.

'this is the sort of pocket our great grandmothers used to wear'

The Demise and Afterlife of Tie-On Pockets

For a book devoted to a full story 'in the round' of the tie-on pocket, it is appropriate that we end by tracing its demise. While it is undeniable that the everyday use of the detachable pocket declined and disappeared between the last decades of the nineteenth century and the first of the twentieth, like many other sartorial practices and common habits, it had no tidy end point, just as it had no exact start date. As we track the complex process of the object's descent into obsolescence, we find a tension between the apparent dimming of its popularity towards the end of the nineteenth century and numerous individual instances of its persistence in practice. The coincidental appearance of handbags around the same time makes it appealing to believe that the latter quickly replaced the tie-on pocket, or that the pocket somehow morphed into the bag. However, as the book has consistently shown, actual sartorial practices disrupt such neat narratives.

By the mid-nineteenth century, it had crept into common parlance that the pocket was looking backwards rather than forwards. However, the case of Yorkshire woman Mary Graves, who lost her purse containing a considerable amount of money as she went home on a London omnibus in 1858, shows the contradictions often apparent at this time.[1] Mary alleged that her purse had been stolen when the accused, Ann Smith, seated next to her, cut a hole in her pocket 'with a sharp instrument'. In court, Mary produced her 'old-fashioned double' pocket (meaning probably an attached pair) to show the actual hole.

Upon seeing the pockets, the lawyer responded 'Why, this is the sort of pocket our great grandmothers used to wear'. He asked: 'How old is it?' Mary drew 'much laughter' when she replied 'I dare say not quite so old as you are.' When the presiding magistrate joined in, 'Perhaps not so old, surely not so deep', more laughter followed. Despite the light relief, the hearing dragged on late and the jury was dismissed after failing to reach a verdict. Her story indeed invites more than one conclusion. From one viewpoint, we could see it as an indication of the decline of the pocket: in the eyes of the lawyers, at least, Mary's pocket was outdated, an amusing spectacle of anachronism. From another, however, the story confirms that pockets persisted, Mary using hers as a matter of course and trusting it to keep her money safe on the omnibus. Imagined by the male lawyers as obsolete when it was actually still in use, Mary's pocket exemplifies the capacity to register different, sometimes conflicting meanings, and underlines a gendered experience of change and continuity.

The demise of tie-on pockets was neither swift nor simple. Protracted over time, their disappearance was not confined to a single downward trajectory and demotion into use only by the poor and the provincial. Thirty years after Yorkshire Mary's experience on the London omnibus, metropolitan Frances Maria Wright, a bank clerk's wife, was wearing a tie-on pocket in 1888. Unbeknownst to her husband, she used it to stash the large sum of £17 10s.[2] Surviving pockets themselves confirm use in the late nineteenth century and into the twentieth. One is recorded as worn by its owner up until 1902 (see fig. 36),[3] and Lady Ponsonby's travelling pocket is known to have been used in South America in the 1930s, indicating an even later date of recorded use among the elite for this evolved form of the tie-on pocket (see fig. 126).[4] Nevertheless, something in the life of the pocket began to change in the mid-nineteenth century. As Mary Graves's court case shows, a sign of perceived obsolescence was its association with grandmothers and earlier generations. In 1883 one author cherished the memory of the grandmother 'dearly beloved of our childish recollections', who went about 'nullifying mamma's punishments by surreptitious gifts and goodies', such as sugar-plums, taking the treats out of her reticule 'or the more mysterious recesses of her unfathomable pocket'.[5]

The most extended account of a grandmother and her pockets, however, comes in Anna Maria Hall's *Grandmamma's Pockets* (1849). In the story, all three generations – Annie, her mother and her grandmother – wear pockets, but Grandmamma's are the biggest and best. Her 'Majestic pockets' and all the substantial well-made things inside are recounted in extensive detail to reinforce the values of hard-wearing things for practical women performing their proper domestic duties.[6] Unexpectedly, Hall inserts an extended dream sequence into the narrative, in which the pockets come alive. As the pockets

159 Thomas Webster RA (1800–1886), *Going to the Fair*, 1837, oil on canvas (55.9 × 76.1 cm). Victoria and Albert Museum, London, FA.220[O].

seem to 'swell and heave', they disgorge various figures, setting alternately good and bad examples to the dreaming Annie. The narrative relies on juxtaposing the left and right pockets and forces that repel and attract in equal measure to demonstrate to the dreamer her own failings and the means of amending her wayward behaviour. Towards the end of the dream comes an 'incongruous multitude' of everyday things that women routinely carried in their pockets, but they are unnervingly transformed and animated. The nutmeg grater began 'grating of itself what seemed cart-loads of ginger upon acres of pin-cushions; the purse became an hammock, and the money therein was transformed into frying pans [. . .] the bodkin marched out of the needle-book, and commanded a regiment of pins'.[7] This last scene serves as a kind of allegory of chaos and abundance, a clash between disorder and order in a series of anxieties about material things. Refusing to represent the grandmother as a saccharine little old lady handing out treats, Hall's work can be placed in a tradition of moralising and instructive literature for children, but at the same time it conjures up the material world in the form of the pockets and their contents in rare, almost graphic detail. Investing the pockets with a compelling story-telling capacity, Hall makes them vividly present rather than merely remembered, but at the mid-century she may have anticipated their loss or demise and intended her story as a call to arms in their defence. Ambivalent and liminal, Hall's pockets are looking forwards and backwards at the same time.

Relatively discreet in eighteenth-century paintings, tie-on pockets became more visible in paintings of the early and mid-nineteenth century.

160 Pocket, late 19th century, found inside a Victorian sofa in the early 21st century (L 34 cm). Private collection.

Worn by children and other guileless characters, they increasingly feature in scenes that are lit by the warm glow of a rural, simple life beyond the reach of the impending shadows of industrialisation and modernisation.[8] *The Hop Garland* (1834) by William Frederick Witherington RA situates the pocket worn by a small girl in a hop field, which is depicted as an indeterminate rural place outside the modern world. An older girl winds a garland of fresh hops onto her straw hat and a boy, at rest on hop baskets, looks on smiling (fig. 158). In his indulgent scene, the painter imagines a place and era when labour was wholesome in the fresh air and children had time to play and enjoy childish pleasures; this idyllic picture is in marked contrast to contemporary concerns over child labour in the enclosed, dangerous mills and factories.[9] Wearing the pocket loosely and forwards over a simple pinafore, the healthy rosy-cheeked girl appears the image of candour, far removed from the realities of toil or the urban dangers of chancers and pickpockets.[10] Set in a pleasant, green land that is populated with kindly adults, pockets become affectionate imaginings, free of their more contentious status as sites of disorder, sex or subversion. In Thomas Webster's *Going to the Fair* (1837), another young girl is shown, this time wearing a disproportionately large adult pocket, as she sets off excitedly on her hobby horse for the fair in the village below, in high expectation of carrying treats home in her pocket (fig. 159).[11] Equally benign and generous is the pocket in the centre of George Smith's painting *Temptation: A Fruit Stall* (1850), where a young child eagerly awaits the coins its mother is reaching for in her patchwork pocket (see fig. 1). The old woman's stall sets out the objects of desire, while the colourful pocket provides the hinge for the whole pictorial narrative. With its array of pieced and colourful printed fabrics, the pocket serves as an emblem of thrift and an indication that virtuous economy holds the promise of small innocent treats. In an age of seemingly excessive consumption, the well-regulated pocket takes centre stage to signal the imagined virtues of the past, when pleasures were simple and satisfaction was at hand.

Although still visible on canvas, pockets, in practice, had reached tipping point and were increasingly discarded. Individual obsolescence can be read in some pockets, such as one with its top loop broken. This may have been the

161 Embroidered pocket, early to mid-18th century, re-used as part of a 'Dolly Varden' fancy-dress costume, late 19th century (L 68.8cm, including 'handle'). Royal Albert Memorial Museum, Exeter, EXEMS 50/1943/34/1.

last straw for its owner, who decided to discard it rather than repair it, and it was relegated to stuffing for a sofa at some time at the end of the nineteenth-century (fig. 160). The end of pockets had its own complex dynamic, however. When we read that twelve pockets were part of a large consignment of old clothes 'condemned' in November 1919 by Christ's Hospital school in London, we might think the wardrobe purge was indicative of a definite rejection.[12] But this was not the end of the school's take-up of the tie-on pocket for their girl pupils: it came to serve as part of the school's deliberately anachronistic uniform.[13] Within partially enclosed communities seeking to express and maintain their distinctiveness, the pocket sometimes became a kind of badge, mustering an element of community heritage or folk memory. One such example occurred among the fish women of Cullercoats, a fishing village near Newcastle, whose working costume from the nineteenth century to the late twentieth included a pocket or 'money apron' made of 'any old cloth' worn over their skirts, recalling the early nineteenth-century fishwives of Billingsgate.[14]

A similar survival in this sartorial afterlife and narrative of resistance may be seen in the decorated 'beady pockets' that continued to be worn until recent times by women in the travelling community in Ireland.[15]

The end could mark a new beginning. Eight years before the novel *Grandmamma's Pockets* was published, Charles Dickens's *Barnaby Rudge* appeared (1841). The novel, set in 1780, was very popular, especially its character Dolly Varden, a locksmith's daughter much loved by Victorian readers and represented in several 'portraits' by William Powell Frith in the 1840s.[16] The popularity of the fictional character came to a peak after Dickens's death in 1869 and the sale of his property, including a Dolly Varden portrait, triggering a widespread fashion for 'Dolly Varden' hats and dresses, and the popularity of polka dances in the 1870s.[17] A pocket survives from this fashion that shows how problematic it can be to pinpoint when, or even if, an object has reached its end (fig. 161).[18] The life story of this pocket began in the early to mid-eighteenth century when it was made. Skilfully embroidered in coloured crewel work, it was very much a typical eighteenth-century embroidered tie-on pocket of its time. In the late nineteenth century, however, the pocket's physical integrity was vandalised in a misguided attempt to create a 'Dolly Varden' style bag, probably as part of a fancy-dress costume.[19] Its opening was firmly stitched shut, the ties removed and the whole turned upside down and attached to bands of similar embroidered fabric. At this point, it had reached an ending, in its original capacity at least. Yet at the same time, it was also reinvented into something new as part of the popular 'Dolly Varden' fashion. Deprived of its utility as a tie-on pocket, this 'old-fashioned' pocket was transformed into an elite fancy-dress accessory.[20] The transformations and reversals within its biography saw yet another beginning when, preserved in this mutilated state, it eventually came into the public domain of a museum collection.

The same new chapter opened in the life of many of the pockets discussed in this book when they became museum objects. They were assimilated into a cultural realm, a state of affairs unimaginable to their previous makers and users. If this marked an ending of sorts – the end of their lives as everyday utilitarian objects – it was also the beginning of a new life in which their original utility was exchanged for a kind of cultural and pedagogical utility as exemplars of skills and tools for understanding the past. At a time when pockets were still in use, it was the eighteenth-century embroidered examples that first moved into museum collections, such as the Victoria and Albert Museum in London.[21] Their decorative needlework was their chief value, and made them of interest to the Circulation department of the museum, where some of the earliest collected pockets were billeted. The department, active until 1976, was responsible for circulating suitable museum objects around the country. It often sought embroidered textiles, sometimes pieces or fragments, to satisfy popular interest in English domestic embroidery, which it lent to schools, colleges and other museums as examples of good workmanship and design.[22] The small size of pockets made them obvious candidates for this new life as teaching aids, and several pockets travelled from London in this way, accruing different usefulness, relevance and meaning on their journey.[23] It took longer for undecorated specimens to enter museum collections, but ultimately they did, helped by the acquisition policies of museums with different missions and focus.[24]

It is a measure of how pockets retained an uncertain status that museum taxonomy shifts, classifications varying from 'waist pockets', 'bag pockets' and 'hanging pockets' to 'dress pockets' or simply 'pockets'. In one case the same pair of pockets has been recorded under a succession of five different names since its acquisition in 1910.[25] In some cases, pockets were placed by museums in their bags and accessories collections.[26] Some pockets, registered on arrival into smaller collections, were not fully accessioned, suggesting that they were not a priority call on museum time. They were in the ledger but not in the mind. Outside museums, those individual pockets still lovingly preserved in private hands, their biographies often well known and inherited as family lore, are assured continuity and a special significance. Evidence of pockets' enduring appeal also comes from the art market, where at auction they can fetch considerable sums. All these various players may assign to surviving pockets different cultural, sentimental or monetary values, but collectively they now safeguard an irreplaceable material legacy for future generations.

The fullest possible engagement with objects is crucial to enriching historical understanding. Like Laurel Thatcher Ulrich, we believe attention to material things 'can reveal connections among people, processes, and forms of enquiry that might otherwise remain unnoticed' and 'uncover what would be undetectable lives' otherwise.[27] We started this book with James Deetz's call to historians to remember 'small things forgotten' and we end it with the little pocket made in 1851 by prisoner Margaret Deas and embroidered in human hair with the entreaty 'forGet Me not' (see figs 140, 157).[28] Writing into the artefact the lasting evidence of her skills and aspiration, Margaret created the pocket as a personal act, a plea she sent to another woman to be held in mind; but by its entreaty to be remembered, spelt out uncannily in stitches of hair, it still speaks today. In preserving part of Margaret's life, it articulates how material things can carry and document acts and ideas of the past – a potent reminder of their capacity to help recover obscure lives from oblivion.

APPENDIX
Pockets in the Old Bailey

Cases selected from Tim Hitchcock, Robert Shoemaker, Clive Emsley, Sharon Howard, Jamie McLaughlin et al., *The Old Bailey Proceedings Online, 1674–1913,* www.oldbaileyonline.org, version 7.0, 24 March 2012.

We selected 572 cases between 1676 and 1904 with an association between women and pockets recorded in the indictments or testimonies or both. The cases include pockets being worn and also unworn pockets – for example, those stored or for sale. Our primary focus being the pockets themselves (and not trends in crime or punishment), we included cases regardless of the final verdict. Not all cases contained sufficient internal evidence to establish that the pockets in question were tie-on pockets and not any other type. The cases that did not are excluded from our statistical analysis. But all 572 cases have contributed to our study as background to practices and vocabulary associated with women's pockets in general. The cases are listed below by decade. For the period between April 1674 and 1698, published collections of the cases survive for the vast majority of sessions; between 1699 and 1714 published editions are missing for two-thirds of the sessions, and there are three years for which no *Proceedings* survive – 1701, 1705 and 1706. (See 'Published History of the Proceedings: Early History, 1678–1729', www.oldbaileyonline.org/static/Publishinghistory.jsp#a1678-1729.)

1670–79
t16760117-6
t16770601-2

1680–89
t16800707-9
t16810526-0
t16810706-1
t16820224-4
t16820426-2
t16820601-4
t16820601a-1
t16820601a-4
t16830418-5
t16840116-21
t16861013-28
t16880831-12

1690–99
t16920115-6
t16920831-13
t16930426-25
t16930531-9
t16930906-13
t16940524-8
t16950508-7
t16950828-28
t16951203-14
t16951203-42
t16961014-12
t16980720-66

1710–19
t17160517-1
t17160906-20

t17161010-24
t17161105-8
t17161105-29
t17161105-30
t17161105-31
t17161105-49
t17161105-75
t17170111-34
t17170111-41
t17170227-19
t17170227-20
t17170227-47
t17170227-54
t17170501-9
t17170501-15
t17170501-34
t17170606-23
t17171016-9
t17171204-24
t17171204-43
t17180110-55
t17180227-33
t17180423-22
t17180423-28
t17180423-42
t17180423-43
t17180423-45
t17180530-2
t17180530-8
t17180530-18
t17180530-19
t17180910-16
t17180910-75
t17181015-14
t17181015-17
t17190115-43
t17190514-20
t17190708-44
t17190708-57
t17191204-4
t17191204-38

1720–29
t17200115-25
t17200303-23
t17200427-33
t17200427-66
t17200602-13
t17200712-37
t17201012-5
t17201012-21
t17201207-10
t17210301-27
t17210419-29
t17210419-51
t17210525-33
t17210712-52
t17211206-43
t17220112-40
t17220228-11
t17220228-12
t17220228-34

t17220228-59
t17220704-69
t17220907-40
t17220907-80
t17221010-18
t17230710-16
t17230828-14
t17240117-38
t17240117-44
t17240226-3
t17240415-8
t17240415-10
t17240708-37
t17240812-21
t17240812-27
t17240812-28
t17241204-34
t17250115-2
t17250513-12
t17250630-28
t17250630-32
t17250827-15
t17251208-35
t17251208-52
t17260114-8
t17260114-32
t17260302-5
t17260302-8
t17260302-22
t17260302-59
t17270517-37
t17271206-21
t17280228-1
t17280228-43
t17280501-41
t17280605-14
t17281204-64
t17290709-4
t17291203-5
t17291203-8

1730–39
t17300704-23
t17301014-71
t17301204-9
t17310428-16
t17310602-36
t17310908-8
t17310908-9
t17310908-51
t17311208-5
t17320223-1
t17320223-10
t17320705-6
t17320906-26
t17320906-27
t17321011-31
t17321011-45
t17321206-38
t17340227-52
t17341204-54
t17350116-6

t17350702-4
t17350702-6
t17350702-10
t17350911-51
t17351210-55
t17360115-21
t17360610-23
t17370216-20
t17371012-33
t17380222-6
t17381011-18
t17391017-16
t17391205-37

1740–49
t17401015-53
t17410405-31
t17410701-4
t17410701-19
t17410828-11
t17410828-29
t17411014-45
t17420115-9
t17420714-11
t17420909-33
t17430519-6
t17431207-2
t17431207-4
t17440113-13
t17440404-27
t17441205-41
t17480224-7
t17490222-9
t17490411-24

1750–59
t17500425-60
t17500711-46
t17500912-47
t17501205-57
t17530221-6
t17530221-47
t17530221-51
t17530718-36
t17531024-38
t17540424-60
t17550515-30
t17550702-27
t17550702-29
t17560528-12
t17570914-50
t17580913-12
t17580913-13
t17591024-12

1760–69
t17600227-3
t17600521-17
t17600521-25
t17610225-17
t17640222-22
t17640502-58

t17641017-20
t17650417-5
t17650417-22
t17650710-56
t17660409-58
t17661217-34
t17670115-9
t17670218-36
t17670218-38
t17670715-3
t17670715-38
t17670715-54
t17680224-65
t17680518-19
t17690405-10
t17690628-16
t17690628-37

1770–79
t17700221-30
t17701024-51
t17701205-3
t17710116-18
t17710703-57
t17710911-34
t17710911-40
t17730626-31
t17730626-33
t17730626-45
t17730707-1
t17730908-87
t17740907-23
t17750111-27
t17750712-40
t17751018-31
t17751018-42
t17760710-68
t17770115-13
t17770409-14
t17771015-35
t17771015-51
t17780429-40
t17780429-103
t17780603-48
t17780715-19
t17780916-63
t17791020-9

1780–89
t17800112-15
t17800112-28
t17800628-51
t17800913-56 A
t17800913-56 B
t17801018-10
t17801206-25
t17810110-4
t17810222-17
t17810222-44
t17810530-40
t17810711-30
t17810912-68

t17820410-35
t17820410-54
t17820703-2
t17820703-4
t17820703-38
t17821016-20
t17830115-14
t17830226-7
t17830226-73
t17830723-17
t17830723-94
t17831210-2
t17840114-54
t17840114-72
t17840114-76
t17840225-35
t17840421-24
t17840526-45
t17840707-76
t17841208-31
t17850406-61
t17850629-72
t17851019-2
t17860222-88
t17860426-4
t17860531-8
t17860531-78
t17861025-86
t17861025-117
t17861213-114
t17870418-67
t17880227-10
t17880625-1
t17880625-2
t17880910-40
t17890114-42

1790–99
t17900424-68
t17900526-50
t17900915-45
t17900915-51
t17900915-79
t17910720-11
t17910720-27
t17910914-21
t17930109-1
t17930220-2
t17930220-7
t17930220-38
t17930220-76
t17930529-30
t17930911-31
t17930911-101
t17931030-11
t17940115-7
t17940219-62
t17940219-74
t17940430-66
t17940716-69
t17940716-70
t17940917-24

t17940917-67
t17941111-36
t17941208-22
t17950916-2
t17950916-8
t17950916-31
t17960406-20
t17960914-103
t17961026-4
t17961130-35
t17961130-36
t17961130-40
t17970111-51
t17970531-41
t17971025-5
t17971025-18
t17980110-33
t17980110-43
t17980214-25
t17980912-37
t17980912-39
t17981024-16
t17981205-34
t17990508-22
t17990508-30
t17990619-53
t17990911-18

1800–09
t18000115-40
t18000115-51
t18000402-4
t18000402-14
t18000402-59
t18000709-13
t18001029-6
t18001029-31
t18010218-17
t18010415-51
t18010916-59
t18010916-109
t18011202-37
t18020217-28
t18020217-65
t18020428-54
t18020428-90
t18020918-12
t18020918-32
t18020918-50
t18021027-102
t18021201-11
t18021201-16
t18021201-71
t18021201-74
t18030420-36
t18030525-7
t18030525-68
t18030914-52
t18030914-85
t18031130-47
t18040215-22
t18040704-14

t18041024-36
t18041205-2
t18041205-41
t18050529-5
t18050710-17
t18050710-41
t18050710-42
t18050918-50
t18060115-28
t18060219-41
t18060917-16
t18060917-18
t18060917-19
t18061203-52
t18070218-37
t18070218-47
t18070408-21
t18070408-42
t18070513-3
t18070513-49
t18070701-42
t18070701-56
t18070916-61
t18070916-67
t18070916-91
t18071028-2
t18071028-46
t18071202-12
t18080113-50
t18080113-65
t18080217-25
t18080217-71
t18080406-35
t18080601-26
t18080713-19
t18080914-41
t18090215-102
t18090412-44
t18090626-5
t18090626-11
t18091101-24
t18091206-31

1810–19
t18100110-39
t18100110-67
t18100221-37
t18100221-38
t18100718-27
t18100919-51
t18101031-25
t18101205-98
t18110109-7
t18110403-6
t18110403-40
t18110710-7
t18111204-57
t18120115-108
t18120916-148
t18130217-13
t18131201-90
t18140112-38

t18140420-143
t18140420-168
t18140525-44
t18150621-9
t18160110-25
t18160214-43
t18160529-77
t18160918-42
t18170115-138
t18170521-9
t18170702-11
t18170702-83
t18170917-1
t18170917-28
t18170917-162
t18170917-176
t18180114-195
t18180401-133
t18180506-120
t18180909-203
t18190915-52
t18190915-93

1820–29
t18210606-172
t18210912-76
t18210912-116
t18220220-21
t18220522-65
t18230115-100
t18230409-66
t18230625-42
t18231203-107
t18240114-148
t18240114-176
t18240916-262
t18250113-11
t18251027-85
t18260914-62
t18261026-150
t18270405-26
t18270913-349
t18271025-166
t18271025-236
t18280110-33
t18280110-40
t18280911-89
t18281204-76
t18281204-243

1830–39
t18300415-157
t18300527-79
t18301028-223
t18310407-135
t18310407-203
t18310630-244
t18310630-326
t18311020-85
t18311201-210
t18320105-22
t18320705-175

t18320906-220
t18320906-446
t18330103-165
t18330411-59
t18330704-30
t18330704-123
t18330905-50
t18340220-75
t18340904-79
t18340904-227
t18341016-10
t18341124-10
t18350105-371
t18350921-2024
t18350921-2049
t18351123-119
t18351214-273
t18360713-1445
t18361024-2289
t18361128-186
t18370508-1159
t18370814-1957
t18370918-2212
t18371127-112
t18380514-1199
t18380820-1831
t18380917-2185
t18390617-1746
t18390617-2002
t18390916-2425

1840–49
t18400106-523
t18400106-536
t18410510-1361
t18411129-285
t18430403-1198
t18430821-2249
t18431211-312
t18440408-1178
t18440819-2138
t18450407-970
t18460105-409
t18460511-1179
t18470510-1271
t18480515-1280

1850–59
t18500204-435
t18500204-479
t18500506-943
t18500610-1101
t18500819-1467
t18500819-1511
t18501216-279
t18510407-855
t18510512-1185
t18510512-1213
t18510616-1396
t18510707-1470
t18510707-1487
t18520105-199

t18530131-286
t18560514-541
t18561215-140
t18580222-327

1860–69
t18600102-142
t18610408-328
t18641024-981
t18660813-720

1870–79
t18700228-278

1880–89
t18870627-714
t18881022-977
t18891021-859

1890–1904
t18960420-366
t19040208-196

NOTES

Introduction

Title quotation: Deetz 1977, 161.

1   'Lucy Locket lost her pocket, / Kitty Fisher found it; / Not a penny was there in it, / Only ribbon round it.' Opie and Opie 1951/1997, 328.

2   *Mist's Weekly Journal* (London), 22 May 1725.

3   The early connoisseurial interest in pockets has often focused on their embroidery (see Hughes n.d.), and embroidered examples were the first to be acquired by museums; see the Conclusion of this book, pp. 216–23). Embroidered examples have tended to be the most referenced and illustrated: for instance, Burrows Swan 1977; Reiter-Weissman and Lavitt, 1987; Beck 1992: Marsh 2006. For the more general idea of 'reading' artefacts see Prown 1980; Prown 1982. More recently, and specifically on dress, see Mida and Kim 2015; Edwards 2017.

4   On cotton as a global fibre see Lemire 2003a; Lemire 2003b; Riello and Parthasarathi 2009; Riello and Tirthankar 2009; Riello 2013. On marcella see Chapter Two, pp. 57, 79.

5   On recent contributions to the history of the industrial development of textiles see Styles 2016; Styles 2018.

6   Reddy 1986, 282.

7   For an account of these tensions see Styles 1998. For an example of a material culture approach to dress see Küchler and Miller 2005.

8   Deetz 1977; Weiner and Schneider 1989; Mackenzie 1991; Tilley 1991; Miller 1998; Tilley 1999; Ingold 2000; Tilley 2006; Ingold 2010; Ingold 2013.

9   Object-centred scholarship first developed in the USA – in particular within art history and folk history: Prown 1980; Prown 1982; Smart-Martin and Garrison 1997; Glassie 1999; Thatcher Ulrich 2001. Social and economic historians have also started increasingly to turn to objects: Richardson 2004; Riello 2006; Styles 2007; Brook 2008; Harvey 2009; Pennell 2009; Trentmann 2009; Hamling and Richardson 2010; Anishanslin 2016; Richardson, Hamling and Gaimster 2016; Hamling and

Richardson 2017. A similar material turn has taken place in other areas of academia. In philosophy see, for instance, Dagognet 1989; Pol-Droit 2005; Sennett 2009. In literary studies see Fumerton 1991; Jones and Stallybrass 2000; Batchelor and Kaplan 2007; Goodman and Norberg 2007; Goggin and Tobin 2009. Bruno Latour and Bill Brown have been influential in this material turn: Brown 2001–2; Brown 2003; Latour 2004; Latour 2005a; Latour 2005b.

10   Hamling and Richardson 2010, 9.

11   Examples of connoisseurial or descriptive approaches are Hughes n.d.; Foster 1982; Baumgarten, Watson and Carr 1999; Marsh 2006. Examples of social historians' work touching on pockets or their contents are Cobb 1978; Bayard 1989; Farge 2003; Palk 2003; Tickell 2015; Tickell 2018. These studies rarely mention pockets as objects. Literary scholars who have shown an interest in pockets similarly focus more on their representation than on their materiality, usually considering pockets in general, whether male or female, attached or detached: Razzall 2006; Carlson 2007; Carlson 2008; Carlson 2009; Todd Matthews 2010; Myers 2014. The rare examples of object-attentive scholarship that contextualise pockets are Thatcher Ulrich 1991; Van de Krol 1994; Baumgarten 2002; Unsworth 2017.

12   Thatcher Ulrich 1991, 34.

13   See, for instance, Stewart 1993; Mack 2007; Findlen 2013, 15.

14   'Auguries of Innocence' in Blake 1979, 209.

15   On the global histories of material culture see, for instance, Lemire 2015; Anishanslin 2016; Gerritsen and Riello 2016; Lemire 2016. See also Brook 2008; Findlen 2013.

16   Our work was made possible by funding provided by the Arts and Humanities Research Council in 2003–6. The research resulted in an exhibition, 'Pockets of History', at the Museum of Costume, Bath (now the Fashion Museum Bath) in 2006–7 and a catalogue of the same name, Burman and Denbo 2006. It also resulted in an online database, which can be found at www.vads.ahds.ac.uk/collections/pocketsofhistory. See also Burman and White 2007. Both authors have also carried out other work, see Burman 2002; Fennetaux 2008.

17   On the practical constraints of working

with objects, see Steele 1998; Taylor 1998; Gerritsen and Riello 2015, 8. See also Brooks 2000; Hayward and Kramer 2007. For an account of trends in the study of dress in museums see Tarrant 1999; Taylor 2002; Taylor 2004. For more recent developments in the field see Mida and Kim 2015; Nicklas and Pollen 2015; Bide 2017.

18   In many cases, firm identification was provided by exemplary museum documentation; in others documentation was limited or non-existent and we used visual identification.

19   Deetz 1977, 161.

20   The correlation between actual things and their names in written documents is a notorious difficulty of working on material culture: Adamson 2009. On the particular difficulties for textiles and dress see Montgomery 1984, pp. xii–xiii.

21   For example, Spufford 1984; Weatherill 1988; Overton et al. 2004.

22   On the representation of 'common people' in paintings in the pre-Victorian and early Victorian periods see Solkin 2008.

23   Shesgreen 2002, 148.

24   Our research was greatly facilitated by the digitised version of *The Proceedings*, https://www.oldbaileyonline.org (last accessed, 12 June 2018). A full list of the cases used is given in the Appendix, pp. 224–5.

25   See www.oldbaileyonline.org/static/Value.jsp (last accessed, 12 June 2018).

26   On jean (a linen or cotton twilled cloth) and denim see Montgomery 1984, 216, 271; Gorguet-Ballesteros 1994, 24–41.

27   Naji and Douny 2009, 420.

28   Unsworth 2017.

29   Earle notes the presence of pairs of pockets in colonial inventories around 1650: Earle 1971, vol. 2, 585. For authoritative overviews of surviving clothing in this period and related sources see Arnold 1985; Arnold, Tiramani and Levey 2008; Tiramani and North 2011; Tiramani and North 2013; Braun et al. 2016; Arnold and Tiramani 2018. See also Arnold 1988.

30   This is usually how fashion and dress historians have accounted for pockets. In exhibitions, for instance, pockets often feature as antecedents to handbags: Foster 1982; Chenoune 2004; Pietsch 2013.

31   On consumption see McKendrick, Brewer and Plumb 1982; Brewer and Porter 1993; Berg and Clifford 1999;

Berg and Eger 2003; Berg 2005; Lemire 1997; Lemire 2003a; Lemire 2003b. On globalised trade see Berg 2015; Gerritsen and Riello 2016; Trentmann 2016. And on industrialisation see Berg 1994; Styles 2016; Styles 2018.

32   Staves 1984; Staves 1990; Erickson 1993, 229. For more on variants of women's relations to property see Wright, Ferguson and Buck 2004.

33   On the capacity of objects to derail 'big narratives' see Riello 2009.

34   Turkle 2007, 6. See also Richardson 2010; Styles 2015; Dolan and Holloway 2016. See also Reddy 2001.

Chapter One

Title quotation: Cady Stanton 1895.

1   Fine 1989, 49.

2   On men's dress see Byrde 1979; Harvey 1996; Breward 1999; Wilcox 1999; Kuchta 2002; Staniland 2003; Staniland 2005; Styles 2007; Clatworthy 2009; Breward 2016. On male non-elite clothing in the late seventeenth century, including its several pockets, see Wilcox 2016; Wilcox 2017.

3   OBP t17210419-10. For an extended discussion of men's watches, their significance and association with pendant seals, see Styles 2007, 97–107.

4   Perkins Gilman 1914/1998, 263.

5   For an analysis of the construction techniques of male pockets see Tarrant 1994, 109–10, 111–12.

6   Sherman 1996, 84–6.

7   On men's coats in the nineteenth century see Stallybrass 1994. More specifically on the greatcoat see Johnston, Kite and Persson 2006, 54.

8   Woodforde 1924, vol. 2, 77, 5 June 1783.

9   Oracle and Daily Advertiser (London), 24 December 1798.

10   Sala 1859, 59.

11   Todd Matthews 2010.

12   New York Times, 28 August 1899; on the number of pockets in men's clothes see also Flügel 1930, 186–7, 206. A twentieth-century take on this is Bernard Rudofsky's art installation 24 Pockets, shown at the MoMA exhibition 'Are Clothes Modern?', 1944: Carlson 2017; see also Rudofsky 1947, 120–21, 124, 126, 217.

13   OBP t18030914-85.

14   WAAS, Worcestershire Quarter Sessions, 1814, 1/1/616/91; OBP t18350921-2049.

15   OBP t17650417-22.

16   Verney and Verney 1904, vol. 1, 224.

17   OBP t17960406-20.

18   OBP t18470510-1271.

19   OBP t17730626-31, OBP t17930220-7.

20   OBP t17961130-36, OBP t17830115-14. See also OBP t18510616-1396, in which a servant was caught wearing her pocket 'not where a pocket is usually worn but in front of her, under her skirt'; OBP t18460105-409, in which a thief was found with a pocket 'tied under her gown behind her'.

21   OBP t17661217-34.

22   On pocket hoops see Arnold and Tiramani 2018.

23   In a letter of 1773, Mrs Delany discusses the stays of her 2-year-old great-niece: Delany 1862, vol. 2, 352. For an analysis of the cultural importance of stays see Steedman 2009, 332–41.

24   For a detailed study of eighteenth-century stays and stay-making see Sorge-English 2005; Sorge-English 2011; see also Sorge 1998.

25   OBP t17420714-11.

26   Hurst 2009, 229, 4 November 1761.

27   For further information on the construction of stays see Arnold and Tiramani 2018.

28   OBP t17980912-39.

29   OBP t18311020-85.

30   Elite women could have numerous aprons in their wardrobes. Mary Churchill, 2nd Duchess of Montagu, had 38 aprons in her dress inventory in 1747: Llewellyn 1997.

31   WYAS, Quarter Sessions Records of the West Riding of Yorkshire, Quarter Session Rolls, QS1/73/4.

32   OBP t18340904-79.

33   OBP t18110403-40.

34   OBP t17791020-9.

35   OBP t18111204-57.

36   Read's Weekly Journal or British Gazeteer [sic] (London), 21 August 1736.

37   Dolls or 'babies', dressed in the fashion of the day with multiple accessories and sometimes very elaborate dolls' houses were used by children and grown-ups alike. Although they are thought to have existed before, they became very fashionable at the end of the seventeenth century. See Peers 2004; Pasierbska 2008; Fennetaux 2018.

38   Doll with pocket, V&A, T.846-1974. City of London Coroners Court, Inquests, Coroner's inquest into the death of Catherine Conway, née Eddowes, LMA, CLA/041/IQ/03/065/135.

39   For an earlier example see a bodice and skirt silver-tissue dress, c.1660, in the Fashion Museum Bath, which has a pocket; it is illustrated in Ribeiro 2005, 245. FMB, (LOAN) VFT.I.09.1032 & A. A recent study of sewn-in pockets for men

and women underlines their presence in the sixteenth century: Unsworth 2017.

40   On the history of riding habits see Buck 1979, 52–5; see also Blackman 2001. For examples of surviving riding habits see V&A, T.554-1993, T.670-1913, T.197-1984, T.198-1984, T.269.B-1890; MoL, A12984.

41   Anon. 1796, 115.

42   David Norie, Account book, NAL, 86.ZZ.148, cited in Blackman 2001, 50. The riding jacket in the Snowshill collection documented by Nancy Bradfield has deep pockets on both sides: Bradfield 1968, 11–12; the jacket is also studied in Arnold 1977, 24–5.

43   Althorp Papers, William Hagelston's bills for these garments, Personal expenditure, chiefly clothing, of Lady Georgiana Spencer, 1771–5, BL, Add. MS 75754.

44   See note 61 below.

45   See note 39 above.

46   See, for instance, OBP t17780429-40. James Bonus, Slop Seller, Bills for items of clothing for the Cold Bath House of Correction in Clerkenwell, LMA, MJ/SP/1795/04/099.

47   A Lady' 1840/1975.

48   OBP t18520105-199.

49   OBP t18600102-142.

50   For example, a cloak, 1850–60, has small front inside pocket, and a caped pelisse, 1820, has male-style side pockets: Charles Paget Wade Collection, Berrington Hall, National Trust; see Bradfield 1968, 97–8, 193–4.

51   See woman's double-breasted reefer, c.1892–7, V&A, T.70-1954. On late nineteenth-century tailored outfits for women see North 2008.

52   Myers 2014.

53   Ann Buck asserts that pockets in side seams were 'very usual' by the 1850s: Buck 1984, 31. For surviving examples see Bradfield 1968, 209, 221–2, 231–2, 237–40. Patch pockets also featured on seaside costumes: V&A, T.128-1923, discussed in Johnston, Kite and Persson 2006, 28–9.

54   For example, Bradfield 1968, 241–7, 283–4. 'An outside pocket was sometimes added low down the skirt at the back in dresses of 1876 to 1878', Buck 1984, 63. This is confirmed by Burman's research on nineteenth-century collections of the Hampshire Cultural Trust. Similar research was carried out in the collections of MoL and AC-NMW.

55   Douglas 1895, 77.

56   Another example of the type of reticule illustrated is V&A, T.227-1966.

57 Ham 1945, 54. Many surviving examples of muslin dresses *c*.1800–10 survive with side openings to access tie-on pockets: V&A T.110 to B-1969; see also Bradfield 1968, 87–92.

58 Fashion historians have traditionally explained the supposed disappearance of tie-on pockets *c*.1800 by their becoming unfashionable: Cunnington 1937, 73. Our argument is that pockets never were fashionable.

59 Press studs appeared in the late nineteenth century: Tarrant 1994, 22. On the evolution of fastening systems see Tarrant 1994, 16–24. For late, dated pockets see, for instance, BCHM, T.9807 (dated 1858); MAG, MCAG.1947.1264/2 (dated 1863); YCM, YORCM: 1946.484.d (dated 1873); NM, NWHCM.1970.171.59 (dated 1877); NCMG, NCM 2005-188 (dated 1892).

60 Garsault 1771, 21.

61 Althorp Papers, Personal expenditure, chiefly clothing, of Lady Georgiana Spencer, 1771–5, BL, Add. MS 75754.

62 Llewellyn 1997, 65.

63 'A Lady' 1840/1975, *passim*.

64 UStA, msdep36; 'waltening' possibly refers to 'welting' – that is, binding with a narrow strip of fabric or ribbon.

65 There are other examples. Embroidery on pockets shared similarities with women's stomachers, suggesting possible pairing: Beck 1992, 21–2. A stomacher of 1709, embroidered with human figures and a deer, has similarities to one of the pockets in our survey (Private collection): Seligman and Hughes 1926.

66 Fashion at the time often involved matching.

67 On quilting in general see Colby 1972. On dressing during pregnancy see Baumgarten 1996; Waterhouse 2007.

68 Eliot 1859/1985, 88.

69 Anon. 1827. This debate was also present in fashionable novels, such as Barrett 1817; Gore 1831.

70 Anon. 1809, vol. 1, 166.

71 Tidy 1817, 22.

72 Ibid., 23. The same advice is found in Anon. 1825, 251–2.

73 Hall 1849. For a fuller discussion of pockets in Hall's novel see Burman and White 2007.

74 Hall 1849, 36.

75 Ibid., 119.

76 Edgeworth 1821, 211.

77 Rochester 1714.

78 Bridges 1770, vol. 1, 45. In the novel, the narrator is the banknote itself. It-narrator novels were a popular genre in

the eighteenth century: Douglas 1993–4; Flint 1998; Blackwell 2007; Park 2009.

79 Van de Krol 1994, 83.

80 Buck 1984, 89–90; Fields 2002; Cunnington 1951.

81 Fashionable muslin dresses such as these were often criticised by satirists. See the anonymous engraving *Full Dress, or Parisian Ladies in Their Winter Dress for 1800*, reproduced in Ribeiro 2003, 118. For other versions of the motif of the flimsy muslin dress see Donald 2002; see also Gatrell 2006; Day 2017.

82 On the use of the milliner motif see, for instance, Chrisman-Campbell 2002; Batchelor 2005, 52–83; Wigston Smith 2013, 162–3.

83 George 1870–1954/1978, vol. 7: *1793–1800*, 640–41.

84 As Thomas Laqueur explains, men's and women's bodies were previously seen as essentially similar, women's being an inferior version of men's. Increasingly, though, anatomical differences between the sexes became foregrounded in the definition of gender: Laqueur 1990, 149–92. The association of pockets with women's reproductive organs, and thus with womanhood itself, made them particularly shocking when they were discovered on cross-dressers. On cross-dressing in the period see Steinberg 2001.

85 See, for instance, Thomas Rowlandson, *The Devonshire or Most Approved Method of Securing Votes*, 1784. For other examples see George 1870–1954/1978, nos 6493–4, 6520, 6527, 6532, 6541, 6544, 6565. For a discussion of the motif of the duchess trading kisses for votes see Rauser 2002.

86 Cady Stanton 1895.

87 Cady Stanton 1901.

88 *The Graphic*, 9 March 1907.

89 *Draper's Record*, 1 November 1916, 325; 23 September 1916, 655; 1 July 1916, 27.

90 'The Unwomanly Pocket', *Huddersfield Daily Examiner*, 3 June 1914.

91 Alice Duer Miller, 'Why We Oppose Pockets for Women', *New York Tribune*, reprinted in Duer Miller 1915.

92 Papers of Emily Wilding Davison, Incendiarism, 1911, TWL, 7EWD/A/4/02.

93 For the return ticket see Papers of Emily Wilding Davison, TWL, 7EWD/M/30, and for her purse TWL, 7EWD/M/27. For the police report see Papers of Emily Wilding Davison, List of possessions found on Emily Wilding Davison, TWL, 7EWD/A/7/2.

94 Raverat 1952, 267.

Chapter Two

Title quotation: Savile 1997, 47.

1 OBP t18320105-22.

2 On the importance of haptic skills in consumer practices see Smith 2012; see also Dyer 2016; Dyer and Wigston Smith forthcoming.

3 Reddy 1986; Weiner and Schneider 1989; MacKenzie 1991; Thatcher Ulrich 2001, 208–339, 374–412; Hayward and Kramer 2007.

4 Spufford 1984, 21. On the global reach of the textile trade see Riello and Parthasarathi 2009; Riello and Tirthankar 2009; Riello 2013.

5 Berg 1994, 40. On the spread of cotton see Lemire 1991a; Lemire 2009; Lemire 2011; see also Gorguet-Ballesteros 1994; Gorguet-Ballesteros 2000. On changes in markets and product development in textiles see Styles 2009; Styles 2016; Styles 2018; see also Farnie 2003; Farnie and Jeremy 2004.

6 J. F. 1696, 1.

7 Lemire 2005, 91.

8 Letter from Jane Austen to Cassandra Elizabeth Austen, 24 May 1813, in Austen 1932, vol. 2, 310. More generally on Jane Austen and dress see Buck 1970; Byrde 2008. More examples of Jane Austen's needlework are cited in Davidson 2015.

9 Vries 2008, 25.

10 There are some exceptions. For pockets with elaborate surface decoration see V&A, 1437-1871, 1438-1871 (probably originating in continental Europe); MoL, A21980b, A21980c (masquerade dress).

11 Lady Arabella Furnese, Personal expenditure, 1714–27, KHLC, EK/U471/A50.

12 For silk pockets in the probate inventory of a middling woman see probate inventory of Edith Carr, widow, of St Michael le Quern, London, February 1731, TNA PROB 31/89/86. For an inventory with a number of silk gowns, cloaks and petticoats but pockets of a more modest material see probate inventory of Mary Pope, widow of Greenwich, Kent, March 1774, TNA PROB 31/606/230.

13 Styles 2010b.

14 OBP t17220228-34.

15 Another leather pocket is in the Burrell Collection, BCG, E1977.43.3.

16 OBP t17610225-17, OBP t18031130-47.

17 For example, inventory of Elizabeth Lawrence, 1752, in George and George 2008, no. 97. Her pair of leather pockets had the lowest value of all her apparel.

18 'Total consumption of cotton first

surpassed that of flax in the 1820s and then, in the 1850s, outdistanced that of all other fibres put together', Farnie 2003, vol. 2, 721. On the cotton trade and industry see Farnie and Jeremy 2004; Lemire 2009; Riello and Parthasarathi 2009; Riello 2013.

19 For example, OBP t17161105-30, OBP t17200602-13, OBP t17500912-47, OBP t17810110-4.

20 'A Lady' 1840/1975, 73.

21 Dimity was a family of cloth whose yarn content changed over time from wholly linen to combined linen and cotton and eventually to all cotton. In common usage, 'dimity' could encompass any of these. On the difficulty of fixing nomenclature and terminology for cloths see Montgomery 1984, pp. xii–xiii.

22 J. F. 1696, 8.

23 Martha Dodson, Account Book, 1746–65, MoL, 80.71; see also Ehrman 2006.

24 Vouchers for sundry payments made on account of the maintenance of Lady Louisa Fitzpatrick, 1765–70, BARS, RO32/16.

25 Based on 107 provincial and metropolitan newspaper advertisements published between 1717 and 1800; advertising was likely to reflect better-off owners and the need to identify exactly goods that were missing.

26 'Dimity', Rees 1819, vol. 11, unpaginated. On Rees as a source see Harte 1974.

27 On corded quilting see Berenson 2010. On quilting in general see Colby 1972. On Marseilles quilting see Lanier 1978; Rose 1999.

28 *Public Advertiser* (London), 5 March 1782; the crime was tried at the Old Bailey, OBP t17820410-54.

29 H. Nisbet identified this later 'Marseilles quilting' as coming from Bolton's early power-loom weavers, whose manufacturing capabilities for such products were not in place until the mid-1840s; Nisbet 1927. J. Z. Munby concurs with this view. Her argument that the quilted woven cottons of Lancashire were resistant to design innovation is borne out by the pockets' 'antique' design style; Munby 1986, 94.

30 On printed cottons, especially after the 1800s, see Sykas 1999; Sykas 2005; see also Eaton 2014; Greene 2014.

31 Hayden 1988, 37. Fustian was originally made from wool then variously from cotton or cotton and linen, including types with corded or tufted surfaces, and was used for furnishing and male and female clothing.

32 OBP t17860222-88.

33 For more on patchwork pockets see below, pp. 61–2, 205–9; see also note 53.

34 Defoe 1729, 50, cited in Lemire 2003c, 196. On linen in England see Dolan 2015.

35 Doll, 1740–60, MAG, MCAG.1955.21.

36 Lemire 2003c.

37 Styles 2009, 326. Styles believes that in most Lancashire 'cottons', linen warps predominated until the later 1780s: personal communication.

38 Lemire 2003c, 187–8.

39 Lady Arabella Furnese, Personal expenditure, 1714–27, KHLC, EK/U471/A50.

40 Hudson 2009, 350.

41 Also conspicuously absent from the survey, though present in other sources, are red pockets. Repeatedly represented in paintings – see, for example, fig. 142, or David Wilkie RA (1785–1841), *The Gentle Shepherd*, 1823, oil on canvas (30 × 40.8 cm), AAGM, ABDAG003541 – they do not seem to have survived. This may have to do with moths or the dyestuffs used to obtain the vibrant colour we see on paintings. On Scottish Turkey red, the dyestuff potentially used, see Tarrant 1978; Tuckett and Nenadic 2012. For a methodological reflection on the absence of certain artefacts see Adamson 2009.

42 OBP t17371012-33, OBP t17431207-2. Outside the metropolis, other sources mention 'Calamanca' pockets – for instance, a pocket made of 'striped calamanca' in WAAS, Worcestershire Quarter Sessions, 1743, 1/1/334/42, 1/1/334/43.

43 *Daily Journal* (London), 17 July 1730.

44 Alongside her checked wool detached pair of pockets (for one of which see fig. 42), she had another pair, AC-NMW, 31.31.3, 31.31.4 (see fig. 132). Biographical information provided by the museum.

45 Stevens 2002.

46 AC-NMW, 59.357; AC-NMW, 31.31.3, 31.31.4; CARM, CAASG.1976.3668; and Private collection.

47 OBP t17900526-50.

48 According to Philip Sykas, there could be a time lag of 'some five to ten or more years' between the production and end use of printed dress fabric in the nineteenth century: Sykas 1999, 65.

49 Jervoise of Herriard Family Papers, Inventory taken on the death of Eliza Jervoise, 1821, HRO, 44M69/M2/1/16.

50 St Sepulchre, Holborn, City of London, Vestry Workhouse, Stock Books of Clothing, 1727–1838, LMA, P69/

SEP/B/080/004, fol. 167, fol. 260.

51 Mary Young Papers, Household Commonplace Book, 1830–36, MoL 48.85/3.

52 Practices of recycling for good economy are evidenced, for instance, in the day book (1694–1703) of Edward Clarke, MP for Taunton in Somerset: Clarke 2009, 43, 44. On textile recycling see Woodward 1985, 177–9; Fennetaux 2014.

53 Our survey includes seven patchwork pockets: BMBC, CST.2.523.1981.25.5; CPW, SNO 1454; MAG, MCAG.1947.1262; MCAG.1947.1250; NMS, H.UF 91; private collection; RSN, RSN 211. Another without a location is illustrated in Colby 1976, fig. 153. More survive in museum collections in the USA: see, for example, The Art Museums of Colonial Williamsburg; Museum of Fine Arts, Boston; Winterthur Museum, DE.

54 OBP t17941208-22.

55 OBP t18070916-67. On patchwork and quilting see Prichard 2010; Long 2014. On the use of patchwork in dress see Swain 1984. Patchwork is further discussed in Chapter Seven.

56 Styles 2010a.

57 'A Lady' 1840/1975, 16. A pedagogical novel by Mary Ann Kilner (1753–1831) makes the salvaging of small bits and their re-use a paramount feminine virtue for girls to learn; M. A. Kilner 1780. The story, told by the pincushion itself, opposes a lazy, wasteful girl to a thrifty, virtuous one.

58 Such marks were normally cut off at export to denote refund of duties paid: Dagnall 1996. Further examples of practical appropriation of officially stamped cloth include what is probably cut-off cloth used to line the back of a rare 1720s stomacher, Winterthur Museum, DE, 1960.0097.

59 Savile 1997, 43, 47, 50, 53.

60 Vickery 1998, 150. Anne Buck regards shirt-making for fathers and brothers to have been 'an accepted duty'; Buck 1979, 183; see also Garry 2005. The practice of making body linen continued well into the nineteenth century and beyond: Burman 1999; Richmond 2013, 93–120.

61 Sanders 2000, 96.

62 'A Lady' 1840/1975, 73. Modern assembly instructions can be found in Baumgarten, Watson and Carr 1999, 65–8.

63 Baumgarten 2002, 40.

64 OBP t17840225-35.

65 Between 1746 and 1791, 32 London newspaper advertisements for linen

lost or stolen in transit cited 96 pairs of pockets, an average of three pairs per container lost; these results come from our analysis of 107 provincial and metropolitan newspaper advertisements published between 1717 and 1800. Our survey of pockets found more than 50 pairs, but these are greatly outnumbered by single pockets.

66 For more on the evolved pocket see pp. 158–61.

67 Long 2016.

68 Austen-Leigh 1870/2002, 77–9.

69 Hurst 2009, 139.

70 For instance, V&A, T.208-1970; OBP t18341124-10.

71 Papendiek 1887, vol. 1, 280.

72 Hall 1849, 44.

73 Martineau 1877/1983, vol. 1, 26.

74 In 1783 Lady Wallingford was delighted to receive such gifts from her young relatives: 'I shall value them the more been [sic] their own work', Lady Wallingford, Letter to her nephew Thomas Woods Knollis, 22 February 1783, HRO, 1M44/7/43. Earlier she had sent them needlework equipment: HRO, 1M44/7/34.

75 Esther Duché, Letter to her aunt Mrs John Morgan, Philadelphia, dated from London, 19 April 1782, cited in Earle 1971, vol. 2, 587.

76 Instructions for making miniature clothing was part of girls' education in the nineteenth century. For an example of an instruction book, with miniature samples, see National Society for Promoting the Education of the Poor in the Principles of the Established Church, 1832 (republished in 1838); see also a needlework instruction book, V&A, T.2 to C-1942. On the use of these needlework exercises in girls' education see Richmond 2009; Richmond 2016. 'Dressed babies', as they were sometimes known, could be bought with all their accessories, including pockets: Fennetaux 2018. They could be very elaborate. A finely dressed doll of 1747, wearing two embroidered pockets, is said to have been given to Marianna Hart, aged 3, after her recovery from illness: Bonhams, London, doll, lot 261, sale 19031, 15 November 2011.

77 D. Kilner 1780, vol. 1, 21.

78 Anon. 1809, vol. 1, 249.

79 'A Lady' 1840/1975, p. v. The same link between learning plain sewing, cutting out and mending and finding appropriate employment as servants or wives is made in Wakefield 1817, 138–9.

80 'A Lady' 1840/1975, p. iv.

81 An early work codifying in print the construction of apparel (though not covering pockets) was *The Art of Cutting out Shifts*, 'A Work never before Attempted', which was advertised as added to J. F. 1696; it is now seemingly lost. See also Anon. 1789; Arnold 1999. *The Workwoman's Guide* was imitated but never equalled: for example, Anon. n.d. [*c*.1842]; Anon. 1852. On the rise of published tailoring manuals see Aldrich 2000. On making clothes see Buck 1979, 180–85. For sewing skills among the poor in the eighteenth century see Styles 2007, 157–61.

82 Hall 1849, 37.

83 Private collection. FITZ, T.67-1938. Surviving embroidered pockets (twice as many singletons as pairs) constitute just 25 per cent of the survey, so existing literature on domestic needlework probably over-represents them. Van de Krol found a similar proportion – 43 embroidered pockets in her survey of 181 pockets in American collections: Van de Krol 1994, 42. These findings are matched in that 'worked' pockets are uncommon in Old Bailey trials and newspaper advertisements. The earliest reference to embroidered pockets we have come across is in the day book of Edward Clarke MP, when his two eldest daughters, Anne and Betty, were given embroidered pockets in the mid-1690s: Clarke 2009, 49.

84 Beck 1992, 21–2.

85 On the transformative effect of the importation of Indian calicos on European aesthetics and taste see Lemire 2003a; Lemire 2003b; Lemire 2003c.

86 For more on the aesthetic of containment see Chapter Seven, pp. 210–11.

87 Van de Krol also found human figures to be rare on pockets in American collections. An early eighteenth-century pocket shows a shepherdess, MFA, 53.521: Van de Krol 1994, 44. Perhaps more such pockets remain in private hands as family heirlooms. Their presence in public collections may be limited because vernacular domestic needlework of this kind was not always welcomed by museums in the past. Human figures embroidered on pockets are described in some detail in a newspaper report of an attack on a travelling woman: *London Evening Post*, 24 March 1752; see also *London Evening Post*, 13 February 1752.

88 For example, Shorleyker 1632/1998.

89 Family history has it that the son of the maker of this pocket was a cleric.

90 Woodforde 1932, 63–4. Paper patterns from about the 1780s in the V&A carry the handwritten note on the back: 'I have not worked these but I thought mayhaps you might like them – Return all when you Have done with them': V&A, E.246-1973.

91 Cited in Isaac 2007.

92 Advertisement, *General Evening Post* (London) 25 July 1772. The pattern itself, believed lost, was discovered recently by Jennie Batchelor in the Bayerische Staatsbibliothek, inv: Per 123 m-3. In September 1786 the *New Lady's Magazine* reported the death of Lunardi's assistant. *Wheble's Lady's Magazine* and the *New Lady's Magazine* regularly included embroidery patterns, sheet music and engravings. For the history of patterns see Thunder 2014. On women's periodicals see Batchelor and Powell 2018.

93 12 samplers, each made by a different hand in the Ipswich area between 1691 and 1710, clearly show the effect of their being the work of pupils of a single tutor – Judith (or Juda) Hayle: Ehrman 2007.

94 Hall 1849, 44.

95 OBP t18000115-40.

96 Moore 1971, 71, 73; Brockman Papers, Household Accompts of Anne, wife of Sir William Brockman, BL, Add. MS 45208. On Giles Moore see Tankard 2015.

97 She paid 2s. 6d. Sara Hurst Account books, Private collection.

98 On the development of retail shops see Mui and Mui 1989; Walsh 1995; Cox 2000; Walsh 2003; Walsh 2006; Cox and Dannehl 2007; Mitchell 2014. On the persistence of pedlars see Fontaine 1996; Toplis 2011.

99 Middlesex Sessions of the Peace: Court in Session, Session Papers, Papers for 1709, December 1709, LMA, MJ/SP/1709/12.

100 Will of Stephen Lawrence, shopkeeper, of Tregony, Cornwall, 1721, CRO, AP/L/1249.

101 Morgan's Haberdashery, BL, Banks and Heal collections of trade cards; trade card of Robert Blunt, LMA, SC/GL/TCC/001; see also Blunt's advertisement in *The Times*, 30 May 1789, p. 4, col. A.

102 OBP t18100221-37.

103 OBP t17500912-47.

104 Finn 2003, 93.

105 Toplis notes that itinerant sellers continued to be an important element of working-class clothing consumption in the period 1800–50, filling retail gaps rather than competing with shops: Toplis 2011, 85.

106 Trimmer 1787; Garry 2005, 96–7. For more on sewing in schools and charitable institutions see Gray 1927; see also Richmond 2013, 93–120. The use of children's labour within institutions was common also for laundry and spinning.

107 National Society for Promoting the Education of the Poor in the Principles of the Established Church 1832, 26; *North Wales Chronicle* (Bangor), 7 May 1833.

108 In 1781 John Haighton, 'millener and haberdasher', was trading in Minster Yard, York: *Bailey's Northern Directory* 1781. Acco't of the Miss Haightons Stock and the Agreement between them and Mr W. Atkinson and Daughters, 1783, LMA, CLC/B/025/MS100033A, 13–14.

109 *Bristol Mercury*, 23 March 1844; see Mitchell 2014, 129–51.

110 Mabyn advertises stock from these sources: for example, *Bristol Mercury*, 9 May 1840, 26 March 1842, 13 May 1843.

111 Lemire 1991a, 187; Lemire 1994; Lemire 1999.

112 OBP t17550702-27.

113 Lemire 1997, 43–4. On needlewomen see also Lemire 1994; Lemire 1999.

114 'Slops' were cheaply produced, ready-made basic garments such as shirts, chemises and petticoats, including clothing made for soldiers and sailors.

115 Althorp Papers, Personal expenditure, chiefly clothing, of Lady Georgiana Spencer, 1771–75, BL, Add. MS 75754.

116 OBP t17840225-35.

117 Jervoise of Herriard Family Papers, Settled bill from Sarah Randell, 31 January 1807, HRO, 44M69/13/13/9.

118 This type of pocket front is thought to be from Bolton in the 1840s. The group comprises AC-NMW, 47.132.11, 47.132.12; AHML, LEEDM.E.X.0171, LEEDME.X.0172; BMBC, CST.2.762.1986.29.3; BMGA, IND.46.1983; HCT, HMCMS:CRH.1973.16.2; HMS, HSS 2339; MoL, 32.112/2, 32.112/3; NCMG, NCM 2005-188; NM, NWHCM:1970.171.59; RAMM, KIL/W/03596; V&A, T.150-1970; YCM, YORCM: 1942.150, YORCM: BA5718, YORCM: BA4530 (doll's pocket). Two are in private hands.

119 On second-hand clothing see Ginsburg 1980; Lemire 1990–91; Lemire 1991b; Sanderson 1997; Lambert 2004; Lemire 2012. More generally on second-hand goods see Stobart and Van Damme 2010.

120 Lemire 2005, 86.

121 Cited in Vickery 1998, 144.

122 Müller 1871, 86.

123 WYAS, Quarter Sessions Records of the West Riding of Yorkshire, QS1 94/3.

124 On pawnbroking, second-hand goods and crime see Palk 2006, 39, 58.

125 Lemire 1991b. On pawnbroking see K. Hudson 1982; Tebbutt 1983.

126 George Fettes of Stonegate, York, pawnbroker, Pledge book, 1777–8. YCA, Acc. 38.

127 OBP t18021201-16.

Chapter Three

Title quotation: Collier, 1739, 10.

1 Anna Margaretta Larpent, Diaries, HL, MS HM 31201, vol. 2, 22 April 1796.

2 Mary Collier (c.1688–1762), Hampshire washerwoman and poet, 'The Woman's Labour: an Epistle to Mr. Stephen Duck', 1739, her riposte to Duck's 'The Thresher's Labour', 1730, which belittled the role of working women.

3 Weatherill 1993, 214.

4 Flather 2007, 92.

5 Except for household management books, which may indicate ideals rather than practices, sources are hard to come by. Exceptions to the academic neglect of housekeeping are Dickerson 1995; Dibbits 1996; Vickery 1998, 147–51; Davidoff and Hall 2002, 380–88; Henderson 2006; Ponsonby 2007; Flather 2011; McEwan and Sharpe 2011; Whittle 2011; Reinke-Williams 2014. More specifically on common domestic chores see Verdier 1979; Davidson 1982; Strasser 1982; Strasser 1999; Steedman 2009.

6 On textile objects and the question of maintenance and upkeep see Kelley 2009; Kelley 2010; Kelley 2015. On 'use' as involving constant care and attention see Riello 2010, 63. Recent professional codes within conservation and museum practices encourage the preservation of an object's physical integrity, thus allowing accumulated traces of past damage or modifications to provide valuable evidence of its history. Many surviving pockets, in museum collections for decades but deemed of marginal importance, escaped earlier more invasive approaches to conservation, happily ensuring that more of the evidence survives.

7 Berg 1996, 428.

8 Vries 2008, 126. A study of household consumption in Kent notes that 'considerable accumulation of extra linen' resulted in an increase in the average number of spare sheets per bed from one set to three sets between the early seventeenth century and the

1740s: Overton et al. 2004, 110.

9 Roche 1994, 366; see also Ashelford and Tobin 1999.

10 The conceptual depth of cleanliness is analysed pre-eminently by Douglas 1966. For accounts of cleanliness as discourse, representation and practice in the period see Walkley and Foster 1978; Smith 1985; Thomas 1994; Smith 2007; North 2012; see also Vigarello 1988. For a study of the practices of cleanliness in the nineteenth century see Kelley 2009; Kelley 2010. The period saw an increase in household management books; see, for instance, Macleane 1981; Attar 1987.

11 Roche 1994, 381.

12 Anon. 1817, 263.

13 This is also borne out by a collection of American inventories, 1796–1835 in Van de Krol 1994, 61.

14 Waller of Bursledon family records, Inventory of the late Mrs Waller's apparel, 1835, HRO, 29M67/57.

15 Jervoise of Herriard Family Papers, Inventory taken on the death of Eliza Jervoise, 1821, HRO, 44M69/M2/1/16; see also inventories of 1814, HRO, 44M69/F10/88/49, and 1816, HRO, 44M69/F10/88/50.

16 Mary Young Papers, Commonplace Book, 1823, MoL, 51.86, fol. 44.

17 An analysis of costs of living for workers in the Lyon silk industry in 1786 claimed a woman needed only one new pocket a year, a meagre allowance compared to the numbers often cited in actual use in English sources, but in keeping with an analysis that also supposed only two chemises a year and two pairs of stays to last three years: Morineau 1972, 472. On under-linen see Brooke 1958; Ewing 1978; Buck 1984; Carter, 1992; Arnold, Tiramani and Levey 2008; Wearden 2010; Ehrman 2017.

18 OBP t17440113-13.

19 Inventory of Sarah Bagg, 27 December 1847, Birmingham, TNA, IR 19/91.

20 OBP t18041024-36.

21 Probate inventory of Hester Clifford, 10 January 1775, WSA, P1/C/984. Her goods and chattels were valued at £9 15s. 5d. in total.

22 Hellman 2007, 140, 147.

23 Bradfield 1968, 113.

24 For further discussion and selected photographs of Fanny's wardrobe see Tozer and Levitt 1983, 67–74; see also Burman and White 2007.

25 Parkes 1825, 183.

26 Haywood 1756, 191–2. A story circulated in 1834 about a servant in Stamford,

Lincolnshire, who found that a pet cat had 'actually crept into her pocket whilst she sat in the kitchen, and *kittened there*': *Bristol Mercury*, 13 September 1834.

27 Roche 1994, 382.

28 *Public Advertiser* (London), 5 January 1781.

29 Baillie 1911, 280.

30 Roche 2000, 168; on furniture and ordering see also 170. On the linen cupboard see Dibbits 1996; Thatcher Ulrich 1997.

31 Llewellyn 1997.

32 Jervoise of Herriard Family Papers, Inventory taken on the death of Eliza Jervoise, 1821, HRO, 44M69/M2/1/16.

33 Mary Young's rules for her children insisted that personal and domestic neatness should run through everything. 'Be truly neat and orderly when you are alone as well as when you are in company.' Her children's possessions, if found out of place or 'lying about', were put into a large bag, released only when they paid a fine that was passed to the poor. Mary Young Papers, Education scheme by Mrs Mary Young for her children, 1825, MoL, 48.85/6. On the regulation of her servants see Mary Young Papers, Commonplace Book 1823-7, MoL, 51.86; Household Commonplace Book, 1830-36, MoL, 48.85/3.

34 Mary Young Papers, Commonplace Book, 1823, MoL, 51.86, fol. 44.

35 For storage as privacy and security see Vickery 2009, 38-41. For a more extended description of Victorian storage of clothing in general see Walkley and Foster 1978, 162-76; see also Richmond 2013, 156-9.

36 Jervoise of Herriard Family Papers, Inventory taken on the death of Eliza Jervoise, 1821, HRO, 44M69/M2/1/16.

37 OBP t17440113-13.

38 OBP t17191204-4; see also Styles 2006.

39 Sarah Hurst, Almanac, brief jottings, lists of clothes, 1803, Private collection.

40 *Public Advertiser* (London), 26 January 1774.

41 Richmond 2013, 156-9.

42 George Fettes of Stonegate, pawnbroker, Pledge book, 1777-8, YCA, Acc. 38.

43 On storage and ownership see Thatcher Ulrich 1997. For storage in the context of genteel housekeeping see Vickery 1998, 147-8.

44 In a guide to help consumers buy linen, the maker's mark on a particular Dutch cloth was reproduced to warn readers that, without it, they were not getting the genuine article: J. F. 1696, 1.

45 Lemire 2005, 188.

46 Burman 2007.

47 On literacy and numeracy in the period see Hunt 1996; Houston 2013.

48 Pocket, AHML, LEEDM.E.1968.0061. 0020.A; Pocket, HCT, HMCMS:BWM. 1957.105; Pocket, V&A, T.150-1970.

49 Coventry was long famed for the production of blue thread. Susan North notes the presence of 'Coventry blue' in inventories from the mid-sixteenth century: North 2012. On the symbolism of marking in red thread in a later period see Verdier 1979, 186-9.

50 *Gazetteer and New Daily Advertiser* (London), 22 December 1777. Coronets surmounting other marks denoted the owner's noble rank.

51 A clout was a piece of cloth used for sundry basic purposes around the house or the person; OBP t17840707-76.

52 *Public Advertiser* (London), 3 October 1769.

53 In 1843, after the ship *Pegasus* was lost off the Farne Islands, the family of two young children on board advertised for the recovery of their bodies, citing not only their facial characteristics but the exact linen marks to be found on their clothing: Printer's proofs of William Davison of Alnwick, NoA, ZMD 167/22. For marks on corpse clothing *not* corresponding to the wearer see Cobb 1978, 21; see also Dickens 1860/2007, 18.

54 Jervoise of Herriard Family Papers, 'A List of Mrs Jervoises Cloathes committed to the care of Elizabeth Thompson November 1814', HRO, 44M69/F10/88/49.

55 Jervoise of Herriard Family Papers, 'A List of Mrs Jervoises Cloathes, August 1816', HRO, 44M69/F10/88/50.

56 For example, in 1811, 1812 and 1818: Jervoise of Herriard Family Papers, HRO, 44M69/e13/11, 44M69/e13/12, 44M69/e13/11/17 respectively.

57 On Eliza's responsibilities in running the estate see Pink 2013.

58 Another example of a doll's pocket with marked handkerchief is FMB, BATMC VIII.01.2.

59 'A Lady' 1840/1975, 217.

60 Mary Young Papers, Household Commonplace Book, 1830-36, MoL, 48.85/3.

61 Staniland 1997, 166.

62 For example, Messrs Wilton advertised a 'new-invented instrument for marking all kinds of linen, books, &c. [. . .] the best contrivance ever thought of for that purpose, being composed of printing letters fixed in manner of an office seal, and capable of being readily changed to

all the different names which may be in a family. As much linen may be mark'd with it in a few minutes, as would take a month to mark with a needle, with this material difference, that the letters and numbers made with the instrument never can be got out, whereas those made with the needle easily may, and are frequently picked out, by which many persons are defrauded of a valuable part of their property.' *Dublin Mercury*, 7-9 December 1769.

63 Cunnington and Lucas 1978, 109.

64 Oliver 1938, 28-9.

65 *North Wales Chronicle* (Bangor), 7 May 1833. Schools of Industry used pupils' needlework or spinning for income, an idea promoted in Trimmer 1787.

66 National Society for Promoting the Education of the Poor in the Principles of the Established Church 1832, 5.

67 Ibid., 21.

68 Among the 90 extant marked pockets in the survey, only one has a pre-woven name tape: FMB, BATMC.VI.14.8.

69 Althorp Papers, Personal expenditure, chiefly clothing, of Lady Georgiana Spencer, 1771-5, BL, Add. MS 75754.

70 Letter from Jane Austen to Cassandra Elizabeth Austen, 17 May 1799, in Austen 1908, 61. On Jane Austen and dress and needlework see Chapter Two, n. 8.

71 Eliot 1860/1985, 282.

72 Dickens 1837-8/2003, 73.

73 OBP t18380820-1831.

74 OBP t17840225-35.

75 'A Lady' 1840/1975, 187.

76 Maybe as a reaction to today's throw-away society, there has been a renewal of academic interest in mending: Graham and Thrift 2007; Pennell 2010; Pennell 2014; Findlen Hood 2015; Kelley 2015; Richmond 2016.

77 'Time and time again, witnesses in criminal trials identified otherwise unremarkable items of stolen clothing by the way they had been mended': Styles 2007, 73-4. For an extended, illustrated account of how clothes were altered, mended and recycled see Baumgarten 2002, 181-207; see also Baumgarten 1998; Fennetaux 2014. For an account of changes made to an eighteenth-century dress see Anon. 1972. For discussion of mending in the household of Elizabeth Shackleton (1726-81) see Vickery 1998, 151. Mending instructions were commonly included in 'how-to' dressmaking books up to the mid-twentieth century.

78 Davies 1795, 28. Frequent consumption of sewing thread was echoed in reports

of similar household budgets gathered by him from nearly 30 other parishes.

79 Lady Arabella Furnese, Personal expenditure, 1714–27, KHLC, EK/U471/A50. Similar practices of regular mending are evidenced in the day book (1694–1703) of Taunton MP Edward Clarke, see Clarke 2009, 43–4; and in the accounts of Elizabeth Jervis of Meaford (1746–1779), see Hayden 1988, 38.

80 Anon. 1789, p. vii.

81 Anon. 1829, 72.

82 Mary Young Papers, Household Commonplace Book, 1830–36, MoL, 48.85/3.

83 For example, in 1819 Mary Young's expenditure on seamstresses alone was £15 9s. 9d. Mary Young Papers, Housekeeping Account, MoL 49.15.

84 Hutton 1891, 213; Catherine Hutton, Diary and scrapbook, July 1779, CRL, MS15/1.

85 Eliot 1858/2003, 74, 24.

86 Martineau 1877/1983, vol. 1, 29.

87 Woodforde 1932, 63, 69, 29 June and 18 August 1792.

88 Cited in Garry 2005, 98.

89 Anna Margaretta Larpent, Diaries, HL, MS HM 31201, vol. 2, *passim*; see, for instance, entries for 7 January and 4 April 1796.

90 The two other pockets, besides those shown in fig. 85, are AC–NMW 59.285.6, 59.285.8.

91 OBP t18320105-22.

92 OBP t17431207-2.

93 Vries 2008, 140, 145.

94 OBP t18000402-59.

95 Washing was only one method of cleaning available; others included scouring, etc., sometimes done by the makers of clothes. We focus here on washing because it was the regime to which pockets were mainly subjected. For the prominence of washing in the working life of female servants see Meldrum 2000, 146–8. For an account of the work of washing see Hill 1989, 155–60.

96 Vickery 1998, 330 n.50, see also Vickery 1993, 298 n. 63.

97 Probate inventory of Hester Clifford, 10 January 1775, WSA, P1/C/984. Waller of Bursledon family records, Inventory of the late Mrs Waller's apparel, 1835, HRO, 29M67/57; Catalogue of the household furniture and effects of the late Mrs Waller, 1831, HRO, 29M67/50.

98 Jervoise of Herriard Family Papers, Inventory taken on the death of Eliza Jervoise, 1821, HRO, 44M69/M2/1/16.

99 McPherson 1805, vol. 4, 81.

100 On the history of bleaching see Gauldie 1969; Ron 1981. On the use of chemicals in the fashion industries see Matthews David 2015.

101 Kelley 2010, 5.

102 OBP t18281204-76.

103 Mary Young Papers, Housekeeping Account, MoL, 48.85/1.

104 'A Lady' 1840/1975, 188–90.

105 Ibid., 178

106 Ibid., 188.

107 Anon. 1790, vol. 2, 107.

108 OBP t18030420-36.

109 *Stamford Mercury*, 5 November 1819.

110 Walkley and Foster 1978, 163.

111 Brockman Papers, Household Accompts of Anne, wife of Sir William Brockman, BL, Add. MS 45208.

112 Frances Tyrwhitt's papers contain records of washing expenses that indicate weekly washes, but some items, such as '11 prs sheets' were washed in alternate weeks, and household linen was washed separately from body linen: Frances Tyrwhitt, Tradesmen's bills and receipts, 1760–61, CBS, D-DR/7/37/2.

113 Elizabeth also continued to make and repair clothes for the family after Mary's death: Waller of Bursledon family records, HRO, 29M67/80.

114 OBP t17861213-114.

115 For example, Jervoise of Herriard Family Papers, Eliza Jervoise, Housekeeping Account Book, 1799, HRO, 44M69/E13/11/133.

116 Hardy 1968, 78.

117 Baillie 1911, 358, 359.

118 'A Lady' 1840/1975, 181.

119 Starke 1828, 500. See also Starke 1800, vol. 2, 311.

120 Shelley 1987, vol. 1, 277–8.

121 Webster's *Duties of the Laundry Maid* explains how completing all the laundry processes for the household and body linen of a large family could occupy a single laundry maid full-time from Monday to Saturday, with some assistance, but in a smaller household only until Thursday. This excludes servants' laundry. It suggests a heavy workload indeed. Webster 1844, vol. 1, 340. For a detailed account of the labour of hand-laundering see Malcolmson 1986, 23–34.

122 For a remarkable ethnographic account of washing practices and sociability in early twentieth-century rural France, see Verdier 1979, 108–56. Verdier notes (135) how a woman's pregnancy might be guessed by washerwomen examining the contents of their baskets when they washed regularly for her.

123 Anon. 1790, vol. 2, 108.

124 Hurst 2009, 201.

125 Letter from Dorothy Wordsworth to Jane Pollard, 10 September 1800, in Wordsworth 1985, 200.

126 OBP t17860531-8.

127 OBP t17820703-38.

128 OBP t17840225-35.

129 For the control householders could exert over their spaces see Flather 2007; outbuildings were 'especially hazardous', ibid., 54

130 OBP t17431207-4.

131 *Stamford Mercury*, 5 July 1844.

132 The laundry was not the only place of potential disorder while also a site of 'moral capital': Pennell 2016, 127.

133 Collier 1739, 13.

Chapter Four

Title quotation: OBP t17940219-74.

1 *Public Advertiser* (London), 12 March 1754. Advertisers often cited higher-value contents inside lost or stolen pockets than those in the Old Bailey indictments.

2 OBP t17530221-51; 'ticking' is a variant spelling of the cloth ticken.

3 Eliot 1859/1985, 381–2.

4 Clifford 1999; Styles 2000; Fennetaux 2009; Clifford 2011; Hilaire-Pérez 2012; Hilaire-Pérez 2013.

5 For exceptions see Cobb 1978; Bayard 1989; Van de Krol 1994.

6 OBP t17800112-28.

7 See the Appendix, pp. 224–5.

8 See Introduction, p. 18.

9 Kopytoff 1986, 90.

10 Ibid., 64.

11 Ibid., 87.

12 Ibid., 88.

13 Certeau 2011, 117.

14 Adam Smith 1759/2002, 211.

15 One such voice was Eliza Haywood's (see Chapter Five, n. 1). On anxieties over consumption and in particular female consumption see Kowaleski-Wallace 1997; Berg and Eger 2003; Berg 2005; Wigston Smith 2013.

16 Hitchcock and Shore 2003, 3. Anxieties about property were matched by the perception of a crime-ridden metropolis: Beattie 1986; King 1996; Beattie 2001; Shore 2003; Palk 2006; Hitchcock and Shoemaker 2015.

17 OBP t17840114-76, OBP t18070701-56, respectively; see also Anon. 1818.

18 Beattie 2001, 459.

19 OBP t17940219-74.

20 Anon. 1735, vol. 1, 115–16. Jones was said to be disappointed that the weight in this pocket consisted of 'no more' than

a small prayer book, a needle-case and a silver thimble.

21 OBP t17220228-59 and OA 17220314, March 1722.

22 OBP t17240415-10.

23 Anon. 1795b, vol. 2, 196–200.

24 Letter from Susan Edmonstone Ferrier to Janet Ferrier Connell, 17 January 1802, in Ferrier 1898, 36.

25 At 61.5 cm, the longest pockets in our survey are RAMM, EXEMS 10/1965/39/1, closely followed by NCMG, NCM 1983-728. Other examples of very long pockets are attached pairs, WORTH, WMAG.1961.924 (47.7 cm and 48.4 cm); MAG, MCAG.1947.1253/2 (51 cm). In her study of 181 pockets, Yolanda Van de Krol found the average length was between 'fifteen and sixteen inches' (38–41 cm): Van de Krol 1994, 19.

26 In 2004, to explore aspects of use not apparent from other sources, University of Southampton postgraduate student Katharine Wheaton wore a pair of replica pockets for a day, carrying in them what would normally be in other pockets or her handbag; she reported the importance of touch and an instinctive need to make left and right pockets into different domains to help locate her things.

27 OBP t17770409-14.

28 Washerwoman and murder victim, also called Frances Pigburn: *Jackson's Oxford Journal*, 3 December 1831; *The Times*, 28 November 1831.

29 A safety pin remains attached to a nineteenth-century adult's pocket; its purpose was said to be to secure money inside when the pocket was worn by a child sent on errands. Personal communication with a descendant of the child. An eighteenth-century pocket has also been preserved with a pin, though its precise function is unknown: VDM, WANVD:1981.85.2.

30 OBP t17890114-42.

31 Hall 1849, 38–9.

32 Goldsmith 1783, 150. Although not often cited in court because of their low monetary value, foodstuffs were sometimes carried in pockets. Sarah Childish had 'two Crusts of Bread', OBP t17190708-44; Elizabeth Canning had 'a penny mince-pye' in her pocket, OBP t17530221-47; Caroline Walsh had 'a biscuit', OBP t18320105-22.

33 OBP t17661217-34.

34 OBP t17350911-51.

35 Johnson 1755, vol. 2, unpaginated.

36 OBP t17200602-13.

37 OBP t17930529-30.

38 OBP t17841208-31.

39 OBP t17610225-17.

40 For a discussion of differentiating and earmarking personal money in the twentieth century see Zelizer, 1994.

41 OBP t17670715-3. Keeping valuables inside boxes was not exclusively a female habit. For example, Francis Williams of Kendal carried 19 guineas in his nutmeg grater in 1790: Records of Justices of Assize, Northern and North-Eastern Circuits, Criminal Depositions and Case Papers, TNA, ASSI 45/37/1/252. It seems also to have been a recognised practice among children. In a story for children of 1832, a girl 'took out of her pocket an old-fashioned nut-grater, and emptied on her lap what little money' she had: Bourne 1832, 61.

42 OBP t17301014-71.

43 OBP t17840114-54, OBP t17940917-67.

44 OBP t17530221-6; Surrey Quarter Sessions, Michaelmas Sessions 1772, SHC, QS2/6/1772/Mic/30.

45 Coroners' inquests into suspicious deaths, 9 May 1766, CoW, LL WACWIC652060292.

46 OBP t17360115-21.

47 Margaret Richards, a convicted thief, was a well-equipped statistical outlier when she carried 98 keys in her pocket in 1760 – 'one parcel to open large door locks, the other such as chests and trunks': OBP t17600521-25.

48 OBP t17650710-56.

49 For examples of keys not in pockets see OBP t17190514-20, OBP t17880227-10, OBP t18220522-65, OBP t18280110-33.

50 OBP t17900424-68.

51 OBP t17841208-31. For a view of domestic security and space see Vickery 2008; Vickery 2009, 25–48.

52 *Morning Post and Daily Advertiser* (London), 6 April 1778. James Boswell visited her bagnio, which was, like others, 'established for the trade in women of the town': White 2012, 356.

53 OBP t17770409-14.

54 OBP t17650710-56.

55 Vickery 1998, 133.

56 Raven 2014, 201–5.

57 Coroners' inquests into suspicious deaths, 4 May 1778, CoW, LL WACWIC652180152.

58 OBP t17770409-14.

59 Lady's Pocket Book for 1757, with notes by Sarah Gatehouse, 1757–1808, HRO, 35M63/66.

60 Thompson 1967; Glennie and Thrift 1996; Glennie and Thrift 2002; Glennie and Thrift 2009.

61 Voth 2000, 58.

62 OBP t17780429-103.

63 For a fuller discussion of watch adoption by men and women, see Styles 2007, 97–107; Donald 2000. Pocket watches were an established part of the male elite's self-fashioning practices by the second half of the seventeenth century. Danae Tankard notes that fashion-conscious Samuel Jeake purchased a 'pendulum watch' in 1681: Tankard 2016, 30.

64 D. Kilner 1780, vol. 1, 41–3.

65 OBP t17161105-49.

66 OBP t17171016-9.

67 It seems putting items of apparel in pockets when travelling was also common: Bayard 1989.

68 OBP t17280605-14, OBP t17180530-18.

69 OBP t17600227-3.

70 The Scots word 'fleerish' means a steel used for striking sparks to ignite tinder.

71 Such a practical item was a pincushion, which could be carried in the pocket, as described in D. Kilner 1780, or hung outside it, as shown in figs 106, 153.

72 OBP t17930529-30.

73 OBP t17940716-69.

74 OBP t18320906-446. Ann O'Dell was referring to her laundry blue, the substance that was normally added to the final rinse to help with whitening.

75 For an account of needlework tools and sundries of the period, including attention to out-of-place objects, see Beaudry 2006.

76 OBP t17190708-44; the trial took place a year after the alleged crime.

77 Beaudry 2006, 68, also 81–5. And see her account of links between prostitutes and needlework: Beaudry 2006, 173–4; see also Thatcher Ulrich 1991, 63–5. In the seventeenth century, 'bodkin' also referred to a large, often decorative, pin used to dress the hair: for example, the decorative silver bodkin, MoL, A21345.

78 De Grazia and Furlough 1996, 16.

79 OBP t17501205-57.

80 Eliot 1859/1985, 382–5.

81 Smart-Martin 2006, 188, 187.

82 Beverly Lemire notes that among people of irregular or limited income 'women were disproportionately responsible for the management of small-scale credit for activities based in the household': Lemire 2005, 17. John Styles argues that among 'smaller outlets' credit seems to have been 'almost universal': Styles 1994, 150.

83 Finn 2003, 80; see also Muldrew 1998. Lemire also argues that cash transactions made slow progress in the eighteenth century: Lemire 2006, 246.

84 OBP t17180227-33.

85 OBP t17990619-53.

86 OBP t17840526-45.

87 Mayhew 2000; Muldrew 2001; Kent 2005, 49–89; Valenze 2006, 31–43.

88 Mayhew 2000, 79.

89 OBP t17831210-2. The reference is to the American War of Independence.

90 Martineau 1877/1983, vol. 1, 25.

91 OBP t17990508-22.

92 OBP t17260302-8.

93 OBP t17600227-3.

94 OBP t17431207-2.

95 OBP t17780715-19.

96 Zelizer 1994, 19.

97 Lemire 2006, 246.

98 OBP t18040704-14.

99 Tomkins 2006, 228–9.

100 OBP t17810530-40.

101 OBP t17940115-7.

102 OBP t17211206-43.

103 OBP t17380222-6.

104 OBP t17990619-53, OBP t17310908-8.

105 OBP t18040704-14.

106 Davies 2015.

107 *Notes and Queries*, 4th series, 3, 13 March 1869, 238.

108 OBP t17501205-57.

109 Coroners' inquests into suspicious deaths, 21 March 1796, CoW, LL WACWIC652360120.

110 Eastop 2001; Harrison and Gill 2002; Eastop 2006. Another concealed pocket with a child's cap inside came to light in the same county: pocket, VDM, WANVD:1981.85.2, and cap WANVD:1981.85.1. For more deliberately concealed garments see http://www.concealedgarments.org (last accessed, 15 June 2018).

111 OBP t17600227-3, OBP t18030420-36.

112 Erickson 1993, 229. For more on variants of women's relations to property see Berg 1993; Wright, Ferguson and Buck 2004; see also Froide 2005.

113 Erickson 1993, 235–6.

114 Richmond 2013, 298.

115 On coverture see Finn 1996; Erickson 2005; Stretton and Kesselring 2013.

116 Staves 1990, 198.

117 OBP t17840114-72.

118 OBP t17970531-41.

119 *Public Advertiser* (London), 2 May 1764.

120 OBP t17670715-38.

121 OBP t16930906-13.

122 OBP t17810222-17.

123 OBP t17310908-9.

124 OBP t17670115-9.

125 OBP t18140420-143.

126 OBP t18270405-26.

127 OBP t18100718-27. For an account of other such lives see Hurl-Eamon 2005.

128 OBP t17351210-55.

129 Breen 1993, 251.

130 Haywood 1743, 26.

131 OBP t17670715-38.

132 OBP t17650417-5.

133 OBP t17580913-12.

134 OBP t17961130-36

135 MacKay 1999. This is echoed in the period 1590–1660: Walker 1994.

136 On shoplifting see Tickell 2015; Tickell 2018. Clothing was also 'a crucial hiding place' for female shoplifters, but, in Deirdre Palk's findings, pockets were used less often than larger items of clothing to conceal stolen goods: Palk 2003, 136. This may be due to rates of detection as much as rates of use.

137 OBP t18070701-56.

138 *The Times*, 11 April 1849, 7, col. A.

139 *The Times*, 19 January 1911, 4, col. B.

Chapter Five

Title quotation: Ann Heatley, Personal expenditure, HL, MS HM 81757.

1   Haywood 1745, vol. 2, 104.

2   For an example of a woman with many of these articles in her pockets see the case of the 'Lady in a Coach' at the start of Chapter Four.

3   Fashionable men, as well as women, used their pockets to keep at hand various props for social intercourse. Fashionable Samuel Jeake carried combs and a copper tobacco box in his pocket: Tankard 2016, 31.

4   On dress and the appropriation of space see Riello 2006, 60.

5   On the changes to perceptions of time and space brought about by rail travel see Schivelbusch 1977; Kern 1983; Beaumont and Freeman 2007; Ferguson 2013; Gavin and Humphries 2015.

6   Bernasconi 2015; see also Hilaire-Pérez 2012; Hilaire-Pérez 2013.

7   Such a pack of conversation cards was advertised in *The World* (London), 14 December 1791.

8   On pocketbooks and almanacs as highly competitive fields of publishing see Raven 2014, 201–5.

9   On pocketbooks, almanacs and memorandum books see Buck and Matthews 1984; Batchelor 2003; Colclough 2015. On pocketbooks and accounting practices see Connor 2004, 28–9. For an example of a pocketbook with 'rules of precedency' see Anon. 1795a.

10 Anon. 1831, vol. 2, 162.

11 Bernasconi 2015; Hilaire-Pérez 2012; Hilaire-Pérez 2013. On miniaturisation see Stewart 1993.

12 Fennetaux 2009.

13 Anon. 1773, p. ix. On directories see Corfield and Kelly 1984.

14 For other examples of such maps see Bowles's 'New Travelling Map of England and Wales', 1778, MoL, 85.571a, and 'London and its Environs', 1832, MoL, 31.107/1. When the railway developed, printed handkerchiefs adapted: see, for instance, MoL, 87.216.

15 Ann Heatley, Letters and personal expenditure, HL, MSS 81748–81770.

16 Ibid.

17 Lady Arabella Furnese, Personal expenditure, 1714–27, KHLC, EK/U471/A50. See also her Household accounts, KHLC, EK/U471/A49.

18 Letter to Georgiana, Duchess of Devonshire, from her mother Lady Spencer, 1 November 1776, Chatsworth MSS, cited in Foreman 1998, 43.

19 Mary Young Papers, Household Cash Book, 1832–9, MoL, 48.85/4; Housekeeping Account, 1817–25, MoL, 48.85/1. For another woman's expansive economic network based on her shopping habits, this time outside the capital, see Berry 2003. On female consumption see also Berry 2002; Dyer 2016.

20 Mary Young Papers, Commonplace Book, 1823, MoL, 51.86, fol. 44.

21 For example, Mary Young Papers, Commonplace Book, 1823, MoL, 51.86; Household Commonplace Book, 1830–36. MoL, 48.85/3.

22 'Pocket Money', Countess of Guilford, Clothing and Pocket Accounts, KHLC, EK/U471/A54, EK/U471/A55.

23 Sarah Sophia Banks's collections of printed ephemera included visiting cards: see, for instance, BM, Department of Prints and Drawings, C,1.5346, C,1.2225. On her paper collections see Leis 2013.

24 Vickery refers to this guide: Vickery 2009, 274-5.

25 Anon. 1800, p. v.

26 On the increasing formalisation of visiting see Heyl 2002; see also Vickery 2009, 274.

27 Ann Heatley, Personal expenditure, HL, MSS HM 81753, 81757.

28 Lady Arabella Furnese, Personal expenditure, 1714–27, KHLC, EK/U471/A50.

29 Lloyd 2002, 31. On urban culture in the eighteenth century see Borsay 1984; Borsay 1989; see also Klein 2003.

30 Borsay 1989.

31 Lloyd 2002, 24, 28. On women and charity see also Andrews 1995.

32 Lloyd 2002, 30. See also Wilson 1990.

33   *London Packet, or New Lloyds Evening Post*, 30 January 1795.

34   Raven 2007, 273.

35   For instance A. Lane produced almanacs and Gothic novels in small formats, which were promoted to a female audience.

36   J. T. Smith 1845, 211.

37   Hoffman 1791.

38   Bryant 1783, p. ix.

39   Wordsworth 2002, 12, 16 May 1800.

40   Bellanca 2007, 113.

41   Withering 1796, vol. 1, 18.

42   Bellanca 2007, 114; Wordsworth 2002, 96. On the comparison between Dorothy Wordsworth's journal and naturalists' notations see Bellanca 2007, 116–18. The Wordsworths also wrote poetry on their outings. Rather amusingly, the notes they were seen taking on their walks, as they were working on a poem entitled 'The Brook', were misconstrued by the Home Office agent in charge of spying on them as some kind of pro-French Revolutionary activity: Holmes 1989, 160, 161; see also Roe 1988, 248–62.

43   Mavor 1800, unpaginated.

44   On the interplay between botany, embroidery and textiles see Laird and Weisberg-Roberts 2009, 150–71, 66–79; see also Beck 1992; Isaac 2007; Anishanslin 2016. On the impact of global trade on floral aesthetics see Lemire 2003a.

45   Writing while on the move was not restricted to women. Famously Jean-Jacques Rousseau preferred writing when on walks, and he wrote his *Rêveries du promeneur solitaire* on the backs of 27 playing cards. Rousseau 1959; Rousseau 2010; Rousseau 2014, 593-672.

46   On the representation of dress in *Pamela* see Buck 1992. On dress in novels see also Wigston Smith 2013.

47   In a royalist newspaper published during the English civil war, Lady Waller being pillaged 'even to her pocket ink-horne' was used as propaganda to illustrate the ruthless plunders of the rebels: *Mercurius Aulicus* (Oxford), 21 July 1644. On nomadic writing practices see Stallybrass et al. 2004; Colclough 2015.

48   Woodforde 1924-31, vol. 2, 107.

49   BM, Department of Prints and Drawings, Heal collection, 92.6, 92.11. On the history of writing implements see Finlay 1990.

50   Jervoise of Herriard Family Papers, Eliza Jervoise, Account book, recording income and expenditure accounts, 16 January 1812 – 31 December 1819, HRO, 44M69/E13/13/12.

51   Burney 1854, vol. 3, 205, 18 August 1789.

52   Raverat 1952, 267.

53   Walpole 1937– , vol. 37, 21–2.

54   Anon. 1795b, vol. 2, 198–9.

55   Murray of Stanhope 1821, 13; see also Baillie 1911, 309–83.

56   Murray of Stanhope 1821, 80–81. It was customary for women to be in charge of accounts, whether at home or away: see Connor 2004, 64–5; Vickery 2009, 108–28; see also Clark 1919; Hunt 1996; Day 2007; Colclough 2015.

57   Murray of Stanhope 1821, 80.

58   Ibid., 81.

59   In Amsterdam, on 18 June 1731, Lady Grisell paid 4s. 2d. 'for baggage', 6d. 'For guid', 5s. 11d. 'for a coach', and £5 18s. 8d. 'for lodging and intertainment': Baillie 1911, 311. In May she bought in Rotterdam 'a pair pockets' for 2s. 5d. and 'a pair pockets' for 2s. 4d.: ibid. 350, 351.

60   Ibid., 329.

61   Memorandums for Earl Hadinton and Mr Baillie in their Travelling', in ibid., 384–410.

62   Ibid., 393.

63   Burton 1875, vol. 1, 71.

64   Starke 1800, vol. 2, 266–7.

65   North 1892, vol. 1, 259–60.

66   Starke 1800, vol. 2, 311. In *The Charterhouse of Parma* (1839), Stendhal refers to the English in Italy who 'would not pay for the merest trifle without looking up the price in the travel journals of one Mrs Starke which had achieved its twentieth edition by indicating to the prudent Englishman the cost of a turkey, an apple, a glass of milk and so on', Stendhal 1839/1999, 211.

67   *The Queen* (London), 7 August 1880.

68   Anon. 1909, 51.

69   For pockets similar to no. 37 in the trade catalogue see, for instance, AC–NMW, F76.342.11; HCT, HMCMS:C2004.79; MAG, MCAG.1947.845, MCAG.1961.186; OX, OXCMS:1980.115.1; YCM, YORCM: 1946.1129, YORCM: BA5708; the Fashion Museum Bath has an example of an evolved pocket very similar to the one featured in the Elliston & Cavell catalogue as no. 39: FMB, BATMC VI.14.11. In his *English Women's Clothing in the Nineteenth Century*, C. W. Cunnington cites for 1857 'Patent Railway Pockets 1/6', so they existed in some form from the 1850s: Cunnington 1931, 191.

70   Besides those cited in note 69, the surviving railway or travelling pockets are AHML, LEEDM.E.X.0174; BMH, 1975.620.4; FMB, BATMC VI.14.8; WORTH, WMAG.1972.361; YCM,

YORCM: 1945.229.

71   *The World* (New York), 4 August 1893. *The Lewiston Evening Journal* (Maine) ran a word-for-word copy of the article on 26 August 1893. Slightly different wording was used in a later American fashion magazine, *The Delineator*, when in 1898 it repeated the description of the 'travelling pocket': *The Delineator* (New York), 52 (1898), no. 5, p. ix.

72   John Binny, in Mayhew 2005, 170–71. The real or perceived increased risk to possessions that accompanied the development of travel led to various attempts at making pockets safer. See, for instance, a patent registered for a safety pocket on 8 December 1857, Registers of the Board of Trade, TNA, BT45 21-4035.

73   Ponsonby 1965, 55.

Chapter Six

Title quotation: OBP t17250513-12.

1   OBP t17441205-41.

2   Thatcher Ulrich noted pockets as emblems of women's diverse work: Thatcher Ulrich 1991, 34.

3   Mendelson and Crawford 2000, 259. On women's work in the period see Clark 1919; Pinchbeck 1930; Hill 1989; Hill 1996; Sharpe 1996; Sharpe 1998; Lane, Raven and Snell 2005; Baudino, Carré and Révauger 2005; Erickson 2008.

4   King 2004, 121.

5   OBP t18510707-1487.

6   OBP t17260302-8.

7   For a cultural history of the night see Halimi 2008; Cabantous 2009; Bronfen 2013.

8   On night-time crime in London see Palk 2003, 141–2.

9   OBP t17690628-37, OBP t17880625-1.

10   *The Times*, 7 August 1826.

11   OBP t17810711-30, OBP t17670115-9.

12   OBP t16950828-28.

13   OBP t18070408-21.

14   See, for instance, OBP t17281204-64, OBP t17350116-6.

15   OBP t17550515-30.

16   OBP t17280501-41.

17   Gay 1728/2013, 54, Act III, scene 5.

18   OBP t17700221-30.

19   OBP t17780715-19.

20   OBP t18351123-119.

21   Alexander Smith 1719, vol. 2, 183.

22   OBP t17220907-80.

23   Records of Justices of Assize, Northern and North-Eastern Circuits: Criminal Depositions and Case Papers, TNA, ASSI 45/14/3/36B–C.

24   In the proceedings, these terms were cited in equal numbers.

25   Respectively OBP t16820601a-4, OBP t17641017-20, OBP t17650417-22, OBP t17840421-24.

26   Probate inventory of Sarah Price, 29 December 1743, Diocese of London, Archdeaconry of Middlesex, Probate inventories (2nd series), LMA, DL/AM/P1/02/1744/002.

27   OBP t17661217-34.

28   Fontaine 1996, 164–82. On pedlars in England see also Spufford 1984; Spufford 1985.

29   OBP t17940917-67.

30   Amgueddfa Cymru–National Museum Wales, museum documentation.

31   A detached pair, AC-NMW, 31.31.1, 31.31.2, and an attached pair 31.31.3, 31.31.4. Amgueddfa Cymru–National Museum Wales, museum documentation.

32   Information recorded at the time of accession in 1930: see Amgueddfa Cymru–National Museum Wales, museum documentation. For Mary Davis see Carmarthenshire County Museum documentation.

33   *Read's Weekly Journal or British Gazetteer* [*sic*] (London), 21 August 1736.

34   Roberts 2006, 29. This multi-tasking was not restricted to Welsh market women. Françoise Bayard's study of eighteenth-century pockets has a woman with knitting needles and a partly finished stocking in her pocket: Bayard 1989, 17. The author of *The Workwoman's Guide* (1840) recommended keeping one's ball of wool in the pocket: 'A Lady' 1840/1975, 238. An early nineteenth-century French costume plate by Camus entitled *La Tricotteuse* ('The knitter'), 1793, shows a woman knitting, with her wool coming out of her pocket: LACMA, M.86.266.9.

35   Latham 1990, 68.

36   For examples of such purchases see ibid., 22, 24. Still the Latham girls were working on the farm. Sara for instance received 2*d*. for three days of 'working in hay' in 1764: ibid., 116.

37   Ibid., 67, 68, 71.

38   Woodforde 1924–31, vol. 5, 166–7.

39   Anon. 1799/2000, 5. After her rescue, Elizabeth became a national celebrity. She survived in poor health until July 1799.

40   For examples of these dolls wearing the traditional garb of pedlars see AHML, LEEDM.E.1956.0164 (female doll); MAG, MCAG.1922.566, MCAG.1954.35; NMS A.1914.1013. On the importance of pedlars for the circulation of goods see Spufford 1984; Spufford 1985; Fontaine

1996, 164–82; see also Lemire 1991b.

41   Inquisition at Cowgrove, Wimborne Minster. Coroner Nicholas Russell, gentleman. Body: Elizabeth Gatehouse of Shaston, 29 August 1729, DRO, D-BKL/C/F/1/3/3/48; Inventory of the goods of Elizabeth Gatehouse, DRO, D-BKL/C/F/1/3/3/50.

42   *London Evening Post*, 24 March 1752. A virtually identical story had appeared little more than a month before in the same newspaper, also involving a travelling woman, though the location and names were different: *London Evening Post*, 13 February 1752.

43   OBP t18530131-286.

44   OBP t17961130-40.

45   Ann Yeats, May 1778, St Helen's, Bishopsgate, Settlement examinations, 1738–96, MS 6886, cited in Hitchcock 2004, 145–47.

46   Hitchcock 2004, 148.

47   Saxby 1806, 15.

48   OBP t17401015-53 and OA 17401124.

49   Sharpe 1996, 100–29.

50   OBP t17910914-21.

51   Earle 1989; Hill 1996; Meldrum 2000; Steedman 2004.

52   OBP t18370918-2212.

53   North Riding of Yorkshire Quarter Sessions Bundles, NYCRO, QSB 1736.

54   OBP t18380820-1831.

55   On illiterate people's uses of written documents see Farge 2003.

56   OBP t17990619-53.

57   Dickens 1850/1990, 59.

58   Humfrey 1998, 59. Low wages, migration and insecure employment were some of the factors that drove women to crime, see Durston 2007.

59   Anon. 1764, 50, 82.

60   Anon. 1850, 51.

61   In our analysis of Old Bailey cases, of the 50 per cent of thieves who used pockets in their crime and had a named occupation, 66 per cent were servants.

62   OBP t18220220-21.

63   OBP t17961026-4.

64   OBP t17650417-5.

65   Leadbeater 1811, 237.

66   Certeau 2011, 37.

67   Worcestershire Quarter Sessions, 1777, WAAS, 1/1/470/32.

68   Quarter Sessions Records of the West Riding of Yorkshire, Quarter Session Rolls, WYAS, QS1/131/8.

69   Worcestershire Quarter Sessions Records, 1818, WAAS, 1/1/635/172, 1/1/635/173.

70   OBP t18460105-409.

71   OBP t18310407-203.

72   OBP t18230409-66.

73   Hitchcock 2004, 93.

74   Earle 1994, 118–19.

75   OBP t17250513-12.

76   Mayhew 1850.

77   King 2004, 124.

78   Coroners' inquests into suspicious deaths, 4 May 1778, CoW, LL WACWIC652180152.

79   Farge 2003.

80   See the extended analysis of her story in Chapter Two.

81   OBP t18320105-22.

82   Mayhew 1971, 175.

83   *The Times*, 14 September 1888, 20 September 1888. See also Case papers of the Whitechapel murders, TNA, MEPO 3/140.

84   City of London Coroners Court, Inquests, Coroner's inquest into the death of Catherine Conway, née Eddowes, LMA, CLA/041/IQ/03/065/135.

85   Ibid. See also *The Times*, 1 October 1888.

86   City of London Coroners Court, Inquests, Coroner's inquest into the death of Catherine Conway, née Eddowes, LMA, CLA/041/IQ/03/065/135; *Daily News* (London), 5 October 1888.

87   This account is taken from John Kelly's testimony at the inquest: LMA, CLA/041/IQ/03/065/135.

88   Lévi-Strauss 1966, 22, 17.

89   Ibid., 21.

Chapter Seven

Title quotation: Burney 1988, vol. 1, 18–19.

1   OBP t17701024-51; Elizabeth Warner was acquitted.

2   On gender and the domestic interior, see Styles and Vickery 2006; Flather 2007; Flather 2011; Harvey 2012.

3   Seligman and Hughes 1926, 37. On pockets and women's experience of privacy see Fennetaux 2008.

4   Eliot 1859/1975, 149–50.

5   Gosden 2004, 39.

6   Girouard 1978; Stone 1991; Ariès, Duby and Chartier 1993; Bold 1993; Saumarez Smith 1993; Ayres 2003; Vickery 2009.

7   OBP t17861025-117.

8   Vickery 2008; Vickery 2009, 25–48.

9   Melville 1999; Flather 2007, 47–52.

10   Styles 2006; Vickery 2009, 25–48.

11   This is dramatised in Samuel Richardson's *Clarissa*, where the heroine's gradually restricted spatial control underpins the escalating infringement made on her privacy. Richardson 1748/1985. Real-life stories of embattled women also existed: see Vickery 2009, 191.

12   Woolf 1929/2000.

13   Mary Young Papers, Commonplace Book, 1823, MoL, 51.86.

14   Famously, her nephew said: 'she had no separate study to repair to, and most of the work must have been done in the general sitting-room, subject to all kinds of casual interruptions', cited in Woolf 1929/2000, 60–61. However, as a young girl, Jane Austen did experience the joy of having a separate room, shared with her sister Cassandra. See Byrne 2013, 55.

15   Austen 1814/1996, 126.

16   Shore 1891, 216–17.

17   Le Faye 2006, 171, cited in Byrne 2013, 267. In the 1780s Mrs Papendiek, Assistant Keeper of the Robes to Queen Charlotte, had no room for her own use but only a writing-table: Papendiek 1887, vol. 1, 181.

18   Goodman 2003; Goodman 2007; Sargentson 2007; Sargentson 2015.

19   Eliot 1866/1998, 58–9.

20   'Une femme [. . .] qui nous chargeait de quelque gage de sa confiance, était en toute sécurité, nous ne la quittions pas, tout le jour à ses côtés, la nuit sous son chevet, et jamais une main téméraire n'aurait osé fouiller les replis où nous enveloppions ses secrets', Desarps 1815, 11–12 [our translation].

21   Elizabeth Isham, Book of Remembrance, autobiography, c.1638, PUL, MS RTC01 (no. 62), fol. 14r.

22   Ibid., fol. 11r.

23   H. Smith 2014, 23–5.

24   OBP t18881022-977.

25   OBP t18280110-33.

26   OBP t17680224-65.

27   See, for instance, OBP t18280110-33. For a male example see OBP t18170917-1, cited in Vickery 2009, 165. For more on nesting practices see Chapter Four.

28   OBP t18060917-19.

29   OBP t18501216-279.

30   Hamlett 2015, 130.

31   Ham 1945, 54.

32   Burney 1988, vol. 1, 18–19.

33   Richardson 1740/1985, 260.

34   OBP t18510616-1396.

35   Gray 1927, 64–6.

36   Hesketh 1997, 76.

37   Brontë 1847/1996, 56. On sewing in the novel see Brain 2014.

38   Magdalen Charity 1759, 18. Matrons' clothing books for workhouses in the capital: St Mary at Lambeth, Workhouse, Matron's clothing book, 1800–25, LMA P85/MRY1/318; St Mary at Lambeth, Norwood Workhouse, Matron's clothing book, April 1790 - October 1792, LMA, P85/MRY1/315, October 1792 – January

1797, LMA, P85/MRY1/316. See also St Sepulchre, Holborn, City of London, Vestry and Parish Officers, Workhouse stock books of clothing, 1727–1838, P69/SEP/B/080/001-008. On clothing distribution in workhouses see Brogden 2002.

39   Angus 1981, 31–2.

40   Hamlett 2015, 10.

41   Clarke 2003, 152.

42   Sarah Hurst, Diary, HMA, cat. nos 3542–45.

43   Hurst 2009, 17.

44   Fumerton 1986; Coombs 2005.

45   This practice was noted as particularly widespread in England by the French painter Jean-André Rouquet: Rouquet 1755/1972, 52. As noted by the painter Jonathan Richardson, miniatures maintained relationships in case of long separations: Richardson 1725/1971, 13. The ledgers of miniature painters testify to the importance of this exchange of miniatures, as orders often come in pairs. See, for instance, Richard Crosse, Diary and account book, NAL, 86 KK 41; William Wood, Memorandum of miniatures painted and finished by William Wood, NAL, 86 KK.3, 86.KK.4, 86.KK.5, 86.KK.5a On miniatures in the eighteenth-century see Pointon 2001.

46   See the entry in Sarah Hurst's diary for 22 July 1759, when she lost her pocket and the miniatures inside it: Hurst 2009, 101.

47   Ibid., 82, 91, 3 April 1759, 25 May 1759.

48   Ibid., 89, 91, 11 May 1759, 23 May 1759.

49   Fielding 1749/1985, 467–73.

50   Sarah Hurst, Diary, HMA, cat. no. 3542, 22 July 1759. The comma between 'pocket' and 'memorandum book' was omitted in the transcription in Hurst 2009, 101; it clarifies that Sarah lost her whole pocket and its contents.

51   Ibid.

52   Hampshire Chronicle, 16 August 1773.

53   John Styles identified hearts as one of the recurring motifs in the textile tokens left with foundlings in the Foundling Hospital: Styles 2010b; Styles 2015. They also occur widely on a variety of objects (see for instance fig. 99).

54   AC-NMW, 47.132.9, 47.132.10; BMH, 1935.122a-b; YCM, YORCM: BA5718. One pocket, decorated with a large heart near its opening and said to be of Scottish origin, is illustrated in Seligman and Hughes 1926. Its present whereabouts are unknown.

55   Mary Granville, letter to Lady Margaret Cavendish, Delany 1861, vol. 1, 84.

56   This is the only known letter from Christopher Wren to Faith Coghill; reprinted in Wren Society 19 (1942), 152–3, cited in Tinniswood 2002, 184.

57   Wordsworth and Wordsworth 1967, 16–17.

58   On gift giving and reciprocation in the early modern period, see Zemon Davis 2000; Heal 2014. On the culture of gift giving in eighteenth-century England see Zionkowski and Klekar 2009. On literary representations of gifts in the same century see Zionkowski 2016.

59   Delany 1862, vol. 2, 496; Delany 1862, vol. 3, 76; see also R. Hayden 1992, 155-7; Laird and Weisberg-Roberts 2009, 228–9.

60   Hall 1969.

61   Mavor 1986, 24, 31. Quilted cases and knitted purse made by Eleanor Butler and Sarah Ponsonby and given to Frances, Lady Douglas, 1788. Houghton Library, Harvard University, MS Eng 1225. On the purse and drawings see Thatcher Ulrich et al. 2015, 80–85.

62   Mavor 1979, 150.

63   For examples of pockets made for relatives see Chapter Two. Alice Morse Earle cites a will in which a New Englander left to her lifelong friend her pocket and its contents 'kept within it': Earle 1971, vol. 2, 589. On the bequest of clothing items in wills in general see Lambert 2004 ; Lambert 2004–5 ; Lambert 2014. On women gifting objects see Berg 1996 ; Pointon 1997.

64   Will of the Honourable Margarett or Margaret Mugge, widow, of Saint George Hanover Square, 8 April 1747, TNA, PROB 11/754/59, cited in Pointon 1997, 344–5.

65   Berg 1996, 421.

66   Bristol Mercury, 29 November 1831; Derby Mercury, 30 November 1831.

67   OBP t18080601-26.

68   AC-NMW, 31.31.3, 31.31.4.

69   AC-NMW, 59.357, 31.31.3, 31.31.4; CARM, CAASG.1976.3668; Private collection.

70   Private collection.

71   On the value of female signatures in eighteenth-century art see Guichard 2018, 187–220. On women's relationship to writing see Daybell 2012; Smith 2014. Elizabeth Parker's stitched 'sampler diary' in the V&A is an extraordinary example of a woman using her needle to stitch her life story: V&A, T.6-1956, discussed in Goggin 2002; Goggin 2009.

72   Patchwork was also used on other garments: Swain 1984.

73   Fennetaux 2014.

74 Vickery 1998, 185.

75 Kirshenblatt-Gimblett 1989, 333.

76 A work-box worked by Hannah Downes at the end of the seventeenth century contains examples of needlework made by four generations of women from the seventeenth to the nineteenth centuries. A pair of unfinished pockets worked by Hannah Haines, as well as a single finished pocket included in our survey, belong to this heirloom, now in the V&A, T.31-1935; for the pair of unfinished pockets see fig. 59. On the gifting of textiles see Lambert 2004; Lambert 2004–5; Lambert 2014.

77 Weeton 1939, vol. 2, 325.

78 The 70th Foot regiment, raised in 1758 as the Glasgow Greys, later became the Surreys. The change in uniform in 1768 would have made the grey coat redundant past that date. On military uniforms see Franklin 2016.

79 NAM documentation. It has been said that the pocket may be the work of the drummer as a present to his sweetheart.

80 Chapter Four, pp. 134–5, see figs 107 and 108.

81 Pocket, VDM, WANVD:1981.85.2, cap WANVD:1981.85.1. On these finds see Eastop 2001; Harrison and Gill 2002; Eastop 2006.

82 Warnier 2006; Warnier 2009.

83 Warnier 2006, 200.

84 Warnier 2001.

85 See Schilder 1935. About bags, purses and pockets as metaphorical extensions of the human body see Tilley 1999, 36–77.

86 See, for instance, OBP t17841208-31, OBP t17360610-23, OBP t18470510-1271, OBP t17690628-37, OBP t17490222-9.

87 OBP t17240117-44, OBP t17930529-30, OBP t17940219-74.

88 See, for instance, OBP t18030525-7; see also OBP t18091101-24.

89 Merleau-Ponty 1945/2010; Stewart 1999; Burman 2002, 460; Classen 2012.

90 OBP t18050710-17.

91 Ash 1996; Kwint, Breward and Aynsley 1999; Stallybrass 2012; Bide 2017.

92 Harrold 2008, 52; see also Lambert 2004–5; Fennetaux 2014.

93 Anon. 1826, 90. This description was made on the occasion of the reopening of the prison after major work. It was in this building that Margaret would have been confined in 1851.

94 Hunter 1993; Pointon 1999a; Pointon 1999b; Holm 2004; Pointon 2009; Lutz 2015.

95 Goggin 2009.

96 Stallybrass 2012, 69.

Conclusion

Title quotation: *The Times*, 4 March 1858.

1 Ibid., 11, col. c.

2 OBP t18881022-977.

3 The documented provenance of this pocket identifies Miss Pheysey of Stourport-on-Severn, Worcestershire, as the owner.

4 Museum documentation and personal communication with descendants.

5 Linton 1883, vol. 2, 32. The same association of grannies' pockets and sweets is found in Leigh Hunt 1903.

6 Hall 1849, 37, 38.

7 Ibid., 133–51.

8 On questions of painting everyday life in the period see Solkin 2008. See also for literature Chapman 1986.

9 Various authors started to raise concerns about child labour in the 1830s. See, for instance, Norton 1836; [A Templar] 1840; Barrett Browning 1843; Dickens 1843. The 1833 Factory Act, which had begun to regulate child labour, had limited impact.

10 In stark contrast, this painting and others like it are contemporaneous with Charles Dickens's *Oliver Twist*, published serially in 1837–9 (Dickens 1837–9/2003). Dickens put his hungry child from the poorhouse to work picking pockets in the metropolis.

11 In the companion piece of the same year, *Returning from the Fair*, oil on canvas (559 x 761 mm), V&A, FA.221[O], the outing proves disappointing and the child returns in tears.

12 Hertford Schools, Christ's Hospital, Wardrobe ledger, 1907–26, LMA, CLC/210/F/040/MS22571, fol. 264.

13 For pockets in the uniform of Christ's Hospital see Angus 1981, 31–2. Pupils at the school today, now moved to Horsham, continue to wear uniforms with historical references.

14 Hamer 1984a, 27–28; see also Hamer 1984b. Numerous paintings and drawings made in Cullercoats in the 1880s by Winslow Homer (1836–1910) – for example, in Harvard Art Museums – depict the fish women.

15 http://kildare.ie/Library/SpecialProjects/ThreadingTales/Workshops/ThreadingTales/TheBeadyPocketasCulturalSymbol/html (last accessed, 15 June 2018); see also Carson Williams 2008.

16 See, for instance, William Powell Frith (1819–1909), *Dolly Varden*, c.1842–9, oil on wood (273 × 216 mm), Tate, T00041. On Dickens and painters see Bills and Penny 2012.

17 On the afterlife of Dolly Varden see England 2017, 272–300.

18 Pocket, RAMM, EXEMS 50/1943/34/1.

19 On the vogue for fancy dress in the nineteenth century see Stevenson and Bennett 1978; Jarvis 1982. For the earlier period see Ribeiro 1984, Castle 1986.

20 It carries an old handwritten note associating it formerly with 'Miss Carslake of Cotmaton' (Devon), on the back of a visiting card of Mrs Samuel Woolcott Brown; it was latterly with Lady Lockyer, whose visiting card is also attached. Both Mrs Woolcott Brown and Lady Lockyer lived in Kensington, London, and perhaps jointly participated in the fancy-dress occasion.

21 The V&A first acquired pockets in 1871 – a lavishly decorated pair almost certainly originating in continental Europe. From 1900 to 1913 six more entered the collection, one of which was French; after a lull, acquisitions recommenced in 1935. VAMA, acquisition files MA/1/C/1032/1, MA/1/C2965, MA/1/D783, MA/1/D1520, MA/1/G1/78, MA/1/H926, MA/1/3222, MA/1N360, MA/9/3, MA/10/2/12. For an account of the establishment of nineteenth- and early twentieth-century dress collections in Britain see Taylor 2004, 106–55.

22 The Circulation department had a reputation as a progressive force within the museum: Sandino 2013.

23 V&A, T.1411-1900, 492-1907, T.730.B-1913, CIRC.86-1938. They are all single, embroidered pockets.

24 For example, an unusually high proportion of the large collection of pockets in Amgueddfa Cymru–National Museum Wales have a documented provenance, reflecting the museum's mission to represent the culture and history of the people of Wales. By contrast, numerous pockets in the large collection at Platt Hall, part of Manchester Art Gallery and originally known as the Gallery of English Costume (Britain's first museum of dress when it opened in 1947), were irretrievably deprived of their provenance by their original collectors – a result of their primary interest in mass rather than personal trends: see Jarvis 1999.

25 V&A, T.281&A-1910.

26 In one case, a pocket was classified as a peg-bag.

27 Thatcher Ulrich et al. 2015, 2, 4.

28 Deetz 1977, 161.

ARCHIVES

For the 572 Old Bailey trial accounts used in our study see the Appendix, pp. 224–5.

Material Sources

Many of the pockets listed below can be viewed on *Pockets of History* (https://vads.ac.uk/collections/POCKETS.html), where their measurements and materials are provided.

Abbey House Museum, Leeds (AHML)
Pocket, single LEEDM.E.1950.0022
Pocket, single LEEDM.E.1967.0011.0025.1
Pocket, single LEEDM.E.1967.0011.0025.2
Pocket, single LEEDM.E.1968.0061.0020.A
Pocket, single LEEDM.E.1968.0061.0020.B
Pocket, single LEEDM.E.1968.0061.0020.C
Pocket, single LEEDM.E.1973.0151.0003.A
Pocket, single LEEDM.E.1973.0151.A
Pocket, single LEEDM.E.1975.0123.0003.1
Pocket, single LEEDM.E.1981.0011.0001
Pocket, single LEEDM.E.1992.0158
Pocket, single LEEDM.E.X.0171
Pocket, single LEEDM.E.X.0172
Pocket, single LEEDM.E.X.0173
Pocket, single LEEDM.E.X.0174
Pocket, single LEEDM.E.X.0175
Pocket, single LEEDM.E.X.0177
Pocket, single LEEDM.E.Y.5496
Pedlar doll with pocket LEEDM.E.1956.0164

Abingdon County Hall Museum, Abingdon-on-Thames (ABING)
Pocket, single OXCMS:1997.7.1

Amgueddfa Cymru–National Museum Wales, St Fagans, Cardiff (AC-NMW)
Pockets, pair 31.31.3, 31.31.4
Pockets, pair 47.132.9, 47.132.10
Pockets, pair 47.132.11, 47.132.12
Pockets, pair 49.469.133, 49.469.134
Pockets, pair 51.27.34.A, 51.27.34.B
Pocket, single 31.31.1
Pocket, single 31.31.2
Pocket, single 31.545
Pocket, single 59.245.30
Pocket, single 59.285.6
Pocket, single 59.285.7
Pocket, single 59.285.8
Pocket, single 59.285.9
Pocket, single 59.357
Pocket, single 60.504
Pocket, single 64.385.10
Pocket, single 67.66.10
Pocket, single F72.331.21
Pocket, single F72.381.27

Pocket, single F73.404.30
Pocket, single F76.342.11
Pocket, single F77.282.82
Pocket, single F78.259.1
Pocket, single F78.4.5
Pocket, single F78.4.14,
Pocket, single F78.4.15
Pocket, single F80.280.9
Pocket, single F92.89

Banbury Museum
Pockets, pair OXCMS:BM985.71.18

Bankfield Museum, Halifax (BMH)
Pockets, pair 1935.122.a–b
Pocket, single 1967.46.2.a
Pocket, single 1970.451.20
Pocket, single 1975.620.4

Blaise Castle House Museum, Bristol (BCHM)
Pockets, pair T.9808
Pocket, single T.9807
Pocket, single TA.6517

Bolton Museums, Art Gallery and Aquarium (BMGA)
Pocket, single IND.46.1983
Apron pocket INV.4326

Bowes Museum, Barnard Castle, County Durham (BMBC)
Pocket, single CST.127
Pocket, single CST.2.161.1976.46.4
Pocket, single CST.2.523.1981.25.5
Pocket, single CST.2.689.1983.20.28
Pocket, single CST.2.762.1986.29.3
Doll with pocket TOY 301.1970.187A

Burrell Collection, Glasgow (BCG)
Pocket, single E1938.92h
Pocket, single 1919.26.b
Pocket, single E1977.43.3

Carmarthenshire County Museum, Carmarthen (CARM)
Pockets, pair CAASG.1976.3668

Charles Paget Wade Collection, Berrington Hall (Herefordshire), National Trust (CPW)
Pockets, pair SNO 1453
Pocket, single SNO 1452
Pocket, single SNO 1454
Pocket, single SNO 1748
Pocket, single SNO 1951

Clare Ancient House Museum, Suffolk
Pocket, single CLREM 1997.98
Pocket, single CLREM 2018.5

Dorset County Museum, Dorchester
Pockets, pair [no inventory number]
Pocket, single 1983.20.5

Embroiderers' Guild
Pockets, pair EG959, EG784

Fashion Museum Bath (FMB)
Pockets, pair BATMC 2004.468
Pocket, single BATMC 93.311A
Pocket, single BATMC 93.311B
Pocket, single BATMC VI.14.1
Pocket, single BATMC VI.14.2
Pocket, single BATMC VI.14.4
Pocket, single BATMC VI.14.5
Pocket, single BATMC VI.14.6
Pocket, single BATMC VI.14.7
Pocket, single BATMC VI.14.8
Pocket, single BATMC VI.14.9
Pocket, single BATMC VI.14.11
Pocket, single BATMC VI.14.100
Pocket, single BATMC VI.14.101
Pocket, single BATMC VI.14.102
Pocket, single BATMC VI.14.103
Pocket, single BATMC VI.14.104
Pocket, single BATMC VI.14.105
Pocket, single BATMC VI.14.106
Pocket, single BATMC VI.14.107
Doll with pocket BATMC VIII.01.2

Fitzwilliam Museum, Cambridge (FITZ)
Pocket, single T.67-1938

Gawthorpe Textiles Collection, Gawthorpe Hall, Lancashire
Pockets, pair RBKS4430
Pockets, pair RBKS4445
Pockets, pair RBKS13408
Pocket, single RBKS4433
Pocket, single RBKS13065
Pocket, single RBKS13067
Pocket, single RBKS13407

Hampshire Cultural Trust, Winchester (HCT)
Pockets, pair HMCMS:CNM.1966.4
Pocket, single HMCMS:BWM.1957.105
Pocket, single HMCMS:BWM.1963.163
Pocket, single HMCMS:C2004.79
Pocket, single HMCMS:CRH.1967.113.12
Pocket, single HMCMS:CRH.1973.16.2
Pocket, single HMCMS:CRH.1978.10.5
Doll with pocket HMCMS:ACM.1949.97

Hereford Museum Service (HMS)
Pockets, pair HSS 2339
Pockets, pair HSS 3950
Pockets, pair HSS 5449
Pocket, single HSS 2784
Pocket, single HSS 2797.1
Pocket, single HSS 2797.2
Pocket, single HSS 2808
Pocket, single HSS 5035
Pocket, single HSS 5683
Doll's pockets, pair HSS 3670 (part A)
Doll's pocket HSS 3670 (part B)
Doll, clothes and two pockets HSS 3744

Maidstone Museum and Art Gallery
Pockets, pair [no inventory number]
Pockets, pair [no inventory number]
Pocket, single MNEMG.19.1960.B

Manchester Art Gallery (MAG)
Pockets, pair MCAG.1922.2150/2
Pockets, pair MCAG.1947.1251
Pockets, pair MCAG.1947.1264/2
Pockets, pair MCAG.1951.107/2
Pockets, pair MCAG.1986.57/2
Pocket, single MCAG.1938.449
Pocket, single MCAG.1941.123
Pocket, single MCAG.1947.845
Pocket, single MCAG.1947.860
Pocket, single MCAG.1947.1250
Pocket, single MCAG.1947.1252
Pocket, single MCAG.1947.1253
Pocket, single MCAG.1947.1253/2
Pocket, single MCAG.1947.1254
Pocket, single MCAG.1947.1258
Pocket, single MCAG.1947.1259
Pocket, single MCAG.1947.1260
Pocket, single MCAG.1947.1261
Pocket, single MCAG.1947.1262
Pocket, single MCAG.1947.1265
Pocket, single MCAG.1948.247
Pocket, single MCAG.1948.248
Pocket, single MCAG.1960.239
Pocket, single MCAG.1961.186
Pocket, single MCAG.1965.154
Pedlar doll with pocket MCAG.1922.566
Pedlar doll with pocket MCAG.1954.35
Doll with pair of pockets and single pocket
    MCAG.1955.21

Museum of Fine Arts, Boston (MFA)
Pocket, single 40.80

Museum of London (MoL)
Pockets, pair 35.35/2
Pockets, pair 49.23/2
Pockets, pair 49.91/2
Pocket, single 32.112/2
Pocket, single 32.112/3
Pocket, single 39.119/10
Pocket, single 46.8/3
Pocket, single A21980b
Pocket, single A21980c
Doll with pocket A21165
Doll with pocket A25315

National Army Museum, London (NAM)
Pocket, single NAM. 2006-08-53-1

National Museums Scotland (NMS)
Pockets, pair K.2002.322
Pocket, single H.RHB 11
Pocket, single H.RHE 10
Pocket, single H.TND 11
Pocket, single H.TND 12
Pocket, single H.UF 45
Pocket, single H.UF 91
Pedlar doll with pocket A.1914.1013

**Norfolk Museums Service, Norwich
Costume and Textile Collections** (NM)
Pockets, pair NWHCM:1935.53.107
Pockets, pair NWHCM:1937.89.42
Pockets, pair NWHCM:1938.166.2.1

Pockets, pair NWHCM:1938.166.2.2
Pockets, pair NWHCM:1953.80.9
Pockets, pair NWHCM:1972.227
Pocket, single NWHCM:1967.305.3
Pocket, single NWHCM:1968.873.9
Pocket, single NWHCM:1968.873.10
Pocket, single NWHCM:1970.171.59
Pocket, single NWHCM:1972.226.2
Pocket, single NWHCM:1972.226.3
Pocket, single NWHCM:1982.259.5

**Nottingham City Museums and
Galleries** (NCMG)
Pockets, pair NCM 1965-92
Pockets, 3 single NCM 1963-256
Pocket, single NCM 1964-35
Pocket, single NCM 1974-185
Pocket, single NCM 1976-195
Pocket, single NCM 1977-497
Pocket, single NCM 1978-22/1
Pocket, single NCM 1978-22/2
Pocket, single NCM 1978-22/3
Pocket, single NCM 1978-22/4
Pocket, single NCM 1980-537
Pocket, single NCM 1983-728
Pocket, single NCM 2005-188

**Oxfordshire County Council Museum
Service, Museum Resource Centre,
Standlake** (OX)
Pocket, single OXCMS:1964.4298
Pocket, single OXCMS:1964.4299
Pocket, single OXCMS:1980.25.3
Pocket, single OXCMS:1980.115.1
Pocket, single OXCMS:1982.117.4

Private collections
Pockets, 3 pairs
Pockets, 14 single

**Royal Albert Memorial Museum
and Art Gallery, Exeter** (RAMM)
Pockets, pair EXEMS 10/1965/39/1
Pocket, single EXEMS 10/1965/39/2
Pocket, single EXEMS 10/1965/39/3
Pocket, single EXEMS 50/1943/34/1
Pocket, single EXEMS 74/1964/4
Pocket, single EXEMS 86/1961/6
Pocket, single EXEMS 95/1965
Pocket, single EXEMS 382/2006
Pocket, single EXEMS 567/2006
Pocket, single EXEMS 568/2006
Pocket, single KIL/PR/1368/4
Pocket, single KIL/W/101991
Pocket, single KIL/W/101695
Pocket, single KIL/W/103596
Pocket, single KIL/W/03990

**Royal School of Needlework,
Hampton Court Palace**
Pocket, single RSN.211
Pocket, single RSN.760

**Salisbury and South Wiltshire
Museum** (SSWM)
Pocket, single SBYWM.1938.35.1

Pocket, single SBYWM.1956.61
Pocket, single SBYWM.1999R.70.2
Pocket, single SBYWM.1999R.780.1
Doll's garment with pocket SBYWM.1943.4
Doll with pocket SBYWM.2000R.368

School of Historical Dress, London (SHD)
Pocket, single TSHD-2014-044

**Swaledale Museum, Reeth, North
Yorkshire**
Pockets, pair SM.T.1

**Vale and Downland Museum,
Wantage** (VDM)
Pocket, single WANVD:1981.85.2

Victoria and Albert Museum, London
(V&A)
Pockets, pair T.41-1935
Pockets, pair T.43-1909
Pockets, pair T.87.A-1978, T.87.B-1978
Pockets, pair T.175-1969
Pockets, pair T.198-1958
Pockets, pair T.208-1970
Pockets, pair T.281&A-1910
Pockets, pair T.697.B-1913, T.697.C-1913
Pocket, single 492-1907
Pocket, single 1437-1871
Pocket, single 1438-1871
Pocket, single CIRC.86-1938
Pocket, single T.42-1935
Pocket, single T.150-1970
Pocket, single T.346-1996
Pocket, single T.730.B-1913
Pocket, single T.1411-1900
Doll with pocket T.19-1936
Doll with pocket T.846-1974, T.846.C-1974
Doll with pocket W.42:1-1922
Doll with pocket W.42:2-1922

**Victoria and Albert Museum
of Childhood, London**
Doll's pockets, pair MISC.61-1964
Doll's clothing with pocket MISC.53-1925
Doll's clothing with pocket MISC.264-1978
Doll's pocket T.143H-1929
Doll with pocket T.186-1931

**Wilson Art Gallery and Museum,
Cheltenham** (WILS)
Pockets, pair CMAG.1940.29
Pockets, pair CMAG.1954.37.7
Pockets, pair CMAG.1956.98.60
Pocket, single CMAG.1951.83.10
Pocket, single CMAG.1965.19.10
Pocket, single CMAG.1967.76.8

Worthing Museum and Art Gallery
(WORTH)
Pockets, pair WMAG.1961.924
Pockets, pair WMAG.1966.389
Pocket, single WMAG.66.891
Pocket, single WMAG.1962.1949
Pocket, single WMAG.1963.766

Pocket, single WMAG.1965.18
Pocket, single WMAG.1966.891
Pocket, single WMAG.1972.361
Pocket, single WMAG.2029
Pocket, single WMAG.2412
Doll with pocket WMAG.927.1
Doll with pocket WMAG.927.2

York Castle Museum (YCM)
Pockets, pair YORCM: 1945.186
Pocket, single YORCM: 1941.356
Pocket, single YORCM: 1942.150
Pocket, single YORCM: 1945.186
Pocket, single YORCM: 1945.229
Pocket, single YORCM: 1946.296.a
Pocket, single YORCM: 1946.484.a
Pocket, single YORCM: 1946.484.b
Pocket, single YORCM: 1946.484.c
Pocket, single YORCM: 1946.484.d
Pocket, single YORCM: 1946.1129
Pocket, single YORCM: 1952.766
Pocket, single YORCM: 1952.767
Pocket, single YORCM: 1953.284.9
Pocket, single YORCM: BA260
Pocket, single YORCM: BA741
Pocket, single YORCM: BA5707
Pocket, single YORCM: BA5708
Pocket, single YORCM: BA5709
Pocket, single YORCM: BA5715
Pocket, single YORCM: BA5716
Pocket, single YORCM: BA5717
Pocket, single YORCM: BA5718
Pocket, single YORCM: BA5719
Pocket, single YORCM: BA5720
Pocket, single YORCM: BA5721
Doll's pocket YORCM: BA4530

Documentary Sources

Bedfordshire Archives and Record Service, Bedford (BARS)
Vouchers for sundry payments made on account of the maintenance of Lady Louisa Fitzpatrick by Richard Vernon esquire, 1765–70, RO32/16

British Library, London (BL)
Althorp Papers, vol. cdliv, unbound, Personal expenditure, chiefly clothing, of Lady Georgiana Spencer, 1769–1775, Add. MS 75754
Brockman Papers, Household Accompts of Anne, wife of Sir William Brockman, 26 December 1700 – 2 October 1704, Brockman Papers, Add. MS 45208

British Museum, London (BM)
Department of Prints and Drawings, Banks and Heal collections of trade cards
Department of Prints and Drawings, Sarah Sophia Banks collections, visiting cards, C,1.5346, C,1.2225

Cadbury Research Library, University of Birmingham (CRL)
Diary and Scrapbook of Catherine Hutton, 1779–[20th century], 2 vols, MS15

Centre for Buckinghamshire Studies, Aylesbury (CBS)
Frances Tyrwhitt, Tradesmen's bills and receipts, 1742–68, D-DR/7/37

City of Westminster Archives (CoW)
All the inquests listed here may be consulted at www.londonlives.org, version 1.1, April 2012, hereafter LL.

City of Westminster, Coroners' inquests into suspicious deaths, 3 January 1766 – 29 December 1766, 9 May 1766, LL, WACWIC652060292
City of Westminster, Coroners' inquests into suspicious deaths, 7 January 1773 – 28 December 1773, 9 June 1773, LL, WACWIC652130279
City of Westminster, Coroners' inquests into suspicious deaths, 2 January 1775 – 28 December 1775, 2 January 1775, LL, WACWIC652150007
City of Westminster, Coroners' inquests into suspicious deaths, 1 January 1778 – 31 December 1778, 4 May 1778, LL, WACWIC652180152
City of Westminster, Coroners' inquests into suspicious deaths, 31 January 1782 – 22 December 1782, 29 July 1782, LL, WACWIC652220275; 13 September 1782, LL, WACWIC652220359
City of Westminster, Coroners' inquests into suspicious deaths, 5 January 1789 – 29 December 1789, 15 April 1789, LL, WACWIC652290243
City of Westminster, Coroners' inquests into suspicious deaths, 5 January 1792 – 31 December 1792, 1 February 1792, LL, WACWIC652320079
City of Westminster, Coroners' inquests into suspicious deaths, 9 January 1794 – 27 December 1794, 17 April 1794, LL, WACWIC652340159
City of Westminster, Coroners' inquests into suspicious deaths, 2 January 1795 – 28 December 1795, 27 February 1795, LL, WACWIC652350143
City of Westminster, Coroners' inquests into suspicious deaths, 4 January 1796 – 28 December 1796, 21 March 1796, LL, WACWIC652360120; 14 July 1796, LL, WACWIC652360418
City of Westminster, Coroners' inquests into suspicious deaths, 9 January 1797 – 29 December 1797, 9 August 1797, LL, WACWIC652370554

Cornwall Record Office, Truro (CRO)
Stephen Lawrence, shopkeeper of Tregony, Cornwall, will, 1721, AP/L/1249

Dorset Record Office, Dorchester (DRO)
Bankes of Kingston Lady and Corfe Castle, Manorial and Hundretal Court Rolls, Papers, books and accounts, Badbury Hundred, Inquisition Papers, 1719–30, D-BKL/C/F/1/3/3

Hampshire Archives and Local Studies (formerly Hampshire Record Office), Winchester (HRO)
Bonham Carter Family, Bundle of bills, 1735–1807, 94M72/F655
Pocket book / Diary of Lady Catherine Fellowes, 1847, 15M84/5/6/4
Lady's Pocket Book for 1757, with notes by Sarah Gatehouse, 1757–1808, 35M63/66
Lady's Pocket Book for 1771, with notes by Sarah Gatehouse, February 1771–1792, 35M63/67
Account book of Lady Betty [Elizabeth] Heathcote, April 1720 – March 1733, 43M87/D1
Jervoise of Herriard Family Papers, 44M69
Waller of Bursledon, Shipping and timber business and family records, 1778–1840, 29M67
Letter from Lady Wallingford to her nephew Thomas Woods Knollis, 1 November 1780, 1M44/7/34
Letter from Lady Wallingford to her nephew Thomas Woods Knollis, 22 February 1783, 1M44/7/43

Horsham Museum and Art Gallery (HMA)
Sarah Hurst, Diary, HMS 3542–3545

Huntington Library, San Marino, CA (HL)
Ann Heatley, Letters and personal expenditure, MSS HM 81748–81770
Anna Margaretta Larpent, Diaries, 1773–1830, 17 vols, MS HM 31201

Kent History and Library Centre, Maidstone (KHLC)
Lady Arabella Furnese, Household accounts, EK/U471/A49
Lady Arabella Furnese, Personal expenditure, 1714–27, EK/U471/A50
Clothing and pocket accounts kept by the Countess of Guilford, 1748–51, EK/U471/A54
Clothing and pocket accounts kept by the Countess of Guilford, 1762–6, EK/U471/A55
Expenditure by Katherine, Countess of Rockingham (later of Guilford), 1750–66, EK/U471/A57

London Metropolitan Archives, City of London (LMA)
Acco't of the Miss Haightons Stock and the Agreement between them and Mr W.

Atkinson and Daughters, 1783, Records of Major Blundell, Haberdasher and Warehouseman at Cheapside, late of Holborn Hill, 1774–1801, CLC/B/025/MS100033A

City of London Coroners Court, Inquests, London, 1838 – 21 June 1901, CLA/041/IQ/03/065

Collection of trade cards, SC/GL/TCC/001

Diocese of London, Archdeaconry of Middlesex, Probate inventories (2nd series), DL/AM/P1/02

Hertford Schools, Christ's Hospital, Wardrobe ledger, 'a record of linen, clothing, household goods and other items taken into stock with names of suppliers, to whom issues, and costs', 1907–26, CLC/210/F/040/MS22571

James Bonus, Slop Seller of the Woolpack and Lion, Thames Street, opposite Billingsgate: Bills for items of clothing bought by Thomas Aris, Governor of the House of Correction, Clerkenwell, for the use of the prisoners in his custody, Middlesex Sessions of the Peace: Court in Session, Sessions Papers, MJ/SP/1795/04/099

Middlesex Sessions of the Peace: Court in Session, Session Papers, MJ/SP

St Mary at Lambeth, Lambeth Road, Parish Records, Norwood Workhouse, Matron's clothing book, April 1790 – October 1792, P85/MRY1/315

St Mary at Lambeth, Lambeth Road, Parish Records, Norwood Workhouse, Matron's clothing book, October 1792 – January 1797, P85/MRY1/316

St Mary at Lambeth, Lambeth Road, Parish Records, Norwood Workhouse, Matron's clothing book, 1800–25, P85/MRY1/318

St Sepulchre, Holborn, City of London, Vestry and Parish Officers, Workhouse stock books of clothing, 1727–1838, P69/SEP/B/080/001-008

Museum of London (MoL)

Martha Dodson, Account Book, 1746–65, 80.71

Mary Young Papers, 1817–54:
Mrs Abbott's Personal Commonplace Book, 1738–91, 48.107/1
Housekeeping Account of Mrs Mary Young, 1817–25, 48.85/1
Housekeeping Account of Mrs Mary Young, 1818–20, 49.15
Commonplace Book kept by Mrs Mary Young, 1823, 51.86
Education scheme by Mrs Mary Young for her children William, Frederick, Sidney, Horace, Lucy, Jane and Emma, including daily schedules, 1825–31, 48.85/6
Household Commonplace Book, 1830–36, 48.85/3
Household Cash Book, 1832–9, 48.85/4

Household and Cash Book, 1840–44, 48.85/5
Mrs Young's travelogue, letters to her husband, 1852, 52.90/1
Mrs Young's Continental Journal, 1853-4, 52.90/2

National Art Library, Victoria and Albert Museum, London (NAL)

Richard Crosse, Diary and account book, 1776–1810, 86 KK 41

David Norie, Account Book, 86.ZZ.148

William Wood, Memorandum of miniatures painted and finished by William Wood, of the Royal Academy, 1790–1808, 86.KK.3, 86.KK.4, 86.KK.5, 86.KK.5a

Northumberland Archives, Ashington (NoA)

Printer's proofs of William Davison of Alnwick, 1781–1858, ZMD 167/1-36

North Riding of Yorkshire County Record Office, Northallerton (NYCRO)

North Riding of Yorkshire Quarter Sessions Bundles, QSB

Princeton University Library, Princeton, NJ (PUL)

Elizabeth Isham, Book of Remembrance, autobiography, c.1638, MS RTC01 (no. 62)

Private collections

Sarah Hurst, Account books
Sarah Hurst, Almanac, brief jottings, lists of clothes, 1803–6

Surrey History Centre, Woking (SHC)

Surrey Quarter Sessions, Records, Sessions Bundles, QS2/6

The National Archives, Kew (TNA)

Board of Stamps: Legacy Duty Office and successors: Specimens of Death Duty Account, 1796–1903, IR 19

Registers of the Board of Trade, BT45 21-4035

Home Office Registered Papers, Criminal, Whitechapel murders, HO 144/221/A49301C

Metropolitan Police Office, Case papers of the Whitechapel murders, MEPO 3/140, MEPO 3/141

Northern and North-Eastern Circuits: Criminal Depositions and Case Papers, 1613–1800, ASSI 45/1/1 – ASSI 45/40/2

Prerogative Court of Canterbury, Main Exhibits, February 1731, PROB 31/89

Records of the Prerogative Court of Canterbury, Prerogative Court of Canterbury and Related Jurisdictions, Will Registers, Name of Register: Potter Quire Numbers 99-146, April 1747, PROB 11/754

Prerogative Court of Canterbury, Exhibits, Main Class, March 1774, PROB 31/606

The Women's Library, London School of Economics (TWL)

Papers of Emily Wilding Davison, Emily

Wilding Davison Personal Papers, Death of Emily Wilding Davison, List of possessions found on Emily Wilding Davison, 7EWD/A/7/2

Papers of Emily Wilding Davison, Emily Wilding Davison Personal Papers, Emily Wilding Davison's Writings, Incendiarism, 1911, 7EWD/A/4/02

Papers of Emily Wilding Davison, Objects, purse of Emily Wilding Davison, 7EWD/M/27

Papers of Emily Wilding Davison, Objects, Emily Wilding Davison's rail tickets, 7EWD/M/30

University of St Andrews, Special Collections (UStA)

Graham Morphie Papers, 1733-1952, msdep36

Victoria and Albert Museum Archive, Blythe House, London (VAMA)

MA/1/C1032/1
MA/1/C2965
MA/1/D783
MA/1/D1520
MA/1/G1/78
MA/1/H926
MA/1/H3222
MA/1/N360
MA/9/3
MA/10/2/12

West Yorkshire Archive Service, Wakefield (WYAS)

Quarter Sessions Records of the West Riding of Yorkshire, Quarter Session Rolls, QS1

Wiltshire and Swindon Archives (WSA)

Probate Records of the Consistory Court of Salisbury, P1/C

Worcestershire Archive and Archaeology Service, Worcester (WAAS)

Worcestershire Quarter Sessions, Quarter Sessions General Rolls, Sessions 1743 Midsummer, 1743, 1/1/334

Worcestershire Quarter Sessions, Quarter Sessions General Rolls, Sessions 1777 Michaelmas, 1777, 1/1/470

Worcestershire Quarter Sessions, Quarter Sessions General Rolls, Sessions 1814 Midsummer, 1814, 1/1/616

Worcestershire Quarter Sessions, Quarter Sessions General Rolls, Sessions 1818 Michaelmas, 1818, 1/1/635

York City Archives (YCA)

George Fettes of Stonegate, York, pawnbroker, Pledge book, 1777-8, Acc. 38

BIBLIOGRAPHY

Electronic Sources

Tim Hitchcock, Robert Shoemaker, Clive Emsley, Sharon Howard, Jamie McLaughlin et al., *The Old Bailey Proceedings Online, 1674–1913*, www.oldbaileyonline.org, version 7.0, 24 March 2012.

Ordinary of Newgate's Accounts: Biographies of Executed Criminals, 1676–1772, www.oldbaileyonline.org/static/Ordinarys-accounts.jsp.

London Lives, 1690–1800: Crime, Poverty and Social Policy in the Metropolis, www.londonlives.org

Printed Primary Sources

Ackerman, Rudolph, 1816. *Ackermann's Repository of Arts, Literature, Commerce, Manufactures, Fashions and Politics. Second Series*. London: R. Ackermann.

'A Lady' 1840/1975. *The Workwoman's Guide*. Facsimile of the 1840 edition. London: Bloomfield Books.

Anon. 1728. *A Genuine Narrative of All the Street Robberies Committed since October Last by James Dalton*. London: J. Roberts.

—— 1735. *The Lives of the Most Remarkable Criminals. Who Have Been Condemn'd and Executed*. 2 vols. London: n.pub.

—— 1764. *Low-Life, or One Half of the World Knows How the Other Half Lives, Being a Critical Account of What Is Transacted in the Twenty-Four Hours between Saturday Night and Monday Morning, in a True Description of a Sunday as It Is Usually Spent within the Bills of Mortality*. 3rd edition. London: J. Lever.

—— 1773. *The London Companion, or an Account of the Fares of Hackney Coachmen, Chairmen and Watermen, with the Rates of Cartmen and Porters Plying in London, Westminster or Southwark*. London: Printed for T. Carnan.

—— 1789. *Instructions for Cutting Out Apparel for the Poor; Principally Intended for the Assistance of the Patronesses of Sunday Schools, and Other Charitable Institutions, but Useful in All Families*. London: Published for the benefit of the Sunday School Children at Hertingfordbury, in the county of Hertford.

—— 1790. *The Ladies' Library: or, Encyclopaedia of Female Knowledge, in Every Branch of Domestic Economy [. . .] Necessary for Servants and Mistresses of Families*. 2 vols. London: Printed for J. Ridgway.

—— 1795a. *Crosby's Royal Fortune-Telling Almanack; or, Ladies' Universal Pocket-Book*. London: Crosby.

—— 1795b. *The Observant Pedestrian, or Traits of the Heart [. . .] by the Author of The Mystic Cottager*. 2 vols. London: Printed for William Lane.

—— 1796. *The Taylor's Complete Guide; or, A Comprehensive Analysis of Beauty and Elegance in Dress. Containing Rules for Cutting out Garments of Every Kind. With Copper Plates*. London: n.pub.

—— 1799/2000. *A Full True and Clear Account of Eliz. Woodcock of the Parish of Impington near Cambridge*. Cambridge: F. Hodson; reprinted Histon and Impington Village Society.

—— 1800. *The Ladies' Complete Visiting Guide Containing Directions for Footmen and Porters, Being Calculated for the Purpose of Receiving and Delivering Visiting Cards, and Answering Letters, with Dispatch & Punctuality*. London: P. Boyle.

—— 1809. *Celia in Search of a Husband*. 2 vols. London: Minerva Press.

—— 1817. *The Housekeeper's Receipt Book: or, The Repository of Domestic Knowledge Containing a Complete System of Housekeeping Formed upon Principles of Experience and Economy*. London: J. Haddon.

—— 1818. *The London Guide, and Stranger's Safeguard against the Cheats, Swindlers and Pickpockets That Abound within the Bills of Mortality*. London: n.pub.

—— 1825. 'Memoirs of a Reticule'. *Atheneum, or Spirit of the English Magazines* 17: 251–2.

—— 1826. *Glasgow Delineated in Its Institutions, Manufactures & Commerce with a Map of the City*. Glasgow: Wardlaw & Cunninghame.

—— 1827. 'The Wardrobe of the Nations'. *La Belle Assemblée, or Bell's Court and Fashionable Magazine* 6, July: 245–7.

—— 1829. *The Home Book; or, Young Housekeeper's Assistant: Forming a Complete System of Domestic Economy, and Household Accounts*. London: Smith, Elder & Co.

—— 1831. *Pin Money*. 3 vols. London: Colburn and Bentley.

—— n.d. [*c*.1842]. *The Worktable and Embroidery Frame Companion*. London: n.pub.

—— 1850. 'Nooks and Corners of Character: The Charwoman'. *Punch* 18: 51.

—— 1852. *The Ladies Worktable Book*. London.

—— 1909. 'A Month's Tour with a Handbag'. *Fashions for All*, July.

—— 1914. 'The Unwomanly Pocket'. *Huddersfield Daily Examiner*, 3 June.

[A Templar] 1840. *'Infant Slavery', or The Children of the Mines and Factories. [A Poem]*. London: n.pub.

Austen, Jane, 1814/1996. *Mansfield Park* [1814]. Harmondsworth: Penguin.

——, 1908. *The Letters of Jane Austen: Selected from the Compilation of Her Great Nephew, Edward, Lord Bradbourne*, edited by Sarah Chauncey Woolsey. Boston: Little, Brown, & Company.

——, 1932. *Jane Austen's Letters to Her Sister Cassandra and Others*, edited by Robert William Chapman. 2 vols. Oxford: Clarendon Press.

Austen-Leigh, J. E., 1870/2002. *A Memoir of Jane Austen and Other Family Recollections* [1870], ed. Kathryn Sutherland. Oxford: Oxford University Press.

Bailey's Northern Directory, or Merchant's and Tradesman's Useful Companion for the Year 1781. Warrington: William Ashton.

Baillie, Grisell, 1911. *Lady Grisell Baillie's Household Book, 1692–1733*, edited by Robert Scott-Moncrieff. Edinburgh: Scottish History Society.

Barrett, E. S., 1817. *Six Weeks at Long's*. 2nd edition. 3 vols. London: Printed for the author.

Barrett Browning, Elizabeth, 1843. 'The Cry of the Children'. *Blackwood's Edinburgh Magazine*, August.

Blake, William, 1979. *Blake's Poetry and Designs*, edited by Mary Lynn Johnson and John E. Grant. New York and London: Norton.

Bourne, Jane, 1832. *The Crooked Sixpence, or The Adventures of Little Harry*. Swaffham: F. Skill.

Bridges, Joseph, 1770. *The Adventures of a Bank-Note*. London: T. Davies.

Brontë, Charlotte, 1847/1996. *Jane Eyre* [1847]. Harmondsworth: Penguin.

Bryant, Charles, 1783. *Flora Diaetetica*. London: n.pub.

Burney, Fanny, 1854. *Diary and Letters of Madame d'Arblay*, edited by Charlotte Barrett. London: H. Colburn.

——, 1988. *The Early Journals and Letters of Fanny Burney*, vol. 1, edited by Lars E. Troide. Oxford: Clarendon Press.

Burton, Elizabeth, 1875. *The Inner Life of Syria, Palestine and the Holy Land from My Private Journal*. 2 vols. London: Henry S. King.

Cady Stanton, Elizabeth, 1895. 'The Pocket Problem'. *Utica Sunday Journal*, 26 May.

——, 1901. 'Make Pockets unto Yourselves'. *Geneva NY Advertiser*, 22 January.

Campbell, R., 1747. *The London Tradesman. Being a Compendious View of All the Trades, Professions, Arts, Both Liberal and Mechanic*

Now Practised. London: n.pub.

Caulfeild, Sophia Frances Anne, and Blanche C. Saward, 1882. *The Dictionary of Needlework, an Encyclopaedia of Artistic, Plain and Fancy Needlework*. London: Upcott Gill.

Clarke, Mary Jepp, ed., 2003. *Clarke Family Letters*. Alexandria, VA: Alexander Street Press.

Coleridge, Samuel Taylor, 1956. *Collected Letters of Samuel Taylor Coleridge*, edited by Earl Leslie Griggs. Oxford: Clarendon Press.

Collier, Mary, 1739. *The Woman's Labour: an Epistle to Mr. Stephen Duck; in Answer to his Late Poem, Called The thresher's Labour. To which are Added, the three wise sentences, taken from the first book of Esdras, Ch. III. and IV. By Mary Collier, Now a Washer-Woman, at Petersfield in Hempshire*. London: J. Roberts.

Davies, David, 1795. *The Case of Labourers in Husbandry*. London: C. G. & J. Robinson.

Defoe, Daniel, 1729. *A Humble Proposal to the People of England*. London: n.pub.

Delany, Mary, 1861. *Autobiography and Correspondence of Mary Granville, Mrs Delany, with Interesting Reminiscences of King George III and Queen Charlotte*, edited by Lady Llanover. 3 vols. London: Richard Bentley.

——, 1862. *Autobiography and Correspondence of Mary Granville, Mrs Delany, Second Series*, edited by Lady Llanover. 3 vols. London: Richard Bentley.

Desarps, M., 1815. *Le Ridicule et les poches. Dialogue en prose*. Paris: Delaunay.

Dickens, Charles, 1837-9/2003. *Oliver Twist* [1837-9]. Harmondsworth: Penguin.

——, 1843. *A Christmas Carol in Prose. Being a Ghost Story of Christmas*. London: n.pub.

——, 1850/1990. *David Copperfield* [1850]. London & New York: Norton.

——, 1860/2007. 'The Shipwreck'. In *The Uncommercial Traveller* [1860]. London: Nonesuch Press, 13-27.

Douglas, Fanny, 1895. *The Gentlewoman's Book of Dress*. London: n.pub.

Duer Miller, Alice, 1915. *Are Women People? A Book of Rhymes for Suffrage Times*. New York: George H. Doran.

Edgeworth, Maria, 1821. 'Mademoiselle Panache'. In *Moral Tales*, vol. 3. London: R. Hunter.

Eliot, George, 1858/2003. *Amos Barton* [1858]. London: Hesperus Press.

——, 1859/1985. *Adam Bede* [1859]. Harmondsworth: Penguin.

——, 1860/1985. *The Mill on the Floss* [1860]. Harmondsworth: Penguin.

——, 1866/1998. *Felix Holt, the Radical* [1866]. Oxford: Oxford University Press.

Ferrier, Susan, 1898. *Memoir and Correspondence of Susan Ferrier, 1782-1854*, edited by John A. Doyle. London: J. Murray.

Fielding, Henry, 1749/1985. *Tom Jones, or the History of a Foundling* [1749]. Harmondsworth: Penguin.

Fine, Anne, 1989. *Bill's New Frock*. London: Methuen.

Garsault, François-Alexandre de, 1771. *L'Art de la lingère*. Paris: L. F. Delatour.

Gay, John, 1728/2013. *The Beggar's Opera* [1728], edited by Hal Gladfelder. Oxford: Oxford University Press.

George, Edwin, and Stella George, eds, 2008. *Bristol Probate Inventories Part III: 1690-1804*. Bristol: Bristol Record Society.

Goldsmith, Oliver, 1783. *Essays by Dr. Goldsmith. Collecta Revirescunt*. London: Printed for J. Wenman, Fleet Street.

Gore, Catherine, 1831. *Pin Money. A Novel*. London: Colburn and Bentley.

Gray, Mrs Edwin, 1927. *Papers and Diaries of a York Family, 1764-1839*. London: Sheldon Press.

Greville, Lady Beatrice Violet, 1892. *The Gentlewoman in Society*. London: n.pub.

Hall, Anna Maria, 1849. *Grandmamma's Pockets*. Edinburgh: William and Robert Chambers.

Ham, Elizabeth, 1945. *Elizabeth Ham by Herself*, edited by Eric Gillett. London: Faber and Faber.

Hardy, Mary, 1968. *Mary Hardy's Diary*, edited by Basil Cozens-Hardy. Norwich: Norfolk Record Society.

Harrold, Edmund, 2008. *The Diary of Edmund Harrold, Wigmaker of Manchester, 1712-1715*, edited by Craig Horner. Farnham: Ashgate.

Haywood, Eliza, 1743. *A Present for a Serving Maid: or, The Sure Means of Gaining Love and Esteem. Under the Following Heads. Observance. Avoiding Sloth. Sluttishness Etc.* London: T. Gardner.

——, 1745. *The Female Spectator*. 4 vols. London: T. Gardner.

——, 1756. *The Wife. By Mira, One of the Authors of the 'Female Spectator' Etc.* London: T. Gardner.

Histon and Impington Village Society 2000. *The Story of Elizabeth Woodcock*. n.p.: Histon and Impington Village Society.

Hodgson's New Double-Check Family Washing Book, 1845. London: Hodgson's.

Hoffman, George Francis, 1791. *Germany's Flora, or A Botanical Pocket-Companion for the Year 1791*. London: n.pub.

Hurst, Sarah, 2009. *The Diaries of Sarah Hurst, 1759-1762: Life and Love in Eighteenth-Century Horsham*, edited by Susan C. Djabri. Stroud: Amberley Publishing.

Hutton, Catherine, 1891. *Reminiscences of a Gentlewoman of the Last Century*, edited by Mrs C. H. Beale. Birmingham: Cornish Bros.

J. F., 1696. *The Merchant's Ware-House Laid Open, or The Plain Dealing Linnen-Draper*. London: Printed for John Sprint at the Bell, and Geo. Conyers at the Golden Ring in Little Britain.

Johnson, Samuel, 1755. *A Dictionary of the English Language*. 2 vols. London: Strahan.

Kilner, Dorothy, 1780. *Dialogues and Letters on Morality, Oeconomy and Politeness*. 3 vols. London: John Marshall & Co.

Kilner, Mary Ann, 1780. *The Adventures of a Pincushion. Designed Chiefly for the Use of Young Ladies*. London: J. Marshall & Co.

Latham, Richard, 1990. *The Account Book of Richard Latham, 1724-1767*, edited by Lorna Weatherill. Oxford: Oxford University Press.

Leadbeater, Mary, 1811. *Cottage Dialogues among the Irish Peasantry, with Notes and a Preface by Maria Edgeworth*. London: J. Johnson & Co.

Leigh Hunt, James Henry, 1903. 'The Old Lady'. In *The Essays of Leigh Hunt*, edited by Arthur Symons. London: Dent [first published in *La Belle Assemblée*, August 1817, 78-80].

Linton, E. Lynn, 1883. 'Old Ladies'. In *The Girl of the Period and Other Social Essays*. 2 vols. n.p.: n.pub.

McPherson, David, 1805. *Annals of Commerce, Manufactures, Fisheries and Navigation*. 4 vols. Edinburgh: Mundell and Son.

Magdalen Charity, 1759. *The Rules, Orders and Regulations of the Magdalen House for the Reception of Penitent Prostitutes by Order of the Governors*. London: n.pub.

Martineau, Harriet, 1877/1983. *Autobiography* [1877]. Reprinted with introduction by Gaby Weiner. 2 vols. London: Virago.

Mavor, William, 1800. *The Lady's and Gentleman's Botanical Pocket Book*. London: J. Crowder.

Mayhew, Henry, 1850. 'Letter LV'. *Morning Chronicle* (London), 6 June.

——, 1971. *The Unknown Mayhew, Selections from the Morning Chronicle, 1849-50*, edited by Edward Palmer Thompson and Eileen Yeo. London: Merlin Press.

——, 2005. *The London Underworld in the Victorian Period*. New York: Dover.

Montagu, Elizabeth R., 1923 *Mrs Montagu, Her Letters and Friendships from 1762 to 1800*, edited by Reginald Blunt and Emily Climenson. London: Constable and Company Limited.

Moore, Giles, 1971. *The Journal of Giles Moore, 1656-1679*, edited by Ruth Bird. Lewes: Sussex Record Society.

Müller, George, 1871. *Supplement to the Thirty-*

Second Report of the Scriptural Knowledge Institution for Home and Abroad Containing Every One of the Donations. Bristol: George Müller Foundation.

Murray, Alexander, 1826. The Domestic Oracle; or, A Complete System of Modern Cookery and Family Economy. London: H. Fisher.

Murray of Stanhope, Lady, 1821. Memoirs of the Lives and Characters of the Honourable George Baillie and Lady Grisell Baillie of Jerviswood by Their Daughter. Edinburgh: n.pub.

National Society for Promoting the Education of the Poor in the Principles of the Established Church 1832. Instructions on Needle-Work and Knitting, as Derived from the Practice of the Central School of the National Society for Promoting the Education of the Poor in the Principles of the Established Church. London: Roake & Varty, J. G. and F. Rivington, and Hatchard & Son.

North, Marianne, 1892. Recollections of a Happy Life: Being the Autobiography of Marianne North. 2 vols. London and New York: Macmillan & Co.

———, 1893. Some Further Recollections of a Happy Life Selected from the Journals of Marianne North. London: Macmillan & Co.

Norton, Caroline, 1836. A Voice from the Factories in Serious Verse. London: n.pub.

Oliver, Edith, 1938. Without Knowing Mr Walkley. London: Faber and Faber.

Papendiek, Mrs, 1887. Court and Private Life in the Time of Queen Charlotte: Being the Journals of Mrs Papendiek, Assistant Keeper of the Wardrobe and Reader to Her Majesty, edited by Mrs Vernon Delves Broughton. 3 vols. London: Richard Bentley & Son.

Parkes, Frances, 1825. Domestic Duties; or, Instructions to Young Married Ladies, on the Management of Their Households, and the Regulation of Their Conduct in the Various Relations and Duties of Married Life. London: Longman, Hurst, Rees, Orme, Brown & Green.

Pepys, Samuel, 1983. The Diary of Samuel Pepys, edited by Robert Latham and William Matthews. London: Bell & Hyman.

Perkins Gilman, Charlotte, 1914/1998. 'If I Were a Man'. In The Yellow Wall-Paper and Other Stories [1914]. Oxford: Oxford University Press.

Ponsonby, Charles, 1965. Ponsonby Remembers. Oxford: Alden Press.

Raverat, Gwen, 1952. Period Piece: A Cambridge Childhood. London: Faber and Faber.

Rees, Abraham, 1819. The Cyclopaedia; or, Universal Dictionary of Arts, Sciences, and Literature. London: Longman, Hurst, Rees,

Orme & Brown.

Richardson, Jonathan, 1725/1971. An Essay on the Theory of Painting. Facsimile of the 2nd edition, 1725. Menston: Scolar Press.

Richardson, Samuel, 1740/1985. Pamela, or Virtue Rewarded [1740]. Harmondsworth: Penguin.

———, 1748/1985. Clarissa, or The History of a Young Lady [1748]. Harmondsworth: Penguin.

Rochester, Earl of, 1714. Cabinet of Love. n.p.: n.pub.

Rouquet, Jean-André, 1755/1972. L'État des arts en Angleterre [1755]. Geneva: Minkoff Reprint.

Rousseau, Jean-Jacques, 1959. 'Mon portrait'. In Œuvres complètes, vol. 1, Les Confessions – Autres textes autobiographiques, edited by Bernard Gagnebin and Marcel Raymond. La Pléiade. Paris: Gallimard, 1020–29.

———, 2010. Les Rêveries du promeneur solitaire. Paris: Honoré Champion.

———, 2014. Oeuvres complètes, edited by Jacques Berchtold, François Jacob, Christophe Martin and Yannick Séité. Paris: Classiques Garnier.

Sala, George, 1859. Gaslight and Daylight. London: Chapman and Hall.

Savile, Gertrude, 1997. Secret Comment: The Diaries of Gertrude Savile, 1721-1757, edited by Alan Saville. Nottingham: Kingsbridge History Society.

Saxby, Mary, 1806. Memoirs of a Female Vagrant, Written by Herself. London: Dunstable.

Shelley, Mary, 1987. The Journals of Mary Shelley, 1814–1844, edited by Paula R. Feldman and Diana Scott-Kilvert, 2 vols. Oxford: Oxford University Press.

Shore, Emily, 1891. The Journal of Emily Shore. London: Kegan Paul.

Shorleyker, Richard, 1632/1998. A Schole-House for the Needle [1632]. Much Wenlock: R J L Smith.

Smith, Adam, 1759/2002. The Theory of Moral Sentiments [1759], edited by Knud Haakonssen. Cambridge: Cambridge University Press.

Smith, Alexander, 1719. A Compleat History of the Lives and Robberies of the Most Notorious Highway-Men, Foot-Pads, Shop-Lifts of Both Sexes in and about London and Westminster. 3 vols. London: A. Dodd.

Smith, John Thomas, 1845. A Book for a Rainy Day, or Recollections of the Events of the Last Sixty-Six Years. London: Richard Bentley.

Stanley, Kate, 1888. Needlework and Cutting-Out: Being Notes of Lessons Specially Adapted for the Use of Teachers in Preparing Pupils for Examination in the Government Schedule III. London: Edward Stanford.

Starke, Marianna, 1800. Letters from Italy

between the Years 1792 and 1798. 2 vols. London: R. Phillips.

———, 1828. Travels in Europe between the Years 1824 and 1828. London: Murray.

Stendhal, 1839/1999. The Charterhouse of Parma [1839], translated by Richard Howard. London: Random House.

Tidy, Theresa, 1817. Eighteen Maxims of Neatness and Order to which is Prefixed an Introduction. 2nd edition. London: J. Hatchard.

Tillotson, Marjory, 1931. The School Knitting-Book. London: n.pub.

Trimmer, Sarah, 1787. The Oeconomy of Charity; or, An Address to Ladies Concerning Sunday-Schools; the Establishment of Schools of Industry Under Female Inspection; and the Distribution of Voluntary Benefactions. London: n.pub.

Trusler, John, 1819. Trusler's Domestic Management, or The Art of Conducting a Family with Economy, Frugality and Method, the Result of Long Experience; with Full Instructions to Servants of Various Denominations, How to Time and Execute Their Work Well. London: n.pub.

Verney, Frances Parthenope, and Margaret M. Verney, eds, 1904. Memoirs of the Verney Family during the Seventeenth Century. 2 vols. London: Longmans, Green and Co.

Wakefield, Priscilla, 1817. Reflections on the Present Condition of the Female Sex with Suggestions for Its Improvement [1798]. 2nd edition. London: n.pub.

Walpole, Horace, 1937– . Correspondence, edited by Wilmarth Sheldon Lewis. London and New Haven: Yale University Press.

Webster, Thomas, 1844. The Encyclopaedia of Domestic Economy. 2 vols. London: Longmans.

Weeton, Ellen, 1939. Miss Weeton's Journal of a Governess, 1807-1825, edited by Edward Hall. Oxford: Oxford University Press.

Withering, William, 1796. An Arrangement of British Plants. 4 vols. Birmingham: M. Swinney.

Woodforde, James, 1924–31. The Diary of a Country Parson, 1758-1802, edited by John Beresford. 5 vols. London: Humphrey Milford; and Oxford: Oxford University Press.

Woodforde, Nancy, 1932. 'A Diary for the Year 1792'. In Woodforde Papers and Diaries, edited by Dorothy Heighes Woodforde. London: Peter Davies.

Woolf, Virginia, 1929/2000. A Room of One's Own [1929]. Harmondsworth: Penguin.

Wordsworth, Dorothy, 1985. Letters of Dorothy Wordsworth: A Selection, edited by Alan G. Hill. London: Clarendon Press.

———, 2002. The Grasmere and Alfoxden

Journals. Oxford: Oxford University Press.

Wordsworth, William, and Dorothy Wordsworth, 1967. *The Early Letters of William and Dorothy Wordsworth (1787–1805)* [1935], edited by Ernest de Sélincourt. 2nd edition. Oxford: Clarendon Press.

——, 1969. *The Letters of William and Dorothy Wordsworth*, vol. 2: *The Middle Years, 1806–1811*, edited by Ernest de Sélincourt and Mary Moorman. 2nd edition. Oxford: Clarendon Press.

Secondary Sources

Adamson, Glenn, 2009. 'The Case of the Missing Footstool: Reading the Absent Object'. In *History and Material Culture: A Student's Guide to Approaching Alternative Sources*, edited by Karen Harvey. London: Routledge, 192–207.

Aldrich, Winifred, 2000. 'Tailors' Cutting Manuals and the Growing Provision of Popular Clothing, 1770–1870'. *Textile History* 31: 163–201.

Andrews, Donna T., 1995. 'Noblesse Oblige: Female Charity in an Age of Sentiment'. In *Early Modern Conceptions of Property*, edited by John Brewer and Susan Staves. London: Routledge, 275–300.

Angus, Louie, 1981. *Blue Skirts into Blue Stockings, or Recollections of Christ's Hospital by [. . .] a Child in the House from 1916 to 1925 in Ward Three*. London: Ian Allan.

Anishanslin, Zara, 2016. *Portrait of a Woman in Silk, Hidden Histories of the British Atlantic World*. New Haven and London: Yale University Press.

Anon. 1972. 'Notes and Queries: Tale of a Satin Puce Dress'. *Costume* 6: 100.

Appadurai, Arjun, ed., 1986. *The Social Life of Things: Commodities in Cultural Perspective*. Cambridge: Cambridge University Press.

Ariès, Philippe, George Duby and Roger Chartier, eds, 1993. *A History of Private Life*, vol. 3: *Passions of the Renaissance*. Cambridge, MA: Harvard University Press.

Arnold, Janet, 1977. *Patterns of Fashion 1. Englishwomen's Dresses and Their Construction, c.1660–1860* [1964]. New edition. London: Macmillan.

——, 1985. *Patterns of Fashion. The Cut and Construction of Clothes for Men and Women, c.1560–1620*. London: Macmillan.

——, 1988. *Queen Elizabeth's Wardrobe Unlock'd*. Leeds: Maney.

——, 1999. 'The Lady's Economical Assistant of 1808'. In *The Culture of Sewing: Gender, Consumption and Home Dressmaking*, edited by Barbara Burman. Oxford: Berg, 223–33.

Arnold, Janet, and Jenny Tiramani, 2018. *Patterns of Fashion 5. The Content, Cut, Construction and Context of Bodies, Stays, Hoops and Rumps, c.1595–1795*. London: School of Historical Dress

Arnold, Janet, with Jenny Tiramani and Santina M. Levey, 2008. *Patterns of Fashion 4. The Cut and Construction of Linen Shirts, Smocks, Neckwear, Headwear and Accessories for Men and Women, c.1540–1660*. London: Macmillan.

Ash, Juliet, 1996. 'Memory and Objects'. In *The Gendered Object*, edited by Pat Kirkham. Manchester: Manchester University Press, 219–24.

Ashelford, Jane, and Shelley Tobin, 1999. *The Care of Clothes*. London: National Trust.

Attar, Dena, 1987. *A Bibliography of Household Books Published in Britain, 1800–1914*. London: Prospect Books.

Attfield, Judy, 2000. *Wild Things: The Material Culture of Everyday Life*. Oxford: Berg.

Ayres, John, 2003. *Domestic Interiors: The British Tradition, 1500–1850*. New Haven and London: Yale University Press.

Batchelor, Jennie, 2003. 'Fashion and Frugality: Eighteenth-Century Pocket Books for Women'. *Eighteenth-Century Studies* 32: 1–18.

——, 2005. *Dress, Distress and Desire: Clothing and the Female Body in Eighteenth-Century Literature*. Basingstoke: Palgrave Macmillan.

Batchelor, Jennie, and Cora Kaplan, 2007. *Women and Material Culture, 1660–1830*. Basingstoke: Palgrave Macmillan.

Batchelor, Jennie, and Manushag N. Powell, eds, 2018. *Women's Periodicals and Print Culture in Britain, 1690–1820s: The Long Eighteenth Century*. Edinburgh: Edinburgh University Press.

Baudino, Isabelle, Jacques Carré and Cécile Révauger, eds, 2005. *The Invisible Woman: Aspects of Women's Work in Eighteenth-Century Britain*. Aldershot: Ashgate.

Baumgarten, Linda, 1996. 'Dressing for Pregnancy: A Maternity Gown of 1780–1795'. *Dress* 23: 16–24.

——, 1998. 'Altered Historical Clothing'. *Dress* 25: 42–56.

——, 2002. *What Clothes Reveal: The Language of Clothing in Colonial and Federal America, the Colonial Williamsburg Collection*. New Haven and London: Yale University Press.

Baumgarten, Linda, John Watson and Florine Carr, eds, 1999. *Costume Close-Up: Clothing Construction and Pattern, 1750–1790*. Williamsburg, VA: Colonial Williamsburg Foundation.

Bayard, Françoise, 1989. 'Au cœur de l'intime: les poches des cadavres. Lyon, Lyonnais,

Beaujolais, XVIIe–XVIIIe siècles'. *Bulletin du Centre Pierre Léon d'Histoire Économique et Sociale de la Région Lyonnaise* 2: 5–41.

Beattie, John Maurice, 1986. *Crime and the Courts in England, 1660–1800*. Oxford: Clarendon Press.

——, 2001. *Policing and Punishment in London, 1660–1750: Urban Crime and the Limits of Terror*. Oxford: Oxford University Press.

Beaudry, Mary C., 2006. *Findings: The Material Culture of Needlework and Sewing*. New Haven and London: Yale University Press.

Beaumont, Matthew, and Michael Freeman, eds, 2007. *The Railway and Modernity: Time, Space and the Machine Ensemble*. Oxford: Peter Lang.

Beck, Thomasina, 1992. *The Embroiderer's Flowers*. Newton Abbot: David and Charles.

Bellanca, Mary Ellen, 2007. *Daybooks of Discovery: Nature Diaries in Britain, 1770–1870*. Charlottesville and London: University of Virginia Press.

Berenson, Kathryn, 2010. *Marseille: The Cradle of White Corded Quilting*. Lincoln, NE: International Quilt Study Center and Museum.

Berg, Maxine, 1993. 'Women's Property and the Industrial Revolution'. *Journal of Interdisciplinary History* 24: 233–50.

——, 1994. *The Age of Manufactures, 1700–1820: Industry, Innovation and Work in Britain* [1985]. 2nd edition. London and New York: Routledge.

——, 1996. 'Women's Consumption and the Industrial Classes of Eighteenth-Century England'. *Journal of Social History* 30: 415–34.

——, 2005. *Luxury and Pleasure in Eighteenth-Century Britain*. Oxford: Oxford University Press.

——, ed., 2015. *Goods from the East: Trading Eurasia, 1600–1800*. London: Palgrave.

Berg, Maxine, and Helen Clifford, 1999. *Consumers and Luxury: Consumer Culture in Europe*. Manchester: Manchester University Press.

Berg, Maxine, and Elizabeth Eger, eds, 2003. *Luxury in the Eighteenth Century: Debates, Desires and Delectable Goods*. Basingstoke: Palgrave Macmillan.

Bernasconi, Gianenrico, 2015. *Objets portatifs au siècle des Lumières*. Paris: Éditions du Comité des Travaux Historiques et Scientifiques.

Berry, Helen, 2002. 'Polite Consumption: Shopping in Eighteenth-Century England'. *Transactions of the Royal Historical Society* 12: 375–94.

——, 2003. 'The Metropolitan Tastes of

Judith Baker, Durham Gentlewoman'. In *On the Town: Women and Urban Life in Eighteenth-Century Britain*, edited by Penelope Lane and Rosemary Sweet. Aldershot: Ashgate, 131–55.

Bide, Bethan, 2017. 'Signs of Wear: Encountering Memory in the Worn Materiality of a Museum Fashion Collection'. *Fashion Theory: The Journal of Dress, Body and Culture* 21: 449–76.

Bills, Mark, and Nicholas Penny, 2012. *Dickens and the Artists*. New Haven and London: Yale University Press.

Blackman, Cally, 2001. 'Walking Amazons: The Development of the Riding Habit in England during the 18th Century'. *Costume* 35: 47–58.

Blackwell, Mark, 2007. *The Secret Life of Things: Animals, Objects and It-Narratives in Eighteenth-Century England*. Lewisburg, PA: Bucknell University Press.

Bold, John, 1993. 'Privacy and the Plan'. In *English Architecture Public and Private: Essays for Kerry Downes*, edited by John Bold and Edward Chaney. London: Hambledon Press, 107–19.

Borsay, Peter, 1984. 'All the Town's a Stage: Urban Ritual and Ceremony, 1660–1800'. In *The Transformation of English Provincial Towns, 1600–1800*, edited by Peter Clark. London: Hutchinson, 228–58.

——, 1989. *The English Urban Renaissance: Culture and Society in the Provincial Town, 1660–1770*. Oxford: Clarendon Press.

Bradfield, Nancy, 1968. *Costume in Detail: Women's Dress, 1730–1930*. London: Harrap.

Brain, Tracy, 2014. 'Stitching a Life, Telling a Story: Sewing in Jane Eyre'. *Women's Writing* 21: 464–87.

Braun, Melanie, Luca Costiglio, Susan North, Claire Thornton and Jenny Tiramani, 2016. *Seventeenth-Century Men's Dress Patterns, 1600–1630*. London: Thames & Hudson.

Breen, Timothy H., 1993 'The Meaning of Things: Interpreting the Consumer Economy in the Eighteenth Century'. In *Consumption and the World of Goods*, edited by John Brewer and Roy Porter. London: Routledge, 249–60

Breward, Christopher, 1999. *The Hidden Consumer: Masculinities, Fashion and City Life*. Manchester: Manchester University Press.

——, 2016. *The Suit: Form, Function and Style*. London: Reaktion Books.

Brewer, John, and Roy Porter, eds, 1993. *Consumption and the World of Goods*. London: Routledge.

Brogden, Anne, 2002. 'Clothing Provision by the Liverpool Workhouse'. *Costume* 36: 50–55.

Bronfen, Elizabeth, 2013. *Night Passages: Philosophy, Literature and Film*. New York: Columbia University Press.

Brook, Tim, 2008. *Vermeer's Hat: The Seventeenth Century and the Dawn of a Global World*. London: Bloomsbury Publishing.

Brooke, Iris, 1958. *Dress and Undress: The Restoration and Eighteenth Centuries*. London: Methuen.

Brooks, Mary M., ed., 2000 *Textiles Revealed: Object Lessons in Historic Textile and Costume Research*. London: Archetype Publications.

Brown, Bill, 2001–2. 'Thing Theory'. *Critical Enquiry* 28: 1–22

Browne, Claire, 2009. 'Mary Delany's Embroidered Court Dress'. In *Mrs Delany and Her Circle*, edited by Mark Laird and Alicia Weisberg-Roberts. New Haven and London: Yale University Press, 66–79.

Buck, Anne, 1970. 'The Costume of Jane Austen and Her Characters'. *Costume* 4, sup. 1: 36–45.

——, 1979. *Dress in Eighteenth-Century England*. London: Batsford.

——, 1984 *Victorian Costume and Costume Accessories*. London: Ruth Bean.

——, 1992. 'Pamela's Clothes'. *Costume* 26: 21–31.

Buck, Anne, and Harry Matthews, 1984. 'Pocket Guides to Fashion: Ladies' Pocket Books Published in England, 1760–1830'. *Costume* 18: 35–58.

Burman, Barbara, ed., 1999. *The Culture of Sewing: Gender, Consumption and Home Dressmaking*. Oxford and New York: Berg.

Burman, Barbara, 2002. 'Pocketing the Difference: Gender and Pockets in Nineteenth-Century Britain'. *Gender and History* 14: 447–69.

——, 2007. '"A Linnen Pockett, a Prayer Book & Five Keys": Approaches to a History of Women's Tie-on Pockets'. In *Textiles and Text: Re-Establishing the Links between Archival and Object-Based Research*, edited by Maria Hayward and Elizabeth Kramer. London: Archetype Publications, 157–63.

Burman, Barbara, and Seth Denbo, 2006. *Pockets of History: The Secret Life of an Everyday Object*, exh. cat. Bath: Museum of Costume.

Burman, Barbara, and Jonathan White, 2007. 'Fanny's Pockets: Cotton, Consumption and Domestic Economy, 1780–1850'. In *Women and Material Culture, 1660–1830*, edited by Jennie Batchelor and Cora Kaplan. Basingstoke: Palgrave Macmillan, 31–51.

Burrows Swan, Susan, 1977. *Plain and Fancy: American Women and Their Needlework, 1700–1850*. New York: Routledge.

Byrde, Penelope, 1979. *The Male Image: Men's Fashion in Britain*. London: B. T. Batsford.

——, 2008. *Jane Austen Fashion: Fashion and Needlework in the Works of Jane Austen*. Ludlow: Moonrise Press.

Byrne, Paula, 2013. *The Real Jane Austen: A Life in Small Things*. London: Harper Perennial.

Cabantous, Alain, 2009. *Histoire de la nuit, XVII–XVIIIe siècle*. Paris: Fayard.

Carlson, Hannah, 2007. 'Vulgar Things: James Fennimore Cooper's "Clairvoyant" Pocket Handkerchief'. *Common Place* 7, no. 2. www.common-place-archives.org/vol-07/no-02/carlson/ (last accessed, 27 June 2018).

——, 2008. 'Stella Blum Grant Report. Idle Hands and Empty Pockets: Postures of Leisure'. *Dress* 35: 7–27.

——, 2009. 'Pocket Book: A Cultural History of the Pocket and Pocketed Possessions'. Unpublished PhD thesis, University of Boston.

——, 2017. 'Fashion and Function at MoMA: Bernard Rudofsky's "24 Pockets"'. *Design Observer.org* [blog]. https://designobserver.com/feature/fashion-and-function-at-moma/39653 (last accessed, 13 June 2018).

Carson Williams, Fionnuala, 2008. 'Beady Pockets: Symbolism and Practicality in Irish Traveller Culture'. In *Travellers and Showpeople: Recovering Migrant History*, edited by Mícheál Ó hAodha. Cambridge: Cambridge Scholars Publishing, 7–18.

Carter, Alison, 1992. *Underwear: The Fashion History*. London: Batsford.

Castle, Terry, 1986. *Masquerade and Civilisation: The Carnivalesque in Eighteenth-Century Culture and Fiction*. London: Methuen.

Certeau, Michel de, 2011. *The Practice of Everyday Life* [1984]. 3rd edition. Berkeley, Los Angeles: University of California Press.

Chapman, Raymond, 1986. *The Sense of the Past in Victorian Literature*. London and Sydney: Croom Helm.

Chenoune, Farid, 2004. *Le Cas du sac: histoire d'une utopie portative*. Paris: Le Passage.

Chrisman-Campbell, Kimberly, 2002. 'The Face of Fashion: Milliners in Eighteenth-Century Visual Culture'. *Journal for Eighteenth-Century Studies* 25: 157–71.

Clark, Alice, 1919. *Working Life of Women in the Seventeenth Century*. London and New York: G. Routledge & Sons.

Clarke, Bridget, 2009. 'Clothing the Family of an MP in the 1690s: An Analysis of the Day Book of Edward Clarke of Chipley, Somerset'. *Costume* 43: 38–54.

Classen, Constance, 2012. *The Deepest Sense: A Cultural History of Touch*. Urbana: University of Illinois Press.

Clatworthy, Lee, 2009. 'The Quintessential Englishman? Henry Temple's Town and Country Dress'. *Costume* 43: 55–65.

Clifford, Helen, 1999. 'Concepts of Invention, Identity and Imitation in the London and Provincial Metal-Working Trades, 1750–1800'. *Journal of Design History* 12: 241–55.

——, 2011. 'English Ingenuity, French Imitation and Spanish Desire: The Intriguing Case of Cut Steel Jewellery from Woodstock, Birmingham and Wolverhampton, c.1700–1800'. In *L'Acier en Europe avant Bessemer*, edited by Philippe Dillmann, Liliane Pérez and Catherine Verna. Toulouse: Presses Universitaires du Mirail, 481–93.

Cobb, Richard, 1978. *Death in Paris: The Records of the Basse-Geôle de la Seine, October 1795 – September 1801, Vendémiaire Year IV – Fructidor Year IX*. Oxford: Oxford University Press.

Colby, Averil, 1972. *Quilting*. London: B. T. Batsford.

——, 1976. *Patchwork* [1958]. London: B. T. Batsford.

Colclough, Stephen, 2015. 'Pocket Books and Portable Writing: The Pocket Memorandum Book in Eighteenth-Century England and Wales'. *Yearbook of English Studies* 45: 159–77.

Connor, Rebecca Elizabeth, 2004. *Women, Accounting and Narrative: Keeping Books in Eighteenth-Century England*. London: Routledge.

Coombs, Katie, 2005. *Portrait Miniatures in England*. London: V&A Publications.

Corfield, Penelope, and Serena Kelly, 1984. 'Giving Directions to the Town: The Early Town Directories'. *Urban History* 11: 22–35.

Cox, Nancy, 2000. *The Complete Tradesman: A Study of Retailing, 1550–1820*. Aldershot: Ashgate.

Cox, Nancy, and Karin Dannehl, 2007. *Perceptions of Retailing in Early Modern England*. Aldershot: Ashgate.

Cunnington, Cecil Willett, 1937. *Englishwomen's Clothing in the Nineteenth Century*. London: Faber.

——, 1951. *The History of Underclothes*. London: Michael Joseph.

Cunnington, Phillis, and Catherine Lucas, 1978. *Charity Costumes of Children, Scholars, Almsfolk, Pensioners*. London: Adam & Charles Black.

Dagnall, Henry, 1996. *The Marking of Textiles for Excise and Customs Duty: The Historical Background and Legislative Framework*. Edgware: the author.

Dagognet, François, 1989. *Éloge de l'objet: pour une philosophie de la marchandise*. Paris: J. Vrin.

Davidoff, Leonore, and Catherine Hall, 2002. *Family Fortunes: Men and Women of the English Middle Class, 1780–1850*. Revised edition. London: Routledge.

Davidson, Caroline, 1982. *A Woman's Work Is Never Done: A History of Housework in the British Isles, 1650–1950*. London: Chatto & Windus.

Davidson, Hilary, 2015. 'Reconstructing Jane Austen's Silk Pelisse, 1812–1814'. *Costume* 49: 193–223.

Davies, Owen, 2015. 'The Material Culture of Domestic Magic in Europe: Evidence, Interpretations, Comparisons'. In *The Materiality of Magic*, edited by Dietrich Boschung and Jan N. Bremmer. Paderborn: Wilhelm Fink Verlag, 379–417.

Day, Carolyn A., 2017. *Consumptive Chic: A History of Beauty, Fashion and Disease*. London: Bloomsbury.

Day, Julie, 2007. 'Elite Women's Household Management: Yorkshire, 1680–1810'. Unpublished PhD thesis, University of Leeds.

Daybell, James, 2012. *The Material Letter in Early Modern England: Manuscript Letters and the Culture and Practices of Letter Writing, 1512–1635*. Basingstoke: Palgrave Macmillan.

Deetz, James, 1977. *In Small Things Forgotten: The Archaeology of Early American Life*. New York: Anchor Books.

De Grazia, Victoria, and Ellen Furlough, eds, 1996. *The Sex of Things: Gender and Consumption in Historical Perspective*. Berkeley: University of California Press.

Dibbits, Hester, 1996. 'Between Society and Family Values: The Linen Cupboard in Early-Modern Households'. In *Private Domain, Public Inquiry: Families and Life-Styles in the Netherlands and Europe, 1550 to the Present*, edited by Anton Schuurman and Pieter Spierenburg. Hilversum: Verloren, 125–45.

Dickerson, Vanessa D., ed., 1995. *Keeping the Victorian House: A Collection of Essays*. New York and London: Garland Publishing.

Dolan, Alice, 2015. 'The Fabric of Life: Linen and Life Cycle in England, 1678–1810'. Unpublished PhD thesis, University of Hertfordshire.

Dolan, Alice, and Sally Holloway, 2016. 'Emotional Textiles: An Introduction'. *Textile: Cloth and Culture* 14: 152–9.

Donald, Diana, 2002. *Followers of Fashion: Graphic Satires from the Georgian Period*, exh. cat. London: Hayward Gallery.

Donald, Moira, 2000. 'The Greatest Necessity for Every Rank of Men: Gender, Clocks and Watches'. In *Gender and Material Culture in Historical Perspective*. Basingstoke: Palgrave Macmillan, 54–75.

Douglas, Aileen, 1993-4. 'Britannia's Rule and the It-Narrator'. *Eighteenth-Century Fiction* 6: 65–82.

Douglas, Mary, 1966. *Purity and Danger: An Analysis of Concepts of Pollution and Taboo*. London: Routledge.

Durston, Gregory, 2007. *Victims and Viragos: Metropolitan Women, Crime and the Eighteenth-Century Justice System*. Bury St Edmunds: Arima.

Dyer, Serena, 2016. 'Trained to Consume: Dress and the Female Consumer in England, 1720–1820'. Unpublished PhD thesis, University of Warwick.

Dyer, Serena, and Chloë Wigston Smith, eds, forthcoming. *Material Literacies: A Nation of Makers*. London: Bloomsbury.

Earle, Alice Morse, 1971. *Two Centuries of Costume in America, 1620–1820*. 2 vols. Rutland, VT: Charles E. Tuttle.

Earle, Peter, 1989. 'The Female Labour Market in London in the Late Seventeenth and Early Eighteenth Centuries'. *Economic History Review*, 2nd series, 42: 328–53.

——, 1994. *A City Full of People: Men and Women of London, 1650–1750*. London: Methuen.

Eastop, Dinah, 2000. 'Textiles as Multiple and Competing Histories'. In *Textiles Revealed: Object Lessons in Historic Textile and Costume Research*, edited by Mary M. Brooks. London: Archetype Publications, 17–28.

——, 2001. 'Garments Deliberately Concealed in Buildings'. In *A Permeability of Boundaries? New Approaches to the Archaeology of Art, Religion, and Folklore*, edited by Robert J. Wallis and Kenneth Lymer. Oxford: British Archaeological Reports, 79–83.

——, 2006. 'Outside In: Making Sense of the Deliberate Concealment of Garments within Buildings'. *Textile: Cloth and Culture* 4: 238–55.

Eaton, Linda, 2014. *Printed Textiles: British and American Cottons and Linens, 1700–1850*. New York: Monacelli Press.

Edwards, Lydia, 2017. *How to Read a Dress: A Guide to Changing Fashion from the 16th to the 20th Century*. London: Bloomsbury.

Ehrman, Edwina, 2006. 'The Accounts of Martha Dodson, 1746–1765'. *Costume* 40: 28–38.

——, 2007. *The Judith Hayle Samplers*. London: Needleprint.

——, 2017. *Undressed: A Brief History of Underwear*. London: V&A Publishing.

England, Maureen Bridget, 2017. 'Inimitable? The Afterlives and Cultural Memory of Charles Dickens's Characters'. Unpublished PhD thesis, King's College London.

Erickson, Amy L., 1993, *Women and Property in Early Modern England*. New York: Routledge.

——, 2005. 'Coverture and Capitalism'. *History Workshop Journal* 59: 1–16.

——, 2008. 'Married Women's Occupations in Eighteenth-Century London'. *Continuity and Change* 23: 267–307.

Ewing, Elizabeth, 1978. *Dress and Undress: A History of Women's Underwear*. London: B. T. Batsford.

Farge, Arlette, 2003. *Le Bracelet de parchemin: l'écrit sur soi au XVIIIe siècle*. Paris: Bayard.

Farnie, Douglas, 2003. 'Cotton, 1780–1914'. In *The Cambridge History of Western Textiles*, edited by David Jenkins. Cambridge: Cambridge University Press.

Farnie, Douglas, and David Jeremy, eds, 2004. *The Fibre that Changed the World: The Cotton Industry in International Perspective, 1600–1990s*. Oxford: Oxford University Press.

Fennetaux, Ariane, 2008. 'Women's Pockets and the Construction of Privacy in the Long Eighteenth Century'. *Eighteenth-Century Fiction* 20: 307–34.

——, 2009. 'Toying with Novelty: Toys in Eighteenth-Century Britain'. In *Between Novelties and Antiques: Mixed Consumer Patterns in Western European History*, edited by Ilja Van Damme, Natacha Coquery, Jon Stobart and Bruno Blondé. Turnhout: Brepols, 17–28.

——, 2014. 'Sentimental Economics: Recycling Textiles in Eighteenth-Century Britain'. In *The Afterlife of Used Things: Recycling in the Long Eighteenth Century*, edited by Ariane Fennetaux, Amélie Junqua and Sophie Vasset. London and New York: Routledge, 122–41.

——, 2015. 'Les Poches ou la voie / voix moyenne: valeurs et pratiques des femmes de la *middling sort* en Grande-Bretagne au XVIIIe siècle'. *XVII-XVIII: Revue d'Études Anglo-Américaines des XVIIe et XVIIIe Siècles* 72: 129–50.

——, 2018. 'Transitional Pandoras: Dolls in the Long Eighteenth Century'. In *Childhood by Design: Toys and the Material Culture of Childhood*, edited by Megan Brandow Faller. New York and London: Bloomsbury Academic, 47–66.

Ferguson, Trish, ed., 2013. *Victorian Time: Technologies, Standardizations, Catastrophes*. Basingstoke: Palgrave Macmillan.

Fields, Jill, 2002. 'Erotic Modesty: (Ad)dressing Female Sexuality and Propriety in Open and Closed Drawers, USA, 1800–1930'. In *Material Strategies: Dress and Gender in Historical Perspective*, edited by Barbara Burman and Carole Turbin. Oxford:

Blackwell Publishing, 492–515 [special issue: *Gender and History*, 14, no. 3].

Findlen, Paula, ed., 2013. *Early Modern Things: Objects and Their Histories, 1500–1800*. London: Routledge.

Findlen Hood, Suzanne, 2015. 'Broken Objects: Using Archaeological Ceramics in the Study of Material Culture'. In *Writing Material Culture History*, edited by Anne Gerritsen and Giorgio Riello. London: Bloomsbury Academic, 67–72.

Finlay, Michael, 1990. *Western Writing Implements in the Age of the Quill Pen*. Wetheral, Carlisle: Plains Books.

Finn, Margot, 1996. 'Women, Consumption and Coverture in England, c.1760–1860'. *Historical Journal* 39: 703–22

——, 2003. *The Character of Credit: Personal Debt in English Culture, 1740–1914*. Cambridge: Cambridge University Press.

Flather, Amanda, 2007. *Gender and Space in Early Modern England*. Woodbridge: Boydell Press.

——, 2011. 'Gender, Space, and Place: The Experience of Service in the Early Modern English Household, c.1580–1720'. *Home Cultures* 8: 171–88.

Flint, Christopher, 1998. 'Speaking Objects: The Circulation of Stories in Eighteenth-Century Prose Fiction'. *PMLA* 113: 212–26.

Flügel, John C., 1930. *The Psychology of Clothes*. London: Hogarth Press.

Fontaine, Laurence, 1996. *History of Pedlars in Europe*. Cambridge: Polity Press.

Foreman, Amanda, 1998. *Georgiana, Duchess of Devonshire*. London: HarperCollins.

Foster, Vanda, 1982. *Bags and Purses*. London: Batsford.

Franklin, Carl, 2016. *British Army Uniforms from 1751 to 1783, Including the Seven Years' War and the American War of Independence*. Barnsley: Pen and Sword.

Froide, Amy M., 2005. *Never Married: Single Women in Early Modern Society*. Oxford: Oxford University Press

Fumerton, Patricia, 1986. 'Secret Arts: Elizabethan Miniatures and Sonnets'. *Representations* 15: 57–97.

——, 1991. *Cultural Aesthetics: Renaissance Literature and the Practice of Social Ornament*. Chicago: Chicago University Press.

Garry, Mary Anne, 2005. '"After they went I worked": Mrs Larpent and Her Needlework, 1790–1800'. *Costume* 39: 91–9.

Gatrell, Vic, 2006. *City of Laughter: Sex and Satire in Eighteenth-Century London*. London: Atlantic.

Gauldie, Enid, 1969. 'Mechanical Aids to Linen Bleaching in Scotland'. *Textile History* 1: 129–57.

Gavin, Adrienne E., and Andrew F. Humphries, eds, 2015. *Transport in British Fiction: Technologies of Movement, 1840–1940*. Basingstoke: Palgrave Macmillan.

George, Dorothy, 1870–1954/1978. *Catalogue of Political and Personal Satires Preserved in the Department of Prints and Drawings in the British Museum*. 11 vols. London: Trustees of the British Museum.

Gerritsen, Anne, and Giorgio Riello, eds, 2015. *Writing Material Culture History*. London: Bloomsbury Academic.

——, 2016. *The Global Lives of Things: The Material Culture of Connections in the Early Modern World*. London and New York: Routledge.

Ginsburg, Madeleine, 1980. 'Rags to Riches: The Second-Hand Clothes Trade, 1700–1978'. *Costume* 14: 121–35.

Girouard, Mark, 1978. *Life in the English Country House: A Social and Architectural History*. London and New Haven: Yale University Press.

Glassie, Henry, 1999. *Material Culture*. Bloomington: Indiana University Press.

Glennie, Paul, and Nigel Thrift, 1996. 'Reworking E. P. Thompson's "Time, Work-Discipline, and Industrial Capitalism"'. *Time & Society* 5: 275–300.

——, 2002. 'The Spaces of Clock Time'. In *The Social in Question: New Bearings in History and the Social Sciences*, edited by P. Joyce. London and New York: Routledge, 151–74.

——, 2009. *Shaping the Day: A History of Timekeeping in England and Wales, 1300–1800*. Oxford: Oxford University Press.

Goggin, Maureen Daly, 2002. 'One English Woman's Story in Silken Ink: Filling in the Missing Strands in Elizabeth Parker's circa 1830 Sampler'. *Sampler and Antique Needlework Quarterly* 8, no. 4: 8–49.

——, 2009. 'Stitching a Life in "Pen of Steele and Silken Inke": Elizabeth Parker's circa 1830 Sampler'. In *Women and the Material Culture of Needlework and Textiles, 1750–1950*, edited by Maureen Daly Goggin and Beth Fowkes Tobin. Farnham: Ashgate, 36–48.

Goggin, Maureen Daly, and Beth Fowkes Tobin, eds, 2009. *Women and Things, 1750–1950: Gendered Material Strategies*. Farnham: Ashgate.

Goodman, Dena, 2003. 'Furnishing Discourses: Readings of a Writing Desk in Eighteenth-Century France'. In *Luxury in the Eighteenth Century: Debates, Desires and Delectable Goods*, edited by Maxine Berg and Elizabeth Eger. Basingstoke: Palgrave Macmillan, 71–88.

——, 2007. 'The Secrétaire and the Integration of the Eighteenth-Century

Self'. In *Furnishing the Eighteenth Century: What Furniture Can Tell Us about the European and American Past*, edited by Dena Goodman and Kathryn Norberg. New York and London: Routledge, 183–203.

Goodman, Dena, and Kathryn Norberg, eds, 2007. *Furnishing the Eighteenth Century: What Furniture Can Tell Us about the European and American Past*. New York and London: Routledge.

Gorguet-Ballesteros, Pascale, 1994. *Histoire du jeans de 1750 à 1994*. Paris: Paris Musées.

——, 2000. *Le Coton et la mode: 1000 ans d'aventure*. Paris: Paris Musées.

Gosden, Chris, 2004. 'Aesthetics, Intelligence and Emotions: Implications for Archaeology'. In *Rethinking Materiality: The Engagement of Mind with the Material World*, edited by Elizabeth DeMarrais, Chris Gosden and Colin Renfrew. Cambridge: McDonald Institute for Archaeological Research, 33–9.

Graham, Stephen, and Nigel Thrift, 2007. 'Out of Order: Understanding Repair and Maintenance'. *Theory, Culture & Society* 24, no. 3: 1–25.

Greene, Susan W., 2014. *Wearable Prints, 1760-1860: History, Materials, and Mechanics*. Kent, Ohio: Kent State University Press.

Guichard, Charlotte, 2018. *La Griffe du peintre: la valeur de l'art (1730-1820)*. Paris: Seuil.

Halimi, Suzy, ed., 2008. *La Nuit dans l'Angleterre des Lumières*. Paris: Presses Sorbonne Nouvelle.

Hall, Edward Twitchell, 1969. *The Hidden Dimension: Man's Use of Space in Public and Private*. London: Bodley Head.

Hamer, Louise, 1984a. *The Cullercoats Fishwife*. Sunderland: Tyne and Wear County Council Museum.

——, 1984b. 'The Cullercoats Fishwife'. *Costume* 18: 66–73.

Hamlett, Jane, 2015. *At Home in the Institution: Material Life in Asylums, Lodging Houses and Schools in Victorian and Edwardian England*. Basingstoke: Palgrave Macmillan.

Hamling, Tara, and Catherine Richardson, eds 2010. *Everyday Objects: Medieval and Early Modern Material Culture and Its Meanings*. Farnham: Ashgate.

Hamling, Tara, and Catherine Richardson, 2017. *A Day at Home in Early Modern England: Material Culture and Domestic Life, 1500-1700*. New Haven and London: Yale University Press.

Harrison, Anna, and Kathryn Gill, 2002. 'An Eighteenth-Century Detachable Pocket and Baby's Cap Found Concealed in a Wall Cavity: Conservation and Research'. *Textile History* 33: 177–94.

Hart, Avril, and Susan North, 2009.

Seventeenth and Eighteenth-Century Fashion in Detail. London: V&A Publishing.

Harte, N. B., 1974. 'On Rees's Cyclopaedia as a Source for the History of the Textile Industries in the Early Nineteenth Century'. *Textile History* 5: 119–27.

Harvey, John, 1996. *Men in Black*. Chicago: University of Chicago Press.

Harvey, Karen, ed., 2009. *History and Material Culture: A Student's Guide to Approaching Alternative Sources*. London: Routledge.

——, 2012. *The Little Republic: Masculinity and Domestic Authority in Eighteenth-Century Britain*. Oxford: Oxford University Press.

Hayden, Peter, 1988. 'Records of Clothing Expenditure for the Years 1746-1779 Kept by Elizabeth Jervis of Meaford in Staffordshire'. *Costume* 22: 32–8.

Hayden, Ruth, 1992. *Mrs Delany, Her Life and Her Flowers*. London: British Museum Press.

Hayward, Maria, and Elizabeth Kramer, eds, 2007. *Textiles and Text: Re-Establishing the Links between Archival and Object-Based Research*. London: Archetype Publications.

Heal, Felicity, 2014. *The Power of Gifts: Gift Exchange in Early Modern England*. Oxford: Oxford University Press.

Hellman, Mimi, 2007. 'The Joy of Sets: The Uses of Seriality in the French Interior'. In *Furnishing the Eighteenth Century: What Furniture Can Tell Us about the European and American Past*, edited by Dena Goodman and Kathryn Norberg. New York and London: Routledge, 129–53.

Henderson, Amy H., 2006. 'A Family Affair: The Design and Decoration of 321 South Fourth Street, Philadelphia'. In *Gender, Taste and Material Culture in Britain and North America, 1700-1830*, edited by John Styles and Amanda Vickery. New Haven and London: Yale University Press, 267–91.

Hesketh, Sally, 1997. 'Needlework in the Lives and Novels of the Brontë Sisters'. *Brontë Society Transactions* 22: 72–85.

Heyl, Christoph, 2002. 'We Are Not at Home: Protecting Domestic Privacy in Post Fire Middle Class London'. *London Journal* 27, no. 2: 12–33.

Hilaire-Pérez, Liliane, 2012. 'Techno esthétique de l'économie Smithienne: valeur et fonctionnalité des objets dans l'Angleterre des Lumières'. *Revue de Synthèse* 133: 495–524.

——, 2013. *La Pièce et le geste: artisans, marchands et savoir technique à Londres au XVIIIe siècle*. Paris: Albin Michel.

Hill, Bridget, 1989. *Women, Work, and Sexual Politics in Eighteenth-Century England*. Oxford: Basil Blackwell.

——, 1996. *Servants: English Domestics in the Eighteenth Century*. Oxford: Clarendon Press.

Hitchcock, Tim, 2004. *Down and Out in Eighteenth-Century London*. London: Hambledon Press.

Hitchcock, Tim, and Robert Shoemaker, eds, 2015. *London Lives: Poverty, Crime and the Making of a Modern City, 1690-1800*. Cambridge: Cambridge University Press.

Hitchcock, Tim, and Heather Shore, eds, 2003. *The Streets of London from the Great Fire to the Great Stink*. London: Rivers Oram Press.

Holm, Christiane, 2004. 'Sentimental Cuts: Eighteenth-Century Mourning Jewelry with Hair'. *Eighteenth-Century Studies* 38: 139–43.

Holmes, Richard, 1989. *Coleridge: Early Visions*. London: Penguin.

Horne, H. Oliver, 1947. *A History of Savings Banks*. Oxford: Oxford University Press.

Houston, Robert Allan, 2013. *Literacy in Early Modern Europe: Culture and Education, 1500-1800* [1988]. 2nd edition. London: Routledge.

Hudson, Kenneth, 1982. *Pawnbroking: An Aspect of British Social History*. London: Bodley Head.

Hudson, Pat, 2009. 'The Limits of Wool and the Potential of Cotton in the Eighteenth and Early Nineteenth Century'. In *The Spinning World: A Global History of Cotton Textiles, 1200-1850*, edited by Giorgio Riello and Prasannan Parthasarathi. Oxford: Oxford University Press, 327–49.

Hughes, Therle, n.d. *English Domestic Needlework, 1660-1860*. n.p.: Abbey Fine Arts.

Humfrey, Paula, 1998. 'Female Servants and Women's Criminality in Early Eighteenth-Century London'. In *Criminal Justice in the Old World and the New: Essays in Honour of J. M. Beattie*, edited by Greg T. Smith, Allyson N. May and Simon Devereaux. Toronto: University of Toronto Press, 58–84.

Hunt, Margaret, 1996. *The Middling Sort: Commerce, Gender and the Family in England, 1680-1780*. Berkeley and London: University of California Press.

Hunter, Margaret, 1993. 'Mourning Jewellery: A Collector's Account'. *Costume* 27: 9–22.

Hurl-Eamon, Jennine, 2005. 'Insights into Plebeian Marriage: Soldiers, Sailors and Their Wives in the Old Bailey Proceedings'. *London Journal* 30, no. 1: 22–38.

Ingold, Tim, 2000. 'On Weaving a Basket'. In *The Perception of the Environment: Essays on Livelihood, Dwelling and Skill*. London: Routledge, 339–48.

——, 2010. 'The Textility of Making'.

Cambridge Journal of Economics 34: 91–102.
——, 2013. *Making: Anthropology, Archaeology, Art and Architecture*. London: Routledge.

Isaac, Amanda, 2007. 'Ann Flower's Sketchbook: Drawing, Needlework, and Women's Artistry in Colonial Philadelphia'. *Winterthur Portfolio* 41: 141–60.

Jarvis, Anthea, 1982. '"There was a young man of Bengal . . .": The Vogue for Fancy Dress, 1830–1950'. *Costume* 16: 33–46.
——, 1999. 'An Agreeable Change from Ordinary Medical Diagnosis: The Costume Collection of Drs C. Willet and Phillis Cunnington'. *Costume* 33: 1–11.

Johnston, Lucy, with Marion Kite and Helen Persson, 2006. *Nineteenth-Century Fashion in Detail*. London: V&A Publishing.

Jones, Ann Rosalind, and Peter Stallybrass, 2000. *Renaissance Clothing and the Materials of Memory*. Cambridge: Cambridge University Press.

Kelley, Victoria, 2009. 'The Interpretation of Surface: Boundaries, Systems and Their Transgression in Clothing and Domestic Textiles, *c*.1880–1939'. *Textile: Cloth and Culture* 7: 216–35.
——, 2010. *Soap and Water: Cleanliness, Dirt and the Working Classes in Victorian and Edwardian Britain*. London: I. B. Tauris.
——, 2015. 'Time, Wear and Maintenance: The Afterlife of Things'. In *Writing Material Culture History*, edited by Anne Gerritsen and Giorgio Riello. London: Bloomsbury Academic, 191–7.

Kent, John, 2005. *Coinage and Currency in London from the London and Middlesex Records and Other Sources: From Roman Times to the Victorians*. London: Baldwin.

Kern, Stephen, 1983. *The Culture of Time and Space, 1880–1918*. Cambridge, MA: Harvard University Press.

King, Peter, 1996. 'Female Offenders, Work and Life-Cycle Change in Late Eighteenth-Century London'. *Continuity and Change* 11: 61–90.
——, 1997. 'Pauper Inventories and the Material Lives of the Poor in the Eighteenth and Early Nineteenth Centuries'. In *Chronicling Poverty, the Voices and Strategies of the English Poor, 1640–1840*, edited by Tim Hitchcock, Peter King and Pamela Sharpe. Basingstoke: Macmillan, 155–91.

King, Steven, 2004. '"Meer pennies for my baskitt will be enough": Women, Work and Welfare, 1770–1830'. In *Women, Work and Wages in England, 1600–1850*, edited by Penelope Lane, Neil Raven and K. D. M. Snell. Woodbridge: Boydell Press, 119–40.

Kirshenblatt-Gimblett, Barbara, 1989. 'Objects of Memory: Material Culture as Life Review'. In *Folk Groups and Folklore Genres: A Reader*, edited by Elliott Oring. Logan: Utah State University Press, 329–38.

Klein, Laurence E., 2003. 'The Polite Town: Shifting Possibilities of Urbanness, 1660–1715'. In *The Streets of London: From the Great Fire to the Great Stink*, edited by Tim Hitchcock and Heather Shore. London: Rivers Oram Press, 27–39.

Kopytoff, Igor, 1986. 'The Cultural Biography of Things: Commoditization as a Process'. In *The Social Life of Things: Commodities in Cultural Perspective*, edited by Arjun Appadurai. Cambridge: Cambridge University Press, 64–91.

Kowaleski-Wallace, Elizabeth, 1997. *Consuming Subjects: Women, Shopping, and Business in the Eighteenth Century*. New York: Columbia University Press.

Küchler, Susanne, and Daniel Miller, eds, 2005. *Clothing as Material Culture*. Oxford: Berg.

Kuchta, David, 2002. *The Three-Piece Suit and Modern Masculinity: England, 1550–1850*. Berkeley and London: University of California Press.

Kwint, Marius, Christopher Breward and Jeremy Aynsley, eds, 1999. *Material Memories: Design and Evocation*. Oxford: Berg.

Laird, Mark, and Alicia Weisberg-Roberts, eds, 2009. *Mrs Delany and Her Circle*. New Haven and London: Yale University Press.

Lambert, Miles, 2004. '"Cast off Wearing Apparell": The Consumption and Distribution of Second-Hand Clothing in Northern England during the Long 18th Century'. *Textile History* 35: 1–26.
——, 2004–5. '"Small Presents Confirm Friendship": The "Gifting" of Clothing and Textiles in England from the Late Seventeenth to the Early Nineteenth Centuries'. *Text* 32: 24–32.
——, 2014. 'Death and Memory: Clothing Bequests in English Wills, 1650–1830'. *Costume* 48: 46–59.

Lane, Penelope, Neil Raven and K. D. M. Snell, eds, 2004. *Women, Work and Wages in England, 1600–1850*. Woodbridge: Boydell Press.

Lanier, Mildred B., 1978. 'Marseilles Quilting of the Eighteenth and Nineteenth Centuries'. *CIETA Bulletin* 47–8: 74–82.

Laqueur, Thomas, 1990. *Making Sex: Body and Gender from the Greeks to Freud*. Cambridge, MA: Harvard University Press.

Latour, Bruno, 2004. 'Why Has Critique Run Out of Steam? From Matters of Fact to Matters of Concern'. In *Things*, edited by Bill Brown. Chicago: University of Chicago Press, 151–73.
——, 2005a. 'From Realpolitik to Dingpolitik or How to Make Things Public'. In *Making Things Public: Atmospheres of Democracy*, edited by Bruno Latour and Peter Weibel, exh. cat. Cambridge, MA: MIT Press, 14–41.
——, 2005b. *Reassembling the Social: An Introduction to Actor-Network-Theory*. Oxford: Oxford University Press.

Le Faye, Deirdre, 2006. *A Chronology of Jane Austen and Her Family, 1700–2000*. Cambridge: Cambridge University Press.

Leis, Arlene, 2013. 'Displaying Art and Fashion: Ladies' Pocket Book Imagery in the Paper Collections of Sarah Sophia Banks'. *Journal of Art History* 82: 252–71.

Lemire, Beverly, 1990–91. 'The Theft of Clothes and Popular Consumerism in Early Modern England'. *Journal of Social History* 24: 255–76.
——, 1991a. *Fashion's Favourite: The Cotton Trade and the Consumer in Britain, 1660–1800*. Oxford: Oxford University Press; New York: Pasold Research Fund.
——, 1991b. 'Peddling Fashion: Salesmen, Pawnbrokers, Taylors, Thieves and the Second-Hand Clothes Trade in England, *c*.1700–1800'. *Textile History* 22: 67–82.
——, 1994. 'Redressing the History of the Clothing Trade in England: Ready-Made Clothing, Guilds, and Women Workers, 1650–1800'. *Dress* 21: 61–74.
——, 1997. *Dress, Culture and Commerce: The English Clothing Trade before the Factory, 1660–1800*. London: Macmillan Press.
——, 1999. '"In the hands of work women": English Markets, Cheap Clothing and Female Labour, 1650–1800'. *Costume* 33: 23–35.
——, 2003a. 'Domesticating the Exotic: Floral Culture and the East India Calico Trade with England, *c*.1600–1800'. *Textile: Cloth and Culture* 1: 64–85.
——, 2003b. 'Fashioning Cottons: Asian Trade, Domestic Industry and Consumer Demand, 1660–1780'. In *The Cambridge History of Western Textiles*, edited by David Jenkins. Cambridge: Cambridge University Press, vol. 2, 493–512.
——, 2003c. 'Transforming Consumer Custom: Linens, Cottons and the English Market, 1660–1800'. In *The European Linen Industry in Historical Perspective*, edited by Brenda Collins and Philip Ollerenshaw. Oxford: Oxford University Press, 187–208.
——, 2005. *The Business of Everyday Life: Gender, Practice and Social Politics in England, c.1600–1900*. Manchester: Manchester University Press.
——, 2006. 'Plebeian Commercial Circuits and Everyday Material Exchange in England, *c*.1600–1900'. In *Buyers & Sellers: Retail Circuits and Practices in*

Medieval and Early Modern Europe, edited by Bruno Blondé, Peter Stabel, Jon Stobart and Ilja Van Damme. Brussels: Brepols, 245–66.

——, 2009. *The British Cotton Trade, 1660–1815*, 4 vols. London: Pickering & Chatto.

——, 2011. *Cotton*. Oxford and New York: Berg.

——, 2012. 'The Secondhand Clothing Trade in Europe and Beyond: Stages of Development and Enterprise in a Changing Material World, *c*.1600–1850'. *Textile: Cloth and Culture* 10: 144–63.

——, 2015. '"Men of the World": British Mariners, Consumer Practice, and Material Culture in an Era of Global Trade, *c*.1660–1800'. *Journal of British Studies* 54: 288–319.

——, 2016. 'A Question of Trousers: Seafarers, Masculinity and Empire in the Shaping of Male Dress, *c*.1600–1800'. *Cultural and Social History* 13, no. 1: 1–22.

Lévi-Strauss, Claude, 1966. *The Savage Mind* [1962]. London: Weidenfeld and Nicolson, 1966.

Llewellyn, Sacha, 1997. '"Inventory of Her Grace's Things, 1747": The Dress Inventory of Mary Churchill, 2nd Duchess of Montagu'. *Costume* 31: 49–67.

Lloyd, Sarah, 2002. 'Pleasing Spectacles and Elegant Dinners: Conviviality, Benevolence, and Charity Anniversaries in Eighteenth-Century London'. *Journal of British Studies* 41, no. 1: 23–57.

Long, Bridget, 2014. 'Anonymous Needlework: Uncovering British Patchwork, 1680–1820'. Unpublished PhD thesis, University of Hertfordshire.

——, 2016. 'Regular and Progressive Work Occupies My Mind Best: Needlework as a Source of Entertainment, Consolation and Reflection'. *Textile: Cloth and Culture* 14: 176–87.

Lutz, Deborah, 2015. *Relics of Death in Victorian Literature and Culture*. Cambridge: Cambridge University Press.

McEwan, Joanne, and Pamela Sharpe, eds, 2011. *Accommodating Poverty: The Housing and Living Arrangements of the English Poor, c.1600–1850*. Basingstoke: Palgrave Macmillan.

Mack, John, 2007. *The Art of Small Things*. Cambridge, MA: Harvard University Press.

MacKay, Lynn, 1999. 'Why They Stole: Women in the Old Bailey, 1779–1789'. *Journal of Social History* 32: 623–39.

McKendrick, Neil, John Brewer and J. H. Plumb, 1982. *The Birth of a Consumer Society: The Commercialization of Eighteenth-Century England*. London: Hutchinson.

Mackenzie, Maureen A., 1991. *Androgynous Objects: String Bags and Gender in Central New Guinea*. London: Routledge.

Macleane, Virginia, 1981. *A Short-Title Catalogue of Household and Cookery Books Published in the English Tongue, 1701–1800*. London: Prospect Books.

Malcolmson, Patricia E., 1986. *English Laundresses: A Social History, 1850–1930*. Urbana: University of Illinois Press.

Marsh, Gail, 2006. *Eighteenth-Century Embroidery Techniques*. Lewes: Guild of Master Craftsman.

Matthews, Harry, 2004. 'The Fashionable Image: A Celebration of the Harry Matthews Collection of Prints and Pocket Books at the Museum of London'. *Costume* 38: 112–15.

Matthews David, Alison, 2015. *Fashion Victims: The Dangers of Dress Past and Present*. London: Bloomsbury.

Mavor, Elizabeth, ed., 1979. *The Ladies of Llangollen: A Study in Romantic Friendship*. London: Michael Joseph.

——, 1986. *A Year with the Ladies of Llangollen*. Harmondsworth: Penguin.

Mayhew, Nicholas, 2000. *Sterling: The History of a Currency*. London: Penguin.

Meldrum, Tim, 2000 *Domestic Service and Gender, 1660–1750: Life and Work in the London Household*. Harlow: Longman.

Melville, Jennifer, 1999. 'The Use and Organization of Domestic Space in Late 17th Century London'. Unpublished PhD thesis, University of Cambridge.

Mendelson, Sara Heller, and Patricia Crawford, 2000. *Women in Early Modern England: 1550–1720*. Oxford: Oxford University Press.

Merleau-Ponty, Maurice, 1945/2010. *Phenomenology of Perception* [1945], translated by Donald A. Landes. Paris: Gallimard.

Mida, Ingrid, and Alexandra Kim, 2015. *The Dress Detective: A Practical Guide to Object-Based Research in Fashion*. London: Bloomsbury.

Miller, Daniel, ed., 1998. *Material Cultures*. London: UCL Press.

Mitchell, Ian, 2014. *Tradition and Innovation in English Retailing, 1700–1850: Narratives of Consumption*. Aldershot: Ashgate.

Montgomery, Florence M., 1984. *Textiles in America, 1650–1870: A Dictionary Based on Original Documents, Prints and Paintings, Commercial Records, American Merchants' Papers, Shopkeepers' Advertisements, and Pattern Books with Original Swatches of Cloth*. New York and London: Norton.

Morineau, Michel, 1972. 'Budgets populaires en France au XVIIIe siècle, II'. *Revue d'Histoire Économique et Sociale* 2: 449–81.

Mui, Hoh-Cheung, and Lorna H. Mui, 1989. *Shops and Shopkeeping in Eighteenth-Century England*. London: Routledge.

Muldrew, Craig, 1998. *The Economy of Obligation: The Culture of Credit and Social Relations in Early Modern England*. Basingstoke: Macmillan.

——, 2001. '"Hard Food for Midas": Cash and Its Social Value in Early Modern England'. *Past and Present* 170: 78–120.

Munby, Jenepher Zoe, 1986. 'Nineteenth-Century Lancashire Woven Cottons: Studies in the Role of the Designer in the Production Process'. Unpublished PhD thesis, Manchester Polytechnic.

Myers, Janet C., 2014. 'Picking the New Woman's Pockets'. *Nineteenth-Century Gender Studies* 10, no. 1. www.ncgsjournal.com (last accessed, 27 June 2018).

Naji, Myriem, and Laurence Douny, 2009. 'Editorial'. *Journal of Material Culture* 14: 411–32.

Nicklas, Charlotte, and Annebella Pollen, 2015. *Dress History: New Directions in Theory and Practice*. London: Bloomsbury.

Nisbet, Harry, 1927. 'The Textile Industry of Bolton (1827–1927)'. *Textile Recorder* 45 (June): 51–4.

North, Susan, 2008. 'John Redfern and Sons, 1847–1892'. *Costume* 42: 145–68.

——, 2012. 'Dress and Hygiene in Early Modern England: A Study of Advice and Practice'. Unpublished PhD thesis, Queen Mary University of London.

Opie, Iona and Peter Opie, 1951/1997. *The Oxford Dictionary of Nursery Rhymes* [1951]. New edition. Oxford: Oxford University Press.

Overton, Mark, Jane Whittle, Darron Dean and Andrew Hann, eds, 2004. *Production and Consumption in English Households, 1600–1750*. London and New York: Routledge.

Palk, Deirdre, 2003. 'Private Crime in Public and Private Spaces: Pickpockets and Shoplifters in London, 1780–1823'. In *The Streets of London from the Great Fire to the Great Stink*, edited by Tim Hitchcock and Heather Shore. Rivers Oram Press, 135–51.

——, 2006. *Gender, Crime and Judicial Discretion, 1780–1830*. Woodbridge: Royal Historical Society / Boydell Press.

Park, Julie, 2009. *The Self and It: Novel Objects in Eighteenth-Century England*. Stanford, CA: Stanford University Press.

Pasierbska, Halina, 2008. *Dolls' Houses from the V&A Museum of Childhood*. London: V&A Publishing.

Peers, Juliette, 2004. *The Fashion Doll from Bébé Jumeau to Barbie*. London: Berg Publishing.

Pennell, Sara, 2009. 'Mundane Materiality, or Should Small Things Still Be Forgotten? Material Culture, Micro-Histories and the Problem of Scale'. In *History and Material

Culture: A Student's Guide to Approaching Alternative Sources*, edited by Karen Harvey. London: Routledge, 173–91.

——, 2010. '"For a Crack of Flaw Despis'd": Thinking about Ceramic Durability and the "Everyday" in Late Seventeenth- and Early Eighteenth-Century England'. In *Everyday Objects: Medieval and Early Modern Material Culture and Its Meanings*, edited by Tara Hamling and Catherine Richardson. Farnham: Ashgate, 27–40.

——, 2014. 'Invisible Mending? Ceramic Repair in Eighteenth-Century England'. In *The Afterlife of Used Things: Recycling in the Long Eighteenth Century*, edited by Ariane Fennetaux, Amélie Junqua, and Sophie Vasset. London: Routledge, 107–21.

——, 2016. *The Birth of the English Kitchen, 1600–1850*. London: Bloomsbury Academic.

Phillips, Nicola, 2006. *Women in Business, 1700–1850*. Woodbridge: Boydell Press.

Pietsch, Johannes, 2013. *Taschen: eine Europäische Kulturgeschichte, 1500–1930*, edited by Renate Eikelmann, exh. cat. Munich: Bayerisches Nationalmuseum.

Pinchbeck, Ivy, 1930. *Women Workers and the Industrial Revolution, 1750–1850*. London: G. Routledge & Sons.

Pink, Nicola, 2013. 'Improving Herriard: George and Eliza Purefoy Jervoise's Public Image'. Unpublished MA thesis, Faculty of Humanities, University of Southampton.

Pointon, Marcia, 1997. *Strategies for Showing: Women, Possession and Representation in English Visual Culture, 1665–1800*. Oxford: Clarendon Press.

——1999a. 'Materializing Mourning: Hair, Jewellery, and the Body'. In *Material Memories: Design and Evocation*, edited by Marius Kwint, Christopher Breward and Jeremy Aynsley. Oxford: Berg, 39–57.

——, 1999b. 'Wearing Memory: Mourning, Jewellery, and the Body'. In *Trauer Tragen – Trauer Zeigen: Inszenierungen der Geschlechter*, edited by G. Ecker. Munich: Wilhelm Fink Verlag, 65–81.

——, 2001. '"Surrounded with Brilliants": Miniature Portraits in Eighteenth-Century England'. *Art Bulletin* 83: 48–71.

——, 2009. *Brilliant Effects: A Cultural History of Gem Stones and Jewellery*. New Haven: Yale University Press.

Pol-Droit, Roger, 2005. *How Are Things? A Philosophical Experiment*, translated by Theo Cuffe. London: Faber.

Ponsonby, Margaret, 2007. *Stories from Home: English Domestic Interiors, 1750–1850*. Aldershot: Ashgate.

Prichard, Sue, ed., 2010. *Quilts, 1700–2010: Hidden Histories, Untold Stories*. London: V&A Publishing.

Prown, J. D., 1980. 'Style as Evidence'. *Winterthur Portfolio* 15: 197–210.

——, 1982. 'Mind in Matter: An Introduction to Material Culture Theory and Method'. *Winterthur Portfolio* 17: 1–19.

Rauser, Amelia, 2002. 'The Butcher-Kissing Duchess of Devonshire: Between Caricature and Allegory in 1784'. *Eighteenth-Century Studies* 36: 23–46.

Raven, James, 2007. *The Business of Books*. London: Yale University Press.

——, 2014. *The Publishing Business in Eighteenth-Century England*. Woodbridge: Boydell and Brewer.

Razzall, Lucy, 2006. 'The Pockets of Henry Fielding's Writing'. *Cambridge Quarterly* 35: 361–77.

Reddy, William M., 1986. 'The Structure of a Cultural Crisis: Thinking about Cloth'. In *The Social Life of Things: Commodities in Cultural Perspective*, edited by Arjun Appadurai. Cambridge: Cambridge University Press, 261–84.

——, 2001. *The Navigation of Feeling: A Framework for the History of Emotions*. Cambridge: Cambridge University Press.

Reinke-Williams, Tim, 2014. *Women, Work and Sociability in Early Modern London*. Basingstoke: Palgrave Macmillan.

Reiter-Weissman, Judith, and Wendy Lavitt, 1987. *Labors of Love: America's Textiles and Needlework, 1650–1930*. New York: Wings Books.

Ribeiro, Aileen, 1984. *The Dress Worn at Masquerades in England, 1730–1790, and Its Relation to Fancy Dress in Portraiture*. London: Taylor and Francis.

——, 2003. *Dress and Morality*. New York: Berg.

——, 2005. *Fashion and Fiction: Dress in Art and Literature in Stuart England*. New Haven and London: Yale University Press.

Richardson, Catherine, 2004. *Clothing Culture, 1350–1650*. Farnham: Ashgate.

——, 2010. '"A Very Fit Hat": Personal Objects and Early Modern Affection'. In *Everyday Objects: Medieval and Early Modern Material Culture and Its Meanings*, edited by Tara Hamling and Catherine Richardson. Farnham: Ashgate, 289–99.

Richardson, Catherine, Tara Hamling and David Gaimster, eds, 2016. *The Routledge Handbook of Material Culture in Early Modern Europe*. London: Routledge.

Richmond, Vivienne, 2009. 'Stitching the Self: Eliza Kenniff's Drawers and the Materialization of Identity in Late-Nineteenth-Century London'. In *Women and Things, 1750–1950: Gendered Material Strategies*, edited by Maureen Daly Goggin and Beth Fowkes Tobin. Farnham: Ashgate, 43–54.

——, 2013. *Clothing the Poor in Nineteenth-Century England*. Cambridge: Cambridge University Press.

——, 2015. 'Stitching Women: Unpicking Histories of Victorian Clothes'. In *Gender and Material Culture in Britain since 1600*, edited by Hannah Greig, Jane Hamlett and Leonie Hannan. Basingstoke: Palgrave Macmillan, 90–103.

——, 2016. *A Remedy for Rents: Darning Samplers and Other Needlework from the Whitelands College Collection*, exh. booklet. London: Goldsmiths. https://www.researchgate.net/publication/303346866_A_Remedy_for_Rents_Darning_Samplers_and_Other_Needlework_from_the_Whitelands_College_Collection (last accessed, 28 June 2018).

Riello, Giorgio, 2006. *A Foot in the Past: Consumers, Producers and Footwear in the Long Eighteenth Century*. Oxford: Oxford University Press.

——, 2009. 'Things that Shape History: Material Culture and Historical Narratives'. In *History and Material Culture: A Student's Guide to Approaching Alternative Sources*, edited by Karen Harvey. London: Routledge, 24–36.

——, 2010. 'Fabricating the Domestic: The Material Culture of Textiles and the Social Life of the Home in Early Modern Europe'. In *The Force of Fashion in Politics and Society: Global Perspectives from Early Modern to Contemporary Times*, edited by Beverly Lemire. Farnham: Ashgate, 41–66.

——, 2013. *Cotton: The Fabric that Made the Modern World*. Cambridge: Cambridge University Press.

Riello, Giorgio, and Prasannan Parthasarathi, 2009. *The Spinning World: A Global History of Cotton Textiles, 1200–1850*. Oxford: Oxford University Press.

Riello, Giorgio, and Roy Tirthankar, eds, 2009. *How India Clothed the World: The World of South Asian Textiles, 1500–1850*. Leiden: Brill.

Roberts, Huw, 2006. *Pais a becon, gẁn stwff a het silc: y wisg Gymreig ym Môn yn y bedwaredd ganrif ar bymtheg* ['Traditional Welsh costume in nineteenth-century Anglesey']. Llangefni: Oriel Ynys Môn.

Roche, Daniel, 1994. *The Culture of Clothing: Dress and Fashion in the Ancien Régime*. Cambridge: Cambridge University Press.

——, 2000. *A History of Everyday Things: The Birth of Consumption in France, 1600–1800*. Cambridge: Cambridge University Press.

Roe, Nicholas, 1988. *Wordsworth and Coleridge: The Radical Years*. Oxford: Clarendon Press.

Ron, Moshe, 1981. 'The Sidney M. Edelstein Collection of the History of Dyeing,

Bleaching and Dry-Cleaning Textiles'. *Textile History* 12: 118-28.

Rose, Clare, 1999. 'The Manufacture and Sale of "Marseilles" Quilting in Eighteenth-Century London'. *CIETA Bulletin* 76: 105-14.

———, 2007. 'Bought, Stolen, Bequeathed, Preserved: Sources for the Study of Eighteenth-Century Petticoats'. In *Textiles and Text: Re-Establishing the Links Between Archival and Object-Based Research*, edited by Maria Hayward and Elizabeth Kramer. London: Archetype Publications, 114-21.

Rothstein, Natalie, ed., 1987. *Barbara Johnson's Album of Fashions and Fabrics*. London: Thames & Hudson.

Rudofsky, Bernard, 1947. *Are Clothes Modern? An Essay on Contemporary Apparel*. Chicago: Paul Theobald.

Sanders, Valerie, ed., 2000. *Records of Girlhood: An Anthology of Nineteenth-Century Women's Childhoods*. Aldershot: Ashgate.

Sanderson, Elizabeth, 1997. 'Nearly New: The Secondhand Clothing Trade in Eighteenth-Century Edinburgh'. *Costume* 13: 38-48.

Sandino, Linda, 2013. 'Art School Trained Staff and Communists in the V&A Circulation Department, *c.*1947-1958'. In *Artists Work in Museums: Histories, Interventions, Subjectivities*, edited by Matilda Pye and Linda Sandino. Bath: Wunderkammer Press, 92-102.

Sargentson, Carolyn, 2007. 'Looking at Furniture Inside Out: Strategies of Secrecy and Security in Eighteenth-Century French Furniture'. In *Furnishing the Eighteenth Century: What Furniture Can Tell Us about the French and American Past*, edited by Dena Goodman and Kathryn Norberg. New York and London: Routledge, 205-36.

———, 2015. 'Reading and Writing the Restoration History of an Old French Bureau'. In *Writing Material Culture History*, edited by Anne Gerritsen and Giorgio Riello. London: Bloomsbury Academic, 265-74.

Saumarez Smith, Charles, 1993. *Eighteenth-Century Decoration: Design and the Domestic Interior in England*. New York: Harry N. Abrams.

Schilder, Paul, 1935. *The Image and Appearance of the Human Body: Studies in the Constructive Energy of the Psyche*. London: Kegan Paul.

Schivelbusch, Wolfgang, 1977. *The Railway Journey: The Industrialization of Time and Space in the Nineteenth Century*. Berkeley and Los Angeles: University of California Press.

Seligman, G. Saville, and E. Talbot Hughes,

1926. *Domestic Needlework: Its Origins and Customs throughout the Centuries*. London: Country Life.

Sennett, Richard, 2009. *The Craftsman*. Harmondsworth: Penguin.

Sharpe, Pamela, 1996. *Adapting to Capitalism: Working Women in the English Economy, 1700-1850*. Basingstoke: Macmillan Press.

———, 1998. *Women's Work: The English Experience, 1650-1914*. London: Edward Arnold.

Sherman, Stuart, 1996. *Telling Time: Clocks, Diaries and the English Diurnal Form, 1660-1785*. London and Chicago: University of Chicago Press.

Shesgreen, Sean, 2002. *Images of the Outcast: The Urban Poor in the Cries of London*. Manchester: Manchester University Press.

Shore, Heather, 2003. 'Crime, Criminal Networks and the Survival Strategies of the Poor in Early Eighteenth-Century London'. In *The Poor in England, 1700-1850: An Economy of Makeshifts*, edited by Steven King and Alannah Tomkins. Manchester: Manchester University Press, 137-65.

Smart-Martin, Ann, 2006. 'Ribbons of Desire: Gendered Stories in the World of Goods'. In *Gender, Taste, and Material Culture in Britain and North America, 1700-1830*. New Haven and London: Yale University Press, 179-200.

Smart-Martin, Ann, and J. R. Garrison, eds, 1997. *American Material Culture: The Shape of the Field*. Knoxville: University of Tennessee Press.

Smith, Helen, 2014. 'Women and the Materials of Writing'. In *Material Cultures of Early Modern Women's Writing*, edited by Patricia Pender and Rosalind Smith. Basingstoke: Palgrave Macmillan, 14-34.

Smith, Kate, 2012. 'Sensing Design and Workmanship: The Haptic Skills of Shoppers in Eighteenth-Century London'. *Journal of Design History* 25: 1-10.

Smith, Virginia, 1985. 'Cleanliness: Idea and Practice in Britain, 1770-1850'. Unpublished PhD thesis, London School of Economics.

———, 2007. *Clean: A History of Personal Hygiene and Purity*. Oxford. Oxford University Press.

Solkin, David, 2008. *Painting Out of the Ordinary: Modernity and the Art of Everyday Life in Early Nineteenth-Century Britain*. New Haven and London: Yale University Press.

Sorge, Lynn, 1998. 'Eighteenth-Century Stays: Their Origins and Creation'. *Costume* 32: 18-32.

Sorge-English, Lynn, 2005. '"29 Doz and 11 Best Cutt Bone": The Trade in Whalebone

and Stays in Eighteenth-Century London'. *Textile History* 36: 20-45.

———, 2011. *Stays and Body Image in London: The Staymaking Trade, 1680-1810*. London: Pickering & Chatto.

Spufford, Margaret, 1984. *The Great Reclothing of Rural England: Petty Chapmen and Their Wares in the Seventeenth Century*. London: Hambledon Press.

———, 1985. *Small Books and Pleasant Histories: Popular Fiction and Its Readership in Seventeenth-Century England*. Cambridge: Cambridge University Press.

Stallybrass, Peter, 1994. 'Marx's Coat'. In *Border Fetishisms: Material Objects in Unstable Spaces*, edited by Patricia Spyer. New York: Routledge, 183-207.

———, 2000. 'Fashion, Fetishism, and Memory in Early Modern England and Europe'. In *Renaissance Clothing and the Materials of Memory*, edited by Ann Rosalind Jones and Peter Stallybrass. Cambridge: Cambridge University Press, 1-14.

———, 2012. 'Worn Worlds: Clothes, Mourning and the Life of Things'. In *The Textile Reader*, edited by Jessica Hemmings. New York: Berg Publishing, 68-77.

Stallybrass, Peter, Roger Chartier, John Franklin Mowery and Heather Wolfe, 2004. 'Hamlet's Tables and the Technologies of Writing in Renaissance England'. *Shakespeare Quarterly* 55: 379-419.

Staniland, Kay, 1997. *In Royal Fashion: The Clothes of Princess Charlotte of Wales and Queen Victoria, 1796-1901*. London: Museum of London.

———, 2003. 'Samuel Pepys and His Wardrobe'. *Costume* 37: 41-50.

———, 2005. 'Samuel Pepys and His Wardrobe'. *Costume* 39: 53-63.

Staves, Susan, 1984. 'Pin Money'. *Studies in Eighteenth-Century Culture* 14: 47-77.

———, 1990. *Married Women's Separate Property in England, 1660-1833*. London and Cambridge, MA: Harvard University Press.

Steedman, Carolyn, 2004. 'The Servant's Labour: The Business of Life, England, 1760-1820'. *Social History* 29: 1-29.

———, 2009. *Labours Lost*. Cambridge: Cambridge University Press.

Steele, Valerie, 1998. 'A Museum Is More than a Clothes-Bag'. *Fashion Theory: The Journal of Dress, Body and Culture* 2: 327-35.

Steinberg, Sylvie, 2001. *La Confusion des sexes: le travestissement de la Renaissance à la Révolution*. Paris: Fayard.

Stevens, Christine, 2002. 'Welsh Peasant Dress. Workwear or National Costume?' *Textile History* 33: 63-78.

Stevenson, Sara, and Helen Bennett, 1978. *Van*

Dyck in Check Trousers: Fancy Dress in Art and Life, 1700–1900. Edinburgh: Scottish National Portrait Gallery.

Stewart, Susan, 1993. *On Longing: Narratives of the Miniature, the Gigantic, the Souvenir, the Collection.* Durham, NC, and London: Duke University Press.

——, 1999. 'Prologue: From the Museum of Touch'. In *Material Memories: Design and Evocation*, edited by Marius Kwint, Christopher Breward and Jeremy Aynsley. Oxford: Berg, 17–36.

Stobart, Jon, 1998. 'Shopping Streets as Social Space: Leisure, Consumerism and Improvement in an Eighteenth-Century County Town'. *Urban History* 25: 3–21.

Stobart, Jon, and Bruno Blondé, eds, 2014. *Selling Textiles in the Long Eighteenth Century: Comparative Perspectives from Western Europe.* Basingstoke: Palgrave Macmillan.

Stobart, Jon, and Ilja Van Damme, eds, 2010. *Modernity and the Second-Hand Trade: European Consumption Cultures and Practices, 1700–1900.* Basingstoke: Palgrave Macmillan.

Stone, Lawrence, 1991. 'The Public and the Private in the Stately Homes of England, 1500–1990'. *Social Research* 58: 227–51.

Strasser, Susan, 1982. *Never Done: A History of American Housework.* New York: Pantheon Books.

——, 1999. *Waste and Want: A Social History of Trash.* New York: Holt.

Stretton, Tim, and Krista J. Kesselring, eds, 2013. *Married Women and the Law: Coverture in England and the Common Law World.* Montreal: McGill-Queen's University Press.

Styles, John, 1994. 'Clothing the North: The Supply of Non-Elite Clothing in the Eighteenth-Century North of England'. *Textile History* 25: 139–66.

——, 1998. 'Dress in History: Reflections on a Contested Terrain'. *Fashion Theory: The Journal of Dress, Body and Culture* 2: 383–92.

——, 2000. 'Product Innovation in Early Modern London'. *Past and Present* 168: 124–69.

——, 2006. 'Lodging at the Old Bailey: Lodgings and Their Furnishing in Eighteenth-Century London'. In *Gender, Taste, and Material Culture in Britain and North America, 1700–1830*, edited by John Styles and Amanda Vickery. New Haven and London: Yale University Press, 61–80.

——, 2007. *The Dress of the People: Everyday Fashion in Eighteenth-Century England.* London and New Haven: Yale University Press.

——, 2009. 'What Were Cottons For in the Early Industrial Revolution ?' In *The Spinning World: A Global History of Cotton Textiles, 1200–1850*, edited by Giorgio Riello and Prasannan Parthasarathi. Oxford: Oxford University Press.

——, 2010a. 'Patchwork on the Page'. In *Quilts, 1700–2010: Hidden Histories, Untold Stories*, edited by Sue Prichard. London: V&A Publishing, 49–52.

——, 2010b. *Threads of Feeling: The London Foundling Hospital's Textile Tokens, 1740–1770.* London: Foundling Museum.

——, 2015. 'Objects of Emotion: The London Foundling Hospital Tokens, 1741–1760'. In *Writing Material Culture History*, edited by Anne Gerritsen and Giorgio Riello. London: Bloomsbury Academic, 165–71.

——, 2016. 'Fashion, Textiles and the Origins of the Industrial Revolution'. *East Asian Journal of British History* 5: 165–93.

——, 2018. 'The Rise and Fall of the Spinning Jenny: Domestic Mechanisation in Eighteenth-Century Cotton Spinning'. Paper presented at the conference 'Explaining the British Industrial Revolution: Textiles, Technology, and Work', California Institute of Technology, Pasadena, March.

Styles, John, and Amanda Vickery, eds, 2006. *Gender, Taste, and Material Culture in Britain and North America, 1700–1830.* New Haven and London: Yale University Press.

Swain, Margaret, 1984. 'The Patchwork Dressing Gown'. *Costume* 18: 59–65.

Sykas, Philip, 1999. 'Calico Catalogues: Nineteenth-Century Printed Dress Fabrics from Pattern Books'. *Costume* 33: 57–67.

——, 2005. *The Secret Life of Textiles: Six Pattern Book Archives in North West England.* Bolton: Bolton Museums.

Tankard, Danae, 2015. 'Giles Moore's Clothes: The Clothing of a Sussex Rector, 1656–1679'. *Costume* 49: 32–54.

——, 2016. '"They tell me they were in fashion last year": Samuel and Elizabeth Jeake and Clothing Fashions in Late Seventeenth-Century London'. *Costume* 50: 20–41.

Tarrant, Naomi E. A., 1978. 'The Collection of Samples of the United Turkey Red Company in the Royal Scottish Museum; Edinburgh'. *CIETA Bulletin* 47–8: 62–5.

——, 1994. *The Development of Costume.* London: Routledge; Edinburgh: National Museums of Scotland.

——, 1999. 'The Real Thing: The Study of Original Garments in Britain since 1947'. *Costume* 33: 12–22.

Taylor, Lou, 1998. 'Doing the Laundry? A Reassessment of Object-Based Dress History'. *Fashion Theory: The Journal of Dress, Body and Culture* 2: 337–58.

——, 2002. *The Study of Dress History.* Manchester: Manchester University Press.

——, 2004. *Establishing Dress History.* Manchester: Manchester University Press.

Tebbutt, Melanie, 1983. *Making Ends Meet: Pawnbroking and Working-Class Credit.* Leicester: Leicester University Press.

Thatcher Ulrich, Laurel, 1991. *Good Wives: Image and Reality in the Lives of Women in Northern New England, 1650–1750.* New York: Vintage Books.

——, 1997. 'Hannah Barnard's Cupboard: Female Property and Identity in Eighteenth-Century New England'. In *Through a Glass Darkly: Reflections on Personal Identity in Early America*, edited by Ronald Hoffman, Mechal Sobel and Fredrika Teute. Chapel Hill: University of North Carolina Press, 238–73.

——, 2001. *The Age of Homespun: Objects and Stories in the Creation of an American Myth.* New York: Alfred A. Knopf.

Thatcher Ulrich, Laurel, Ivan Gaskell, Sara J. Schechner and Sara Anne Carter, 2015. *Tangible Things: Making History Through Objects.* Oxford: Oxford University Press.

Thomas, Keith, 1994. 'Cleanliness and Godliness in Early Modern England'. In *Religion, Culture and Society in Early Modern Britain*, edited by Anthony Fletcher and Peter Roberts. Cambridge: Cambridge University Press, 56–83.

Thompson, Edward Palmer, 1967. 'Time, Work Discipline and Industrial Capitalism'. *Past and Present* 38: 56–97.

Thunder, Moira, 2014. *Embroidery Designs for Fashion and Furnishings.* London: V&A Publishing.

Tickell, Shelley Gail, 2015. 'Shoplifting in Eighteenth-Century England'. Unpublished PhD thesis, University of Hertfordshire.

——, 2018. *Shoplifting in Eighteenth-Century England.* Cambridge: Boydell and Brewer.

Tilley, Christopher, 1991. *Material Culture and Text: The Art of Ambiguity.* London: Routledge.

——, 1999. *Metaphor and Material Culture.* London: Blackwell.

——, ed., 2006. *A Handbook of Material Culture.* London: Sage Publications.

Tinniswood, Adrian, 2002. *His Invention so Fertile: A Life of Christopher Wren.* London: Pimlico.

Tiramani, Jenny, and Susan North, eds, 2011. *Seventeenth-Century Women's Dress Patterns (Book 1).* London: V&A Publishing.

——, 2013. *Seventeenth-Century Women's Dress Patterns (Book 2).* London: V&A Publishing.

Todd Matthews, Christopher, 2010. 'Form and

Deformity: The Trouble with Victorian Pockets'. *Victorian Studies* 52: 561–90.

Tomkins, Alannah, 2006. *The Experience of Urban Poverty, 1723–1782: Parish, Charity and Credit*. Manchester: Manchester University Press.

Toplis, Alison, 2011. *The Clothing Trade in Provincial England, 1800–1850*. London: Pickering & Chatto.

Tozer, Jane, and Sarah Levitt, 1983. *Fabric of Society: A Century of People and Their Clothes, 1770–1870*. Carno, Powys: Laura Ashley.

Trentmann, Frank, 2009. 'Materiality in the Future of History: Things, Practices and Politics'. *Journal of British Studies* 48: 283–307.

——, 2016. *The Empire of Things: How We Became a World of Consumers, from the Fifteenth Century to the Twenty-First*. London: Harper.

Tuckett, Sally, and Stana Nenadic, 2012. 'Colouring the Nation: A New In-Depth Study of the Turkey Red Pattern Books in the National Museums Scotland'. *Textile History* 43: 161–82.

Turkle, Sherry, ed., 2007. *Evocative Objects: Things We Think With*. Cambridge, MA: MIT Press.

Unsworth, Rebecca, 2017. 'Hands Deep in History: Pockets in Men's and Women's Dress in Western Europe'. *Costume* 51: 148–70.

Valenze, Deborah, 2006. *The Social Life of Money in the English Past*. Cambridge: Cambridge University Press.

Van de Krol, Yolanda, 1994. '"Ty'ed about my middle, next to my smock": The Cultural Context of Women's Pockets'. Unpublished MA thesis, University of Delaware.

Verdier, Yvonne, 1979. *Façons de dire, façons de faire: la lessiveuse, la couturière, la cuisinière*. Paris: Gallimard.

Vickery, Amanda, 1993. 'Women and the World of Goods: A Lancashire Consumer and Her Possessions, 1751–81'. In *Consumption and the World of Goods*, edited by John Brewer and Roy Porter. London: Routledge, 274–301.

——, 1998. *The Gentleman's Daughter: Women's Lives in Georgian England*. London: Yale University Press.

——, 2008. '"An Englishman's home is his castle?" Thresholds, Boundaries and Privacies in the 18th-Century London House'. *Past and Present* 199: 147–73.

——, 2009. *Behind Closed Doors: At Home in Georgian England*. London and New Haven: Yale University Press.

Vigarello, Georges, 1988. *Concepts of Cleanliness: Changing Attitudes in France since the Middle Ages* [1985], translated by Jean Birrell. Cambridge: Cambridge University Press.

Voth, Hans-Joachim, 2000. *Time and Work in England, 1750–1830*. Oxford: Clarendon Press.

Vries, Jan de, 2008. *The Industrious Revolution: Consumer Behaviour and the Household Economy, 1650 to the Present*. Cambridge: Cambridge University Press.

Walker, Garthine, 1994. 'Women, Theft and the World of Stolen Goods'. In *Women, Crime and the Courts*, edited by Jenny Kermode and Garthine Walker. Chapel Hill and London: University of North Carolina Press, 81–105.

Walkley, Christina, and Vanda Foster, 1978. *Crinolines and Crimping Irons: Victorian Clothes, How They Were Cleaned and Cared for*. London: Peter Owen.

Walsh, Claire, 1995. 'Shop Design and the Display of Goods in Eighteenth-Century London'. *Journal of Design History* 8: 157–76.

——, 2003. 'Social Meaning and Social Space in the Shopping Galleries of Early Modern London'. In *A Nation of Shopkeepers: Five Centuries of British Retailing*, edited by John Benson and Laura Ugolini. London: I. B. Tauris, 52–79.

——, 2006. 'Shops, Shopping, and the Art of Decision-Making in Eighteenth-Century England'. In *Gender, Taste and Material Culture in Britain and North America, 1700–1830*, edited by John Styles and Amanda Vickery. New Haven and London: Yale University Press, 151–77.

Warnier, Jean-Pierre, 2001. 'A Praxeological Approach to Subjectivation in a Material World'. *Journal of Material Culture* 6: 5–24.

——, 2006. 'Inside and Outside'. In *A Handbook of Material Culture*, edited by Christopher Tilley. London: Sage Publications, 186–95.

Waterhouse, Harriet, 2007. 'A Fashionable Confinement: Whalebone Stays and the Pregnant Woman'. *Costume* 41: 53–65.

Wearden, Jennifer, 2010. *Underwear: Fashion in Detail*. London: V&A Publishing.

Weatherill, Lorna, 1988. *Consumer Behaviour and Material Culture in Britain, 1660–1760*. London: Routledge.

——, 1993. 'The Meaning of Consumer Behaviour in Late Seventeenth and Early Eighteenth-Century England'. In *Consumption and the World of Goods*, edited by Roy Porter and John Brewer. London: Routledge, 206–27.

Weiner, Annette B, and Jane Schneider, eds, 1989. *Cloth and Human Experience*. Washington: Smithsonian Institution.

White, Jerry, 2012. *London in the Eighteenth Century: A Great and Monstrous Thing*. London: Bodley Head.

Whittle, Jane, 2011. 'The House as a Place of Work in Early Modern Rural England'. *Home Cultures* 8: 133–50.

Wigston Smith, Chloe, 2007. '"Callico Madams": Servants, Consumption and the Calico Crisis'. *Eighteenth-Century Life* 31, no. 2: 29–55.

——, 2013. *Women, Work and Clothes in the Eighteenth-Century Novel*. Cambridge: Cambridge University Press.

Wilcox, David, 1999. 'Cut and Construction of a Late Eighteenth-Century Coat'. *Costume* 33: 95–7.

——, 2016. 'Scottish Late Seventeenth-Century Male Clothing: Some Context for the Barrock Estate Finds'. *Costume* 50: 151–68.

——, 2017. 'Scottish Late Seventeenth-Century Male Clothing (Part 2): The Barrock Estate Clothing Finds Described'. *Costume* 51: 28–53.

Wilson, Kathleen, 1990. 'Urban Culture and Political Activism in Hanoverian England: The Example of Voluntary Hospitals'. In *The Transformations of Political Culture: England and Germany in the Late Eighteenth Century*, edited by Hellmuth Eckhart. Oxford: Oxford University Press, 165–84.

Woodward, Donald, 1985. 'Swords into Ploughshares: Recycling in Pre-Industrial England'. *Economic History Review* 38: 175–91.

Wright, Nancy E., Margaret W. Ferguson and A. R. Buck, eds, 2004. *Women, Property, and the Letters of the Law in Early Modern England*. Toronto: University of Toronto Press.

Zelizer, Viviana A., 1994. *The Social Meaning of Money*. New York: Basic Books.

Zemon Davis, Natalie, 2000. *The Gift in Sixteenth-Century France*. Oxford: Oxford University Press.

Zionkowski, Linda, 2016. *Women and Gift Exchange in Eighteenth-Century Fiction: Richardson, Burney, Austen*. New York: Routledge.

Zionkowski, Linda, and Cynthia Klekar, eds, 2009. *The Culture of the Gift in Eighteenth-Century England*. Basingstoke: Palgrave Macmillan.

INDEX

Page numbers in *italic* refer to the illustrations

A

Abingdon, Oxfordshire 134, *134–5*, 210
accessories *see* women's garments and
    accessories
Adelaide, Queen 48–9, *49*
advertisements 11–12, 16, 26, 56, *75*, 76, 115,
    147, 155, 158–9, *159*, 160
advice literature 90, 103, 109
Andrews, Susannah 133
Angus, Louie 196–7
'anti pocketists' 42–3
appliqué decoration 62, *63*, 70
The Art of Cutting out Shifts 230 n.81
Austen, Jane 54, 66, 96, 190
    Mansfield Park 190

B

Bagg, Sarah 87
bags 28, 32, 34, 37, 39, 44, 49, 184, 222
    'Dolly Varden' 221–2, *221*
    handbags 19, 34, 49, 161, 217
    reticules 24, *37*, 39, 42–3, 192
    'underskirt bags' 158–9, *159*
    work-bags 37, 190, 196
Baillie, Lady Grisell 90, 106, 157–8, 236 n.59
Bangor National School 76, 96
Banks, Sarah Sophia 152–3
Barrow, J., *Parliament Security* 48
Basey, Lydia 53–4, 81
baskets *17*, 18, 76, 91, 104, *105*, 108, 170, 173,
    174, 182, *216*, 220
basket women 121, 163, 169–74
Batchelor, Elizabeth 106, *106*
beadwork, stocking purses *119*
'beady pockets' 221
Bedfordshire 176
Beechey, William, *Portrait of Sir Francis Ford's*
    Children Giving a Coin to a Beggar 43–4, *43*
Bell, Mrs 203
Bentham, Jeremy 214
Berkshire 98
Bevan, Elizabeth 121
Beynon, Ann 55, *56*, 169–70
Billingsgate fishwives 167, 221
binding 65, *66*, 100, 106, *118*, 197, 215, 228 n.64
Blake, William 15
bleaching 57, 103
Blunt, Robert 76
body linen 13, 20, 26, 30, 40, 59, 65, 78, 86, 88,
    92, 229 n.60, 231 n.17, 233 n.121
Bolton, Lancashire 57, 79

Boswell, James 234 n.52
botany 151–3
Boulton, Richard 121–2
Bowles, Carington, *Cobler's Hall* 168, *169*
boxes (for storage or transport) 91, 108, 187
Bridgen, Elizabeth 94
Bridges, Joseph, *Adventures of a Bank-Note* 46
Bristol 32, 77, 81, 138, 170
Britford 94
Brockman, Ann 75, 105–6
Brontë, Charlotte, *Jane Eyre* 196
Buckinghamshire 174
bundles 23, 32, 37, 173, 203
Burke, Celia 81
Burn, Robert 40
Burney, Edward Francis, *The Waltz* 45–6, *45*,
    199
Burney, Fanny 155, 195
Butler, Eleanor 202
Buton, Ann 53–4, 81, 100
buttonholes 66
Byron, Lord 191

C

Calais 91
Cambridge 51, 173
Carr, Edith 228 n.12
Carryll, Mary 202
Cato, William 189
Celia in Search of a Husband 44, 68–9
charity 150–1, 174–5
charity schools 196
Charlotte, Queen 67, 201–2, *201*, 238 n.17
charwomen 18, 109, 179, 212
Chichester 91
child labour 220, 239 n.9
Christ's Hospital school, London 196–7, 221
Clapham, Lady (doll) 33–4, *33*, 35
Clarke, Edward 229 n.52, 230 n.83, 233 n.79
Clarke, Mary Jepp 197
cleanliness 57, 86, 88, 89, 103–9, 231 n.10
Clifford, Hester 88, 103
cloth and other materials 54–62
    'Calamanca' ('Callimancoe') pockets 59,
        229 n.42
    canvas pockets 55–6
    cotton pockets 54, 55–9, *65*, 104
        printed cottons 57–8, *59*, *61*
    damask 19, 55, 212
    denim pockets 19
    dimity pockets 38, 54, 56–7, *57*, 79, 103,
        104, 229 n.21
    fustian pockets 57–8, 229 n.31
    jean pockets 19
    Holland (linen) 54, 59, 148, 196
    lace 35, 77, 132, 174
    lawn 103, 136
    leather pockets 19, 55, *56*, *68*, 100, 211
        and trade work 169–70
    linen pockets 58–9
    marcella pockets 13, *14*, *57*, 79, *81*
    poplin 40

    quilting 57, 61, 70, 77, 229 n.29
    silk pockets 19, 55, 117
    ticking 55–6, *75*
    worsted 27, 55, 122
    velvet 37
    woollen pockets 59–60, *60*, 170
clothes *see* women's garments and
    accessories
clouts 94, 232 n.51
coach travel 91, 111, 121, 157
Coghill, Faith 200
Collett, John, *Shop-Lifter Detected* 140
Collier, Mary, 'The Woman's Labour' 109,
    231 n.2
consumption
    and consumer knowledge 54, 79, 149, 151
    and culture of preservation 62, 102
    excessive consumption 113
    undercurrents to 21, 62, 82
    work of/labours of 86, 109
containers, in pockets 119–21, *120–1*
containment 210–11
contents of pockets 111–41
    afterbirth 187
    and agency 123–8
    almanacs 111, 144, 145–7, 173
    amulets 133–4
    balls of wool 170
    bodkins 44, 111, 128, 177, 201, 219, 234 n.77
    bone 134
    books 133, 151–3
    boxes 44, 119–21, *121*
    calling cards 149–50
    coins 32, 43, 116–7, *118*, 119, 129–33, 134,
        135, 166–8
    conversation cards 144
    combs 111, 172
    corkscrews 44, 127
    diaries *see* contents of pockets: journals
    ducks 180
    duplicates (pawnbrokers' tickets) 121, 132,
        133, 136
    etuis 143, 145, *146*, 147
    and female networking 202
    garments and accessories inside pockets
        125–6
    handkerchiefs 12, 51, 96, 121, 122, 126, 142,
        147, 147,158, 163, 173, 180, 184, 200–1
    huswifs 43, 44, 119, *120*, 122, 126, 136, 200,
        202
    ink horns 155
    jewellery 126
    journals 195, 197–9, *198*
    keepsakes 201–2
    keys 111, 123, 138, 177, 190, 193
    knitting needles 170, 237 n.34
    knives 51, 127, 137, 163, 201
    letters 133, 158, 197, 199–201
    memorandum books 144, 199
    microscopes 153, *153*
    miniatures, portrait 197–9, *198*, 238 n.45
    mirrors 126, 148

money 129–33
    old coins 132
necessaires 145
needle-cases *120*, 202, 219
nutcrackers 44, *173*
nutmeg graters 44, 121, *121*, 219, 234 n.41
official documents 133, 176–7
ordering strategies 113–22
    and ownership 135–40
    and nesting 121–2, 194
    pass warrants 175
pincushions 44, 126–7, *127*, 200, 205, 210, 219, 229 n.57, 234 n.71
pins 32, 116, *118*, 126, 193, 219, 234 n.29
pocketbooks 111, 119, 124–5, *125*, 127, 132, 144, 145–7, *145*, 197, 201–2, *201*
prayer books 133–4, 158
'promise of goods' 128–34
purses 37, 111, 118–19, *119*, 121, 127, 148, 150, 160, 168, 174, 181, 193, 194, 200, 202, 217, 219
ready reckoners 124, *124*
scent bottles 111, 142, 143, *144*, 145, 147
scissors 51, 122, 196, 201
snuffboxes 23, 44, 55, 115, 117, 121, *121*, 122, 143, 145, 173
spectacles 44, *122*
thimbles 12, 44, 111–12, 127–8, 130, 135, 200
tools 126–8
toothpicks and cases 111, 126
watches 26, 125, 137, 150, 200, 234 n.63
Conway, Henry Seymour 157
Coventry blue marking thread 94, 232 n.49
coverture 136
crime: assault 163, 165
    murder 183–5, 187–8
    see also infanticide; pickpocketing; shoplifting; theft; victims of crime
crocheted pockets 54, 55, 70
Crosby, Mary 93–4, *94*, 116, *117*
cross-dressing 228 n.84
cross-stitch markings *92*, *93*, 96, *97*
Cuckfield 199
Cullercoats, near Newcastle 221
Cumberland 54

D

dancing 45–6, *45*
Dartford 174
Davies, Revd David 98
Davison, Emily Wilding 50–1, *51*
Deas, Margaret *186*, 213–15, *214*, 223
Defoe, Daniel 58
Delany, Mary 200, 201–2, *201*
deliberately concealed pockets 134, *134–5*, 210, 220–1, *220*
Derbyshire 81
Desarps, M.: *Le Ridicule et les poches* 192
Devonshire, Georgiana, Duchess of 35, 40, 48, 78, *80*, 96, 148
Dickens, Charles: *Barnaby Rudge* 221–2
    David Copperfield 178–9

Oliver Twist 97, 239 n.10
Dighton, Robert: *The Lottery Contrast* 149
    The Return from Margate 91, *92*
Digman, Mary 117
Dodson, Martha 56
dolls 227 n.37
    clothes *13*, 20, 68, *69*, 230 n.76
    'Lady Clapham' 33–4, *33*, 35
    marked linen *95*, *96*
    matching pockets to dresses 40
    muslin dresses 38, *38*
    pedlar dolls 76, *78*, 173, *174*
    pocket contents *126*
    printed cotton dresses 58, *58*
    undergarments *28*, *35*
'Dolly Varden' fashion 221–2, *221*
Dorset 173
Douglas, Frances, Lady 202
Downes, Hannah 238 n.76
Dover 91
Draper's Record 49
du Maurier, George, 'A "New Woman"' *36*
Duché, Esther 68
Duck, Stephen, 'The Thresher's Labour' 231 n.2
Duke Street Prison, Glasgow 213–14

E

Edgeworth, Maria, *Moral Tales* 46
Eliot, George: *Adam Bede* 42, 111–12, 129, 189
    Amos Barton 99
    Felix Holt, the Radical 191
    The Mill on the Floss 96–7
Elliston & Cavell, Oxford 158–9, *159*, 160
embroidered pockets *frontispiece*, *10*, 12, 70–4, *78*, *211*
    children's pockets *68*
    'Dolly Varden' bag 221–2, *221*
    in human hair 213–14
    identification marks 93
    and memory 213–15, *214*, 223
    motifs 52, 70, 72–3, *72–4*, 153, *154*, 199–200, *200*, 205, *206*, 210
    in museums 222–3
    printed patterns 72, *74*, 79
    repairs 100, *101*
    sampler-style pockets 39, *39*, *171*, 185, 203, 204–5
Evans, Mary 106
Eyston and Crooke, Pall Mall, London 179

F

factory workers 180–1
Farne Islands 232 n.53
Fashions for All 158
Female Society for Birmingham 37, *37*
Ferrier, Susan 115
Fettes, George 82, 91–2
Fielding, Henry, *Tom Jones* 178, *178*, 199
Fine, Anne: *Bill's New Frock* 23
Fitzpatrick, Lady Louisa 56
Flora Diaetetica 153

floral motifs 57–8, 70, 153, *154*, 210
fob pockets 26, 36, 117
Ford, Sir Francis 43–4, *43*
Fox, Ann 103–4
Fox, Charles 48
Frith, William Powell, *Dolly Varden* 221, 239 n.16
Furnese, Lady Arabella 55, 59, 98, 148, 150–1
furniture, locked 190–1

G

gambling 148
Gardner, Frances 122
Garsault, François-Alexandre de 40
Gatehouse, Sarah 124–5, *125*, 145
Gay, John: *The Beggar's Opera* 166
gifts 200–3
Gillray, James: *The Man of Feeling, in Search of Indispensibles* 47, *47*
    'Sophia, Honour, & the Chambermaid' 178, *178*
Gilman, Charlotte Perkins, 'If I Were a Man' 24
girls: learning needlework 96
    making pockets 68–9, *68*
    wearing pockets *43*, *58*, 216, *219*, *220*
global trade 13, 15, 20–21, 54–6, *57*, 112
Godwin, Mary 106
Goldsmith, Oliver 118
The Graphic 49
Green, Ann 105
Green, Mrs 91–2
Grey Coat charity school, York 196
Griffiths, Margaret 124, 182

H

hackney coach 145, 164
Hagelston, William 35
Haighton, John 231 n.108
Haighton, Sarah and Ann 77
Haines, Hannah *71*, 238 n.76
hair embroidery 213–15, *214*, 223
Hall, Anna Maria *44*
    Grandmamma's Pockets 44–5, 67–8, 70, 73–4, 117–18, 218–19, 221
Ham, Elizabeth 38
Hampshire 60, 79, 87, 90, 94, 124
Hardy, Mary 106
Harrington, Olivia 116, 123
Hatfield, Hertfordshire 96
Hayle, Judith (Juda) 230 n.93
Haywood, Eliza 89, 138, 143
heart motifs 199–200, *200*
Heath, William, *A Sketch for the Ladies Album!!!* 113
Heatley, Ann 147–8, 150, 151
Heideloff, Nicholas von, *Gallery of Fashion* 152
heirlooms: pockets as 207–10
    textiles as 205–7
Herriard, Hampshire 94, 155
Hibberd, Mary 72, 204
hidden pockets *see* deliberately concealed pockets; pockets: visibility of

Hoare, Mary 75
Hodgson's New Double-Check Family Washing Book 104, *105*
Hogarth, William, *A Harlot's Progress* 175–6, *176*
Holland (country) 157
Homer, Winslow 239 n.14
Horsham 67, 197
household management 44–5, 85–109
    bed linen 231 n.8
    linen 54, 57, 59, 86, 89–96, 98, 103, 105–9, 177
    marking pockets 92–8
    mending pockets 98–102, *100–2*
    multiple pockets 87–90
    pocketbooks 124
    storing pockets 90–2
    washing and cleanliness 103–9, *105–7*
housing 189–90, 193–4
Howe, Lord 49
Howit, Mary 65
Hunter, Eleanor 121
Hurst, Sarah 30–1, 67, 75, 91, 107, *124*, 197–9, *198*
Hutton, Catherine 99

I

Ibbetson, Julius Caesar, *Washing with Ashes* 107
identity 203–15, *205*
'indispensibles' 37, 47
inked markings and inscriptions 13, *14*, 40, 87, 92–4, *93–4*, 95, 96, *96*, 97, *98*, 203–4, *205*
Instructions for Cutting Out Apparel for the Poor 99
internal compartments 116–17, *117–18*, 125, 145, *146*, 212
inventories 16, 40, 77, 87, 94–5, *95*, 103, 167, 228 n.12
Ireland 221
Isham, Elizabeth 192
Isham, Judith 192
Italy 106, 157–8
itinerant work 169–74

J

Jack the Ripper 33, 183–5
jacquard looms 13, 79
Jarvis, Fanny 87, 88, 94, 103, *104*
Jeake, Samuel 234 n.63, 235 n.3
Jervis, Elizabeth 57–8, 233 n.79
Jervoise, Eliza 60, 79, *80*, 87, 90, 91, 94–5, *95*, 103, 106, 155
Johnson, Samuel 119
Jones, Jenkin 108
Jones, Sali *171*, 203

K

Kauffmann, Angelica, *Louisa Hammond 156*
Kent 148, 174
Killick, Mrs 79
Kilner, Dorothy 68, 126
Kilner, Mary Ann, 'A Lady' 229 n.57

Kirby, Elizabeth 58
knitted pockets 55, 205
knitting *162*, 170, *172*, 237 n.34

L

labour *see* work
Ladies' Complete Pocket Book 197
The Ladies' Complete Visiting Guide 150, *150*
Ladies of Llangollen 202
The Lady's and Gentleman's Botanical Pocket Book 153
Lady's Magazine 148
The Lady's New Elegant Pocket Magazine 151
Lancashire 172
Laroon, Marcellus, *The Cryes of the City of London* 32
Larpent, Anna Margaretta 76, 85, 86, 99
Latham family 172
laundry 103–9, *105–7*
laundry maids 107, 233 n.121
laundry marks 96, 203
Laurie & Whittle, *Beauty and Fashion* 29
Lawrence, Elizabeth 228 n.17
Lawrence, Stephen 75–6
Leadbeater, Mary, *Cottage Dialogues* 180
Lincolnshire 109
linen presses *84*, 90, 91, 95
Liverpool 172
Llangwm, Pembrokeshire *170*
locked furniture 190–1
Locket, Lucy 11
locks 91, 119, 123, 179, 187, 189, 190, 193, 194
London 114, 182
    sociability 147–50
London Companion 145
London Evening Post 174
looms, jacquard 13, 79
Loosely, Stephen 28
lotteries 148
Low-Life 179
Lowe, James Cromp 82
luggage 91, 158–9
Lunardi, Vincenzo 72, 204

M

Mabyn, John 77
Maclise, Daniel, *Portrait of Mrs. Anna Maria Hall* 44
Magdalen House, London 196
makeshift economy 140–1, 182–3
making pockets 63–75, *64*, *66*
    construction methods 65
    cross-generation transmission of techniques 68
    as pedagogical 68–9, 230 n.76
marketing tables *124*, 144
markets 166–8, *167*, 169–70, 181–2
marking clothing 92–8, 232 n.62
    doll's pockets 95, *96*
    elaborate systems of 94–5
    identification after theft 93–4
    identification of corpses 94, 232 n.53

    and identity 203–4, *205*
    inked markings and inscriptions 13, *14*, 40, 87, 92–4, *93–4*, 95, *96*, *96*, 97, *98*, 203–4, *205*
    laundry marks 96, 203
    marking thread 94
    numbers 87, 88, 93
    pre-woven name tapes 96
    stitched markings 92, *93*, 94–7, *97*
    unpicking 97–8
Marlborough 88
Marseilles quilting 57
Marshall, Mary 134
Martin, E., *Let sloth adorned with splendid arts 71*
Martineau, Harriet 68, 99, 130
material literacy 19, 53, 54
Mayhew, Henry 182, 183
memory 189, 205–10, 212–15, *213*
mending 98–102, *100–2*
    darning 99–100, *100*
    patching 56, 99–100, *100*, *101*, *102*, 171, 178, *178*, 185
men's clothes and accessories 23, 25–7
    army uniform 207
    breeches 25–6, 165
    coats 26–7, 227 n.12
    greatcoats 26–7
    grenadier's cap *208*, 209–10
    suits 27
    watches 26
men's pockets 25–7, 136, 137, 202
Miller, Alice Duer 49–50
Mills, Wallis, 'Suffragettes at Home' 50
miniature pockets *186*, 213–15, *214*
miniaturisation, pocket contents 145
mobility 143–61, 164–5
money: agency for women 129–33, 134, 147–8, 150
    concealing in pockets 193
    and mobility 143–4, 158
    and ownership 136–8
    traders 166–8
Montagu, Mary Churchill, 2nd Duchess of 40, 90, 227 n.30
Moore, Giles 75
Morgan, Ann 91
Morier, David, *Grenadiers 209*
Moss Alley, from Ladd's Court 194
motifs, embroidered 52, 70, 72–3, *72–4*, 205, *206*
    around openings 70, 210
    exotic 70
    floral 57–8, 70–1, 153, *154*, 210
    hearts 199–200, *200*
    human figures 70, 205
    sampler-style pockets *171*, 185, 203, *204–5*
    women's names 203–4
Mugge, Mrs 202
multiple pockets 28, 87–90, 117
museum acquisitions of pockets 222–3

N

name tapes, pre-woven 96
nature 151–6
needlework 63–75, 79, 96
  as idiosyncratic 74–5, 100, *102*
  different skills at 16, *62*, 74, 96, *97*, 99,
    mending 98–102, *100–2*
  plain sewing 69, 74, *89*
  as sociable 67–9, 72
  see also embroidered pockets
nesting 121–2, 194
New Lady's Magazine 72, 230 n.92
Norfolk 104
Northamptonshire 192
North, Countess 87–8
North, Marianne 158
Nugent, Hesse 202
numbers, marking pockets 87, 88, 93

O

object-centred scholarship 14–15, 226 n.9,
  226 n.11
The Observant Pedestrian 115, 157
O'Dell, Ann 127, 234 n.74
Old Bailey criminal court, London 18, 35–6, 76,
  112, 119, 121–2, 139, 163, 164–7, 175, 189–90,
  211, 224–5
openings in pockets 48, *89*
  decoration around 70, *75*, *76*, 210
  dolls' clothes *20*
  orientation 66, *67*, 167
  reinforcement around 13, *14*, 65, 66
Orton and Stow, London 78, 96
ownership 135–40
Oxford 158
Oxfordshire 134, 160, 210

P

Papendiek, Charlotte 67, 238 n.17
papers, in pockets 133, 176–7
Park School, Wilton House 96
Parker, Elizabeth 238 n.71
patch pockets 36
patchwork pockets 58, 61–2, *62*, 70, *118*,
  205–9, *207*
patterns for pockets 71–2
pawnbrokers 82, 91–2, 132, 133, 136
pawning as credit 129, 132, 182
pawning as storage 91
Pearcy, Rebecca 107
Pearson, Prudence 105, 135
pedlars 76, 77, *78*, 173–4, *174*
Pegasus (ship) 232 n.53
Pemberton, Samuel *121*
Pheysey, Miss *54*
Philip, Anne 77
pickpockets 18, 23, 160, 163, 165–6
Pin Money 144–5
Pitt, William the elder 166
'pocket aprons' ('apron pockets') 166, 167–8,
  168

pockets: accessories 144–5
  and agency 123–34
  at work 166–85
  birth of 19
  buying pockets 75–82
  colour of 40–41, *41*, 229 n.41
  and companionship 200
  contents 111–41, *126–7*
  and crime 139
  decoration 205–10, *206*
  deliberately concealed pockets 134, *134–5*,
    210, 220–1, *220*
  demise of 19, 39, 217–23
  evolved pockets 66, 160, *161*
  as extensions of the body 211–12
  eyelet holes 66, *67*, 79
  and fashionability 36, 39
  and female genitalia 46–8
  and folk beliefs 134, 210
  as gendered 23–4
  as gifts 68, 200–3
  and good housewifery 43, 44, 45
  and identity 203–15, *205*
  imagined chaos in 114–5
  improvised pockets 31–2
  internal compartments 116–17, *117–18*, 125,
    145, *146*
  lost pockets 11–12
  and love 197–200
  made for relatives 202–3, 238 n.63
  and magic 133, 134, 210
  making 63–75, *64*, *66*
  matching to clothes 40, *41*, *58*
  materials 54–62
  and memory 205–10, 212–15, *213*
  mending 98–102, *100–2*
  miniature pockets *186*, 213–15, *214*
  money in 129–32, 134
  multiple pockets 28, 87–90, 117
  and multi-tasking 164, 181–2, 185
  as old-fashioned 36, 38–9, 43, 217–8
  ordering strategies in 116–7
  and ownership 135–40
  pairs of *41*, *93*, *101*, *104*, *116*, *154*, *171*, *204*,
    205
  and politics 48–51
  and portability 144–5, 155
  position worn in 28–9
  and pregnancy 42, 187, 233 n.122
  prices 76–7
  and privacy 187–97
  and protection 134, 210
  quasi-pockets 29–30
  ready-made pockets 75–82, *81*, 96
  represented in paintings *7*, 220
  revealing 40–2
  safety pockets 158
  and secrecy 197–200
  sewn-in pockets 24, 34, 36, 117
  and sexuality 42, 46–8
  signs of wear
    memory of load 100, *114*, 115, 215

    stains on 155, *155*, 184, *185*
    see also broken ties
  size (large) 114, 115–16, *116*
  sociability and mobility 143–61
  in stays 30–1, *31*
  storage of 89–92
  and travel 160–1, 170, 172, 175–7, 218, 221,
    236 n.70
  theft by servants 179–80
  ties 65, *67*, 100, *101*, *114*, 183
  undecorated pockets 78
  under the pillow 27, 28, 130, 192, 194–5, 211
  as undress or undergarments 40–41, 78
  unstable status of 40–2, 90
  versatility 27–8
  visibility of pockets 29, 37, 38, 40–42, 54,
    73–4, 100, 168, 196, 210
  washing and cleanliness 103–9, *105*
  women's male-style pockets 19, 24, 34, 35,
    36, 49, 117
  and women's suffrage 49–51
'pocketists' 42–3
Pollard, Jane 200–1
Pomier, Miss 35
Ponsonby, Sarah 202
Ponsonby, Winifred Marian, Lady 160, *161*,
  218
Pope, Mary 228 n.12
Porter, Thomas 136
portrait miniatures 197–9, *198*, 238 n.45
pregnancy 42, 187, 233 n.122
  Adam Bede 42
  afterbirth 187
Prescot 172
press studs 39, *40*, 228 n.59
printed cottons 57–8, *59*, *61*
privacy 91, 187–97
probate inventories 16, 167, 228 n.12
property: coverture 136
  inventories 16, 40, 87, 94–5, *95*, 103,
    167, 228 n.12
  ownership 135–40
prostitutes 18, 31, 139, 166, 181, 183
proxy possession 136–8
Punch 36, 50, 179

Q

The Queen 158, *158*

R

rag bags 61–2
Rag Fair, Rosemary Lane, London 81, *82*
'railway pockets' *117*
Randell (Randall), Sarah 79, *80*, 106
Raverat, Gwen 51, 155
ready-made 64, 77
recycled fabrics 60–2, *61*, 62, 205–10, *207–8*
red pockets 229 n.41
Rees, Abraham 57
Reform Act (1832) 48–9
Repository of Arts 37
Reynolds, Elizabeth 204, *205*

Reynolds, Jane 87, 91
Richardson, Jonathan 238 n.45
Richardson, Samuel 155
    Clarissa 237 n.11
    Pamela 195
Roberts, Sarah 39, *39*
Rochester 91
Rochester, Earl of 46
Rolland, Miss 212, *213*
Rouquet, Jean-André 238 n.45
Rousseau, Jean-Jacques 236 n.45
Rowlandson, Thomas: *After Sweet Meat Comes
    Sour Sauce* 188
    *The Devonshire or Most Approved Method
        of Securing Votes* 228 n.85
    Rag Fair 82
    Rigging out a Smuggler 110
    A Sudden Squall in Hyde Park 46, *47*

S
Sala, George, 'Things Departed' 26–7
Salisbury, Countess of 96
sampler-style pockets 39, 60, *171*, 185, 203,
    204–5, 230 n.93
samplers 70, 238 n.71
Sandby, Paul: *Asylum for the Deaf* 25, *25*
    Cries of London 22, 30
    'View of the Eagle Tower at Caernarvon'
        162, *172*
    A Wine Seller 17–18, *17*
'Sarah Thrifty' (pedlar doll) 76, *78*, *174*
Savile, Gertrude 63–4, 67
schools 69, 76, 96, 99, 188, 196–7, 221
Scotland 90
second-hand pockets 79–82
secrecy 197–200
selling pockets 75–82
servants: accommodation 189–90
    boxes 91, 176, *176*, 179, 195
    carrying keys 138
    the 'character' 176–7
    charwomen 109, 179, 212
    distinguishing servants' things from
        masters' 104, 107
    lack of privacy 91, 195–7
    laundry 106, 197
    marking pockets 94
    multiple pockets 87
    pockets 176–8
    security of possessions 91
    theft by 87–8, 179–80
sewing *see* mending; needlework
sewing machines 13, 21, 64, 65–6, *66*, 74
sewn-in pockets 24, 34, 36, 117
sexuality 45–8
Shackleton, Elizabeth 81, 103, 205, 210
Shayer, William Sr, *Outside the Royal Oak* 177
Shelley, Percy Bysshe 106
shoplifting 18, 139–40, *140*, 235 n.136
shops selling pockets 75–7, 92
Shore, Daniel 209
Shore, Emily 190

Shropshire 175
Simple Directions in Needlework 97
Sinclair, Eliza 76
'slops' 78, 231 n.114
Smith, Adam 113
Smith, George, *Temptation: A Fruit Stall* 7,
    61, 220
Smith, Captain Henry 197–9, *198*
Smith, Mrs 187
sociability 143–51
    visiting 149–50, *151*
Spencer, Lady Georgiana *see* Devonshire,
    Georgiana, Duchess of
St Sepulchre's workhouse, Holborn, London
    60
Stanton, Elizabeth Cady, 'The Pocket
    Problem' 49
Starke, Mariana, *Letters from Italy* 106, 158
Stendhal, *The Charterhouse of Parma* 236 n.66
Stirling, Annie 213–14
stitches 65–6, 74–5, 88, *89*
    around openings 66, *75*, *76*
    as evidence 76
    marking pockets 92, *93*, 94–7, *97*
    sewing machines 65–6, *66*, 74–5
stocking purses 118–19, *119*
storage 90–2
    boxes and trunks 91, 108, 158, 190–1
    chests of drawers 91
    linen press 84, 90, 91, 95
    pawning as 91
    servants' boxes 91, 176, *176*, 179, 195
suffrage movement 49–51, *50*
Sturminster Marshall 173
Surrey 76
Sussex 67
Sweeney, Mary 165

T
tailors 26, 27, 34–5
Taunt, Henry, *Washing on Hedge in Front
    of a Cottage, Surrey* 108
theft 27, 89–90
    evolved pockets 160, *161*
    from luggage 91
    hiding illicit goods in stays 31
    highway robbery 111, 115, 133, 163, 165,
        173–4
    laundry 32, 103, 107–8
    pickpockets 18, 23, 160, 163, 165–6
    pockets used in 29, 139–40
    by servants 87–8, 179–80
    shoplifting 18, 139–40, *140*, 235 n.136
    see also victims of crime
Thomas, Jane 60, *60*, 203
thread, marking 94, 95, 96, 232 n.49
Tidy, Theresa, *Eighteen Maxims of Neatness
    and Order* 44
tie-on pockets *see* pockets
ties 65, *67*
    broken ties 27, 183, 220
    mending ties 100, *101*, *114*, 183

The Times 139
Tinsley, Elizabeth and Daniel 137
tipping 149
touch, sense of 211–12
tourism 144, 156–61, *158–9*
trade cards 16, *34*, *75*, 76–7, 147, 230 n.101
traders 27–8, 29, 166–8, *167*, 170
    Beynon, Ann 169–70, 185
    Bird, Eleanor 29, 118–19, 168
    Davis, Mary 170, 185
    Gatehouse, Elizabeth 173
    Hollingsworth, Mary 167
    Lee, Mary 181–2
    Plater, Sarah 174
    Price, Sarah 167
    Redmane, Katherine 166
    Stebbing, Elizabeth 28
    Thomas, Jane 170, 185
    Walsh, Caroline 53–4, 182
travel 156–61, *158–9*, 174–6
travelling pockets 66, 158–161
Tregony, Cornwall 75–6
Trimmer, Sarah, *Oeconomy of Charity* 76
trousseau 40, 78, 96

U
Under Petticoat Government 48–9, *49*
undress 24, 40
'The Unwomanly Pocket' 49–50
used pockets 79–82

V
vagrants 175
    Saxby, Mary 175
    Yeats, Ann 175
Verney, Margaret 28
victims of crime: Adams, Elizabeth 121
    Airburg, Margaret 194
    Alloway, Lucy 137
    Anderson, Elizabeth 132, 133
    Baldwin, Mary 119
    Bastin, Margaret 130, 166
    Bennett, Ellen 36
    Bird, Eleanor 29, 118–19, 168
    Birtue, Susanna 166
    Blakeway, Susannah 175
    Bottley, Sarah 181
    Bourne, Bridget 128–9, 134
    Branson, Ann 122
    Buckworth, Ann 193
    Bullen, Richard 127
    Caldcleugh, Elizabeth 119, 127
    Cantell, William 212–13
    Carter, Mary 174
    Chalkley, Elizabeth 119
    Chapman, Annie 183
    Childish, Sarah 128
    Chipperfield, Sarah 194
    Clark, Elizabeth 126
    Clough, Ann 180
    Cock, Mary 129
    Cockburn, Elizabeth 165

Cook, Sarah 165
Cooke, Mary 166
Craggs, Helen 203
Dyke, Elizabeth 165
East, Elizabeth 129–30
Eddowes, Catherine 33–4, 183–5, *183*
Embling, Mrs 32
Essington, Dorcas 137
Ferguson, Mary 133
Footman, Mary 163
Foulkes, Dorothy 193
Frances, Frances 28
Goldsmith, Elizabeth 165
Graves, Mary 217–18
Griffin, Sarah 175
Ham, Elizabeth 195
Harrison, Mary 103
Harrold, Edmund 213
Heath, Sarah 100, 130
Hicks, Ann 165
Hordes, Elizabeth 61
Hudson, Mary 36
Huguenin, Sarah 74–5
Ironmonger, Elizabeth 125
Jackson, Lucy 97, 176
Jones, Jenkin 97–8
Jones, Margaret 114–15
Jones, Mrs 66, 79
Karrsone, Mrs 165
Kensington, Mrs 189
Kidd, Jane 121
King, Jane 111
King, Michael 181
Knowles, Elizabeth 115
Lewis, Matilda 137
Ley, Margaret 136
Lister family 105
Macdonald, Elizabeth 129, 133, 177
Maclode, Esther 132
Maxwell, Mary 123
Morgan, Susanna 127, 130, 135
Morning, Sarah Ann 166
Moses, Amelia 195
Nelson, Margaret 165–6
Norton, Catharine 121, 169
Orris, Mary 137, 165
Parker, Caroline 176
Pearson, Anne 166
Peterson, Catherine 133
Pighorn, Fanny 116, 202–3
Plater, Sarah 174
Pristow, Elizabeth 130
Redmane, Katherine 166
Rowen, Sarah 174
Rowland, Mary 108
Rutherford, Mary 126
Satcher, Sarah 119
Satcher, Susannah 123
Schooler, Susannah 28
Sippel, Ann and Samuel 137–8
Smith, Judith 119
Taylor, Ann 123

Taylor, Elizabeth 27
Taylor, Margaret 139
Torrent, Agnes 136
Turner, William 137
Wade, Daniel 130
Wainwright, Thomas 180
White, Ann 76
Williams, Eleanor 165
Wood, Mary 29
Wood, Sarah 115
Victoria, Queen 95–6
visiting and visiting cards 149–50, 151

W
Wakefield, Mary 66, 79
Wales 60, 76, 169–70, 203–4, *204–5*
walking 151–5, 165
Wall & Browne 34
Waller, Lady 236 n.47
Waller, Mary 87, 103, 106
wallet purses 119
Walpole, Horace 157
Walsh, Caroline 53–4, 81–2 , *182*
Walton, Henry, *A Girl Buying a Ballad 131*
Warner, Elizabeth 187–8
washerwomen 104, 108, 109, 127
washing 65, 88–9, 93, 97, 103–9, *105–7*
    disruption of 104–5, 107, 109
    drying 105, 107–8, *108*
    exposing the intimate 107
    energetic methods of 65, 107
    ironing 107
    putting linen at risk 93, 107, 109
    theft of 107–8
    wash-houses 108–9
    when travelling 106
watch pockets 36
Webster, Thomas: *Going to the Fair 219*, 220
    Returning from the Fair 239 n.11
Weeton (née Stock), Ellen 207–9
Wheble's Lady's Magazine 72, 230 n.92
whiteness 88, 103
Wilkie, David: *The Jew's Harp 57, 58*
    The Refusal 191
William, Prince of Orange *47, 47*
Williams, Anne 203
Williams, Charles, *Scandal Refuted, or Billingsgate Virtue 167*
Williams, Francis 234 n.41
Williams, Thomas 61
Williams, William 55
Wilton House, Wiltshire 96
Wilton, Messrs 232 n.62
Wiltshire 94
Wimborne Minster 173
Withering, William, *Arrangement of British Plants* 153
Witherington, William Frederick, *The Hop Garland 216*, 220
women's garments and accessories
    affording personal satisfaction or pleasure 74, 103, 109

aprons 23, 29, 31–2, 43–4, 167, 168
bustles 36, 39
caps 209–10
chemises 29, 58
cloaks 29
corsets 29, 30
crinolines 29, 39
drawers 46
gloves 28, 76, 77, 106, 122, 125, 139, 172, 189
handkerchiefs 32, 40, 49, 77, 88, 90, 91, 94, 97, 126, *142, 147, 147*, 148, 173, 175, 200–1, 213
muffs 31
muslin dresses 37–8, *38*, 39, 47, 228 n.81
neckerchiefs 126
openings to access pockets 11, 20, 28–9, *29*, 37, 48–9, *48, 49*, 168–9, 197, 227 n.57
petticoats 29, 35, *35*, 36, 65
pocket hoops 29–30
riding habits 34–5, 148
shawls 32
side hoops or pocket hoops 29–30
skirts 29, 36, 44, 47, 49, 126, 168 221
stays 23, 29, 30–1, *31, 34*, 148, 175, 180, 181, 202
stomachers 29, 56, 70, 228 n.65
suits (women's) 36
waistcoats 26, 40, *41, 55*
wedding dresses 40
see also men's clothes
Woodcock, Elizabeth 172–3, *173*
Woodforde, Nancy 72, 99, 155
Woodforde, Parson 26
Woodley, Elizabeth 60
Worcestershire 175
Wordsworth, Dorothy 107, 200–1, 236 n.42
    Grasmere Journal 153
work 166–85
    child labour 220, 239 n.9
    itinerant occupations 169–74
    prostitutes 181, 183
    servants 175–80
    traders 166–8, *167*
work-bags 190–91, 196
work-baskets 190–92, 196
workhouses 60, 188, 196, 238 n.38
The Workwoman's Guide 35, 56, 64, 65, 66, 69, 71, 76, 84, 95, 104–5, 106
The World 160
Wren, Christopher 200
Wright, Charles Cole 192–3
Wright, Frances Maria 192–3, 218
writing 153–5, *155*

Y
York 77, 82, 91–2, 166, 196
Yorkshire 176, 217
Young, Mary 60, 87, 90, 95, 99, 104, 148–9, 150, 151, 190, 232 n.33

PICTURE CREDITS